On the Job

On the Job

Is Long-Term Employment a Thing of the Past?

David Neumark
editor

Russell Sage Foundation
New York

The Russell Sage Foundation

Library of Congress Cataloging-in-Publication Data

On the job: is long-term employment a thing of the past? / David Neumark, editor.
    p. cm.
  Includes bibliographical references and index.
  ISBN 0-87154-618-3
    1. Occupational mobility—Congresses. 2. Organizational change—Congresses. 3. Job security—Congresses. I. Neumark, David.
HD5717.C43 2000
331.12—dc21   00-036617

The paper used in this publication meets the minimum requirements of American National Standard for Information Sciences—Permanence of Paper for Printed Library Materials. ANSI Z39.48-1992.

Text design by Suzanne Nichols

RUSSELL SAGE FOUNDATION
112 East 64th Street, New York, New York 10021
10 9 8 7 6 5 4 3 2 1

Contents

Contents

Contributors

DAVID NEUMARK is professor of economics at Michigan State University and research associate of the National Bureau of Economic Research.

STEVEN G. ALLEN is professor in the College of Management at North Carolina State University and research associate at the National Bureau of Economic Research.

ANNETTE BERNHARDT is a sociologist and senior associate at the Center on Wisconsin Strategy of the University of Wisconsin-Madison. Her research in this volume was completed while at the Institute on Education and the Economy of Columbia University.

PETER CAPPELLI is George W. Taylor Professor of Management, director of the Center for Human Resources, and chairman of the Council on Employee Relations at The Wharton School of the University of Pennsylvania.

ROBERT L. CLARK is professor in the College of Management at North Carolina State University.

HENRY S. FARBER is Hughes-Rogers Professor of Economics and research associate of the Industrial Relations Section of Princeton University. He is also research associate of the National Bureau of Economic Research.

PETER GOTTSCHALK is professor of economics at Boston College and research affiliate of the Institute for Research on Poverty at the University of Wisconsin-Madison.

MARK S. HANDCOCK is professor of statistics and sociology at the University of Washington and research affiliate of the Center for Statistics in the Social Sciences.

DANIEL HANSEN is senior economist at Christensen Associates.

SUSAN N. HOUSEMAN is senior economist at the W.E. Upjohn Institute for Employment Research.

DAVID A. JAEGER is associate professor of economics at Hunter College and the Graduate Center of the City University of New York.

other research, including both earlier papers and those presented at the conference. In addition, some papers began to explore possible explanations of changes in the employment relationship emerging from the ongoing research, adding a vital component to what to that point had been largely a debate about empirical facts—a necessary first step, but an incomplete research agenda. Following the conference, the usual process of review and revision of the papers was accompanied by a deliberate effort to push the contributors in the direction of reconciling, whenever possible, contradictory findings, both among the papers and with respect to other research on job stability and job security. The final product of this process is represented in this volume.

As the title of this chapter suggests, this process was unique in its collective effort to establish a consensus on the empirical evidence across numerous papers using a variety of data sets. Besides assembling a set of new papers that would generally advance our knowledge about changes in job stability and job security, we also set out to push a research "model" that focuses a number of papers simultaneously on the same topic, with a strong emphasis on delineating points of reconciliation, points of continued disagreement, and, wherever possible, the reasons for each. This emphasis gives this conference volume a unique flavor. It is hard to read its chapters and not come away believing that as a whole—but in some sense *only* as a whole—it substantially advances our knowledge of changes in the employment relationship.

In this introductory chapter, I briefly summarize the original findings presented in each chapter and then move on to what each has to say about findings in the previous literature and in the other conference papers. My purpose is to provide a synthesis that is somewhat difficult for the reader to obtain from reading the individual chapters without engaging in his or her own detailed process of comparing and contrasting them, since they are filled with a rather bewildering array of discussions about data issues, measurement problems, alternative estimates, and references to other research findings. I hope this synthesis helps the reader absorb the contributions of this research more easily.[1]

In addition to the contribution this volume makes to the debate over the changing employment relationship, I believe readers will also find in it a wealth of useful suggestions and insights regarding the measurement of worker-employer attachments (tenure, job separations, job loss, and so on) in many of the main data sets that labor economists use in a variety of applications. These contributions have resulted from what is probably the most serious attention such issues have received. This volume may prove indispensable not only in future research on changes in the employment relationship but also in a much wider body of research on job mobility, job attachment, and job loss.

Table 1.1 *Continued*

Authors	Main Data Sets	Sample Period	Coverage	Outcomes	Findings
			non-Hispanic whites, employed (not self-employed)		
Gottschalk and Moffitt	SIPP PSID	1983 to 1995 1981 to 1992	Male (married) heads of households in PSID; all males and females in SIPP, ages twenty to sixty-two, employed	One-year and one-month job separation rates; involuntary job separations and other classifications of reason for separation; characteristics of separations; wage changes upon job changes	One-year separation rates did not increase in SIPP or in PSID with given sample restrictions, variable definitions, and sample period. Involuntary separations in PSID increased, but only from 1970s to 1980s; no increase after 1980. No trend increase in monthly separation rates in SIPP; secular decline from mid-1980s to early 1990s. Little evidence that job endings were more likely to be accompanied by spell of nonemployment, but duration of nonemployment increased for less-educated. No downward drift in wage gains associated with job changes.
Allen, Clark, and Schieber	Database of consulting clients (firms) of Watson Wyatt Worldwide	1990 to 1997	All workers	Change in average tenure; changes in percentages with more than ten and more than twenty years of tenure; five-year retention rate	Average tenure rose over 1990s, although not uniformly across firms. Percentages of workers with more than ten and more than twenty years of tenure rose over 1990s. Most of the lower retention rates associated with downsizing firms relative to growing firms were found among junior workers.

Abbreviations: Panel Study of Income Dynamics (PSID); Current Population Survey (CPS); National Longitudinal Survey of Young Men (NLSYM); National Longitudinal Survey of Youth (NLSY); and Survey of Income and Program Participation (SIPP).

update the evidence on job stability based on CPS tenure supplements by extending into the 1990s the type of estimates presented in our earlier work. Rather than looking at point-in-time distributions of tenure or some transformation thereof (such as the share with tenure below some cutoff), we string together tenure supplements to estimate retention rates, which are free of the influence of factors such as changes in participation.[3] Overall, however, the findings are quite consistent with those of Jaeger and Stevens. Shorter-term (four-year) retention rates were largely unchanged for the sample as a whole over the sample period (1983 to 1995). In contrast, longer-term (eight-year) retention rates fell in the early 1990s; both rates fell for higher-tenure and older workers, and more so for higher-tenure managerial and professional workers. These results point to a weakened tendency, in the short run at least, for managerial and professional workers to remain in long-term jobs.

Annette Bernhardt, Martina Morris, Mark Handcock, and Marc Scott look at job stability in chapter 4 by comparing two-year job separation rates across cohorts of young white men in the National Longitudinal Surveys (NLS). This data source, an alternative to the PSID or CPS, offers some advantages that the authors describe (most important, a unique employer code), but it also presents potential problems of changes over time stemming from differences in the survey methods used for the two NLS cohorts. The authors carefully consider the issues that arise because of differences between the surveys, and they present a compelling case that their findings of substantially higher separation rates in the later NLS cohort reflect a real behavioral change. Their results compare one cohort followed over the period 1966 to 1981 with another cohort followed over the period 1979 to 1994. Thus, their findings of higher separation rates in the more recent cohort to a large extent compare the 1970s with the 1980s and hence are not inconsistent with the evidence reported in other chapters in this volume that job stability declined somewhat over the 1970s and early 1980s (see, for example, Jaeger and Stevens) but not during the 1980s. In addition, their data are restricted to relatively young men, in contrast to most of the other analyses in this volume.

Bernhardt and her colleagues also broach the interesting question of whether the consequences of job changing have shifted over time; they report that the wage returns to job changing have declined and become more unequal. Although there is not enough material in these chapters to reach definitive conclusions on this issue, I would argue that research along these lines has a valuable role to play. Much of the recent debate has been about empirical measurement of changes in the employment relationship, but little if any research has asked, "So what?" To know what to make of the evidence on changes in the employment relationship, we need a better idea of what the consequences of such changes are.

The analysis of Bernhardt and her colleagues of changes in separation rates largely revisits an earlier paper, using the NLS cohorts, by Monks and Pizer (1998), who reported rather sharp declines in two-year retention rates between the NLS cohorts. After considering the role of measurement issues, differences in attrition (which is plausibly associated with measured job retention), and some other empirical issues, they largely confirm the Monks and Pizer results, finding, if anything, an even larger decline in job stability.

Finally, the Gottschalk and Moffitt chapter is not devoted to reconciling conflicting evidence but rather to presenting evidence on short-term dynamics from the SIPP. However, to ensure that any differences they find are not due simply to differences between data sets, they first endeavor to verify that the SIPP and the PSID, when used longitudinally and in a comparable fashion to study yearly turnover, yield similar results. In addition, because past research with the PSID did not treat it as a longitudinal data set but instead as a series of cross-sections, an important by-product of their "benchmarking" of the data is showing that when the PSID data are used longitudinally, they give very similar results to those obtained when using the PSID as a series of cross-sections; although estimated separation rates shift, the time-series pattern of no upward trend remains the same. Again, this finding is of interest to researchers who may be measuring job stability or turnover with other questions in mind that require longitudinal data.

JOB SECURITY

Although the research on job stability focuses on the duration of jobs, another critical dimension is what has come to be labeled "job security." The distinction between job stability and job security was introduced as a means of sharpening the interpretation of different types of changes in the employment relationship.[5] A decline in job durations might be construed as negative or positive depending on whether workers are leaving their jobs involuntarily more often or quitting their jobs more frequently to take better jobs (such as occurs to some extent in an economic expansion). A decline in job security, in contrast, refers specifically to a decline in job durations attributable to increased involuntary job loss, an unambiguous "negative" from the perspective of workers. Tracking changes in both job stability and job security is important for understanding how the employment relationship is changing. As in the previous section, table 1.3 presents the evidence on changes in job security in a condensed form, and table 1.4 summarizes the attempts to reconcile the conflicting evidence.

Table 1.3   Summary of Findings from Studies Focusing on Job Security

Authors	Main Data Sets	Sample Period	Coverage	Outcomes	Findings
Valletta	PSID	1976 to 1992	Workers (not self-employed), ages twenty-one to sixty-four	Dismissals (permanent layoffs and firings), quits, and general turnover	For men, although tenure is negatively associated with dismissal, significant upward time trend in probability of dismissal, stemming from upward trend for high-tenure workers. Negative effect of tenure on dismissals reduced in declining sectors (but no consistent trend toward greater probability of dismissal of high-tenure workers in declining sectors). Downward trend in probability of quit for low-tenure workers and upward trend for high-tenure workers. Similar results for skilled white-collar women.
Stewart	CPS (March)	1967 to 1997	Men and women over nineteen, with one to forty years of potential experience; worked (not self-employed) at least one week in previous year	Employment-to-unemployment transitions (worked in previous year and unemployed in March) as proxy for job loss	Rate of job loss was higher in 1980s than in the 1970s but did not increase in 1990s. Also holds for men in all education groups, for less educated women, and for all experience groups. For most groups, job loss during the 1990 recession was lower than during the more severe 1982 recession. But for some groups—usually more insulated from recessions—1990 recession was as severe, including college-educated men, men with twenty-one or more years of experience, and white-collar workers.
Schmidt	GSS	1977 to 1996	Men and women over eighteen, employed full-time or part-time in survey week	Perceived likelihood of job loss or layoff in next twelve months (fear of job loss) and interaction of this with perceived difficulty of finding job with same income and fringe benefits (fear of costly job loss)	Workers in 1990s were more pessimistic about involuntary job loss and costly job loss than in earlier periods. This is apparent in comparison of economic recovery years 1993 to 1996 to late 1980s, with similarly low unemployment, and in comparison of the 1990 to 1991 recession years to 1982 to 1983 recession years. These perceptions are broadly consistent with patterns of actual job loss in DWS overall and for many demographic subgroups.

Abbreviations: General Social Survey (GSS); Displaced Workers Survey (DWS); see table 1.1 note.

Table 1.4 Reconciling Evidence and Establishing Consistent Results on Job Security

Authors	Studies Addressed	Findings
Gottschalk and Moffitt	Boisjoly et al. (1998) PSID results showing that involuntary terminations rose over 1970s and 1980s.	Results driven by increases from 1970s to 1980s, but not in-creases in 1980s.
Stewart	Farber (1997b) DWS study concluding that rate of job loss increased from 1991 to 1993 period to 1993 to 1995 pe-riod.	Omitting the potentially troublesome category of job loss in the DWS for "other" reasons, job loss rate in March CPS data (employment-to-unemployment rate) falls from 1991 to 1993 period to 1993 to 1995 period, while job loss rate in DWS data remains constant (despite economic recov-ery). Concludes that the job loss rate actually did decline, but that changes in questions in 1996 DWS (covering 1993 to 1995) resulted in more job-leavers being classified as job-losers than in earlier years.
	Boisjoly et al. (1998) PSID results showing that involuntary terminations rose over 1970s and 1980s.	Job security declined over early 1970s, but from mid-1970s through mid- to late 1990s there has been little change.
	Monks and Pizer (1998) reporting increase in rate of job loss between the NLSYM and NLSY cohorts.	CPS data show increased job loss rates for those with at most a high school education, but (in contrast to Monks and Pizer) not for those with some college or college gradu-ates. Suggests that contrast between the two data sets is not due to differences in survey between NLSYM and NLSY, since this would generate contrasting results across all schooling groups.

Abbreviations: see table 1.1 note.

Part II opens with Robert Valletta's chapter on the evidence on changes in the probability of dismissal over the period 1976 to 1992 using the PSID. Valletta estimates how this probability has changed differentially for high- and low-tenure workers; how this probability varies (overall, and with tenure) in declining versus expanding sectors; and how the latter relationships have changed over time. These particular empirical analyses are motivated by what is one of the first attempts in this growing literature to offer a theoretical framework for interpreting the empirical analysis. In particular, Valletta attempts to estimate parameters that might reflect behavior in the context of implicit employment contracts that are designed to overcome incentive problems and imperfect monitoring, as well as changes in the terms of such contracts, although he acknowledges that the theoretical framework does not impose enough structure on the empirical analysis to test sharp hypotheses. Nonetheless, there is evidence consistent with the general "implicit contracts" approach, in particular the diminution of the influence of tenure in reducing the likelihood of dismissal for workers in declining sectors, dismissals that Valletta interprets as employer default on delayed payment contracts in the face of adverse shocks. In light of this framework, the upward trend in dismissals for high-tenure workers and a similar upward trend in quits suggest some change in the incentives or behavior underlying long-term implicit contracts. Valletta's chapter clearly establishes a case for incorporating more theoretical analysis into what has until now been a purely empirical research agenda.

Jay Stewart's contribution to the job security literature is to develop a time series on job loss that can be used as an alternative to those based on the PSID and Displaced Workers Surveys (DWS), which have been used to date. As Stewart points out, neither of these two data sources provides consistent measures of job loss over time. The changes in questions over time in the PSID have received careful attention in previous research (see, for example, Polsky 1999). The changes in the DWS are more recent, but their impact on estimates of changes in job loss in the 1990s is potentially serious (see Polivka and Miller 1998; Farber 1998b; Polivka 1998). Stewart looks instead at the rate of employment-to-unemployment transitions in the CPS over a thirty-year period. Although such transitions are not synonymous with job loss—some job-losers go directly to other jobs—they offer an alternative perspective. Stewart then reports findings that draw some potentially interesting contrasts with the existing literature. He finds that the rate of transition to unemployment increased in the 1980s relative to the 1970s but did not increase in the 1990s. For example, for most groups this rate was lower during the 1990 recession than during the more severe 1982 recession. However, this was

Author	Data source	Years	Sample	Research question	Findings
Houseman and Polivka	CPS contingent work supplements	1995, 1997	All workers	Do workers in flexible staffing arrangements (temporary, on-call, contract, and part-time work) have less stable jobs? Can growth in flexible staffing arrangements account for changes in job stability?	Workers in most flexible staffing arrangements (especially agency temps, on-call workers, direct-hire temps, and contract workers) are less likely to remain in their jobs for one year than workers in full-time arrangements. Simulations based on applying these cross-section results to the growth in temporary help agency employment from 1986 to 1996 suggest that growth in flexible staffing arrangements could explain a substantial share (30 percent or more) of the modest increase in employer switching in this decade.
	Match between CPS contingent work supplement and monthly CPS files	1995 to 1996			
Cappelli	EQW National Employers Survey	1994, 1997	Sample of private establishments with more than twenty employees	What establishment-specific factors are associated with downsizing, and what are the consequences of downsizing?	Downsizing (defined as cuts in employment by firms operating at or above capacity) is related to both management practices and variables reflecting factor prices (such as unionization), but not always in the expected direction. Factors explaining downsizing are not too different from those explaining overall job losses, and overall job reductions are not driven mainly by demand shortfalls. Downsizing is associated with cuts in both sales per employee and labor costs per employee, possibly mitigating overall performance effects.

Abbreviations: National Center on the Educational Quality of the Workforce (EQW); see table 1.1 note.

increasingly "bad" jobs offered to low-skill workers. Although not documented in this chapter (see, however, Henry Farber's chapter in this volume), these jobs are probably less stable and secure, suggesting a link between the types of jobs some firms are offering and changes in job stability and job security.

However, Levenson considers an important alternative hypothesis. We know that the wages of low-skill workers have fallen over the past couple of decades, both absolutely (in real terms) and relative to high-wage workers, and that this decline is in part responsible for the relative declines in labor-force participation among low-skill individuals (see, for example, Katz and Murphy 1992; Juhn 1992). Levenson builds on this research by asking whether the relative rise in involuntary part-time and temporary work among low-skill workers in fact reflects a voluntary labor supply response to lower wages. With respect to part-time work, this would imply, of course, that the "involuntary" distinction used in the CPS is not meaningful; it may reflect an inability to find full-time work at the wage at which the individual would choose to work full-time rather than an inability to find such work per se. Levenson finds that for men, but not for women, the relative increase in involuntary part-time work among the less skilled can be partly understood as a labor supply response, and that only a small amount of the relative increase in temporary employment among low-skill men can be explained as a labor supply response. This finding injects an important perspective into the debate about changes in the employment relationship broadly defined—namely, whether some of the changes reflect market responses to relative wages, or changes in workers' preferences or constraints, rather than changes in the nature of the employment relationship per se driven by corporate restructuring, management strategies, and so on.

Henry Farber looks at a different source of the flow of workers into temporary and involuntary part-time employment. He defines temporary employment more broadly to include on-call and contract work. Matching data from the DWS to the 1995 and 1997 Contingent and Alternative Employment Arrangements Supplements (CAEAS) to the CPS, he finds that workers who lose jobs are more likely to be in temporary or involuntary part-time jobs than workers who have not lost their jobs. Farber goes on to characterize these jobs and the workers who fill them in more detail. In particular, he finds that the relationships between job loss and temporary or involuntary part-time employment weaken with time, suggesting that these jobs are to some extent used as workers make transitions back to full-time, regular employment following a job loss. Indeed, his evidence suggests that those in temporary jobs specifically are of two types: job-losers using them as transitions back to full-time, regular employment; and voluntary part-time workers who prefer these jobs over other alternatives.

Although the nature of Farber's evidence is different, the perspective it yields is in some ways similar to Levenson's. In particular, we should not necessarily view involuntary part-time or temporary employment as "bad" employment relationships foisted on workers who would otherwise have full-time, regular jobs. Job loss is a persistent phenomenon, and the availability of transitional jobs may serve a useful function. Moreover, as Levenson points out, some workers may prefer some types of flexible or nonpermanent employment relationships. The evidence Farber presents is cross-sectional, but coupled with some other evidence suggesting that the rate of job loss has increased it could explain part of the growth in involuntary part-time employment and temporary employment. If the relationship between job loss and employment in these types of jobs has been stable over time, then higher rates of job loss would lead to a higher incidence of these types of employment. However, this cannot be established with the data Farber has available; data on most forms of temporary employment, in particular, are available beginning only with the CPS contingent work supplements in 1995.

Susan Houseman and Anne Polivka study flexible employment arrangements, broadly defined. They begin by presenting evidence from an Upjohn Institute employer survey on why employers use flexible staffing arrangements. They focus on the reasons that are likely to have implications for job stability, in particular whether employers use these arrangements to screen workers for more permanent positions, and whether they actually move employees in flexible arrangements into regular positions. Houseman and Polivka conclude that employers sometimes use flexible arrangements for screening—most notably agency temporaries—but that other factors are generally more important in determining employers' reliance on these employment arrangements.[9]

The main part of their analysis exploits the CPS contingent work supplement, matching the 1995 supplement to other CPS files to obtain evidence on job turnover among workers in flexible and regular employment relationships. Their principal finding is that workers in these flexible employment relationships are less likely to remain in their jobs for an additional year (or an additional month) than workers in full-time employment. Among workers in such flexible arrangements, this is especially true for agency temps, on-call workers, direct-hire temps, and contract workers. Houseman and Polivka are naturally concerned with the possibility that workers in these latter types of jobs are simply higher-turnover workers—that it is not the nature of the jobs per se that reduces job stability. Although more complete panel or work history data might address this issue better, they argue—based on controls they can include (measures of very recent job loss, turnover, unemployment, and nonemployment), as well as on other evidence from longitudinal data for temporary services workers (Segal and Sullivan 1997)—that there is a causal effect of employment in these types of arrangements on job stability.

On the assumption that their evidence points to such a causal effect, Houseman and Polivka also attempt to answer the question of whether the growth of flexible staffing arrangements can explain part of the modest decline in job stability in the 1990s. Because of data limitations and the lack of evidence on the relationship between flexible employment arrangements and job stability in earlier years, this exercise must be viewed cautiously. But based on their estimates, the authors' calculations suggest that the growth in flexible employment arrangements from 1986 to 1996 may explain nearly one-third of the modest decline in job stability over this period.

Finally, Peter Cappelli seeks to shed light in chapter 13 on the corporate downsizing phenomenon, which has been fingered by the media as a prime cause of the decline in job stability and job security in the 1990s, although its contribution to overall trends is difficult to gauge. Cappelli seeks to accomplish two goals with his analysis of establishment-level data from the 1994 and 1997 National Employer Surveys. First, he is interested in understanding some of the characteristics of establishments and their workforces that are related to the incidence and magnitude of downsizings. Second, he examines the consequences of downsizing for productivity and labor costs per employee. To operationalize the concept of downsizing, Cappelli defines such an event as an employment reduction that is not associated with excess capacity. Such employment reductions seem more likely to coincide with events such as corporate reorganizations and management restructurings, which correspond to the popular conception of a downsizing, than to be associated with slack demand.[10] To the best of my knowledge, this chapter is the first establishment-level empirical analysis, based on representative data, of the determinants and consequences of downsizing in terms of workforce and establishment characteristics or outcomes. It is easy to criticize the data for a failure to capture unambiguous downsizings, specific events, or factors that might have spurred them. Nonetheless, it presents some new evidence that helps inform our understanding of downsizing.

Cappelli reports that downsizings are associated not only with reductions in labor costs per worker but also with declines in sales per worker (productivity), suggesting that overall performance is unlikely to be enhanced by downsizing.[11] The failure to find beneficial consequences of downsizing is consistent with the research cited by Cappelli indicating that financial performance on average declines after a downsizing, although this research also indicates that downsizings accompanied by specific features–such as restructuring plans—may have more beneficial financial effects.[12] The apparent absence of beneficial performance effects

Chapter 2

Is Job Stability in the United States Falling? Reconciling Trends in the Current Population Survey and the Panel Study of Income Dynamics

David A. Jaeger and Ann Huff Stevens

The degree of job stability in the U.S. economy is of substantial concern to workers and policymakers and has important implications for a variety of economic applications. Documenting trends in job stability over the past twenty-five years, however, has become a controversial exercise. Press reports continue to emphasize deteriorating job stability, though support for this assertion from empirical economic studies has been limited. One reason for the continuing ambiguity in the literature on trends in job stability is the apparent sensitivity of empirical results to the specific data source used. Results that differ across presumably representative and widely used data sets are always a matter of concern to empirical researchers, but the enormous attention recently paid to job stability makes resolution of this issue of more than methodological interest. This chapter aims to resolve one area of ambiguity by examining whether the Panel Study of Income Dynamics (PSID) and the Current Population Survey (CPS) yield systematically different results with respect to comparable measures of employer tenure.

The suspicion that different data lead to different conclusions about trends in job stability arises from both a review of the growing literature on this topic and specific references within that literature. Several PSID-based studies report an increase in job mobility since the 1970s, while most CPS-based work finds no overall trend through the late 1980s. Dave Marcotte (1995) and Peter Gottschalk and Robert Moffitt (1994), in particular, have noted that the conclusions of studies based on the PSID seem to differ systematically from those using the CPS. Examination of the conclusions of other studies in this area supports the notion of a relationship between findings and the data used. Despite this pattern, there has been no attempt to produce a directly comparable set of results between the PSID and CPS.[1] Moreover, it is not possible to reconcile the inconsistencies solely with reference to existing research. The available studies utilize different measures of job stability, have different sample coverage, and focus on several different time periods, all of which make it difficult to judge whether the different conclusions can be explained by the specific details of each study. Because panel data such as the PSID are often necessary to answer questions relating to the consequences of job instability, it is important to know whether the PSID can produce results consistent with the CPS when changes to the survey are handled appropriately.

Our results suggest that, during the 1980s and 1990s, the two data sets produce similar measures of the level of and trends in employer tenure. We find little evidence in either data set of a reduction in the share of workers with employer tenure of one year or less between 1983 and 1996. We find, however, an increase in the share of workers with tenure of less than ten years between 1983 and 1996, concentrated among older male workers toward the end of the period.

Including the 1970s in our analysis produces greater differences in trends across the two data sets. In the 1970s, the incidence of low tenure in the PSID is generally smaller than in the CPS. We argue that this is probably the result of changes in the CPS question following the 1981 survey that may have caused low tenure rates in the 1970s to be overstated relative to those in the 1980s. Evidence from similar question changes in the early years of the PSID is quite consistent with this hypothesis.

Our focus in this chapter is on cross-sectional tabulations of the fraction of workers with employer tenure below a fixed cutoff of either one year or ten years. This focus is motivated by our desire to have the simplest possible measures of workers' attachment to an employer that will be directly comparable across the two data sets. One drawback of focusing on these aspects of the tenure distribution is that they do not directly measure job stability. In particular, the fraction of individuals with tenure below a fixed cutoff is sensitive to changes in the flows of workers into employment from out of the labor force or unemployment. An increase in the rate at which individuals move from not working to working would increase the fraction of workers with low tenure but would not necessarily indicate a change in the degree of job stability. This distinction between the changes over time in the distribution of employer tenure and in the probability of remaining with a given employer is, in principle, an important one. We find, however, that trends in these simple measures of employer tenure are sensitive neither to conditioning on employment in a previous year nor to other variations in the exact measures used.

THE LITERATURE ON TRENDS IN JOB STABILITY

To clarify the degree to which the data source used is related to observed trends in job stability, we begin by summarizing a number of recent studies of job stability and tenure. Among studies using the tenure data from the CPS, Henry Farber (1998) found that there was no overall change in the distribution of job duration between 1973 and 1993. He did, however, find evidence of a reduction in job duration among less educated men, particularly those with less than a high school education. The results presented by Frank Diebold, David Neumark, and Daniel Polsky (1996, 1997), who also used the CPS tenure data, are generally consistent with these findings of little or no change in job stability. These authors reported a small reduction in four-year job retention rates for men from 1983 through 1991 of just over two percentage points after controlling for the business cycle. Between 1973 and 1991, a sample period more comparable to Farber's, Diebold, Neumark, and Polsky found a small increase in the ten-year job retention rate for men, although the change is essentially zero after controlling for the business cycle.[2] Jay Stewart (1997), employing data from the March CPS to calculate job mobility rates, also found little overall change in job mobility among men.

However, results from several PSID-based studies have presented a different pattern. Marcotte (1999) found reductions in one-year job retention rates for men from the period 1976 to 1978 to the period 1985 to 1988 of just over two percentage points. Although the estimated overall change in this study is relatively modest, Marcotte reported very large increases in mobility for several demographic groups, including blacks and young workers. Two other studies using the PSID have also suggested declining job stability. Steven Rose (1995) reported that the proportion of workers with "strong employment stability," defined as having changed employers no more than once in a decade, fell both overall and for a variety of subgroups from the 1970s to the 1980s.[3] A similar finding of a possible increase in rates of job changing during the late 1980s was reported in Gottschalk and Moffitt (1994). Job changing was not the focus of their study, but they did report an increase in rates of job turnover from the 1970s to the 1980s in the PSID and noted that such an increase "is in contrast to tabulations based on the January CPS" (241).

Also using the PSID, Polsky (1999) reached substantially different conclusions. His point estimates of the change from the 1976 to 1981 period to the 1986 to 1991 period in the probability of job separation were generally one percentage point or less and were statistically significant and positive only for workers in service occupations. Polsky identified changes over time in the "reason for job change" question as a potentially important reason for some of the earlier findings of increased turnover in the PSID.[4] Changes in the questionnaire skip pattern and question wording in the 1984 through 1987 surveys make the responses to this question inconsistent over time. From 1984 through 1987, the "reason for job change" question was asked of all respondents who reported that their current job started after January of the previous year, rather than within the past twelve months, as in prior years.[5] This change artificially inflated the job-changing rates based on this question for these four years. Polsky argued that the discrepancy between his work and the findings of some other PSID-based studies could be attributed to the failure of the earlier work to take the change in the "reason for job change" question into account.

A final set of papers on job stability that deserve some mention here are those focusing exclusively on involuntary job changes, as opposed to all job changes or low tenure. The findings in this literature are somewhat more consistent across different data sets. Johanne Boisjoly, Greg Duncan, and Timothy Smeeding (1998), for example, found an increase between the 1970s and early 1990s in the probability of job displacement, or *involuntary* job changes, using PSID data. Similarly, Farber (1997) used the Displaced Workers Survey (DWS) (a supplement to the main CPS survey) and found a similar increase in displacement rates from the early 1980s through the mid-1990s. This finding of increased rates of involuntary job changes could be consistent either with no overall change in the distribution of employer tenure implied by several CPS studies (if there was an offsetting decrease in voluntary employer changes) or with increases in the total number of employer transitions suggested by some of the PSID studies.

Overall, our reading of the literature on job stability (considering both voluntary and involuntary employer changes) points to many discrepancies across data sets and, to a lesser extent, across studies using the same data set. We next attempt to resolve some of these discrepancies and to understand how they have arisen. Specifically, we consider whether eliminating differences in sample composition, measures of job stability, and time periods also eliminates differences in the measured trends in the PSID and CPS.

DATA AND SAMPLE CONSTRUCTION

In both data sets, we restrict our samples to include heads of household and their spouses, between the ages of twenty and fifty-nine, who were employed but not self-employed at the time of the survey. The restriction to household heads and spouses is driven by data limitations in the PSID; we attempt to generate a comparable CPS sample by including "refer-

The results for men are shown in the upper panels of figure 2.8. The CPS gives consistently higher estimates than the PSID of the share of male workers with employer tenure of less than ten years, particularly for men thirty to thirty-nine years old.[26] Figure 2.8 also shows, however, that the trends in these measures are comparable across data sets. For workers age thirty-nine and under, neither data set shows a sustained trend in this measure through the entire sample period. From 1983 forward, the series for workers in their thirties exhibit a shallow U-shape in both data sets. In contrast, for workers over age forty both data sets show an increase in the fraction of workers with less than ten years of employer tenure. Unlike the results for the fraction of workers with one year or less of tenure, using this measure suggests an upward trend from the early 1980s through the end of the sample that is found in both data sets. This trend is particularly strong during the 1990s, suggesting that the change in the tenure distribution is a fairly recent phenomenon.

The results in the lower panels of figure 2.8 show a decline over time in the percentage of women with tenure of less than ten years. We find this decline in both data sets for all groups except for the thirty- to thirty-nine-year-olds in the PSID; it is stronger in the PSID for the oldest women. Using this measure, we find no evidence consistent with a reduction in job stability for women.

We have also compared the full distributions of tenure in the CPS and PSID samples. To summarize these distributions over time, we followed Farber (1998) and calculated interpolated quantiles of the distributions. Medians and ninetieth percentiles were calculated separately by the age groups shown in figure 2.8. This comparison results in much the same story as the probabilities of tenure of less than ten years.[27]

MULTIVARIATE TREND REGRESSIONS

The characteristics of our samples change somewhat between the 1970s and 1990s. In particular, both samples are more educated and slightly older by 1996 than in the 1970s or 1980s. These changes in the sample composition over time could mask changes in the underlying incidence of low tenure for workers with a fixed set of characteristics. To examine changes in the adjusted incidence of low tenure, holding individual characteristics (age, education, and race) constant, we performed regression analysis of the incidence of low tenure. The regression results presented here are for men only since we have the necessary education and race information for men in all years. Controlling for age and education did not alter our conclusion that there was no increase in rates of low tenure among women.

The estimation proceeded in two steps. In the first step, we estimated a logit model on the probability of having employer tenure of less than one year or less than ten years and controlled for age, age squared, race, education, and calendar year.[28] Using the calendar year coefficients, we then calculated year-specific probabilities.[29] In the second step of the estimation, these probabilities were regressed on a time trend using ordinary least squares. Because the error term in this second-stage regression is heteroskedastic, we present heteroskedasticity-consistent standard errors estimated using the jackknife.[30] We have estimated the model for the full sample as well as separately for each age, education, and race group; the results are presented in table 2.1.

The first four columns of table 2.1 show the estimated trends in the regression-adjusted probabilities of tenure of one year or less for the two data sets. We show results for both the full periods and for 1983 through 1996 only, but we focus our attention on the latter period, in which we view the measures as more comparable to one another. Between 1983 and 1996, for the full sample, neither data set produces a statistically significant trend in rates of tenure of less than or equal to one year. Within certain subgroups, the estimated trend in the CPS is larger, although often not statistically significant. In the PSID, there are statistically significant trends only for forty- to forty-nine-year-olds, high school graduates, and blacks. The trends for forty- to forty-nine-year-olds (as well as for fifty- to fifty-nine-year-olds) and high school graduates are also statistically significant in the CPS. This analysis largely confirms the visual evidence in the previous section of little movement in the probability of having tenure of less than one year.

The results for the period beginning in the 1970s are substantially different from those beginning in the 1980s. First, in the PSID, including the years 1976, 1977, 1981, and 1982 produces a statistically significant and upward trend for almost every subgroup. The pattern of a smaller increase in the CPS from the 1970s to the 1980s is consistent with our hypothesis that the question changes lead to an overstatement of low tenure probabilities prior to 1983. The PSID data are more consistent over the entire period from 1976 through 1996 and provide evidence of a small increase in the fraction of male workers in new jobs from the mid-1970s to the mid-1990s. This evidence also suggests that measured trends in job tenure are sensitive to the exact time period under consideration.

Columns 5 through 8 of table 2.1 present results for the trend in the percentage of workers with employer tenure of less than ten years. The trends here are statistically significant in almost every subgroup from 1983 to 1996. The estimated trend is stronger in the PSID, with the magnitude of the trend coefficient typically equal to approximately twice that from the CPS. After adjusting for age, education, and race, we find strong evidence from both data sets that workers are more likely to be in jobs with tenure of less than ten years in the 1990s relative to the 1980s.

In general, the regression-adjusted probabilities provide stronger evidence of an increase in the probability of having tenure of less than ten years than did the unadjusted figures in the previous section.[31] This is not surprising since the sample is both more educated and older at the end of the period, and both of these characteristics are associated with lower probabilities of being in relatively new jobs.

SENSITIVITY OF ESTIMATED TRENDS IN LOW TENURE

As noted throughout, fractions of employed individuals with tenure of less than one year or less than ten years is not an ideal measure of job stability. Although the two data sets may produce similar trends in these tenure-based measures, the question remains whether preferred measures of job stability would also produce such agreement. We are somewhat limited by the data available in both data sets, but we have also estimated trends in several alternative measures of changes in the tenure distribution.

Our inclusion of only employed individuals may mask business cycle effects on the tenure distribution. For example, if equal shares of individuals with low tenure and with high tenure become unemployed owing to a cyclical downturn, our measures would not capture this obvious decrease in job stability. To check the robustness of our results for nonemployed individuals (that is, those who are unemployed or out of the labor force), we present trends in the share of the population (including both employed and nonemployed individuals) in figure 2.9. These calculations count nonemployed individuals as having zero months of employer tenure.

In the PSID, the population- and employment-based fractions with tenure of less than one year and less than ten years show extremely similar trends from 1981 through 1996. This suggests that the distinction between population- and employment-based fractions of workers with low tenure is unlikely to alter our conclusions. In contrast to the employment-based series, the CPS population-based series shows a slight increase in the fraction of men with low tenure. This population-based trend is mainly driven by the 1979 and 1983 estimated probabilities, which are lower than in other years (and closer to the employment-based probabilities). As we noted earlier, the employment-based probability in 1979 is somewhat anomalous and is substantially higher than the CPS probabilities from 1978 and 1981.[32] This pattern is not repeated in the population-based estimates. Lacking data from the PSID in this year for comparison, it is difficult to say more about the 1979 CPS observation. We note, however, that evidence from the population-based CPS series from 1979 to 1996 is consistent with our finding of an upward trend in the share of men with low tenure in the PSID from 1976 through 1996.

(Text continues on p. 62.)

Table 2.1 Trends in Tenure Probabilities of Employed Male Household Heads

	Coefficient on Linear Trend							
	Tenure Less Than or Equal to One Year				Tenure Less Than Ten Years			
	CPS		PSID		CPS		PSID	
Group	1973 to 1996	1983 to 1996	1976 to 1996	1983 to 1996	1973 to 1996	1983 to 1996	1976 to 1996	1983 to 1996
Full sample	.0015	.0020	.0027	.0011	.0001	.0040	.0046	.0079
	(.0008)	(.0014)	(.0007)	(.0010)	(.0016)	(.0014)	(.0012)	(.0010)
Age								
Twenty to twenty-nine	.0018	.0045	.0039	−.0002				
	(.0014)	(.0027)	(.0016)	(.0022)				
Thirty to thirty-nine	.0014	.0007	.0022	.0015	−.0002	.0030	.0029	.0070
	(.0013)	(.0021)	(.0008)	(.0014)	(.0022)	(.0025)	(.0016)	(.0013)
Forty to forty-nine	.0015	.0014	.0027	.0028	.0004	.0057	.0064	.0109
	(.0005)	(.0006)	(.0007)	(.0010)	(.0016)	(.0009)	(.0012)	(.0008)
Fifty to fifty-nine	.0018	.0020	.0006	−.0017	.0020	.0075	.0060	.0066
	(.0003)	(.0008)	(.0007)	(.0010)	(.0022)	(.0006)	(.0009)	(.0010)

Education								
Less than twelve years	.0022	.0022	.0021	−.0005	.0024	.0060	.0050	.0035
	(.0008)	(.0007)	(.0008)	(.0020)	(.0014)	(.0007)	(.0013)	(.0031)
Twelve years	.0015	.0022	.0031	.0027	.0005	.0046	.0038	.0091
	(.0005)	(.0003)	(.0004)	(.0007)	(.0017)	(.0005)	(.0022)	(.0024)
Thirteen to fifteen	.0009	.0018	.0029	.0008	−.0004	.0031	.0072	.0111
	(.0013)	(.0029)	(.0012)	(.0022)	(.0017)	(.0028)	(.0010)	(.0009)
Sixteen or more years	.0009	.0011	.0019	−.0000	−.0006	.0045	.0057	.0095
	(.0006)	(.0012)	(.0009)	(.0009)	(.0025)	(.0024)	(.0014)	(.0015)
Race								
White	.0014	.0019	.0023	.0006	.0001	.0039	.0045	.0072
	(.0009)	(.0017)	(.0007)	(.0011)	(.0017)	(.0015)	(.0011)	(.0009)
Black	.0022	.0035	.0061	.0048	−.0000	.0041	.0036	.0146
	(.0006)	(.0031)	(.0010)	(.0014)	(.0012)	(.0008)	(.0000)	(.0040)

Note: CPS: Tenure and employee benefits supplements; PSID: weighted full sample. Standard errors in parentheses. "Tenure less than or equal to one year" samples include all individuals ages twenty to fifty-nine; "tenure less than ten years" samples include all individuals ages thirty to fifty-nine. First-stage logit regressions include control variables for age, age squared, education group, and race group (where appropriate). Second stage is regression of adjusted year-specific predicted probabilities on time trend. Predicted probabilities are calculated at the mean value of the control variables. Standard errors are estimated using the jackknife.

Figure 2.9   Employment and Population-Based Estimates of Share of Low Tenure, 1974 to 1997

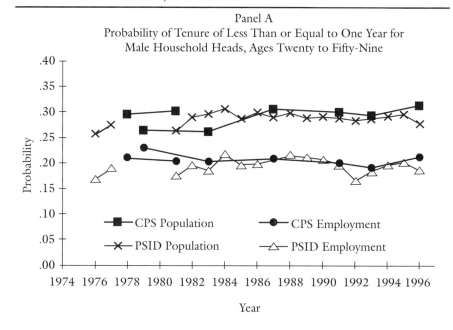

Panel A
Probability of Tenure of Less Than or Equal to One Year for
Male Household Heads, Ages Twenty to Fifty-Nine

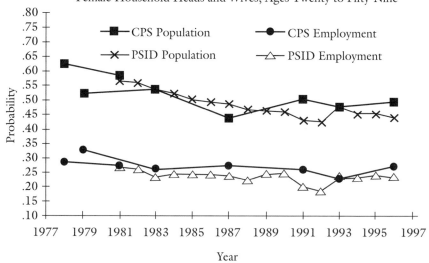

Panel B
Probability of Tenure of Less Than or Equal to One Year for
Female Household Heads and Wives, Ages Twenty to Fifty-Nine

Figure 2.9 *Continued*

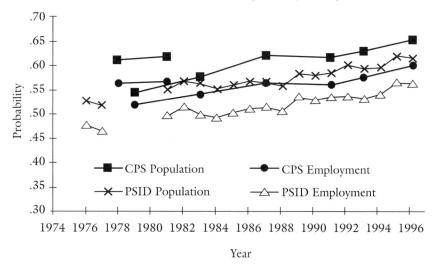

Panel C
Probability of Tenure of Less Than Ten Years for
Male Household Heads, Ages Thirty to Fifty-Nine

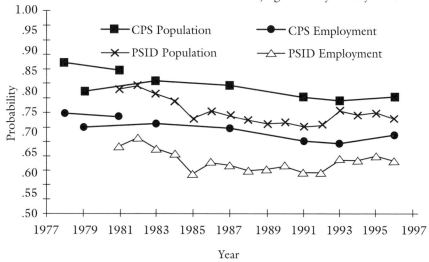

Panel D
Probability of Tenure of Less Than Ten Years for
Female Household Heads and Wives, Ages Twenty to Fifty-Nine

Note: CPS: Tenure and employee benefits supplements; PSID: Weighted full sample. Panels have different horizontal and vertical scales. Male sample includes blacks and whites only; female sample includes all race-ethnic groups.

More generally, the population-based trends confirm our previous results from 1983 through 1996: we find reductions in the fraction of women with one year or less of tenure and increases in the fraction of men with less than ten years of tenure.

We have also directly controlled for the effects of the business cycle in regressions like those presented in the previous section. Including the unemployment rate in these regressions gave estimates that were similar to those presented earlier. This largely reflects that our measures of the incidence of low tenure capture the effects of recent job changes due to both quits and involuntary separations. Because these two categories of job change generally have opposite cyclical patterns, it is not surprising that our measures are relatively unaffected by the business cycle.

Our results might also be sensitive to changes over time in the flow of workers from nonemployment to employment. An increase (decrease) in this inflow would push the share of workers with low tenure up (down), while the underlying trend in job stability would remain unchanged. Using the longitudinal aspect of the PSID, we estimated the fraction of employed individuals in year t who had tenure of less than twelve months in year t + 1. This measure is closer to the retention rate measures reported elsewhere in the literature (see, for example, Diebold, Neumark, and Polsky 1997) and is not sensitive to changes in the flow of workers into employment. Like the population-based series cited earlier, this experiment also produced estimated trends that were essentially parallel to the employment-based results reported in figures 2.2 and 2.3. Conditioning on employment in the previous year lowers the probability of having tenure of less than one year by 5.5 to 6.5 percentage points but has no discernible effect on the trends. We find little evidence that eliminating those workers who have low tenure following a transition into the workforce changes our main conclusions.

DISCUSSION AND CONCLUSION

We conclude by returning to the questions that motivated this work: Has there been a trend toward decreased job stability? Does the answer to this question differ between the CPS and the PSID? In answer to the first question, we find that both data sets show a statistically significant increase in the probability of workers having less than ten years of tenure. We find no similar trend, however, in the fraction of workers with one year or less of tenure. Because the pool of workers with less than one year of tenure is quite small, it is difficult to estimate precisely small changes in this fraction over time, particularly with the sample sizes available in the PSID. In answer to the second question, and perhaps most central to the specific goals of this chapter, we find similar trends in the two data sets once consistent data series, variable definitions, and time periods are used.

We find several explanations for the apparent sensitivity of previous estimates of job stability or turnover to the particular data used. The general tendency for PSID studies to find an upward trend in employment instability where none is found using CPS data may be explained by three factors:

1. Tenure estimates or job-changing rates based on PSID data may be very sensitive to the particular variables used. Some of the increase found in the PSID, as noted by Diebold, Neumark, and Polsky (1997), results from failure to account for the major changes made in the questions regarding job and position changing during the 1980s. As emphasized by figure 2.1, the exact choice and definition of variables in the PSID can substantially affect the resulting trends.

2. Comparison of the PSID and CPS shows some sensitivity of the results to the exact time period studied. Many of the previous PSID studies have included data only through 1988, when the probability of having tenure of one year or less appears to have peaked in those data. This is not, however, inconsistent with the CPS findings once the later years of both surveys are included. The trends we find over the course of the 1980s and 1990s in the PSID are also sensitive to whether we begin the period in 1976, 1981, or 1983.[33] A related point is that individual year estimates of job tenure or job-changing probabilities in the PSID are, by virtue of the sample sizes available, substantially less precise than those in the CPS.

3. Although we cannot say with certainty, our evidence suggests that the CPS question change prior to 1983 may have had an important effect on comparisons across data sets. For comparisons starting in the 1970s, the upward trend in instability found in the PSID for some groups (young workers, for example) may reflect genuine changes (although relatively small) in job mobility. These changes may not have been replicated in the CPS-based studies, either because those studies did not include the 1970s or because the CPS question change masks this increase.

In many cases, a combination of these factors contributes to the apparent differences in findings across data sets. For example, the PSID study by Marcotte (1999) is based on a relatively young sample of workers (under age forty-five) and examines the period 1976 through 1988. Our results from the PSID are quite consistent with his finding of some increase in job instability for young men over this time period. Panel A of figure 2.4 shows a strong increase in the fraction of young men with low tenure from 1976 through 1988. We should also note that two recent studies using the National Longitudinal Survey of Youth (NLSY) (Monks and Pizer 1998; Bernhardt et al., this volume) found an increase in turnover among young men from the 1970s to the 1980s. The lack of CPS-based evidence for such an increase over this period is not necessarily informative given potential comparability problems related to the CPS question change.

Despite beginning his analysis in the 1970s, Polsky (1999) produced the one PSID-based study that found virtually no increase in turnover rates. It is likely that he achieved this result because he included data through 1991 (when some of the temporary increase in the late 1980s had been reversed) and based his measure of turnover on the position tenure question, which measures a somewhat different quantity than employer tenure. More important, however, Polsky corrected for changes over time in heaping patterns; other authors using the PSID position tenure question did not. The comparison of trends in slightly different levels of position tenure shown in figure 2.1 suggests that such a correction may be crucial to making correct inferences based on this question.

Our results from both data sets during the 1980s and 1990s are quite consistent with the findings of Diebold, Neumark, and Polsky (1997) and a recent extension of this work by Neumark, Polsky, and Hansen (this volume). These studies are somewhat unique among those using the CPS in that they explicitly adjusted for the question change after 1983. Diebold, Neumark, and Polsky (1997) produced two main sets of estimates: one covering the period 1983 through 1991, and a second covering 1973 through 1991. In our full samples we find, consistent with Diebold et al., little evidence of an increased incidence of low tenure during the period from 1983 to 1991. Finally, as we show in figures 2.6 and 2.7, much of the increase that we report in the fraction of workers with less than ten years of tenure occurs during the early part of the 1990s, consistent with the findings of Neumark, Polsky, and Hansen (this volume).

Although we view our findings as generally consistent with those of Diebold, Neumark, and Polsky (1997) from the 1980s to the 1990s, we find less agreement in the 1973 to 1991 period. Like Diebold, Neumark, and Polsky, we find no strong overall trend in job stability over this period, but results by education and age subgroups differ somewhat across the two studies. Of course, our PSID results used as the basis for comparison in the 1970s involve only two years in the late 1970s. We are thus not surprised that results focused on the 1980s and later are far more consistent with these previous findings.

Using what we view as the cleanest and most consistent variable to measure tenure in the PSID produces estimates that differ very little from comparable CPS estimates from 1983 to 1996. This is an important find-ing for researchers interested in utilizing either the panel nature of the PSID or the much larger sample sizes available in the CPS to study issues related to job tenure or job stability. Although previous work has focused on the difficulties with the PSID tenure variable, and several recent studies have produced results seemingly at odds with CPS-based studies, we are able to produce consistent results across the two data sets once comparable time frames, variable definitions, and samples are used.

ACKNOWLEDGMENTS

For their helpful comments, the authors thank Charles Brown, Lawrence Kahn, Henry Farber, David Neumark, Daniel Polsky, seminar participants at the City University of New York Graduate Center, the Federal Reserve Bank of New York, the board of governors of the Federal Reserve, the participants in the Cornell-Princeton Policy Conference on Layoffs, Em-ployment Stability, and Job Changing, and the Russell Sage Foundation Conference on Changes in Job Stability and Job Security. They also thank Bob McIntire and Anne Polivka for insightful discussions regarding the tenure questions in the Current Population Survey.

NOTES

1. Jay Stewart (1997) used the CPS March supplements and explicitly com-pared his results to those of Henry Farber (1998) and David Marcotte (1999). His results are quite similar to those of Farber (who used the CPS tenure supplement), but not very similar to those of Marcotte (who used the PSID).

2. Kenneth Swinnerton and Howard Wial (1995, 1996) did find a reduction in retention rates using the CPS data, but a revision of their findings in response to comments by Diebold, Neumark, and Polsky (1996) tempers their estimated change in retention rates. Remaining differences between Swinnerton and Wial's findings and those of Diebold, Neumark, and Polsky appear to be related to how the authors weight the CPS data to account for nonresponse to the tenure question.

3. Diebold, Neumark, and Polsky (1997) have presented evidence that Rose's findings are largely driven by his use of the "reason for job change" ques-tion in the PSID. Later in the chapter, we discuss the important changes in this question during the mid-1980s.

4. Evidence on the extent of this problem is documented in Diebold, Neu-mark, and Polsky (1997) in their replication of the results of Rose (1995).

5. Those who had changed positions within the past twelve months, or since the beginning of the previous calendar year, were asked, "What happened to the job you had before—did the company go out of business, were you laid off, promoted, were you not working, or what?"

6. Most of the previous CPS studies have not been limited to reference persons and their spouses. Calculation of low tenure probabilities in the CPS including nonheads and nonspouses, however, does not result in trends different from those reported here.

7. In the PSID, the male in a two-adult household is automatically considered the "head of household."

8. Because race was asked of wives beginning only in 1984 in the PSID, we do not similarly restrict the female samples.

9. PSID data from 1993 to 1996 are "early release," so these results may be subject to revision upon final release of the data.

10. In particular, prior to 1983 the PSID question was, "How long have you worked for your present employer?" From 1984 to 1987, the PSID employer tenure question was, "How many years altogether have you worked for your present employer?" and after 1987 it was, "How many years' experience do you have altogether with your present employer?" See the appendix in Polsky (1999) for the complete set of PSID tenure questions.

11. This is because the total time measure is from a question asking for a response in months, while the measure of time in the most recent spell comes from a question eliciting the month and year the spell started.

12. Other responses to the "reason for job change" question that might also be applicable to within-employer changes (in addition to promotion) include "wanted a change in jobs," "other or transfer," and "job completed."

13. The exact question changed from, "How long have you been in your present position?" to, "When did you start working in your present position?"

14. Another alternative is to use the "reason for job change" question in the PSID. In addition to the problems with using the variable noted by Polsky (1999), it is triggered from the response to the position tenure question and so has all of the advantages and disadvantages of that question as well.

15. Recognizing this potential problem, Polsky (1999) adjusted for heaping by using the longitudinal aspect of the PSID to identify those who round down to one year from those who round up. Although this may solve some of the problem, the patterns shown in figure 2.1 nonetheless suggest that turnover rates and trends in them that are based on this variable may be quite sensitive to how the heaping issue is handled.

16. We do not include a comparable position tenure series using the eighteen-month cutoff since it is not generally possible to identify promotions that occurred more than twelve months before.

17. We use less than twelve months as the cutoff for this job-based series because job tenure is reported only in bracketed quantities during these years.

18. Information on tenure is also available in the 1983 and 1988 employee benefits supplements.

19. Supplement weights are not available in 1978 and 1981.

20. We also performed the analyses using adjusted supplement weights that take into account nonresponse to the tenure questions. This also made very little

difference to the results. Further details are available from the authors on request.

21. Interviewers were instructed to follow this type of rounding rule if the individual answered the new question with a non-integer response (U.S. Bureau of Labor Statistics 1997).

22. In the CPS, standard errors are estimated as $[p(1-p)/N]^{1/2}$, where p is the share of the sample with one year or less of tenure and N is the number of (unweighted) observations in the cell. To address sample design issues in the PSID, standard errors are estimated using balanced half-sample replication (Wolter 1985).

23. Farber (1998), in his appendix tables, showed similar results for 1979. His estimated rates of tenure of less than one year were also substantially higher in 1979 than in the surrounding years.

24. Because the education question in the CPS changed in January 1992, we use the recoding scheme proposed by David Jaeger (1997) to define consistent groups across the break in question. In particular, Jaeger showed that agreement between the old and new questions is increased if individuals who attended but did not complete their thirteenth year of school are included in the "thirteen to fifteen" group.

25. Because we have been unable to recover complete information on wives' education from the PSID early release data, we have examined education-based differences for women only through 1992, the last year for which final-release, fully documented PSID data are available.

26. Different sample coverage may partially explain the discrepancy. Because of the nature of its sample, the PSID does not include immigrants who entered the United States after the first wave of interviews, and the CPS is a representative sample of the population in the year of the survey. Unfortunately, immigrants are not separately identified in the CPS prior to 1994. Using the 1996 sample, we find that the share of native men with less than ten years of employer tenure was .58, while for immigrants it was .75; for women the shares were .68 and .79 for natives and immigrants, respectively. For the "one year or less of tenure" measure, the differences in share between natives and immigrants were .04 and .01 for men and women, respectively.

27. Tables showing these results are available from the authors on request.

28. We control for education by including dummy variables for the education groups shown in figures 2.6 and 2.7.

29. In creating these probabilities, the logit function is evaluated at the observed mean of the other covariates.

30. J. G. MacKinnon and Halbert White (1985) showed that the small-sample performance (which is certainly relevant here!) of jackknife standard errors is superior to other heteroskedasticity-consistent standard errors, such as those suggested by White (1980).

31. In addition to the evidence from the figures in previous sections, we have also estimated the trend terms shown in table 2.1 without conditioning on

age, education, and race in the first stage. These "unadjusted" trend coefficients are consistently smaller and are often not statistically significant.

32. Recall that in 1979 the CPS asked the new (employer-based) question, which we would have expected to give somewhat smaller estimates of low tenure than in 1978 and 1981, when the old (job-based) question was asked.

33. We do not believe this is the result of different business cycle conditions in the different years. We have also estimated trends holding constant the unemployment rate and alternative business cycle controls and obtained similar results.

REFERENCES

Boisjoly, Johanne, Greg J. Duncan, and Timothy Smeeding. 1998. "The Shifting Incidence of Involuntary Job Losses from 1968 to 1992." *Industrial Relations* 37: 207–31.

Brown, James, and Audrey Light. 1992. "Interpreting Panel Data on Job Tenure." *Journal of Labor Economics* 10: 219–57.

Diebold, Frank X., David Neumark, and Daniel Polsky. 1996. "Comment on Kenneth A. Swinnerton and Howard Wial, 'Is Job Stability Declining in the U.S. Economy?'" *Industrial and Labor Relations Review* 49: 348–52.

———. 1997. "Job Stability in the United States." *Journal of Labor Economics* 15: 206–33.

Farber, Henry S. 1997. "The Changing Face of Job Loss in the United States, 1981–1995." *Brookings Papers on Economics Activity: Microeconomics* 1: 55–128.

———. 1998. "Are Lifetime Jobs Disappearing?: Job Duration in the United States: 1973–1993." In *Labor Statistics Measurement Issues*, edited by John Haltiwanger, Marilyn Mauser, and Robert Topel. Chicago: University of Chicago Press.

Gottschalk, Peter, and Robert Moffitt. 1994. "The Growth of Earnings Instability in the U.S. Labor Market." *Brookings Papers on Economic Activity* (2): 217–72.

Jaeger, David A. 1997. "Reconciling the Old and New Census Bureau Education Questions: Recommendations for Researchers." *Journal of Business and Economic Statistics* 15: 300–309.

MacKinnon, J. G., and Halbert White. 1985. "Some Heteroskedasticity-Consistent Covariance Matrix Estimators with Improved Finite Sample Properties." *Journal of Econometrics* 29: 305–25.

Marcotte, Dave. 1995. "Declining Job Stability: What We Know and What It Means." *Journal of Policy Analysis and Management* 14: 590–98.

———. 1999. "Has Job Stability Declined?: Evidence from the Panel Study on Income Dynamics." *American Journal of Sociology and Economics* 58: 197–216.

Monks, James, and Steven Pizer. 1998. "Trends in Voluntary and Involuntary Job Turnover." *Industrial Relations* 37: 440–59.

Polsky, Daniel. 1999. "Changing Consequences of Job Separations in the United States." *Industrial and Labor Relations Review* 52(4): 565–80.

Rose, Stephen. 1995. "Declining Job Security and the Professionalization of

Opportunity." Research Report 95–4. Washington, D.C.: National Commission for Employment Policy.

Stewart, Jay. 1997. *Has Job Mobility Increased?: Evidence from the Current Population Survey: 1975–1995.* Washington, D.C.: U.S. Bureau of Labor Statistics.

Swinnerton, Kenneth A., and Howard Wial. 1995. "Is Job Stability Declining in the U.S. Economy?" *Industrial and Labor Relations Review* 48: 293–394.

———. 1996. "Is Job Stability Declining in the U.S. Economy?: Reply to Diebold, Neumark, and Polsky." *Industrial and Labor Relations Review* 48: 352–55.

U.S. Bureau of Labor Statistics. 1997. "Employee Tenure in the Mid-1990s." News release, January 30, 1997. Available at ftp://146.142.4.23/pub/news.release/tenure.txt.

White, Halbert. 1980. "Heteroskedasticity-Consistent Covariance Matrix Estimation and a Direct Test for Heteroskedasticity." *Econometrica* 48: 817–38.

Wolter, Kirk. 1985. *Introduction to Variance Estimation.* New York: Springer-Verlag.

Chapter 3

Has Job Stability Declined Yet?
New Evidence for the 1990s

David Neumark, Daniel Polsky, and Daniel Hansen

U ntil recently, little was known about how the stability of jobs has changed over time in the U.S. economy, the nature of the changes (if any), and which groups have been most affected. In the past few years, however, researchers have begun to assemble evidence on these questions. This research was spurred in part by a wave of corporate downsizings and accompanying media stories suggesting that workers could "forget any idea of career-long employment with a big company" (*Time,* November 22, 1993), and that "the notion of lifetime employment has come to seem as dated as soda jerks, or tail fins" (*New York Times,* March 8, 1996). However, a spate of widely publicized downsizings does not necessarily imply that the nature of the employment relationship has changed. The goal of much of the research on job stability is to ask whether, in fact, such changes are evident in labor market surveys based on nationally representative samples.

Earlier work (Diebold, Neumark, and Polsky 1996, 1997) examined the temporal evolution of job stability in U.S. labor markets through the 1980s, using data assembled from a sequence of Current Population Survey (CPS) tenure supplements. In contrast to evidence reported by some other researchers, we found little or no change in aggregate job stability in the U.S. economy. Some groups of workers—in particular, the same lower-skill groups that suffered relative wage declines in the 1980s—experienced decreases in job stability in this period. On the other hand, in contrast to perceptions reflected in the media, white, older, more tenured, more educated, white-collar workers did not experience decreases in job stability in the latter part of the 1980s, and indeed some of these groups experienced increases.

Resolving the disagreements on changes in job stability through the 1980s is important to our efforts to measure long-term trends, but the goal of this chapter is simply to update evidence on job stability through the mid-1990s, using recently released CPS data for 1995 that parallel the earlier job tenure supplements. Updating the evidence from system-

70

atic random samples of the population and workforce through this period is especially important because the media have painted a stark picture of declining job stability in the 1990s, based largely on anecdotal evidence and surveys of subjective assessments of job security (Neumark and Polsky 1998).

In measuring job stability using the CPS, it is critical to ensure comparability of the data over time. Because the CPS survey eliciting information on tenure changed in 1995, we pay particular attention here to the adjustments to the data that may be needed for comparability, and we analyze the sensitivity of the results to alternative adjustment procedures in order to obtain a robust impression of the empirical evidence. Despite some relatively minor ambiguities, we believe that a relatively consistent picture emerges in the data for the 1990s, one that contrasts in some ways with our earlier findings for the 1980s.

In the aggregate, there is some evidence that job stability declined modestly in the first half of the 1990s. Moreover, the relatively small aggregate changes mask rather sharp declines in stability for workers with more than a few years of tenure. These sharp declines are partially offset in the aggregate by gains in job stability for low-tenure workers at the beginning stages of attachment to an employer. The changes by tenure group contrast with the 1980s and are more consonant with the increase in job loss among "career workers" noted in the popular press. The pattern by tenure group is roughly similar for blacks and whites and for males and females (although changes in overall job stability differ by race and sex). However, these data do not permit us to infer how stable the jobs of today's younger, low-tenure workers will be once they reach higher levels of tenure. This factor, coupled with the contradictory results for the 1980s, implies that the data on job stability do not support the conclusion that the downward shift in job stability for more tenured workers and the more modest decline in aggregate job stability reflect long-term trends.

RELATED LITERATURE

In earlier work (Diebold, Neumark, and Polsky 1996, 1997), we studied data from a sequence of CPS tenure supplements, issued periodically by the U.S. Census Bureau, that ask workers how long they have been with their current employer or at their current job. By stringing these supplements together, we studied the evolution of tenure for cohorts, summarized in job retention rates over periods of four and ten years. We generally found retention rates to be stable and concluded that there was little or no change in aggregate job stability in the U.S. economy over the 1980s.

Much of the other research studying this question arrived at a different conclusion. Using the PSID, Johanne Boisjoly, Greg Duncan, and Timothy Smeeding (1998), Stephen Rose (1995), and Dave Marcotte (1996) reported evidence of declines in job stability through sample periods extending into the late 1980s or early 1990s. However, Daniel Polsky (1999) and Diebold, Neumark, and Polsky (1997) examined the evidence from the PSID and concluded that the evidence of decreased job stability reported in at least the first two of these papers is largely attributable to changes over time in the variables used to measure job attachment. Kenneth Swinnerton and Howard Wial (1995) reported evidence of declining job stability based on essentially the same CPS tenure supplements that we have used, but the differences in the findings appear to be due in large part to errors they made in using the CPS data (Diebold, Neumark, and Polsky 1996; Swinnerton and Wial 1996). Comparing findings in the National Longitudinal Surveys of Young Men (NLSYM) and of Youth (NLSY), James Monks and Steven Pizer (1998) and Annette Bernhardt and her colleagues (this volume) reported a large increase in the probability of job turnover in the period from 1971 to 1990. It is not entirely clear, however, that we can consistently compare these probabilities across the surveys: because the NLSY collects information on more jobs per year, it may report a greater number of spurious job changes (relative to the earlier NLSYM); more generally, there are significant differences between the early experiences of these two cohorts (for example, the Vietnam War). Nonetheless, the analyses of the NLSY are restricted to younger cohorts for whom we also find some declines in job stability (Diebold, Neumark, and Polsky 1997, table 3). In contrast, the results in Farber (1995), although based on a different analysis, are similar to ours, indicating the overall stability of cross-section tenure distributions in the CPS tenure supplements.

A second issue raised in recent literature concerns what might be termed "job security" as opposed to job stability. Most of the studies cited thus far, as well as the research presented in this chapter, look at the employment relationship from the perspective of job stability, asking, in one fashion or another, whether the length of time people remain on their jobs has declined. However, job security could be declining even if job stability remains unchanged. For example, Polsky (1999) suggests that even though overall separations have remained constant, a greater proportion of recent job separations may now be involuntary (layoffs, plant closings, and so on) rather than voluntary (quits). Because we think that workers quit to improve their well-being, whereas involuntary separations are more likely to make individuals worse off, a rising proportion of involuntary separations could make workers feel less secure and more anxious about their jobs. Using PSID data to compare the periods 1976 to 1981 and 1986 to 1991 (periods chosen because of similar cyclical behavior), Polsky reports that there were modest increases in the rate of involuntary job separation, and that these increases were more marked for older and more tenured workers. Parallel findings were also reported by Boisjoly and his colleagues (1998), Valletta (1996), and Farber (1996). In addition, Polsky finds that in the 1980s the consequences of job loss were more severe than they were the 1970s. In particular, the probability of a large real wage loss following an involuntary separation had risen significantly, an increase that could also have reduced perceived job security. We think the job security versus job stability question is of interest, but in this chapter we restrict our attention to evidence on job stability.

METHODS

GENERAL APPROACH

The metric we use to measure job stability is the retention rate for a current job, which is the probability of retaining a current job over future periods. Specifically, we define the t-year retention rate, R(t), as the probability that a worker will have an additional t years of tenure t years hence. The t-year retention rate may be defined for any subgroup of the population, such as workers with particular initial tenure levels. Denoting current tenure by c, and other characteristics by x, we write the t-year retention rate for workers with initial tenure c and characteristics x in the base sample year 0 as $R_{xc}^0(t)$.[1] The sequence of retention rates, $R_{xc}^0(t)$, $t = 1, 2, \ldots$, is the survival function, which provides a complete characterization of the probability distribution of eventual tenure.

In the absence of longitudinal data covering workers' entire careers, the estimation of the complete sequence of retention rates (that is, the survival function) requires rather strong assumptions. For example, Robert Hall's (1982) estimation of the survival function required the assumption that the employment survival function is stable over time, and that the overall arrival rate (the number of workers beginning new jobs) is constant (Ureta 1992); the latter assumption would be violated, for example, by the increased labor-force participation rates of women.[2] However, given that we are investigating *changes* in job stability, we cannot assume a stable survival function. Instead, we link together a sequence of CPS tenure supplements and use them to characterize tenure distributions based only on observed historical retention rates across spans of years covered by different supplements.

We then track changes in job stability by examining changes in retention rates over different periods. This is potentially advantageous compared with looking at changes in tenure distributions (as in Farber 1995). The latter can be misleading because mean or median tenure may fall owing to new labor market entrants—the same arrival rate problem discussed earlier. Thus, while it is of interest to compare changes in overall tenure distributions, more information about changes in job stability can be obtained from comparing retention rates over time.

ESTIMATING RETENTION RATES

The basic t-year retention rate for workers with c years of tenure is estimated as the ratio of the number of workers with t + c years of tenure (and t years older) in the tenure supplement t years hence ($N_{x,t+c}^{0+t}$) to the number of workers with c years of tenure in the base year tenure supplement (N_{xc}^0). Formally,

$$\hat{R}_{xc}^0(t) = \frac{N_{x,t+c}^{0+t}}{N_{xc}^0}. \tag{3.1}$$

Retention rates can be estimated for any subgroup that is consistently represented across surveys. Ideally we would like to estimate retention rates from longitudinal data in which we can observe whether individuals remain on their jobs in the future. However, as equation 3.1 indicates, we instead use cross-sectional data sets, studying cohort experiences with respect to job stability by stringing these data sets together.[3]

Because the retention rate estimate is based on ratios of numbers of workers in different CPS samples, the sample of workers from each CPS must be representative of the population if we are to obtain unbiased estimates. The CPS is a stratified sample representative of the U.S. population when the weights provided for each sampled individual are applied. We find, however, that nonresponse to the tenure supplement causes the sample of respondents with tenure data available to be nonrepresentative. Therefore, in constructing the Ns in equation 3.1, we adjust the standard CPS sample weights by multiplying by the reciprocal of the response rate to the tenure question for each race-age-sex subgroup, with age grouped into five-year intervals.[4] We always use the adjusted weights in forming the Ns, which are then rescaled to reproduce the actual sample sizes.

We are also interested in the variance of this estimated retention rate. If we had true longitudinal data, our estimated retention rate would come from the following calculation. We initially draw a sample of size N_{xc}^0 (a number on which we condition), and t years later $N_{x,t+c}^{0,t}$ observations have an additional t years of tenure.[5] Conditioning on N_{xc}^0, $N_{x,t+c}^{0,t}$ can be modeled as a binomial random variable (with $N_{x,t+c}^{0,t}$ the number of "successes" in N_{xc}^0 trials). Then the estimate of $R_{xc}^0(t)$ in equation 3.1 would just be the estimate of the proportion of "successes" (defined as remaining in the job for t years). The estimated retention rate would then be asymptotically normally distributed, with

$$\hat{R}_{xc}{}^0(t) \overset{a}{\sim} N\left(R_{xc}{}^0(t), \frac{R_{xc}{}^0(t)\,(1 - R_{xc}{}^0(t))}{N_{xc}{}^0} \right). \tag{3.2}$$

Of course, we do not have true longitudinal data but rather estimate $N_{x,t+c}{}^{0,t}$ from an independent sample. What we do not know, then, is how many observations from the year 0 sample would have been observed with $t + c$ years of tenure t years later. That is, in contrast to equation 3.1, the retention rate estimate we would like to use (from true longitudinal data) is

$$\hat{Q}_{xc}{}^0(t) = \frac{N_{x,t+c}{}^{0,t}}{N_{xc}{}^0}. \tag{3.3}$$

We can rewrite the retention rate estimate we actually use (equation 3.1) as

$$\hat{R}_{xc}{}^0(t) = \frac{N_{x,t+c}{}^{0,t}}{N_{xc}{}^0} + \frac{N_{x,t+c}{}^{0+t} - N_{x,t+c}{}^{0,t}}{N_{xc}{}^0}, \tag{3.4}$$

which makes clear that our estimated retention rate can be interpreted as a true retention rate in longitudinal data, plus an error (the second term) that comes from the fact that we estimate the number of individuals with $t + c$ years of tenure from an independent sample rather than a true longitudinal sample. This sampling error generally adds variance to the estimated retention rate.[6] To calculate the variance of the retention rate we can estimate, $N_{x,t+c}{}^{0+t}$ can be modeled as a multinomial random variable for the number of observations with characteristics x and tenure $t + c$ out of the entire sample N^{0+t}. Using $p_{x,t+c}{}^{0+t}$ to denote the true proportion with x and $t + c$ in the year $0 + t$ supplement, the variance of the estimated retention rate is

$$\mathrm{Var}(\hat{R}_{xc}{}^0(t)) = \frac{N^{0+t} p_{x,t+c}{}^{0+t}(1 - p_{x,t+c}{}^{0+t})}{(N_{xc}{}^0)^2}. \tag{3.5}$$

We can estimate this variance consistently using the corresponding sample moments.

Because

$$\frac{N^{0+t} p_{x,t+c}{}^{0+t}}{(N_{xc}{}^0)} \cong R_{xc}{}^0(t), \tag{3.6}$$

we can write

$$\text{Var}(\hat{R}_{xc}{}^0(t)) \cong \frac{R_{xc}{}^0(t)(1 - p_{x,t+c}{}^{0+t})}{N_{xc}{}^0} =$$

$$\frac{R_{xc}{}^0(t)(1 - R_{xc}{}^0(t))}{N_{xc}{}^0} \times \frac{(1 - p_{x,t+c}{}^{0+t})}{(1 - R_{xc}{}^0(t))}. \qquad (3.7)$$

When we are estimating the retention rate for the whole sample (that is, when $p_{x,t+c}{}^{0+t}$ is simply the proportion with tenure $t + c$ and we do not distinguish based on characteristics x), $p_{x,t+c}{}^{0+t}$ and $R_{xc}{}^0(t)$ are both estimates of the retention rate, although they have different expectations if the survival function is not stable. (Otherwise, we could just use cross-sectional data to estimate survival functions.) But to a first approximation, in this case the variance of the estimated retention rate using repeated cross-sections, is no higher. However, when we are looking at a subsample with particular characteristics x, the variance is higher than it would be with true longitudinal data, since $p_{x,t+c}{}^{0+t}$, which is the cross-sectional estimate of the retention rate multiplied by the proportion of the sample with characteristics x, is less than $R_{xc}{}^0(t)$, as equation 3.6 shows. Intuitively, this occurs because in the year $0 + t$ sample we also resample on the characteristics x. The smaller the proportion of observations with characteristics x (and hence the smaller $p_{x,t+c}{}^{0+t}$ is relative to $R_{xc}{}^0(t)$), the more the variance is increased because we may get variation in $N_{x,t+c}{}^{0+t}$ owing to sampling variation in the proportion of observations with characteristics x, not solely variation owing to the uncertainty of retaining a job.

We also study changes in retention rates over time. In estimating the variances of these changes, we consider an additional factor: the potential for dependence in sampling errors in the estimated retention rates for different periods. This can arise because in some cases we use the same supplement in the denominator of one retention rate and the numerator of the earlier retention rate. For example, using the surveys in years 0, $0 + t$, and $0 + 2t$ to estimate changes in t-year retention rates from year 0 to year $0 + t$, the estimated change in retention rates is

$$\Delta\hat{R}_{xc}(t) = \frac{N_{x,t+c}{}^{0+2t}}{N_{xc}{}^{0+t}} - \frac{N_{x,t+c}{}^{0+t}}{N_{xc}{}^0}. \qquad (3.8)$$

The variance of this expression involves the covariance of the two estimated retention rates. Depending on the tenure groups we specify, there may be some overlap between the observations counted in $N_{xc}{}^{0+t}$ and those counted in $N_{x,t+c}{}^{0+t}$.[7] However, as explained earlier, in computing each retention rate we condition on the number in the denominator of each rate (the number of individuals with characteristics x and tenure c in the "base" year for calculating the retention rate). Under this assumption, the overlapping observations between the denominator of the first expression and the numerator of the second does not generate a covariance between the two expressions. Obviously, however, the existence of the overlap suggests that this conditioning assumption is not entirely satisfactory, and that the standard errors for the changes in retention rates that we compute are likely to be somewhat understated if we ignore the negative covariance between the estimated retention rates that is generated by the overlapping observations. On the other hand, retention rates may be positively correlated over time as, for example, increases in retention rates affect employers' expectations regarding worker turnover, leading to changes in behavior (such as increased human capital investment) that in turn reduce turnover further. This positive covariance would tend to reduce the variance of the difference in equation 3.8. For these reasons, we must regard statistical inferences regarding some of our estimated changes in retention rates quite cautiously. However, when we compute changes in eight-year retention rates, we use different surveys for the end of the first span over which we compute these rates (1991) and the beginning of the second span (1987), so the problem of negative covariance from overlapping observations does not arise. Similarly, there are some changes in the four-year retention rates we estimate for which this problem does not arise because the periods are nonoverlapping—specifically, changes from the period 1983 to 1987 to the period 1991 to 1995.

Aside from these factors, we make numerous corrections and adjustments to the data in an attempt to obtain more reliable comparisons of job stability over time. These adjustments probably contribute further variance to our estimates of levels of and changes in retention rates. On balance, therefore, we suspect that our estimated variances understate the true variances, which strengthens the evidence when we find no significant changes in estimated retention rates and weakens the evidence when we find significant changes.

DATA

The empirical analysis in this chapter first updates estimates of changes in four-year retention rates, using 1983, 1987, 1991, and 1995 CPS data. Thus, we estimate and compare retention rates for 1983 to 1987, 1987 to 1991, and 1991 to 1995; estimates for the first two spans were reported in our earlier work. In addition, the 1995 tenure data enable us to estimate and compare eight-year retention rates for 1983 to 1991 and 1987 to 1995; we also report evidence on these rates. For 1983, 1987, and 1991, we use the January CPS tenure supplements. For 1995, we use tenure data from the February contingent work supplement. As in our earlier work, there are some problems with tenure data reported in all years in the CPS. We first mention how we handle these, relegating the details to the appendix. We then go on to discuss specific additional problems that arise in the new 1995 data that we use.[8] For all years, we study nonagricultural, non-self-employed workers,[9] either currently working or with a job but not currently at work, age sixteen or older.

Our approach to the data is to attempt to ensure comparability between the different time spans. Comparability may be particularly influenced by different rounding patterns and by changes in the survey instrument.[10] We next describe how we address each of these issues.

ROUNDING AND HEAPING

The empirical probability distributions of reported tenure for each of the four years are shown by the dark bars in figure 3.1. The rough shape of these distributions is the same in each of the four years, with the highest proportion reporting tenure in the range of zero to one year, and the proportion declining nearly monotonically in subsequent years.[11] However, the empirical distributions reveal some other features.

First, for 1983, 1987, and 1991, the proportion reporting tenure of one to two years is lower than the proportion reporting tenure of two to three years. This almost surely arises because the wording of the tenure question has led to a phenomenon we call rounding. In each of these surveys, the tenure question asks how long a person has worked for the present employer. If the answer is less than one year, the respondent is queried as to the length of tenure in months; otherwise, the answer is recorded in years. Thus, if respondents have worked more than one and a half years, they may very well respond that they have been working for two years. So we might expect that approximately one-half of the respondents with twelve to twenty-four months of tenure are coded as having two (that is, two to less than three) years of tenure rather than one (one to less than two). On the other hand, this problem is much less apparent for 1995 because individuals could choose to respond in terms of weeks, months, or years.[12]

A second feature of the empirical tenure distributions is that they have spikes at multiples of five years, which we call heaping. The problem, originally identified by Manuelita Ureta (1992), presumably arises because of rounding with regard to the number of years for which a respondent has worked for the present employer. Our method for adjusting for rounding and heaping is described in the appendix. The graphed lines in figure 3.1 show the adjusted distributions for each year.

THE PROBLEMS WITH 1995 TENURE DATA

The 1983, 1987, and 1991 tenure supplements used a uniform question, in particular, "How long has [_____] been working continuously for his present employer [_____]?" Unfortunately, in 1995 the Census Bureau did not continue to elicit information on tenure in the same way for the same four-year interval between earlier supplements. Because the primary results of our analysis involve comparisons over time, ensuring comparability of the data over time is critical to being able to attribute changes in retention rates to changes in job stability rather than changes in the data instrument. In particular, there were two potentially quite important changes in the tenure questions in the 1995 supplement.[13]

The first important change is that the tenure questions take different forms for individuals classified as contingent workers. Table 3.1 lists the various ways the question is asked, depending on the classification of the worker; in the appendix, table 3A.1 provides the questions and definitions used to classify alternative types of contingent workers. As a general matter, the questions try to clear up some ambiguities that might arise in using the general tenure question from earlier years for contingent workers. For example, if an individual is a temporary worker in an agency (type 4 in the table), defining how long he or she has been working continuously for his or her present employer is ambiguous, since this could refer either to the agency itself or to the present placement. Thus, the contingent work supplement first asks about the amount of time worked at the current place of work. It then asks how long the worker has been accepting assignments from a temporary help agency, although it might be preferable to ask how long the worker has been accepting assignments from the temporary help agency from which he or she now accepts assignments, were there only one. Similarly, contractors are asked about tenure at the place to which they are currently assigned as well as at the company that contracts out their services.[14]

Although these more detailed questions provide less ambiguous information on tenure for contingent workers, it is not immediately obvious which types of answers are most comparable to the tenure responses such workers would have provided on the earlier tenure supplements. Our guess is that the responses that refer to the current place of work are more comparable. Furthermore, we are least likely to reject erroneously the widely held view that job stability has declined if we use these lower-bound responses, which seems the appropriate strategy given that our previous work is at odds with this view. The changes for contingent workers may also have a minor overall impact on the estimates because these workers represent only about 10 percent of the workforce, although this depends, of course, on how much the measurement of ten-

Figure 3.1   Frequency Distributions of Job Tenure in CPS Surveys

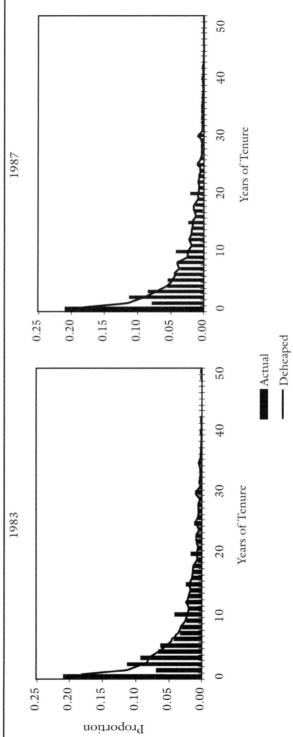

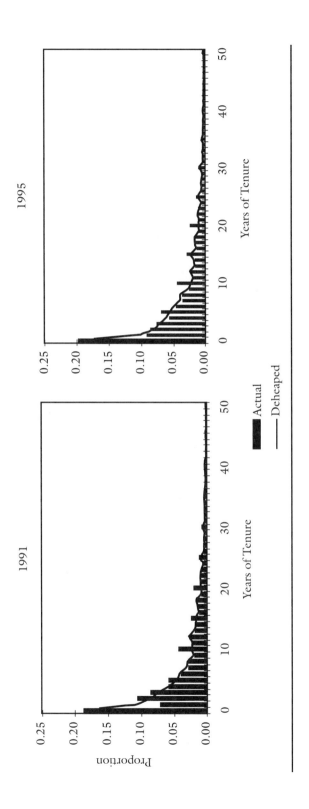

Table 3.1   Tenure Questions in the February 1995 Contingent Work Supplement

Type-Question	Percentage Answering
1. *Incorporated self-employed:* "How long have you been self-employed?"	3.87
2. *Independent contractor:* "How long have you worked for the employer where you worked last week?" (low) or "How long have you been an independent contractor"? (high)	.98
3. *Temporary worker, no agency:* "How long have you worked for (*fill in employer's name from the basic CPS*)?"	3.29
4. *Temporary worker in an agency:* "How long have you worked (*where you are currently working/fill in employer's name from the basic CPS*)?" (low) or "How long have you been accepting assignments from a temporary help agency? If there have been long periods when you have been turning down assignments for reasons such as attending school, only include the time since the last interruption." (high)	.94
5. *Contractor with employer:* "How long have you worked for (*fill in employer's name from basic CPS/the place where you were assigned*)?" (low) or "How long have you worked for the company that contracts out your services?" (high)	.00
6. *On-call worker:* "How long have you worked for the employer where you were working last week?" (low) or "How long have you been an on-call worker?" (high)	1.40
7. *Day laborer:* "How long have you been a day laborer?"	.00
8. *Noncontingent worker:* "How long have you worked for (*fill in employer's name from the basic CPS*)?" or "Excluding your time as a temporary worker, contractor, consultant, free-lancer, or on-call worker, how long have you worked for (*fill in employer's name from the basic CPS*)?"	89.51

ure is affected. Nonetheless, we proceed by defining low and high values of tenure in the 1995 survey, based on the workplace-specific and more general tenure responses, respectively, and report some results both ways.[15]

The second and most important difference in the 1995 tenure data is that in the earlier tenure supplements the question referred to "continuous" work for the same employer, while the question in 1995 drops the word "continuous." Because some employer separations are temporary, this introduces a comparability problem between reported tenure in 1995 and reported tenure in the previous supplements. For example, if we are calculating a four-year retention rate from 1991 to 1995, because people will appear to have higher tenure in 1995 than they actually do (based on the earlier definition), it will appear that more people have stayed on their job for four years. This upward bias would, of course, tend to obscure any decrease in job stability through 1995.

We correct for this bias by using alternative available data sources to adjust the 1995 CPS data. In February 1996, the CPS included the Displaced Worker, Job Tenure, and Occupational Mobility Supplements, which included both "continuous" and "total tenure" questions. In particular, in the 1996 CPS the question pertaining to total tenure asked how long the respondent had been working for his or her present employer. The question pertaining to continuous tenure asked how long he or she had been working continuously for that employer. (The latter is the same question asked in the 1983, 1987, and 1991 supplements.) Our basic strategy is to adjust the 1995 CPS total tenure distribution to represent continuous tenure based on adjustments computed from the 1996 CPS.[16]

These adjustments include three steps. We first calculate the fraction of individuals whose total tenure exceeds continuous tenure. We then calculate the amount of the difference for this subset of individuals. We carry out these calculations at disaggregated levels of total tenure, since it is likely that the two measures diverge more for more tenured workers. Next, we apply these adjustment factors to 1995 reported tenure to approximate the distribution of continuous tenure. Specifically, using the 1996 CPS data for specific tenure groups (encompassing sufficiently large sample sizes), we first estimate the proportion for whom the two measures differ. We then calculate the difference between total and continuous tenure at four quartiles of the distribution of this difference (always weighting the data).[17] In the appendix, table 3A.2 reports these results for the 1996 CPS data. In the final step of the adjustment, we randomly choose this same proportion of respondents in the corresponding total tenure group in the 1995 CPS, divide this chosen group into four equally sized groups, and then adjust tenure by the estimated ratio for one of the quartiles.[18]

The top left-hand panel of figure 3.2 displays the distributions of total and continuous tenure in the 1996 CPS tenure data, as well as the estimated distribution of continuous tenure that results if we apply this procedure to the distributions of total tenure in the 1996 CPS. The top right-hand panel summarizes this information in terms of the implied differences in the distributions of total and continuous tenure. The bottom panels display similar information for the 1995 CPS data (having already applied the deheaping procedure for the 1995 CPS explained in the previous subsection), although in this case there is no actual continuous tenure variable. As we would expect, the adjustment based on the 1996 CPS data moves some individuals from higher tenure to lower tenure; this is reflected in the right-hand panels as a negative difference be-

Figure 3.2   Frequency Distributions of Total Job Tenure and Estimated Continuous Job Tenure Based on the CPS Adjustments

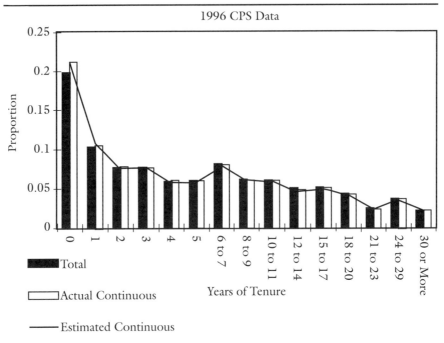

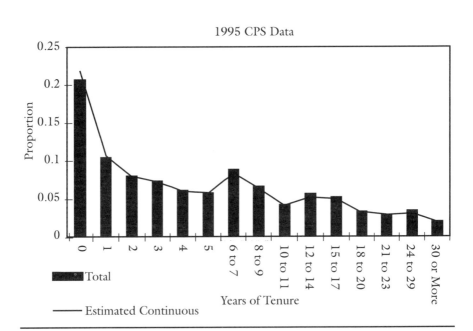

Figure 3.2 *Continued*

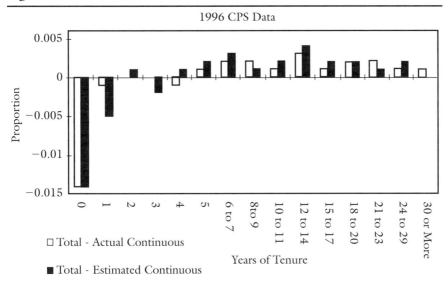

1996 CPS Data

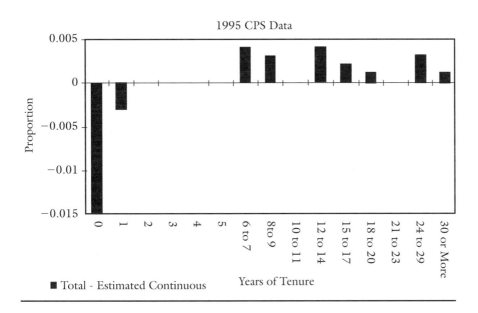

1995 CPS Data

tween the proportion with, for example, total tenure of one to two years and the proportion with continuous tenure in this range, and positive differences at higher tenure levels. Obviously, this adjustment leads to lower retention rates through 1995 than we obtain in the absence of this adjustment.

As a check on the robustness of our results to this adjustment to the 1995 CPS data, we have carried out a similar exercise using adjustment factors estimated from the PSID, which, for the waves covering 1988 to 1992, asks workers to report current tenure in two ways: total time with employer and total time since most recent hire. Although using these data to perform the adjustment is considerably more complicated, the results are qualitatively similar. (For a description of the results, see Neumark and Polsky 1997.)

Finally, as an additional check on the robustness of the results to the tenure correction, we report limited findings in which we simply pretend that the 1996 CPS supplement was administered one year earlier and substitute it for the 1995 supplement. Strictly speaking, this procedure requires that the 1996 sample come from a stable population with a stable survival function for job tenure and a constant arrival rate. Although we do not believe that either of these assumptions holds, violations of this assumption over such a short period may be sufficiently minor that substituting the 1996 data for the 1995 data provides at least an informative check on whether the more complicated adjustments using the 1996 CPS data (or the 1988 to 1992 PSID data) are providing misleading estimates of job retention rates.

A natural question that arises given the preceding discussion is whether we can learn anything reliable from extending the analysis to use the 1995 data, and more significantly, whether there are alternative data sources that might not be plagued by changes in the survey instrument and might provide enhanced comparability of job stability over time. As noted earlier, some of the other data sources that may address this issue are also affected by changes in the survey questions. Problems with the PSID were noted earlier, although Polsky (1999) has demonstrated that it is possible to use the PSID to look at changes in job stability on a consistent basis over time; in addition, however, the much smaller sample size of the PSID prevents much disaggregated analysis. Farber (1996) has used the Displaced Worker Surveys (DWS) to study job loss, in contrast to overall job stability. It turns out, however, that this data source also underwent changes that make comparisons of the 1994 DWS with earlier surveys problematic. Specifically, the recall period covered through the 1992 DWS was five years, compared with three years in the 1994 DWS. Farber used information from the PSID to adjust the data. Thus, researchers interested in measuring changes in job stability or job security over time appear to have little choice but to use data sets that are not entirely consistent over time, and to attempt to develop procedures for making these sources consistent. In our view, it is important to try to update the evidence on changes in job stability, while being cautious about drawing strong conclusions from somewhat different data sources. Finally, we would express the hope that uniform methods of tracking job stability over time will be pursued.

RESULTS

We first report, in table 3.2, estimates of four-year retention rates for 1983 to 1987 and 1987 to 1991 for all workers in our sample, classified by initial tenure; this provides a brief overview of the results reported by Diebold, Neumark, and Polsky (1997). Table 3.2 reveals that taking account of heaping, the estimated four-year retention rate fell modestly, from .561 in 1983 to .539 in 1987.[19] The qualitative pattern by tenure group is similar with or without the adjustments for heaping (and rounding). In particular, job stability fell for those with two to nine years of tenure and for those with nine to fifteen years of tenure, but rose for those with fifteen or more years of tenure. Also, notice that the heaping adjustment has considerably less effect on the estimated changes in retention rates, although it affects their estimated levels. Thus, in what follows using the 1995 data, we focus on results with adjustments for heaping.

Table 3.2   Estimated Retention Rates for All Workers by Tenure Group, in Four-Year Spans: 1983 to 1987 and 1987 to 1991

Time Span	Initial Tenure Group	Raw Data	Deheaped
1983 to 1987	Zero to less than two	.425	.344
	Two to less than nine	.554	.611
	Nine to less than fifteen	.777	.861
	Fifteen or more	.682	.653
	Total	.566	.561
1987 to 1991	Zero to less than two	.422	.348
	Two to less than nine	.508	.552
	Nine to less than fifteen	.747	.821
	Fifteen or more	.724	.706
	Total	.545	.539
Δ 1983–1987 to	Zero to less than two	−.002	.004
1987–1991	Two to less than nine	−.046*	−.059*
	Nine to less than fifteen	−.031*	−.040*
	Fifteen or more	.042*	.053*
	Total	−.021*	−.021*

*Denotes that the estimated difference in the retention rates is significant at the 5 percent level.

As discussed earlier, the tenure questions in the 1995 supplement, on which estimated retention rates through 1995 are based, are not entirely comparable with earlier tenure questions. In table 3.3, we first report estimated retention rates without the adjustments to the 1995 data described earlier. We present results using the upper- and lower-bound tenure responses. We then report results based on the adjusted data. The comparison across the estimates is useful in gauging the degree of uncertainty in the estimates through 1995 stemming from the changes in the tenure questions. However, our preferred estimates are based on the lower-bound tenure question in the 1995 CPS supplement, using the 1996 CPS data to adjust the 1995 data; these are reported in the second column. We also report the estimated changes in retention rates from 1983 and 1987.

The first column of table 3.3 reports results using total tenure in 1995 (that is, unadjusted tenure), based on the lower-bound variables for 1995 tenure; these latter variables correspond to the tenure questions labeled "low" in table 3.1, when there are two questions. As table 3.3 shows, the estimated retention rate for 1991 to 1995 (.571) is higher than for either 1987 to 1991 (.539) or 1983 to 1987 (.561). Although this suggests an increase in aggregate job stability, the total tenure variable in 1995 probably overstates tenure as defined in earlier years and hence biases the estimated retention rates for 1991 to 1995 upward.

The second column therefore adjusts the 1995 data using information on total and continuous tenure in the 1996 CPS supplement. As expected, this lowers estimated retention rates for 1991 to 1995. Nonetheless, aggregate job stability still appears not to have fallen, with an estimated four-year retention rate of .551, a shade higher than for 1987 to 1991, and a shade lower than for 1983 to 1987.

When we disaggregate by tenure, some rather sharp contrasts with the picture of aggregate job stability emerge. Workers with less than two years of tenure experienced significant estimated increases in four-year retention rates (.053 relative to 1983 to 1987, and .048 relative to 1987 to 1991). On the other hand, workers with nine to fifteen years of tenure experienced significant and somewhat larger declines, and for the comparison with 1987 to 1991 the same is true of workers with fifteen or more years of tenure. In contrast, in comparison with 1983 to 1987, workers with two to nine years of tenure experienced smaller but still significant declines in job stability.[20] The qualitative difference between less tenured and more tenured workers is striking. Some of these qualitative findings show a reversal of the evidence through 1991. Specifically, as reported earlier, the four-year retention rate for workers with fifteen or more years of tenure rose from 1983 to 1987, and the four-year retention rate for workers with nine to fifteen years of tenure fell by considerably less over this period. Although the adjustments to the 1995 data

Table 3.3 Estimated Continuous Four-Year Retention Rates for 1991 to 1995: A Comparison of Adjustment Methods

Time Span	Initial Tenure Group	Lower Bound		Upper Bound		
		1995 Total Tenure	1995 Tenure Adjusted to Continuous, Using 1996 CPS	1995 Total Tenure	1995 Tenure Adjusted to Continuous, Using 1996 CPS	1996 CPS Substituted for 1995
1991–1995	Zero to less than two	.397	.396	.398	.396	.392
	Two to less than nine	.595	.572	.600	.574	.601
	Nine to less than fifteen	.801	.758	.809	.768	.767
	Fifteen or more	.669	.641	.685	.654	.664
	Total	.571	.551	.576	.555	.566
Δ 1987–1991 to 1991–1995	Zero to less than two	.049*	.048*	.050*	.048*	.044*
	Two to less than nine	.044*	.021*	.048*	.022*	.050*
	Nine to less than fifteen	−.021	−.064*	−.012	−.053*	−.054*
	Fifteen or more	−.037*	−.065*	−.021	−.052*	−.042*
	Total	.031*	.012*	.037*	.016*	.027*
Δ 1983–1987 to 1991–1995	Zero to less than two	.053*	.053*	.054*	.053*	.049*
	Two to less than nine	−.016*	−.039*	−.011	−.037*	−.010
	Nine to less than fifteen	−.060*	−.103*	−.052*	−.093*	−.094*
	Fifteen or more	.016	−.012	.032*	.001	.011
	Total	.010*	−.010*	.015*	−.006	.005

Note: All retention rates are adjusted for heaping.

*Denotes that the estimated difference in the retention rates is significant at the 5 percent level.

strengthen the declines in retention rates for more tenured workers, the qualitative conclusion is the same with or without the adjustment. The evidence of recent declines in job stability for those with nine to fifteen years of tenure and with fifteen or more years of tenure indicates a shift toward less job stability among long-term, career workers in the first half of the 1990s.

In the next two columns of table 3.3, we show the differences that result from using the upper-bound tenure variables in the 1995 contingent work supplement; these latter variables are based on the tenure questions labeled "high" in table 3.1, when there are two questions. As we would expect, estimated retention rates for 1991 to 1995 are higher using these alternative tenure variables, in the aggregate and for each tenure group, and hence any declines in retention rates are moderated. However, the differences in the results are small. As a consequence of the small differences, and because the lower-bound estimates correspond more closely to tenure with an employer, we focus on the lower-bound estimates in the remainder of the chapter.

Finally, the last column substitutes the 1996 tenure data for 1995, a simpler (but admittedly crude) method of accounting for problems with the 1995 contingent work supplement. By tenure group, the results are qualitatively similar to those based on adjustments to the 1995 data, with increased stability for less tenured workers and decreased stability for more tenured workers. The only difference is that using the data this way indicates a more substantial but still modest (.027) increase in aggregate job stability from the 1987 to 1991 period to the 1991 to 1995 period; this difference hints at an improvement in job stability between 1995 and 1996, since the 1996 tenure data are now used directly rather than to adjust the 1995 data. We have more confidence in the estimates based on explicit adjustments to the 1995 CPS data. But regardless, we have what we regard as robust evidence of essentially no decline in aggregate job stability based on four-year retention rates, moderate increases in job stability for less tenured workers, and sizable decreases in job stability for more tenured workers.[21]

With the tenure data for 1983, 1987, 1991, and 1995, we can also estimate eight-year retention rates for 1983 to 1991 and for 1987 to 1995. These longer-term retention rates may be of particular interest in light of the popular perception that longer-term jobs are becoming more rare; it is possible that the four-year retention rates miss changes in the likelihood of holding longer-term jobs. Table 3.4 reports estimates of these rates, in all cases adjusting for heaping and using the lower-bound tenure variable for 1995. We first report estimates using 1995 total tenure, and then estimates using the adjustment to continuous tenure, based on the 1996 CPS supplement. As expected, this adjustment lowers estimated retention rates for 1987 to 1995. With the adjustment, the evidence suggests a non-negligible decline in aggregate job stability, with the estimated retention rate falling by .032 (based on the adjusted data).[22] Note that the longer the span over which a retention rate is computed, the larger percentage change a given decline represents, because the retention rate over a longer span is lower in the first place; for example, the eight-year retention rate from 1983 to 1991 is .386, whereas the four-year retention rate from 1983 to 1987 is .561. The pattern of changes in eight-year retention rates by tenure group partly mirrors that obtained from four-year retention rates, with job stability increasing for workers with zero to two years of tenure and falling for those with nine to fifteen years of tenure or with fifteen or more years of tenure. However, here stability also falls for those with two to nine years of tenure, providing a relatively consistent picture of decreases in job stability for more tenured workers. Although not reported in the table, using the 1996 CPS file directly gives qualitatively similar (but slightly weaker) results by tenure group and in the aggregate.

We next turn to evidence disaggregated by race, sex, and age. In the disaggregated analysis, we report results using the same adjustments and tenure questions as in table 3.4. Table 3.5 first reports results for four-year retention rates broken down by race. For whites, there is little evidence of an aggregate decline in job stability as measured by four-year retention rates over this period. For blacks, the same is true for the change in the retention rates from the period from 1987 to 1991 to the period from 1991 to 1995. However, over the longer period, between 1983 to 1987 and 1991 to 1995, blacks experienced a relatively sharp decline in aggregate job stability, with the retention rate falling by .066. For both races, at least some groups of more tenured workers suffered sizable declines in job stability over this period, although for blacks, given the sharper aggregate decline, the declines for more tenured workers are larger and more widespread. Less tenured white workers experienced increases in job stability over the longer period, while for less tenured black workers this increase was smaller and not statistically significant.

Similar to race, the results disaggregated by sex reveal rather distinct differences in changes in job stability over the longer period (between 1983 to 1987 and 1991 to 1995), but these differences are due for the most part to changes from the period from 1983 to 1987. Thus, the last column, which computes changes in job stability between 1983 to 1987 and 1991 to 1995, reveals some substantial sex differences. Among both sexes, workers with nine to fifteen years of tenure experienced declines in job stability. But for women, in contrast to men, the job stability of those with fifteen or more years of tenure rose; the changes in aggregate rates are also quite different, falling for men (by .033) but rising for women (by .018). However, the results for men and women are much more similar in comparing the period between 1987 to 1991 and 1991 to 1995.

Table 3.4   Estimated Retention Rates for All Workers by Tenure Group, in Eight-Year Spans: 1983 to 1991 and 1987 to 1995

Time Span	Initial Tenure Group	Retention Rate (with 1995 Total Tenure)	Retention Rate (Continuous Tenure)[a]
1983 to 1991	Zero to less than two	.183	.183
	Two to less than nine	.433	.433
	Nine to less than fifteen	.650	.650
	Fifteen or more	.485	.485
	Total	.386	.386
1987 to 1995	Zero to less than two	.216	.209
	Two to less than nine	.384	.368
	Nine to less than fifteen	.617	.585
	Fifteen or more	.477	.454
	Total	.370	.354
Δ 1983–1991 to	Zero to less than two	.034*	.026*
1987–1995	Two to less than nine	−.049*	−.065*
	Nine to less than fifteen	−.033*	−.065*
	Fifteen or more	−.008	−.032*
	Total	−.016*	−.032*

Note: All retention rates are adjusted for heaping.

[a] 1995 total tenure is adjusted to continuous tenure using the 1996 CPS; the lower-bound tenure variable from the 1995 CPS is used.

*Denotes that the estimated difference in the retention rates is significant at the 5 percent level.

The second panel of table 3.5 also reports aggregate retention rates disaggregated by race and sex. We see that the overall sex differences appear among whites also, with white men experiencing a decline in retention rates and white women an increase between the periods from 1983 to 1987 and 1991 to 1995, although the latter increase was sharper for white women (.029) compared with all women (.018). We also see that among blacks, both men and women experienced declines in retention rates over the longer period, of similar magnitudes. Thus, it is only white women who experienced an increase in job stability over this period, while both black men and black women fared worse than white men.

Thus, although the most recent four years have not witnessed strong race or sex differences in changes in job stability, a longer view suggests that blacks have been hit hardest, and that job stability has actually increased for white females. The differences in results for men and women in particular indicates that a rather strong convergence in job stability among men and (white) women underlies the approximate stability in aggregate four-year retention rates over the 1980s and the first half of the 1990s. One might interpret the cup as either half full or half empty de-

Table 3.5 Estimated Retention Rates for Selected Race, Sex, and Age Subgroups, in Four-Year Spans: 1983 to 1987, 1987 to 1991, and 1991 to 1995

Initial tenure group	Time Span			Difference Between Spans		
	1983 to 1987	1987 to 1991	1991 to 1995	1983–1987 to 1987–1991	1987–1991 to 1991–1995	1983–1987 to 1991–1995
Race						
White						
Zero to less than two	.336	.349	.390	.012*	.041*	.053*
Two to less than nine	.605	.549	.572	−.057*	.024*	−.033*
Nine to less than fifteen	.853	.824	.751	−.029	−.073*	−.102*
Fifteen or more	.651	.698	.648	.046*	−.050*	−.003
Total	.555	.538	.550	−.016*	.012*	−.005
Black						
Zero to less than two	.394	.345	.421	−.049*	.076*	.027
Two to less than nine	.663	.573	.553	−.090*	−.021	−.110*
Nine to less than fifteen	.919	.805	.858	−.114*	.054	−.061
Fifteen or more	.680	.762	.598	.082*	−.164*	−.082*
Total	.623	.559	.557	−.064*	−.002	−.066*
Sex						
Male						
Zero to less than two	.363	.361	.396	−.002	.035*	.033*
Two to less than nine	.654	.567	.588	−.087*	.020*	−.066*
Nine to less than fifteen	.884	.848	.791	−.037	−.056*	−.093*
Fifteen or more	.678	.707	.637	.028*	−.069*	−.041*
Total	.601	.566	.568	−.035*	.002	−.033*

(Table continues on p. 94.)

Table 3.5 *Continued*

	Time Span			Difference Between Spans		
	1983 to 1987	1987 to 1991	1991 to 1995	1983–1987 to 1987–1991	1987–1991 to 1991–1995	1983–1987 to 1991–1995
White	.600	.570	.568	−.030*	−.001	−.031*
Black	.627	.541	.561	−.086*	.020	−.067*
Female						
Zero to less than two	.324	.335	.396	.011	.061*	.072*
Two to less than nine	.568	.535	.555	−.033*	.021*	−.012
Nine to less than fifteen	.830	.789	.720	−.041	−.069*	−.110*
Fifteen or more	.591	.704	.647	.113*	−.058*	.056*
Total	.514	.509	.532	−.005	.023*	.018*
White	.500	.501	.529	.001	.028*	.029*
Black	.619	.575	.553	−.043*	−.022	−.065*
Initial age group						
All workers						
Sixteen to twenty-four	.318	.282	.296	−.036*	.013	−.023*
Twenty-five to thirty-nine	.609	.580	.580	−.029*	.001	−.029*
Forty to fifty-four	.715	.687	.683	−.028*	−.004	−.032*
Fifty-five or older	.489	.471	.457	−.018	−.014	−.032*
Total	.561	.539	.551	−.021*	.012*	−.010*

Note: All retention rates are adjusted for heaping. 1995 total tenure is adjusted to continuous tenure using the 1996 CPS; the lower-bound tenure variable from the 1995 CPS is used.

* Denotes that the estimated difference in the retention rates is significant at the 5 percent level.

pending upon one's perspective (or perhaps on one's sex or race). Declines in job stability among more tenured men in the first half of the 1990s may have dominated the media, but this has been coupled with some longer-term gains among women that appear to have received considerably less attention.

The third panel of table 3.5 reports results disaggregated by age group instead of by tenure. The estimates reveal declines of about .02 to .03 across all age groups. Curiously, estimated retention rates for each subgroup declined by more than the aggregate retention rate (unlike the results when we disaggregated by tenure). This can be explained by the combination of two facts. First, the workforce is aging; the decline in the proportion of workers age sixteen to twenty-four is particularly sharp. Second, for the three youngest age groups retention rates increase with age. Thus, age-specific retention rates have declined, but this decline is masked to some extent by population shifts toward older workers, whose jobs are more stable. This implies that aggregate changes in job stability tell us what is happening to jobs overall, while the age-specific changes are more informative as to what is happening to particular types of workers. As the third panel suggests, this distinction can be of some importance. In particular, the evidence of declines in job stability is a bit stronger when we ask how job stability has changed relative to what workers at similar points in their careers used to experience.

Table 3.6 reports similar disaggregated evidence for the eight-year retention rates. Because these eight-year rates cover the longer period from 1983 to 1995, we might expect the results in this table to parallel the changes between the periods 1983 to 1987 and 1991 to 1995 from the previous table, although this need not be true considering that eight-year and four-year retention rates can behave differently. This expectation is to some extent confirmed. In particular, blacks experienced considerably sharper declines in aggregate job stability than did whites (.068 versus .027), and men experienced considerably sharper declines than women (.041 versus .020); all of these estimated declines are statistically significant. For males and especially for blacks, sharp declines are evident for those with nine to fifteen years of tenure. As in table 3.5, the second panel of table 3.6 reports aggregate retention rates disaggregated by race and sex. Although in this case all groups experienced at least some decline in retention rates, the decline is negligible for white women, and again, black men and black women fared worse than either white women or white men.

The results in the third panel, disaggregated by age, also largely parallel those in table 3.5. These estimates indicate statistically significant declines for all age groups except those age fifty-five and older, although the estimated declines are not sharper for the older "career" employees about whom much has been written.

Table 3.6 Estimated Retention Rates for Selected Race, Sex, and Age Subgroups, in Eight-Year Spans: 1983 to 1991 and 1987 to 1995

Specification	1983 to 1991	1987 to 1995	1983–1991 to 1987–1995
Initial tenure group			
Race			
White			
Zero to less than two	.181	.209	.028*
Two to less than nine	.430	.365	−.065*
Nine to less than fifteen	.634	.592	−.042*
Fifteen or more	.483	.454	−.029*
Total	.381	.354	−.027*
Black			
Zero to less than two	.184	.196	.013
Two to less than nine	.471	.414	−.057*
Nine to less than fifteen	.766	.544	−.222*
Fifteen or more	.514	.456	−.058
Total	.434	.366	−.068*
Sex			
Male			
Zero to less than two	.195	.230	.035*
Two to less than nine	.469	.384	−.085*
Nine to less than fifteen	.699	.619	−.080*
Fifteen or more	.489	.448	−.041*
Total	.420	.379	−.041*
White	.420	.380	−.039*
Black	.429	.371	−.058*
Female			
Zero to less than two	.170	.188	.018*
Two to less than nine	.397	.351	−.046*
Nine to less than fifteen	.585	.542	−.043*
Fifteen or more	.476	.465	−.011
Total	.345	.325	−.020*
White	.334	.322	−.012*
Black	.439	.361	−.078*
Initial age group			
All workers			
Sixteen to twenty-four	.190	.154	−.036*
Twenty-five to thirty-nine	.454	.404	−.050*
Forty to fifty-four	.527	.484	−.043*
Fifty-five or older	.188	.188	.000
Total	.386	.354	−.032*

Note: All retention rates are adjusted for heaping. 1995 total tenure is adjusted to continuous tenure using the 1996 CPS; the lower-bound tenure variable from the 1995 CPS is used.

* Denotes that the estimated difference in the retention rates is significant at the 5 percent level.

Finally, we report results disaggregated by broad industry and occupation groups; changes in four-year retention rates are presented in table 3.7, and changes in eight-year rates in table 3.8. Looking first at the four-year retention rates, the data indicate that aggregate job stability declined in manufacturing industries (by .046) and rose slightly in nonmanufacturing industries (.012) from the period from 1983 to 1987 to the period from 1991 to 1995. However, evidence of declines in job stability among more tenured workers from 1987 to 1991 appears in both industry groups; over the whole period, this decline is strong only in manufacturing and is particularly pronounced for those with nine to fifteen years of initial tenure.

Turning to occupational differences, the data are broken into blue-collar workers and three subgroups of white-collar workers: managerial-professional workers, clerical workers (technical, sales, and administrative), and service workers. Aggregate job stability fell only for blue-collar workers, and this change occurred between the periods from 1983 to 1987 and 1987 to 1991; four-year retention rates for the period between 1987 to 1991 and 1991 to 1995 are similar across the four occupational groups. The results for more tenured workers, however, point to some more interesting findings. Although there is fairly consistent evidence of declines in job stability for more tenured workers among blue-collar, clerical, and service workers from the periods from 1983 to 1987 and 1987 to 1991, for managerial-professional workers it is only for the latter time span that declines in job stability appear. In particular, from the period between 1987 to 1991 and 1991 to 1995, four-year retention rates for more tenured managerial-professional workers fell sharply, by .081 for those with nine to fifteen years of tenure, and by .106 for those with fifteen or more years of tenure. Only because job stability moved in the opposite direction from the period between 1983 to 1987 and 1987 to 1991 for these workers is there evidence of considerably less change over the longer period. Nonetheless, the decline in job stability for this group in the first half of the 1990s is consistent with media stories regarding changes experienced by more tenured managers and related workers, as well as with research based on specialized samples or case studies indicating that management is being streamlined (see, for example, Cappelli et al. 1997).

Table 3.8 presents changes in eight-year retention rates disaggregated in the same fashion. As with the four-year rates, job stability declined relatively sharply for workers in manufacturing and blue-collar workers. Also, for workers in these groups the declines among the more tenured (those with nine to fifteen years of tenure) are apparent, as in the aggregated results. Among managerial-professional and clerical workers, there were modest declines in aggregate job stability (significant only for clerical workers) and no evidence of sharper declines among more tenured workers.[23] In contrast with table 3.7, table 3.8 shows the changes in eight-year retention rates masking the decline in job stability for more

Table 3.7 Estimated Retention Rates for Selected Industry and Occupation Subgroups, in Four-Year Spans: 1983 to 1987, 1987 to 1991, and 1991 to 1995

Specification	Initial Tenure Group	Time Span			Difference Between Spans		
		1983 to 1987	1987 to 1991	1991 to 1995	1983–1987 to 1987–1991	1987–1991 to 1991–1995	1983–1987 to 1991–1995
Industry							
Manufacturing	Zero to less than two	.426	.409	.462	−.017	.053*	.036*
	Two to less than nine	.656	.592	.590	−.064*	−.002	−.066*
	Nine to less than fifteen	.936	.882	.756	−.054*	−.126*	−.180*
	Fifteen or more	.657	.676	.628	.018	−.047*	−.029
	Total	.638	.601	.592	−.037*	−.009	−.046*
Nonmanufacturing	Zero to less than two	.312	.324	.373	.012	.049*	.061*
	Two to less than nine	.588	.531	.563	−.057*	.032*	−.024*
	Nine to less than fifteen	.811	.782	.758	−.028	−.024	−.053*
	Fifteen or more	.648	.735	.651	.088*	−.084*	.003
	Total	.519	.507	.531	−.012*	.024*	.012*
Occupation							
Blue-collar	Zero to less than two	.337	.328	.367	−.008	.039*	.031*
	Two to less than nine	.633	.520	.538	−.112*	.018	−.094*
	Nine to less than fifteen	.890	.801	.734	−.089*	−.067*	−.156*
	Fifteen or more	.653	.637	.645	−.016	.008	−.008
	Total	.580	.516	.531	−.064*	.015*	−.049*

Managerial-professional	Zero to less than two	.542	.567	.625	.025	.058*	.083*
	Two to less than nine	.711	.669	.693	−.043*	.024	−.018
	Nine to less than fifteen	.912	.936	.854	.024	−.081*	−.057*
	Fifteen or more	.690	.787	.682	.097*	−.106*	−.009
	Total	.698	.708	.701	.010	−.007	.003
Clerical	Zero to less than two	.322	.327	.364	.005	.037*	.042*
	Two to less than nine	.569	.524	.536	−.046*	.012	−.034*
	Nine to less than fifteen	.825	.775	.715	−.050	−.060*	−.110*
	Fifteen or more	.621	.665	.621	.044	−.044	.000
	Total	.516	.496	.509	−.020*	.012	−.007
Service	Zero to less than two	.211	.214	.257	.003	.043*	.046*
	Two to less than nine	.487	.451	.463	−.036*	.012	−.024
	Nine to less than fifteen	.749	.665	.621	−.085*	−.044	−.128*
	Fifteen or more	.619	.763	.495	.143*	−.268*	−.125*
	Total	.396	.384	.388	−.012	.004	−.008

Note: All retention rates are adjusted for heaping. 1995 total tenure is adjusted to continuous tenure using the 1996 CPS; the lower-bound tenure variable from the 1995 CPS is used.

* Denotes that the estimated difference in the retention rates is significant at the 5 percent level.

Table 3.8   Estimated Retention Rates for Selected Industry and
             Occupation Subgroups, in Eight-Year Spans: 1983 to 1991
             and 1987 to 1995

		1983 to 1991	1987 to 1995	1983–1991 to 1987–1995
Specification	Initial Tenure Group			
Industry				
Manufacturing	Zero to less than two	.238	.258	.020*
	Two to less than nine	.484	.401	−.084*
	Nine to less than fifteen	.707	.595	−.112*
	Fifteen or more	.466	.428	−.037*
	Total	.449	.395	−.054*
Nonmanu-facturing	Zero to less than two	.162	.190	.028*
	Two to less than nine	.406	.351	−.055*
	Nine to less than fifteen	.611	.578	−.033*
	Fifteen or more	.507	.479	−.028*
	Total	.351	.332	−.019*
Occupation				
Blue-collar	Zero to less than two	.171	.192	.021*
	Two to less than nine	.424	.340	−.084*
	Nine to less than fifteen	.640	.530	−.110*
	Fifteen or more	.432	.424	−.009
	Total	.376	.332	−.044*
Managerial-professional	Zero to less than two	.337	.400	.063*
	Two to less than nine	.569	.497	−.072*
	Nine to less than fifteen	.793	.743	−.050*
	Fifteen or more	.558	.533	−.024
	Total	.546	.518	−.027*
Clerical	Zero to less than two	.159	.188	.029*
	Two to less than nine	.387	.326	−.061*
	Nine to less than fifteen	.564	.526	−.037
	Fifteen or more	.460	.417	−.043*
	Total	.334	.308	−.025*
Service	Zero to less than two	.101	.095	−.006
	Two to less than nine	.313	.268	−.045*
	Nine to less than fifteen	.498	.422	−.076*
	Fifteen or more	.515	.338	−.177*
	Total	.248	.205	−.043*

Note: All retention rates are adjusted for heaping. 1995 total tenure is adjusted to continuous tenure using the 1996 CPS; the lower-bound tenure variable from the 1995 CPS is used.

* Denotes that the estimated difference in the retention rates is significant at the 5 percent level.

tenured managerial-professional workers that occurred over the 1991 to 1995 period relative to the 1987 to 1991 period.

Looking at the evidence disaggregated by subgroups does not provide us with a behavioral explanation of why job stability may have declined for certain groups, although it may provide evidence more consistent with some explanations than with others. One hypothesis discussed by Diebold, Neumark, and Polsky (1997) is that many of the changes that are believed to underlie changes in the wage structure—in particular, shifts in relative demand away from less skilled workers—also underlie changes in job stability. Indeed, we found through 1991 that although aggregate job stability was largely unchanged, those workers who experienced declines in job stability were the same workers whose relative wages had suffered (young, unskilled, minorities, and so on), perhaps consistent with technological change biased against such workers driving down both their wages and job attachment. There is not yet enough work on changes in wage structure in the 1990s to ask whether in this period some of the other groups that experienced declines in job stability (such as more tenured workers) also began to experience declines in relative earnings. Additionally, a prominent theme in the management literature (for example, Cappelli et al. 1997) is that the 1990s witnessed a good deal of restructuring of organizations, entailing, among other things, streamlined managerial structures. This view is consistent with the declines in job stability for managerial-professional workers that we find in the 1990s.[24]

CONCLUSIONS

We update evidence on job stability in the U.S. economy through 1995 by combining information from the 1995 CPS contingent work supplement with earlier CPS tenure supplements. Using these somewhat different data sources requires that we make adjustments to achieve comparability over time. But the general robustness of results across alternative adjustment procedures suggests that we have successfully transformed these supplements into a set of cross-section data sets with comparable tenure data, which we can string together to provide a reasonably accurate empirical description of changes in job retention rates. These retention rates provide measures of job stability that are immune to both changes in the underlying distribution (or survival function) for job tenure and changes in new arrivals in the labor market.

In the aggregate, there is some evidence of modest declines in job stability in the first half of the 1990s, differing somewhat from the 1980s, during which time aggregate job stability remained stable. However, the drop in aggregate job stability might appear somewhat worse if the workforce were not shifting toward ages in which jobs are typically more sta-

ble. More significantly, in the first half of the 1990s more tenured workers experienced significant and perhaps rather large declines in job stability, although less tenured workers experienced gains in job stability. This
contrasts with the 1980s, when the declines in job stability that did appear were concentrated among younger, less skilled, and less tenured
workers.

There are some rather prominent differences in these results by race
and sex. White women appear to have had either an increase or a small
decrease in job stability, depending on the period over which we compute job retention rates. White men, in contrast, have experienced mild
declines in job stability in the aggregate, and rather sharp declines among
those with higher tenure. Looking at race, blacks have experienced the
strongest declines in job stability, with rather pronounced declines
among more tenured workers and in the aggregate.

Disaggregating workers by broad industries and occupations, we find
that declines in job stability occurred among manufacturing workers and
among blue-collar workers. Among these workers, the aggregate findings of sharp declines in the first half of the 1990s among more tenured
workers are apparent. We also find that, relative to the immediately preceding period, the job stability of more tenured managerial-professional
workers fell sharply in this period, representing a reversal from the 1980s.

The main goal of this chapter has been to present new evidence on job
stability through the mid-1990s. Other research has claimed to find evidence of substantial declines in job stability during the 1980s, although
we have disputed many of those findings. On the other hand, looking
through the mid-1990s, we find evidence of more recent declines in job
stability, especially for older, more tenured workers, and more so for
blacks and men than for women. This is consistent with two other studies
that have also looked at recent data. Farber (this volume), using the CPS
tenure supplements, reported declines in the proportions of male workers
with ten or more years of tenure and with twenty or more years of tenure,
especially after 1993; for women, in contrast, these proportions did not
decline. Similarly, using data from both the PSID and the CPS, Jaeger
and Stevens (this volume) reported an increase in the fraction of male
workers aged thirty or older with fewer than ten years of tenure in the
1990s. Thus, the broad trends we find are consistent with this research.
Also, these two papers, as well as ours, point to the emergence of declining stability in the 1990s and hence are in agreement that the decline in
job stability (measured in different ways) is recent. Thus, at this point we
view the evidence as pointing mainly to a drop in job stability for some
groups of workers in the first half of the 1990s. Based on the evidence
available thus far, we do not see this decline as part of a longer-term trend
and can only speculate as to whether it reflects a temporary or permanent
change in U.S. labor markets.

APPENDIX: ADJUSTMENTS FOR HEAPING AND ROUNDING

Following procedures developed by Diebold, Neumark, and Polsky (1997), we adjust the data for rounding and heaping by estimating a mixture model for reported tenure, the estimates of which we then use to reallocate the rounded and heaped data. For this purpose, we model true tenure with a Weibull distribution, and we assume that individuals report true tenure with probability p and report a nearby multiple of five with probability (1 - p).[1] The corresponding Weibull survival function is $\exp[-(\alpha t')^{\beta}]$, where t′ denotes true tenure in years. We expect heaping to be more severe the longer the true length of the tenure spell, so we allow p to depend linearly on reported tenure t, $p = \gamma + \delta t$, where we expect to find $\delta < 0$. We treat the problem of half-year rounding, discussed in the main text, in a similar fashion—by assuming that independently of reported tenure (as long as it exceeds twelve months), individuals report true tenure with probability θ and report one year more than true tenure with probability $1 - \theta$.

Under these assumptions, the reported tenure distribution differs from the true probability distribution for three reasons—rounding, heaping, and sampling variation. We use the minimum chi-square method to estimate the parameters α, β, γ, δ, and θ for each of the four years. First, we divide the possible values of reported tenure into J cells, and then we find the values of the parameters that minimize

$$\sum_{j=1}^{J}(O_j - E_j)^2/E_j, \qquad (3A.1)$$

where O_j is the actual number of observations in cell j, and E_j is the expected number of observations given the parameters. We estimate the parameters using a grid search.[2]

We use the estimates of the parameters of the mixture model to adjust the data for heaping and rounding. With respect to heaping, for each multiple of five years for reported tenure, we calculate the probability that respondents have reported the truth, using the estimates of γ and δ. We then redistribute to adjacent values of tenure the number of respondents estimated to have rounded. The redistribution is in proportion to the percentage shortfall between the expected number of observations at each of the adjacent values based on the estimated Weibull distribution and the expected number of observations based on the mixture of the Weibull distribution and the heaping mechanism.[3] To handle rounding, we shift reported tenure down by one year for the proportion estimated to have rounded up by one year.

Table 3A.1   Classification of Workers in the February 1995 Contingent Worker Supplement

Type-Identification	Percentage Answering
1. Incorporated self-employed S8IC = "Something Else"	3.87
2. Independent contractor S1 = Y, S7 = Y, or S8IC = Independent contractor, independent consultant, or free-lance worker	.98
3. Temporary worker, no agency S1 = Y, S2 = N, S4 = N, S5 = N, and S6 = N or S7EL = Y	3.29
4. Temporary worker in an agency S1 = N and S2 = Y or S1 = Y and S2INS = Y	.94
5. Contractor with employer S1 = Y, S6 = Y	.00
6. On-call worker S1 = Y, S4 = Y	1.40
7. Day laborer S1 = Y, S5 = Y	.00
8. Noncontingent worker S1 = N, S1SCR = Y, S2 = N, S4 = N, S6 = N, S7EL = N, and S7 = N; or in universe for S28 (N: 95.4 percent, Y: 4.6 percent)	89.51

S1: Some people are in temporary jobs that last only for a limited time or until the completion of a project. Is your job temporary?

S1SCR: Provided that the economy does not change and your job performance is adequate, can you continue to work for your current employer as long as you wish?

S2INS: Are you paid by a temporary help agency?

S2: Even though you told me your job is not temporary, are you paid by a temporary help agency?

S4: Some people are in a pool of workers who are *only* called to work as needed, although they can be scheduled to work for several days or weeks in a row, for example, substitute teachers and construction workers supplied by a union hiring hall. These people are sometimes referred to as *on-call* workers. Were you an *on-call* worker last week?

S5: Some people get to work by waiting at a place where employers pick up people to work for a day. These people are sometimes called *day laborers*. Were you a *day laborer* last week?

S6: Some companies provide employees or their services to others under contract. A few examples of services that can be contracted out include security, landscaping, or computer programming. Did you work for a company that contracts out you or your services last week?

S7EL: Are you paid by an employee leasing company?

S7: Last week, were you working as an independent contractor, an independent consultant, or a free-lance worker? That is, someone who obtains customers on their own to provide a product or service.

S8IC: Are you self-employed as an independent contractor, independent consultant, free-lance worker, or something else? (1 = independent contractor, independent consultant, or free-lance worker, 2 = something else)

S28: Did you *ever* work as a temporary worker, contractor, consultant, free-lancer, or on-call worker for (fill: employer's name from basic CPS)?

Table 3A.2 The Difference in Years Between Total and Current Tenure, by Tenure Group, in the 1996 CPS

Years of Total Tenure	Proportion (Continuous Tenure Less Than Total Tenure)	Distribution of the Difference in Years, Conditional on Total Tenure Greater Than Continuous Tenure			
		12.5 Centile	37.5 Centile	62.5 Centile	87.5 Centile
Zero to eleven months	.000	1	1	1	1
One	.049	1	2	2	2
Two	.065	1	2	3	3
Three	.069	1	2	3	3
Four	.065	1	2	4	4
Five	.082	1	2	4	5
Six to seven	.083	1	2	5	6
Eight to nine	.096	1	3	5	7
Ten to eleven	.087	1	3	7	9
Twelve to fourteen	.123	1	4	9	11
Fifteen to seventeen	.085	1	4	8	14
Eighteen to twenty	.096	1	3	8	15
Twenty-one to twenty-three	.092	1	3	8	18
Twenty-four to twenty-nine	.096	1	4	5	23
Thirty or more	.076	2	7	22	29

ACKNOWLEDGMENTS

We thank Robert Mare, Anne Polivka, Peter Schmidt, Mark Schweitzer, Jay Stewart, Rob Valletta, Jeff Wooldridge, and anonymous referees for helpful comments. Neumark gratefully acknowledges support from NIA grant K01-AG00589.

NOTES

1. Current tenure, c, can refer to a range of tenure levels.

2. These assumptions enabled Hall to estimate the survival function using the 1978 CPS tenure supplement because they imply that we can estimate the survival function from synthetic cohorts constructed from a single cross-section; specifically, the t-year retention rate for workers with current tenure c can be computed as the ratio of workers with t + c years of tenure to workers with c years of tenure.

3. When x refers to age, it is increased by t years in each subsequent survey to follow the right cohort over time.

4. The CPS sample weight is the reciprocal of the probability of being sampled, adjusted for non-interview and variation in the sampling of race-age-sex and residence subgroups.

5. Note that here the superscript on $N_{x,t+c}$ is 0,t, indicating the number of workers in the longitudinal sample (drawn in year 0) with characteristics x and t + c years of tenure t years later. This contrasts with the earlier subscript 0 + t, which indicated the number of workers with characteristics x and t + c years of tenure in a new cross-section sample drawn t years after year 0.

6. In Diebold, Neumark, and Polsky (1997), we ignored this additional variation. However, accounting for it would only have reinforced our statistical inference that aggregate job stability had not declined.

7. For example, if we calculate retention rates for those with between one and ten years of tenure in the base year, and t equals 4, then some observations counted in N_{xc}^{0+t} also are counted in $N_{x,t+c}^{0+t}$, where t + c is the range of five to fourteen years of tenure.

8. The February 1996 tenure supplement is more comparable to the earlier surveys, but because it comes five years after the 1991 supplement, it cannot be used directly to estimate four-year retention rates that are comparable to those we estimate for earlier years. Nonetheless, as explained later in the chapter, we do consider some evidence from this supplement.

9. Specifically, the unincorporated self-employed are excluded.

10. In previous work (Diebold, Neumark, and Polsky 1997), we also attempted to correct for the effects of the business cycle. Our cyclical adjustment, which had only minor effects on the estimates, focused on the influence of the cycle on estimates of retention rates as fluctuations in unemployment affect the probability of termination, independently of underlying changes in job retention rates. However, reviewers of this chapter correctly pointed

out that "quits" also have a cyclical dimension (moving procyclically), in contrast to terminations. Indeed, evidence presented in Jaeger and Stevens (this volume) and Gottschalk and Moffitt (this volume) suggested no clear cyclical pattern to overall separations. We therefore omit the business cycle adjustment in this chapter, although incorporating it had little influence on the qualitative conclusions.

11. Our convention is that when a tenure interval is specified, the first value is included in the interval and the second excluded. For example, "0 to 1" means "tenure is greater than or equal to zero and less than one."

12. In fact, the Bureau of Labor Statistics (BLS) recognized this problem and changed the subsequent February 1996 tenure supplement in a similar way to reduce rounding.

13. A third change, while most apparent, is inconsequential. Whereas tenure information for 1983, 1987, and 1991 comes from January, the information for 1995 comes from the February 1995 contingent work supplement. Since there is always some risk of losing one's job in any month, defining workers' tenure as of February leads to downward bias in estimates of retention rates through 1995. However, it is easy to show that this bias is trivial. If we assume a constant risk of losing one's job each month, this biases the estimated four-year retention rate through 1995 downward by $1/48 = .02$ (because there are forty-nine months). Of course, the actual risk is much higher in the early months on a job, and much lower in later months, suggesting that the bias from using data from February is much smaller. For example, if we use estimates of the Weibull parameters of $\alpha = .22$ and $\beta = .80$, based on the estimates obtained in the deheaping procedure, the downward bias is .006.

14. We experimented with using the 1995 data to identify a large number of industry and occupation cells with few or no contingent workers, and with using the tenure data from all of the years to study these cells only. But it turned out that contingent workers were distributed across a wide array of industry and occupation cells.

15. Susan Houseman and Anne Polivka (this volume) reported that 57 percent of temporary workers in the 1995 contingent work supplement claim their temporary agency, rather than their current client, as their employer on the main CPS. This suggests that, for this category of contingent workers, actual tenure as it would be measured in the earlier CPS tenure supplements is most likely to be near the middle of the range given by the high and low values of tenure. On the other hand, Polivka has reported to us internal BLS results indicating that most contractors report their most recent assignment as their main employer on the basic CPS, suggesting that the lower tenure number is most comparable to past tenure supplements for these workers.

16. There is some evidence suggesting that this adjustment may go a bit too far. Jay Stewart has reported to us the results of an internal BLS "behavioral coding" study of responses to the tenure questions. After responding to the continuous tenure question, 13 (of 126 respondents) indicated a previous span of employment with the same employer. Some of these respondents were then given the option of revising downward their response to the con-

tinuous tenure question, and some did so. This suggests that a small percentage of respondents to earlier tenure supplements (when respondents were asked about continuous tenure) may have interpreted continuous tenure as total tenure, in which case our procedure would overadjust. Again, despite the possible ambiguity, we choose to use the adjustment, being careful not to reject erroneously the hypothesis that job stability declined in the 1990s, but the reader should keep in mind that our results may be biased slightly toward finding such a decline.

17. These calculations are made on the deheaped data in order to preserve the relationship between continuous and total tenure at the individual level.

18. The total tenure question in the 1996 CPS is not asked of the self-employed, but this group is not included in the adjustment since the distinction between total and continuous tenure is not applicable to these workers.

19. There are slight differences in the sample and estimation method compared with the results of Diebold, Neumark, and Polsky (1997), in which the corresponding estimated four-year retention rate fell from .554 to .530. With the adjustment for the business cycle used by Diebold and his colleagues (1997), the decline is slight, from .539 to .536.

20. These tenure groups were chosen in our earlier work by combining more disaggregated tenure groups with similar experiences over the 1983 to 1991 period.

21. Although not reported in the tables, these qualitative findings are also robust to whether or not we adjust for the business cycle.

22. In our earlier work, the most comparable evidence was on changes in ten-year retention rates from the period from 1973 to 1983 to the period from 1981 to 1991. As reported by Diebold, Neumark, and Polsky (1997), these retention rates remained stable or rose over time.

23. The data indicate some sharp swings for service workers with fifteen or more years of tenure in both four-year and eight-year retention rates; although statistically significant, we are skeptical of these estimates, which are based on rather small samples of six hundred to seven hundred individuals.

24. It is difficult to address the more fundamental question of whether the employment "contract" has changed. For an interesting attempt to interpret the evidence in light of this question, see Valletta (this volume).

APPENDIX NOTES

1. For at least two reasons, it is unlikely that the rounding and heaping adjustments depend on the Weibull assumption in any important way. First, the Weibull is actually a fairly rich functional form, allowing for both an increasing and a decreasing hazard, as well as a flat hazard in the nested exponential case. Second, the Weibull mixture model is used purely as a smoothing device, and a comparison of the original and adjusted tenure distributions in figure 3.1 reveals that apart from the valleys and peaks corresponding to rounding and heaping—which, of course, hardly appear in the adjusted distributions—the adjusted and unadjusted distributions agree closely.

2. The cells used are zero, one to two, three to four, five, six to nine, ten, eleven to fourteen, fifteen, sixteen to nineteen, twenty, and twenty-one or more. For the four supplements, the estimates of α ranged from .21 to .23, while those of β ranged from .79 to .81. The estimates of γ and δ were consistent with a very low probability of rounding at low levels of tenure, but a rising probability with tenure; the estimates of γ ranged from .94 to .99, and the estimates of δ ranged from $-.005$ to $-.008$, implying that $0 < p < 1$ for all observed values of tenure. Finally, the estimates of θ ranged from .33 to .41 for the 1983 to 1991 tenure supplements, consistent with our conjecture that roughly one-half of respondents round reported tenure upward in these supplements; the estimate was .15 for the 1995 survey, consistent with less evidence of rounding in the 1995 data, as is apparent in figure 3.1.

3. Because the tendency to heap appears to be approximately three times more likely at multiples of five ending in zero (that is, multiples of ten) than multiples ending in five, we use the following adjacent values. For multiples ending in five, we define the adjacent values as one year less or one year more of tenure (for example, for five years of tenure, we use four and six). For multiples ending in ten, we define the adjacent values as one to three years less, and one to three years more.

REFERENCES

Boisjoly, Johanne, Greg J. Duncan, and Timothy Smeeding. 1998. "The Shifting Incidence of Involuntary Job Losses from 1968 to 1992." *Industrial Relations* 37(2): 207–31.

Cappelli, Peter, Laurie Bassi, Harry Katz, David Knoke, Paul Osterman, and Michael Useem. 1997. *Change at Work*. New York: Oxford University Press.

Diebold, Francis X., David Neumark, and Daniel Polsky. 1996. "Comment on Kenneth A. Swinnerton and Howard Wial, 'Is Job Stability Declining in the U.S. Economy?'" *Industrial and Labor Relations Review* 49(2): 348–52.

———. 1997. "Job Stability in the United States." *Journal of Labor Economics* 15(2): 206–33.

Farber, Henry S. 1995. "Are Lifetime Jobs Disappearing?: Job Duration in the United States: 1973–1993." NBER working paper 5014. Cambridge, Mass.: National Bureau of Economic Research.

———. 1996. "The Changing Face of Job Loss in the United States, 1981–1993." Working paper 360. Princeton, N.J.: Industrial Relations Section, Princeton University.

Hall, Robert E. 1982. "The Importance of Lifetime Jobs in the U.S. Economy." *American Economic Review* 72(4): 716–24.

Marcotte, Dave E. 1996. "Has Job Stability Declined?: Evidence from the Panel Study of Income Dynamics." Unpublished paper. Center for Governmental Studies, Northern Illinois University.

Monks, James, and Steven Pizer. 1998. "Trends in Voluntary and Involuntary Job Turnover." *Industrial Relations* 37(4): 440–59.

Neumark, David, and Daniel Polsky. 1997. "Has Job Stability Declined Yet?: New Evidence for the 1990s." NBER working paper 6330. Cambridge, Mass.: National Bureau of Economic Research.

———. 1998. "Changes in Job Stability and Job Security: Anecdotes and Evidence." Proceedings of the fiftieth annual meeting of the Industrial Relations Research Association, Madison, Wisc. (vol. 1, pp. 78–87).

Polsky, Daniel. 1999. "Changing Consequences of Job Separations in the United States." *Industrial and Labor Relations Review* 52(4): 565–80.

Rose, Stephen J. 1995. "Declining Job Security and the Professionalization of Opportunity." Research Report 95–04. Washington, D.C.: National Commission for Employment Policy.

Swinnerton, Kenneth, and Howard Wial. 1995. "Is Job Stability Declining in the U.S. Economy?" *Industrial and Labor Relations Review* 48(2): 293–304.

———. 1996. "Is Job Stability Declining in the U.S. Economy?: Reply to Diebold, Neumark, and Polsky." *Industrial and Labor Relations Review* 49(2): 352–55.

Ureta, Manuelita. 1992. "The Importance of Lifetime Jobs in the U.S. Economy, Revisited." *American Economic Review* 82(1): 322–35.

Valletta, Robert G. 1996. "Has Job Security in the United States Declined?" *Federal Reserve Bank of San Francisco Weekly Letter* 96(7, February 16).

Chapter 4

Trends in Job Instability and Wages for Young Adult Men

Annette Bernhardt, Martina Morris, Mark S. Handcock, and Marc A. Scott

Although the perception of increased job instability is widespread, empirical documentation of this "fact" remains elusive. Data and measurement problems have led to a trail of conflicting findings, and the absence of clear evidence of rising instability has led some to question whether the problem lies instead with public perception. A careful review of the evidence suggests that the question may be premature. The primary sources of cross-sectional data are the tenure and pension supplements of the Current Population Survey (CPS) and the Displaced Workers Survey (DWS). Using the CPS, Kenneth Swinnerton and Howard Wial (1995) found evidence of an overall decline in job stability, whereas Francis Diebold, David Neumark, and Daniel Polsky (1997) and Henry Farber (1998) did not. Changes in the wording of the CPS tenure question and in nonresponse rates over time hamper the building of synthetic age cohorts and duration analysis and make it difficult to resolve the different findings. Adding recent CPS data and making better adjustments for changes in wording and other data problems, Neumark, Polsky, and Hansen (this volume) did find a modest decline in the first half of the 1990s among older workers with longer tenures. Similarly, using the DWS, Farber (1997) found a mild rise in involuntary job loss during the 1990s, but changes in wording and time windows make analysis difficult here as well.

Longitudinal data sets permit more direct measurement of moves between employers, and initial research on the Panel Study of Income Dynamics (PSID) appeared to provide consistent evidence of a general increase in the rate of job changing (see, for example, Rose 1995; Boisjoly, Duncan, and Smeeding 1998). But several recent papers found no such overall trend, and again the disagreement hinges on how one resolves the problem of measuring year-to-year job changes (Polsky 1999). Because employers in the PSID are not uniquely identified, a job change must be inferred using several different questions about length of tenure that have changed over the years (see Brown and Light 1992). This measurement problem does not plague the other main source of longitudinal data, the National Longitudinal Survey (NLS), which provides unique employer identification codes that are consistent over time. Although this would seem to be an important advantage for the analysis of trends in job stability, to date only one study has used the NLS for this purpose: James Monks and Steven Pizer (1998) compared two cohorts of young men and found a significant increase in job instability between 1971 and 1990.

It is somewhat puzzling that the NLS data have been underexploited in this research field. Although the term "young men" may convey a narrow segment of the population, in fact the NLS cohorts are followed from their late teens to their midthirties. Roughly two-thirds of lifetime job changes and wage growth occur during these formative years of labor market experience when long-term relationships with employers are established (Topel and Ward 1992). This observation period is particularly useful because the two NLS cohorts bracket the striking growth in earnings inequality that emerged in the 1980s (Levy and Murnane 1992). The first cohort is tracked through the years just preceding this change (1966 to 1981), and the second cohort through the years following its onset (1979 to 1994). Comparing the two cohorts thus provides an opportunity to explore whether there have been changes in job instability and whether they have contributed to the growth in earnings inequality.

In this chapter, we take another look at the NLS data. In part, we seek to subject the Monks and Pizer (1998) findings to closer scrutiny, since the history of this field suggests that differences in measurement and methods can lead to different conclusions. Monks and Pizer made a number of analytic choices that we find questionable: they did not consistently use the employer codes provided by the NLS; they neither chose an equivalent set of years for each cohort nor used the full range of years available; and they restricted their sample to full-time workers. We address these measurement issues in our analysis, model the job change process differently, and add several important covariates. Our findings suggest that, if anything, the rise in job instability is greater than that estimated by Monks and Pizer.

In addition to critically reanalyzing the NLS data, we seek to integrate our findings into the larger debate in several ways. The first is by validating the NLS data as a source of sound information on job stability. The three main data sources on job instability (CPS, PSID, and NLS) need to be reconciled so that we have a thorough understanding of the limitations of each. The recent papers by Neumark, Polsky, and Hansen (this volume) and Jaeger and Stevens (this volume) have made considerable headway on this task for the CPS and PSID. We take up this task for the NLS data, finding strong agreement between NLS and PSID estimates of instability, but less with the CPS estimates; over time the latter echoes some of the findings of Jaeger and Stevens (this volume). Since the potential bias associated with permanent attrition is always a key problem for longitudinal data, we also conduct an extensive attrition analysis. Even under the most conservative assumptions, we find that the effect of attrition on our estimates appears to be small.

Second, the focus of the field has so far been on identifying a general trend in instability for *all* workers, and this is where the controversy resides. But we also have evidence that specific groups in the labor market—less educated workers, black workers, and older men with long tenures—may in fact have experienced an increase in instability, though the results differ by whether the 1990s are included in the analysis and by whether the analysis is restricted to involuntary job loss (for example, see Diebold, Neumark, and Polsky 1997; Jaeger and Stevens, this volume; Polsky 1999). This evidence suggests that researchers should engage more carefully in group-specific analyses, which we do here by focusing on young adults in depth.

Finally, regardless of whether job instability is on the rise, it is important to ask whether the wage outcomes associated with leaving or not leaving an employer have changed. Only a few researchers have addressed this question because resolving data and measurement problems has dominated so much of the effort (but see Polsky 1999; Stevens 1997). As these problems are resolved, however, wage outcomes should increasingly become the focus of study, since wages help to inform us about the welfare consequences of instability. We therefore test for cohort differences in the wage gains that young workers capture as they engage in job shopping and then eventually settle with one employer. We find that the returns to job changing have declined and become more unequal for the recent cohort, mirroring trends in their long-term wage growth.

DATA

We use two data sets from the National Longitudinal Surveys, both of which provide nationally representative samples of young men age fourteen to twenty-two in the first survey year. From the National Longitudinal Survey of Young Men (NLSYM) we use the sample of young men born between 1944 and 1952, surveyed yearly from 1966 to 1981 except for 1972, 1974, 1977, and 1979. From the National Longitudinal Survey of Youth (NLSY) we use the sample of young men born between 1957 and 1965, surveyed yearly from 1979 to 1994. Throughout we refer to the former as the "original cohort" and to the latter as the "recent cohort." We selected non-Hispanic whites only, because attrition among nonwhites was extreme in the original cohort. We also excluded the poor white supplemental sample and the military supplemental sample from the recent cohort, because there are no comparable supplemental samples available for the original cohort. Monks and Pizer (1998) used the same two cohorts in their research but with a different sample: they included nonwhites but excluded part-time workers.

It is important to note that the NLS data are not representative of the entire population over time, unlike the other main longitudinal data set, the PSID. Instead, the NLS data comprise a representative sample of a moving eight-year age window: from the ages of fourteen to twenty-two at the beginning of the panel to the ages of thirty to thirty-eight at the end. The power of this research design lies in the fact that we observe both cohorts across a full sixteen years, at exactly the same ages, with comparable information on schooling, work history, and job characteristics. This enables us to isolate the impact of potential differences in the economic context of their early career development: the original cohort entered the labor market in the late 1960s at the tail of the economic boom, while the recent cohort entered the labor market in the early 1980s after the onset of economic restructuring.

We conducted a series of analyses to establish the representativeness and comparability of the samples, as well as the impact of differential attrition bias (for details, see Bernhardt et al. 1997). Comparing the initial year samples of the two cohorts (1966 and 1979) to corresponding CPS samples and to each other, we found no problems with representativeness or comparability. The attrition rate, however, is considerably higher for the original cohort than for the recent cohort (25.8 percent versus 7.8 percent).[1] This discrepancy is primarily due to differences in retention rules in the two panels. In the original cohort, any respondent who missed two consecutive interviews was dropped from the survey; such respondents in the recent cohort remained eligible and were pursued for future interviews with great effort.[2] The NLS revised the original base-year weights in each subsequent survey year to account for permanent attrition and nonresponse within any given year, and we use these weights throughout. However, these adjustments were made only along the main sampling dimensions (for example, race), not along the outcome dimensions that are the focus of this chapter. It may be, for example, that respondents who dropped out during the course of the sixteen-year survey period were also more unstable, so that the sample that remains is artificially stable. Later in the chapter, we investigate the extent to which the differential attrition rates between the two cohorts might have affected the cohort differences that we estimate. We also investigate the effect of attrition on wages and find that controlling for age and education removes any attrition bias in wages (as is true with other key variables such as employment status and work experience). We therefore control for age and education in all models.

Finally, about one-third of the original cohort respondents served in the Vietnam War at some point during the survey years. Surprisingly, the timing and rate of attrition is similar for veterans and nonveterans. Of course, the veterans lost several years of experience in the civilian labor market during their military service. They therefore show a clear time lag in their entry into the labor market, with shorter tenures and less accumulated work experience by their early thirties. We adjust for this in the analyses presented here. Beyond this time lag, however, and consistent with other research (Berger and Hirsch 1983), we found no significant bias on other dimensions (for example, employment rates, hourly wages).

MEASURES

The NLS data have a distinct advantage for this field, because unique employer identification codes allow us to measure directly whether an employer change occurred over a given time span. (In the remainder of the chapter, we use the term "job change" to refer to a separation from an employer). James Brown and Audrey Light (1992) found that these employer codes are the best source of employer identification, not only for the NLS data but also compared to the other longitudinal data sets. We use the employer codes for both cohorts, in contrast to Monks and Pizer (1998), who used them only for the recent cohort and relied on other questions for the original cohort. We focus on the respondent's main "CPS" employer at the time of the survey.[3] In the original cohort, the CPS employer is assigned an employer code that is unique across all interview years. In the recent cohort, unique identification of the CPS employer is only possible between any two consecutive years. By successively linking pairs of years, however, we can trace a unique CPS employer over any time span as long as that employer is present in each year. We have restricted our use of the employer codes in the original cohort to match this constraint.

Four noncontiguous years were skipped in the original cohort follow-up surveys. This means that we cannot construct an unbroken series of year-to-year employer comparisons. We therefore construct a series of two-year employer comparisons. These are strictly matched between the two surveys, so that we are comparing job changes at exactly the same ages and at exactly the same time during the survey period. There are six such comparisons for each cohort, and they are evenly spaced across the survey time span. Table 4.1 shows the years that we use for our analyses and defines the six comparisons being made for each cohort. Monks and Pizer (1998) also used two-year employer comparisons, but they constructed only four of them and did not select the same survey years from

Table 4.1   Years Used for Job Change Analysis

| Year of NLS Survey | | | |
Original Cohort	Recent Cohort	Year Number	Years Used for Two-year Comparison
1966	1979	1	
1967	1980	2	2 to 4
1968	1981	3	
1969	1982	4	4 to 6
1970	1983	5	
1971	1984	6	6 to 8
	1985	7	
1973	1986	8	8 to 10
	1987	9	
1975	1988	10	
1976	1989	11	11 to 13
	1990	12	
1978	1991	13	13 to 15
	1992	14	
1980	1993	15	
1981	1994	16	

each cohort. (For example, the fourth and sixth years were used as a comparison for the original cohort but not for the recent.)

We define a job separation as follows. For each two-year comparison, the risk set in year t is all employed respondents, not self-employed or working without pay, who are also observed in year t + 2. If the respondent is unemployed or out of the labor force in year t + 2, an employer separation occurred. If the respondent is employed in year t + 2, then the employer code for the CPS employer in year t is compared to the CPS employer code in year t + 2. An employer separation occurred if these codes differ. The empirical two-year separation rate is thus calculated as the number of respondents who have left their year t employer by year t + 2, divided by the total number of respondents in the risk set in year t. After the risk set was defined, we dropped person-year observations outside the sixteen-to-thirty-four age range to ensure adequate sample sizes within age groups. The resulting sample sizes and mean number of observations contributed by respondents are given at the top of table 4.A1.

We do not disaggregate voluntary from involuntary job changes because data on this variable are missing for a significant fraction of the original cohort person-years and exploratory analysis suggests that there is bias in the missingness. But changes in job stability per se remain an important trend to document, and not only because of the current conflicting findings on this measure. Job stability can confer access to firm-specific training, internal promotion ladders, and health and pension benefits. Similarly, wage growth in the middle and later working years generally accrues from tenure with one employer, rather than from job changing, which may in fact become detrimental. Changing employers thus has potentially strong implications for skills, job security, and wages.

Our second dependent variable, wage, is measured as the respondent's hourly wage at his CPS job at the date of the interview. This measure is constructed by the NLS using direct information if the respondent reported his earnings as an hourly wage, and from questions on the weeks (or months) and hours worked in the last year if the respondent reported in other units. We focus on hourly wages rather than yearly earnings because the latter are confounded by hours and weeks worked and the number of jobs held during the year. Analyses are based on the natural log of real wages in 1992 dollars, using the Personal Consumption Expenditure (PCE) deflator. Cleaning and imputation of missing wages affected less than 6 percent of person-year wage observations in each cohort.

Later in the chapter, we examine the two-year wage changes that correspond to the two-year job changes for the subset of respondents in the risk set who were working in both years. Thus, for any two years that t and t + 2 were used to compute whether or not a job change occurred, we compute the corresponding wage change: $(\ln)\text{wage}_{t+2} - (\ln)\text{wage}_t$. We also compute the total wage growth that each individual experienced over the entire sixteen-year survey period. Total wage growth is measured by specifying a model for the individual-specific *permanent* wage profile over the sixteen years, smoothed of short-term, transitory fluctuations. Specifically, the smoothed wages are predicted hourly wages for each respondent at each age, from a mixed-effects wage model that allows a unique wage profile for each person across his or her work history (cf. Gottschalk and Moffitt 1994; Haider 1997). The appendix contains the technical details of the model.

Finally, table 4A.1 shows the independent variables that are used in this study. All the covariates are measured identically in the two cohorts, and all are time-varying—that is, they are measured at year t for any year t versus t + 2 employer or wage comparison. Although most of these variables are straightforward—see the *NLS Users' Guide* (Center for Human Resource Research 1995) for details on coding—several require elaboration. Industry and occupation are based on 1970 census codes, since these were available for both cohorts. Work experience is not measured with potential experience but rather with cumulative *actual* months worked since age sixteen. For respondents who entered the survey after age sixteen, we imputed the missing months of experience using a model based on observed experience for those who entered the survey before age seventeen. For any years in the remainder of the survey where data on months worked were missing, we imputed the average of the months worked in the surrounding two years. Finally, education is measured using information on both years of education completed and degree received.[4] Thus, respondents coded as high school graduates or college graduates must actually hold those degrees. (A GED is considered equivalent to a high school degree in this coding.)

TRENDS IN JOB INSTABILITY

The key point of interest is whether the two-year separation rates differ between the two cohorts. Figure 4.1 shows the empirical cohort differences, overall and broken down by age, education, and tenure. With no adjustments, 46.4 percent of the original cohort and 52.7 percent of the recent cohort had left their current employer two years later, a 13.6 percent proportionate increase in the rate of job changing. The next three panels illustrate the well-known fact that job instability declines with age, education, and time spent with one employer. In each case, however, the recent cohort shows a higher rate of job changing.

The problem is that all of these dimensions change simultaneously as the cohorts are surveyed over time. We therefore move directly to modeling the separation rates to determine whether there has been a secular increase in the rate of job changing, net of compositional shifts. Let Y_{ijt} indicate whether individual i in job j in year t has left that job by year t + 2. We specify a logistic regression model of the form:[5]

$$\text{logit}(P[Y_{ijt} = 1 \mid X_{ijt}, J_{ijt}, U_{it}, C_i, \phi_i]) = \theta_0 X_{ijt} + \theta_1 J_{ijt} + \theta_2 U_{it} + \theta_3 C_i + \phi_i, \quad (4.1)$$

where $P[Y_{ijt} = 1 \mid X_{ijt}, J_{ijt}, U_{it}, C_i, \phi_i]$ is the probability that an individual in job j in year t has left that job by year t + 2 given that they have characteristics $X_{ijt}, J_{ijt}, U_{it}, C_i$, and ϕ_i, described later, and $\text{logit}(p) = \log[p/(1 - p)]$ is the log-odds of the probability p. Here X_{ijt} represents the time-varying characteristics of the respondent; J_{ijt} represents the time-varying characteristics of the job, including tenure; U_{it} represents the local unemployment rate in the individual's labor market in year t; and C_i represents a cohort indicator variable, coded zero for the original cohort and one for the recent cohort. In their analysis of the two NLS cohorts, Monks and Pizer (1998) fit somewhat different models, namely, a series of probits with a different specification of the cohort difference and with fewer covariates. (In particular they excluded tenure.) We compare our results with theirs at the end of this section.

We include an individual-specific effect (ISE), ϕ_i, to capture un-

Figure 4.1 Cohort Differences in Job Separation Rates

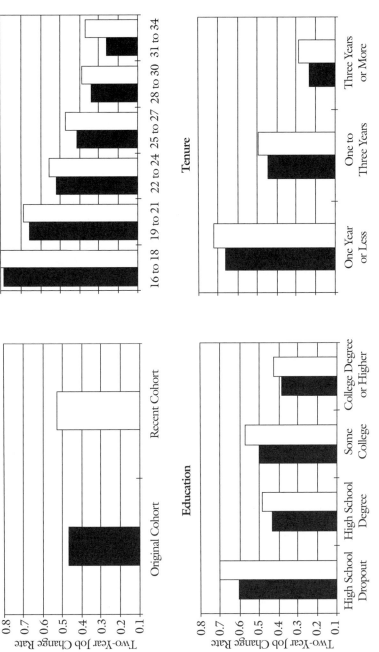

measured characteristics of the individual that are stable over the sample period. Since the main objective of this term is to reflect the longitudinal nature of the sample, we adopt a simple specification, modeling it as independent of the other regressors (Heckman and Singer 1984).[6] The estimate of the cohort difference was robust to this specification of unobserved heterogeneity, as well as others.[7]

Table 4.2 presents the results of several versions of the above model. In model 1, we control for basic compositional differences. For example, we know that the distributions of age, education, and local unemployment differ across the two cohorts. Controlling for work experience is also important—recall that the Vietnam veterans delayed their entry into the labor market, reaching employment stability at a later age and thus "dragging down" the overall stability of the original cohort. The behavior of these "correction" variables is as expected. The odds of a job change strongly decline with age, tenure, and accumulated work experience as young workers begin to form permanent attachments to employers. Higher local unemployment has a mild positive effect on the odds of a job change.[8] Youth without a high school degree are significantly more likely to leave their current employer than are high school graduates, and those with postsecondary education are significantly less likely to do so.

In sum, after adjusting for key compositional differences, we estimate that the odds of a job change are 43 percent higher for the recent cohort. We consider this our best baseline estimate of the increase in job instability experienced by young white men in the 1980s and early 1990s, compared to their counterparts in the late 1960s and 1970s.[9]

In the next four models, we explore several alternative specifications in order to pursue different substantive questions. In model 2, we examine the impact of additional sociodemographic variables. It is not surprising that enrollment in school raises the odds of a job change, since jobs held during schooling are often short-lived. The geographic effect of living in the South works in the expected direction, as does the stabilizing effect of marriage. The impact of these three variables on the cohort difference is strong: the odds of a job change are now 28 percent higher for the recent cohort—still substantial, but clearly lower. Most of this reduction is driven by lower marriage rates in the recent cohort and its longer periods of college enrollment (Morris et al. 1998); both trends are evident in CPS data as well.

In model 3, we ask whether the economywide shift toward the service sector has played a role. Service industries, as a rule, are more unstable than the public sector and the goods-producing and traditionally unionized industries (with the exception of construction, in which the nature of work is inherently transient). On both fronts, the young workers in the

(Text continues on p. 124.)

Table 4.2 Logistic Regression Estimates for Two-Year Job Separations

Variable	(1) β̂	exp(β̂)	(2) β̂	exp(β̂)	(3) β̂	exp(β̂)	(4) β̂	exp(β̂)	(5) β̂	exp(β̂)
Intercept	1.544*** (.052)	4.68	1.173*** (.060)	3.23	1.436*** (.067)	4.20	1.839*** (.070)	6.29	.930*** (.069)	2.53
Recent cohort [original cohort]	.358*** (.052)	1.43	.244*** (.052)	1.28	.176*** (.052)	1.19	.156* (.079)	1.17	.373*** (.067)	1.45
Age	-.146*** (.021)	.86	-.063** (.022)	.94	-.037 (.023)	.96	-.109*** (.021)	.90	-.060 (.034)	.94
Age squared	.005*** (.001)	1.00	.002 (.001)	1.00	.001 (.001)	1.00	.004*** (.001)	1.00	.003 (.002)	1.00
Current education [high school graduate]										
Less than high school	.558*** (.069)	1.75	.542*** (.069)	1.72	.478*** (.068)	1.61	.497*** (.068)	1.64	.747*** (.101)	2.11
Some college	.393*** (.057)	1.48	.205*** (.060)	1.23	.208*** (.061)	1.23	.349*** (.058)	1.42	.088 (.091)	1.09
College degree or more	-.127* (.064)	.88	-.234*** (.065)	.79	-.151* (.071)	.86	-.145* (.066)	.86	-.295*** (.087)	.74
Current tenure [one year or less]										
One to three	-.747*** (.042)	.47	-.725*** (.042)	.48	-.702*** (.042)	.50	-.726*** (.042)	.48	-.807*** (.059)	.45

(Table continues on p. 122.)

Table 4.2 *Continued*

Variable	(1) β̂	(1) exp(β̂)	(2) β̂	(2) exp(β̂)	(3) β̂	(3) exp(β̂)	(4) β̂	(4) exp(β̂)	(5) β̂	(5) exp(β̂)
Three or more years	−.859*** (.055)	.42	−.842*** (.056)	.43	−.811*** (.056)	.44	−.833*** (.055)	.44	−.954*** (.072)	.38
Work experience	−.008*** (.001)	.99	−.006*** (.001)	.99	−.006*** (.001)	.99	−.008*** (.001)	.99	−.008*** (.001)	.99
Local unemployment rate	.008 (.007)	1.01	.009 (.007)	1.01	−.009 (.007)	1.00	.008 (.007)	1.01	.016 (.010)	1.02
Currently enrolled	—		.447*** (.054)	1.56	.402*** (.055)	1.50	—		—	
Living in the South	—		.105* (.052)	1.11	.085 (.051)	1.09	—		—	
Married	—		−.342*** (.045)	.71	−.297*** (.045)	.74	—		—	
Industry [trades, business services]										
Construction, mining, agriculture	—				.115 (.066)	1.12	−.037 (.082)	.96		
Manufacturing, transportation, and communication	—				−.763*** (.051)	.47	−.927*** (.070)	.40		

Finance, insurance, real estate, and other professional services	—	—	−.202** (.066); .82	−.198* (.088); .82	—
Public administration	—	—	−1.334*** (.107); .26	−1.456*** (.116); .23	—
Professional, management, and technical occupations	—	—	−.147** (.053); .86	—	—
Interaction of cohort and industry					
Recent cohort in high-level services	—	—	—	−.043 (.124); .96	—
Recent cohort in traditional industries	—	—	—	.241** (.091); 1.27	—
Individual heterogeneity: standard deviations	1.087*** (.036)	1.080*** (.036)	1.025*** (.035)	1.029*** (.035)	1.259*** (.054)
Change in −2 log likelihood	−2133***	−137***	−427***	−459***	−734***

Note: Standard errors are identified in parentheses. Contrast categories are identified in brackets. Age is rescaled to age sixteen. Work experience is measured in months. Model 5 is fit for a subsample of respondents; see text for full explanation. For model 4, change in −2 log likelihood is relative to model 1; for model 5 it is the change relative to the null model for the subsample.

*** = significant at .001; ** = significant at .01; * = significant at .05 level.

recent cohort are disadvantaged. Mirroring the economywide trend, they are less likely to be employed in the public sector and more likely to be employed in the service sector, especially in low-end, high-turnover industries such as retail trade and business services. Controlling for these compositional shifts further reduces the cohort difference, so that the job change odds are now 19 percent higher for the recent cohort—about half of the baseline estimate.

In these first three models, all of the variables are constrained to have the same effect for both cohorts, so that we are capturing the impact of compositional shifts in the variables, not changes in their impact. We did test whether the rise in job instability for the recent cohort was particularly pronounced for those with less education. Surprisingly, we found no such differential—the rise in instability has been felt by all education groups. (This is consistent with Monks and Pizer's [1998] finding for whites.) There is, however, a further twist to the industry story. In model 4, we fit an interaction between the cohort effect and the industry effect. The cohort dummy now captures the cohort difference in job instability *within* the baseline industries of retail and wholesale trade and business services. The first interaction term indicates that the cohort difference is similar within finance, insurance, real estate, and other professional services. The second interaction term, however, shows a significantly stronger cohort difference in industries that historically have been unionized. Thus, not only are youth in the recent cohort suffering from greater reliance on the "unstable" service sector, but they are not benefiting as much when they are employed in traditionally stable industries such as manufacturing. What we are probably identifying here, albeit indirectly, is the shedding of employment and declines in unionization in the goods-producing and to some extent public sectors.[10]

Finally, we examined whether the greater instability observed in the recent cohort is simply a function of more volatile transitions to the labor market; it could be that the cohort differences in job stability are less pronounced after this transition has been completed. In model 5, we therefore reestimate model 1, but only for workers after they have finished their schooling.[11] The focus, therefore, is on the experience of the young workers once they have permanently entered the labor market. The results are consistent with those from the full sample: in particular, the estimated cohort difference remains strong and significant. (The same finding obtains if we reestimate models 2, 3, and 4.) The increased job instability we have found does not disappear once the young workers "settle down" and is therefore not just a legacy of churning in the labor market early on.

At a general level, our findings match those of Monks and Pizer (1998) in that both studies find greater job instability for the recent cohort. A direct side-by-side comparison of results is not possible: we use different (as well as more) years in our analysis, construct a somewhat different measure of job change, fit different models, and focus on a different sample. A reasonable approximation to their analysis, however, can be obtained if we restrict our sample to full-time workers only and fit a version of model 1 using a continuous linear time trend instead of a cohort dummy and including only education, age, marital status, and the unemployment rate as covariates. Monks and Pizer's (1998) estimate of this time trend for whites, as given in their table 4, is 0.017 (standard error: 0.006), and our estimate is 0.022 (standard error: 0.005), within 1.2 standard errors of their estimate.[12] Thus, there is solid agreement between the two studies to this point, and our attrition analysis in the next section can be seen as commenting on the validity of both.

VALIDATION ANALYSIS

In the context of a research field that has not been able to reach consensus on trends in job instability, the significant increase found above certainly requires a second look. On the one hand, we might expect the NLS data to yield different findings: they focus on young adult men only; they extend from the late 1960s to the early 1990s (thus capturing a longer time span); and they allow for a direct, clean measure of instability. On the other hand, other characteristics of the NLS data may be generating an artificial increase in instability. In particular, the higher attrition rate in the original cohort (25.8 percent versus 7.8 percent in the recent cohort) raises important questions about the interpretation of our findings. If respondents who attrit are also more likely to be unstable in their job change behavior, then our cohort effect for job instability may be upwardly biased by the lower rates of attrition in the recent cohort. We use two strategies to examine the potential confounding effect of attrition. First, we benchmark the NLS job change estimates against estimates based on the PSID and the CPS. This exercise is also important in its own right, since it contributes to cross–data set validation in the field. Second, we develop several model-based adjustments to our instability estimates for the impact of attrition.

We begin by comparing job change estimates from the NLS to estimates from the two other main data sets in the field. We use Polsky's (1999) series for the PSID and Stewart's (1998) series for the CPS; both address some of the well-known problems with changes in measures and question wording over time. If attrition in the original cohort introduces bias, then the job instability estimates from the original cohort will not match up well with the other data sets whereas estimates from the recent cohort will match up well (since attrition in the recent cohort was negligible).

Two factors complicate a simple comparison. First, neither the PSID nor the CPS extend back far enough in time, so they provide only two time points that we can use to compare with the original cohort. Both of these years, however, fall toward the end of the series, when the greater attrition rate in the original cohort is most likely to make itself felt. Second, the two NLS cohorts age throughout the sixteen-year survey period, and because of the skipped interview years in the original cohort, we sometimes have to use two-year instead of one-year job change rates. With these considerations in mind, table 4.3 presents the best comparisons that can be constructed, showing the specific age ranges and years used in each case. For all three data sets, the samples are white working men who are not self-employed. We also reweighted the NLS and PSID distributions to the CPS distribution within age and education cells, so that the analysis is not confounded by differences in composition; in practice, this reweighting has a minor effect.

The first half of the table gives the NLS-PSID comparison, using either one-year or two-year job change rates. For the NLS, these rates are once again calculated using the unique employer codes; for the PSID, the rates are calculated using information on job tenure (Polsky 1999).

Table 4.3   Comparison of Separation Rate Estimates from NLS, PSID, and CPS

Year	Age Range	Measure	Cohort	NLS	PSID[a]	NLS-PSID
1978	Twenty-six to thirty-two	Two-year rate	Original	.3668	.3652	.0016
1980	Twenty-eight to thirty-four	One-year rate	Original	.2292	.2104	.0188
1989	Twenty-six to thirty-two	Two-year rate	Recent	.4078	.4177	− .0100
1991	Twenty-eight to thirty-four	One-year rate	Recent	.2420	.2389	.0031

Year	Age Range	Cohort	NLS One-year rate	CPS[b] Fourteen-month rate	NLS-CPS
1975	Twenty-three to thirty-one	Original	.2721	.3351	− .0630*
1980	Twenty-eight to thirty-six	Original	.2108	.2591	− .0483*
1988	Twenty-three to thirty-one	Recent	.3001	.3452	− .0451*
1989	Twenty-four to thirty-two	Recent	.2942	.3198	− .0256
1990	Twenty-five to thirty-three	Recent	.2653	.3228	− .0575*
1991	Twenty-six to thirty-four	Recent	.2474	.2890	− .0416*
1992	Twenty-seven to thirty-five	Recent	.2546	.2705	− .0159
1993	Twenty-eight to thirty-six	Recent	.2713	.2727	− .0014

[a] Authors' tabulation of data from Polsky (1991).
[b] Authors' tabulation of data from Stewart (1998).
*Difference significant at .05 level.

For both, the measure is the proportion of respondents working at time t who had left their time t employer at time t + 1 or t + 2, depending on which comparison is being made. The two sets of estimates match up remarkably well: none of the differences is statistically significant. Note in particular the close agreement in 1980 for the original cohort, the next to last year of that panel when the rate of attrition peaks. This is a solid indicator that the greater attrition rate in the original cohort is not driving our finding of changes in job stability over time.

The second half of the table shows our comparison of the NLS with the CPS. This comparison is more problematic because the two data sets have different measures and risk sets. Stewart's (1998) CPS measure is (1) a fourteen-and-a-half-month job change rate that (2) is inferred using several decision rules for (3) respondents who worked at least one week in the previous year and who were not students or recent graduates. By contrast, the NLS measure is (1) a one-year job change rate that (2) is calculated directly for (3) respondents who were working during the week of the previous year's survey. The results of comparing across these different measures are not clear. As a rule, the NLS estimates are lower than the CPS estimates, as we might expect given how the measures are defined (one-year change rates for the former, fourteen-and-a-half-month rates for the latter). But the size and significance of the differences vary considerably, both within and between cohorts. Especially worrisome is the variability in the differences *within* the recent cohort, which has very little attrition. Our sense is that it would be difficult to reconcile these two data sets without considerably more analysis, along the lines of Jaeger and Stevens (this volume). It should be noted, however, that these authors also found a divergence between CPS and PSID estimates in the 1970s, though not in the 1980s and 1990s.

Our second attrition analysis is a model-based sensitivity analysis. Specifically, we make several adjustments to our estimate of the cohort difference in job stability, based on potential differences in the behavior of attriters. First, attriters may have higher levels of job instability than non-attriters. Second, attriters may also be less likely to be eligible for the risk set that defines the job change sample. In both cases, attriters do not contribute enough "unstable" observations to the original cohort sample, and as a result the cohort effect is overstated. Our strategy in calculating the adjusted cohort effects therefore is to "add back in" the missing attriter observations. Since we are conducting a hypothetical experiment—"what would the cohort effect have been if the attriters had not attrited?"—we cannot estimate the adjusted cohort effect empirically from the data. Instead, we derive an expression for this adjusted effect that allows us both to incorporate any greater propensity among attriters to change jobs and to equalize the number of observations contributed by attriters and non-attriters.

We begin by adding several terms to model 1:

$$
\begin{aligned}
\text{logit}(P[Y_{ijt} = 1 \mid X_{ijt}, J_{ijt}, U_{it}, C_i, \phi_i, A_{ijt}]) &= \theta_o\, X_{ijt} + \theta_1\, J_{ijt} \\
&\quad + \theta_2\, U_{it} + \theta_3\, C_i + \theta_4\, A_{ijt} \\
&\quad + \theta_5\, CA_{ijt} + \phi_i.
\end{aligned} \tag{4.2}
$$

The model now includes two attrition-related terms: A_{ijt}, a dummy variable indicating whether person i in job j in year t attrits after year $t + 2$ given that he has not attrited before, and CA_{ijt}, the interaction between attrition and cohort. Thus, θ_4 represents the attrition effect for the original cohort. (Later we suppress the references to the characteristics X_{ijt}, J_{ijt}, U_{it}, and ϕ_i.) Under this model, the log-odds of a two-year job change for a randomly chosen person-year with given characteristics from cohort k is:

$$
\begin{aligned}
\text{logit}&(P[Y_{ijt} = 1 \mid C_i = k]) \\
&= \text{logit}(P[Y_{ijt} = 1 \mid C_i = k, A_{ijt} = 0])\, P(A_{ijt} = 0 \mid C_i = k) \\
&\quad + \text{logit}(P[Y_{ijt} = 1 \mid C_i = k, A_{ijt} = 1])\, P(A_{ijt} = 1 \mid C_i = k) \\
&= \theta_0 X_{ijt} + \theta_1 J_{ijt} + \theta_2 U_{it} + \theta_3 k + \phi_i + \theta_4 P(A_{ijt} = 1 \mid C_i = k) \\
&\quad + \theta_5 k P(A_{ijt} = 1 \mid C_i = k)
\end{aligned} \tag{4.3}
$$

The attrition-adjusted cohort effect is then simply represented as:

$$
\begin{aligned}
\text{logit}&(P[Y_{ijt} = 1 \mid C_i = 1]) - \text{logit}(P[Y_{ijt} = 1 \mid C_i = 0]) \\
&= \theta_3 + \theta_4[P(A_{ijt} = 1 \mid C_i = 1) - P(A_{ijt} = 1 \mid C_i = 0)] \\
&\quad + \theta_5\, P(A_{ijt} = 1 \mid C_i = 1)
\end{aligned} \tag{4.4}
$$

The first term (θ_3) represents the cohort effect for a non-attriter. The second term represents the differential odds that an attriter experiences a job separation before being lost, multiplied by the difference in attrition rates between the two cohorts. If attriters are more unstable, θ_4 will be positive, and since the difference in attrition rates is negative, the adjustment will lower the estimate of the cohort effect. The third term represents the differential in the attrition effect for the recent cohort, multiplied by the attrition rate in the recent cohort. If those who attrit in the recent cohort are more unstable than those who attrit in the original cohort, then θ_5 will be positive and this adjustment will increase the estimate of the cohort effect.

To calculate an adjusted cohort effect based on this derivation, we need to estimate two sets of quantities: θ_3, θ_4, and θ_5, and the conditional probabilities of attrition. We estimated the former using the modified logistic regression model described earlier; we obtained $\theta_3 = 0.3478$, $\theta_4 = 0.2902$, and $\theta_5 = 0.0039$. Note that attriters in the recent cohort are in fact relatively more unstable than attriters in the original cohort. We might expect this, since the recent cohort was pursued more rigorously for continued participation in the survey—any respondents who still managed to drop out of the survey are thus likely to be particularly unstable individuals.

We next estimated the conditional probabilities of attrition that we will use in our derivation. The idea here is to construct these probabilities *as though* the attriters' unobserved years had been included in the analysis. We accomplish this by defining the fraction of attriters at the level of the individual rather than at the level of person-years, so that the number of person-year observations contributed by attriters and non-attriters is equalized. There are three ways these fractions can be defined:

1. *The fraction of attriters in the risk set:* The fraction of respondents in the job change risk set who eventually attrit is 0.1603 in the original cohort and 0.0545 in the recent cohort. In using these fractions, we are effectively adding the person-years that attriters would have contributed had they not dropped out of the sample.

2. *The fraction of attriters in the risk set, equalized for eligibility:* In addition to the adjustment made in (1), we also need to account for the fact that recent cohort attriters were more likely to make it into the job change risk set than original cohort attriters. We do so by equalizing the proportion of attriters eligible for the risk set, yielding an adjusted attrition fraction of 0.1996 for the original cohort.

3. *The fraction of attriters in the full sample:* Finally, the strongest adjustment would use the fraction of attriters for each cohort in the full sample (all available survey years). The fraction of persons who ever worked in the full sample and who are lost to attrition is 0.2323 in the original cohort and 0.0658 in the recent cohort.

The adjustments based on each of these three methods are provided in table 4.4, along with the unadjusted estimate from model 1 in table 4.2 for comparison. Although in all cases the attrition adjustment reduces the estimated cohort effect, the reductions are modest. Under method 1, the adjusted cohort effect is 0.3172—an 11.31 percent decrease in the unadjusted value. Under method 2, the adjusted cohort effect is 0.3058—a 14.50 percent decrease in the unadjusted value. We consider this the most accurate adjustment, since it removes both types of attrition bias from the job change sample. Finally, under method 3 the adjusted cohort effect is 0.2996—a 16.23 percent decrease. We feel less comfortable with this adjustment, since it uses estimates from the job change sample (that is, θ_3, θ_4, and θ_5) and applies them to a sample that is not

Table 4.4   Attrition Adjustments to the Cohort Instability Effect

	Unadjusted	Adjustments		
		Method 1	Method 2	Method 3
Fraction of attriters				
Original cohort	.16	.16	.20	.23
Recent cohort	.06	.06	.06	.07
Cohort effect	.3577[a]	.3172	.3058	.2996
Standard error	.052	.042	.042	.042
Adjustment	—	−.0405	−.0114	−.0062
Percentage adjustment	—	11.31	14.50	16.23

[a] Taken from model 1 in table 4.2.

included in the instability analysis conducted here. Even with this most conservative adjustment, however, the recent cohort still has a 35 percent higher odds of a job change.

There are two reasons why the adjustments are modest under all methods. First, because the cohort difference in attrition only ranges from 11 percent (method 1) to 17 percent (method 3), the proportional reweighting is not substantial in any of the methods. Under these conditions, the estimated attrition effect (θ_4) would have to be about five and a half times larger in order to negate fully the size of the cohort effect.

Second, the recent cohort attrition differential (θ_5) is positive, thus offsetting the negative adjustment made by the main attrition effect. That attriters in the recent cohort are more "unstable" than attriters in the original cohort makes sense, given the difference in retention rules in the two panels. In the original cohort, any respondents who missed two sequential interviews were dropped from the survey; such respondents in the recent cohort remained eligible and were energetically pursued for future interviews. Those who did manage to drop out of the recent cohort therefore likely represent "hard-core" attriters. We found support for this conjecture by examining respondents in the recent cohort who would have been dropped from the survey under the rules used in the original cohort (about 9 percent of the sample). These "hypothetical attriters" have attributes and outcomes that fall in between those of the hard-core attriters and the retained sample. This result suggests that the additional respondents lost to attrition in the original cohort are a moderate group.

In sum, both the cross–data set comparisons and the model-based adjustments suggest that although attrition bias exists in the original cohort, it does not alter the statistical significance or the substance of our findings.

WAGE CHANGES

A rise in job instability among young adults in the American labor market does not necessarily signal a problem. In fact, a solid body of research has established that job shopping early in the career is highly beneficial, yielding greater wage gains than staying put with one employer (Borjas and Rosen 1980; Bartel and Borjas 1981). Roughly two-thirds of lifetime wage growth for male high school graduates occurs during the first ten years of labor market experience, and the bulk of it is the result of job changes (Murphy and Welch 1990; Topel and Ward 1992). Although it is in general true that having many employers early on does not impede wage growth (Gardecki and Neumark 1998), in the long term job instability becomes harmful to wage growth, and chronically high levels of job instability are detrimental from the outset (Light and McGarry 1998). In this context, it is important to examine how the wage returns to job shopping have changed for the recent cohort. For example, it is possible that the very nature of career development has changed in recent years. The recent cohort might be changing jobs more frequently and accumulating less tenure with one firm but nevertheless be able to capture consistent wage growth over time. Thus, our appraisal of the rise in job instability must in the end focus on the wage outcomes—specifically, the wage gains that young workers capture as they engage in job shopping and then eventually settle with one employer.

We present a simple descriptive analysis here, not a behavioral model. There is clearly a serious endogeneity problem that must be addressed in any causal analysis of the role that job changes play in wage growth, and this kind of full-scale analysis is beyond the scope of this chapter. Our descriptive findings, however, do provide the first empirical step in establishing whether the association between job stability and wage outcomes has changed.

We continue with the sample used in the job change analysis but select that subset of respondents who were working in both years t and t + 2, so that we can construct the corresponding two-year wage changes.[13] In the top half of figure 4.2, we have plotted median wage changes for workers who left their employer and for workers who stayed with the same employer. This figure confirms that early in the career, job changing pays off more than staying with an employer—in fact, these wage gains are substantially higher than any experienced later on. After the mid-twenties, there is less to be gained from switching employers, and wage growth as a whole slows down.

The recent cohort, however, has failed to capture wage growth precisely where it is most critical: in the early stages of job shopping. This deterioration first appears between the ages of sixteen and twenty-one.

**Figure 4.2   Two-Year Wage Changes, by Age and Job Change Status
(Medians and Variances)**

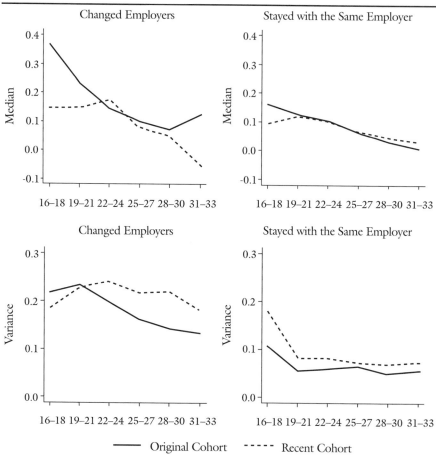

Breakdowns by education show that it is young workers moving directly from high school into the labor market who receive the lowest returns. There is also a noticeable drop in the wage gains resulting from a job change in the early thirties, and this is shared by all except those with a college degree.[14] By contrast, when young workers stay with the same employer, there is little difference in the *absolute* wage gains captured by the two cohorts. In *relative* terms, however, the recent cohort benefits more from staying with the same employer after the midtwenties, because the returns to job changing have declined so steeply at that point.

In table 4.5, we further explore the role of education in these trends, with a model of cohort differences in the wage returns to changing and not changing jobs. (Again, this regression is simply descriptive.) Substan-

Table 4.5   Wage Change Regression Results

Variable	Estimate	Standard Error	Ratio of College to High School[a]
Original cohort			
Did not change jobs			
High school or less (intercept)	.2577	.016	1.42
Some college or more	.0439	.013	
Changed jobs			
High school or less	.0850	.013	1.12
Some college or more	.1084	.014	
Recent cohort			
Did not change jobs			
High school or less	−.0227	.012	1.61
Some college or more	.0264	.014	
Changed jobs			
High school or less	−.0439	.013	3.26
Some college or more	.0915	.015	
Age (rescaled to 16 = 0)	−.0242	.004	
Age squared (rescaled to 16 = 0)	.0010	.000	
Work experience (in months)	−.0006	.000	
Adjusted R^2	.042		
N	11,139		

Note: Dependent variable is two-year change in log wages.

[a] Evaluated at variable means for age, age squared, and experience.

tive findings are summarized in the third column. For the original cohort, the education differentials in wage returns are roughly similar regardless of whether individuals change jobs or not. This is not the case for the recent cohort. Here, young adults with no college experience are getting hit the hardest when they search for jobs—and this, precisely at the time that job changing has become more prevalent. By contrast, those with college experience in the recent cohort have maintained their wage growth when they search for a job.[15]

A second potential impact of job instability is on the variability in wage changes. There has been some debate over the role of transitory wage fluctuations in the overall growth in wage dispersion over the last two decades (Gottschalk and Moffitt 1994). The rise in job instability would seem a natural candidate for explaining an increase in transitory wage variance. In the bottom half of figure 4.2, we have plotted the variances of the observed wage changes. Generally speaking, a job change results in more variable wage changes, as we might expect. The recent cohort, however, consistently shows greater variability in wage gains. This is especially pronounced among job-changers in the later age ranges, yet it is also evident among job-stayers at all ages. This suggests that transitory wage fluctuations associated with job changes are not the only force driving the increase in wage dispersion. Breakdowns by education show consistency in these trends across all education groups.

Finally, we have up to now focused on two-year wage changes and linked them to job change events. The young adult workers observed here, however, have experienced an entire chain of wage changes. Even small differences in single wage changes can cumulate into substantial differences over time. What happens, then, when we examine the total wage growth observed for each individual? Figure 4.3 plots the distribution of total wage growth between the ages of sixteen and thirty-six, using "permanent" wages that have short-term fluctuations smoothed out (see earlier discussion).

Two important trends emerge from this figure. First, young workers who entered the labor force in the 1980s experienced significantly lower *total* wage growth when compared to their predecessors. Translated into real terms, the typical worker in the original cohort saw his hourly wage increase by $8.65 between the ages of sixteen and thirty-six, compared to

Figure 4.3   Change in Permanent (Log) Wages from Age Sixteen to Thirty-Six

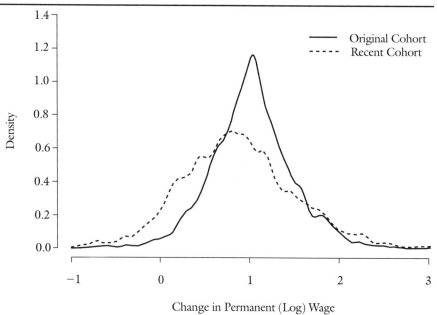

Change in Permanent (Log) Wage

$6.69 for those in the recent cohort—a 23 percent decline (both figures in 1992 dollars). Not surprisingly, this loss of growth has been felt largely by those without a four-year college degree (Handcock and Morris 1998). Second, long-term wage growth has also become significantly more unequal in the recent cohort. There remain some workers who experience high levels of wage growth, but there are now substantially more workers who have minimal or even negative wage growth. We estimate that the percentage of workers experiencing no wage growth or actual real wage declines is 1.7 percent for the original cohort but 7.2 percent for the recent cohort. This polarization becomes progressively stronger as the young workers age, and it is consistent across different levels of education.

To our minds, this figure suggests that there is a connection between trends in job instability and wage inequality, since it mirrors our findings on the wage consequences of job changing. We are currently developing models that will formally test for such a connection.

CONCLUSIONS

In this chapter, we have identified a marked increase in job instability among young white men during the 1980s and early 1990s, compared to the late 1960s and 1970s. The robustness of this finding to different controls is striking. It does not disappear, for example, once the young workers "settle down" and is therefore not just a legacy of job churning early on. It is also not limited to less educated workers. Some of the increase is associated with lower marriage rates in recent years (though it is unclear which is cause and which is effect), as well as with the trend toward longer school enrollment. The shift of the U.S. economy to the service sector—in which jobs are generally more unstable—has also played a role. But in addition, there has been a pronounced decline in job security in manufacturing industries at a time when many young men still depend on this traditional sector for employment. With these and other controls in place, only about half of the overall rise in instability is explained, indicating the presence of additional factors—perhaps linked to the respondents' employers—that we have not been able to measure.

Job instability is not necessarily a bad thing. In fact, previous research has shown that job shopping is actually the main mechanism by which young adults generate wage growth. We find, however, that this process has changed in recent years. Early job search no longer confers the same wage gains it once did, especially on those with less education. It is also yielding more unequal wage gains, and this holds true for all education groups. Our findings therefore suggest that there may be a direct link between job instability and the trends in long-term wage mobility that we and others have documented (Gottschalk and Moffitt 1994; Duncan, Boisjoly, and Smeeding 1996).

The sixteen years covered by the NLS data represent most of the job changes and wage growth that these young adults will experience during their careers. Our findings therefore suggest that public perceptions of rising job instability may not be so far off base, at least for those who entered the labor market during the late 1970s and early 1980s. Their long-term wage trajectories have also changed. Absent a dramatic shift in the American economy, the greater inequality in wage growth that they have experienced will persist over their life course.

APPENDIX

Table 4A.1   Characteristics of Sample for Job Change Analysis

	Pooled Sample	Original Cohort	Recent Cohort
Number of persons	4,616	2,340	2,276
Number of person-years	18,077	8,811	9,266
Mean number of observations contributed per person	3.9	3.8	4.0
Two-year separation rate	.494	.464	.527
Age range	16 to 34	16 to 34	16 to 34
Mean age	24.9	25.0	24.8
Mean work experience, in months	82.1	80.2	84.2
Enrolled in school	22.0%	18.9%	25.3%
Current education			
Less than high school	16.4	16.5	16.4
High school degree	39.2	34.8	44.0
Some college	23.0	24.8	20.9
College degree or more	21.4	23.9	18.7
Current tenure			
One year or less	40.1	40.2	39.9
One to three years	29.9	28.8	31.2
Three or more years	30.0	31.0	28.0
Living in the South	29.2	29.7	28.2
Married	49.9	60.3	38.4
Industry			
Construction, mining, agriculture	14.2	13.6	14.8
Manufacturing, transportation, and communication	34.3	37.1	31.2
Wholesale and retail trade, business services	31.1	26.1	36.6
Finance, insurance, real estate, and other professional services	15.7	17.3	14.0
Public administration	4.7	5.9	3.4
Professional, managerial, technical occupations	26.4	28.4	24.2
Finished with education	59.8	58.9	60.9

Note: All quantities based on person-years, unless otherwise described.

PERMANENT WAGE ESTIMATION

We use the following model to smooth an individual's wages of short-term fluctuations: a set of fixed effects to capture the average curve of the wage profile over age; a set of random effects to isolate the heterogeneity in permanent wage gains among individuals; and a residual term to represent the transitory components of wage change within each individual profile.

The permanent and transitory components of wage-profile heterogeneity are specified as follows:

$$y_{it} = \mu_{it} + e_{it}, \tag{4.5}$$

where y_{it} is the log of the real wage of individual i in year t. The average wage profile μ_{it} is specified by:

$$\mu_{it} = \beta_0 + \beta_1 l_{it} + \beta_2 q_{it} + \gamma X_{it} \tag{4.6}$$

where l_{it} and q_{it} are the linear and quadratic age terms, respectively, and X_{it} represents individual and age-specific covariates. In this application, these are education and experience. The coefficients β_0, β_1, β_2, and γ_{it} are average-level ("fixed-effect") parameters. We have parameterized l_{it} as the age of individual i in year t centered on age sixteen and q_{it} as the quadratic term centered on age sixteen and orthogonal to l_{it}. The random-effects component is specified as:

$$e_{it} = p_{it} + u_{it}, \tag{4.7}$$

where we define p_{it} as the permanent component and u_{it} as the transitory component. Specifically,

$$p_{it} = b_{0i} + b_{1i} l_{it} + b_{2i} q_{it}. \tag{4.8}$$

Thus, p_{it} is a random quadratic representing the deviation of the individual-specific wage profile from the average wage profile. Under this parameterization, b_{0i}, b_{1i}, and b_{2i} represent the deviations from their fixed-effects counterparts. We model b_{0i}, b_{1i}, and b_{2i} as samples from a mean-zero trivariate Gaussian distribution. We suppose u_{it} is mean-zero and allow the variance of u_{it} to vary by calendar year to capture any business cycle effects.

The individual-specific wage profile is the combination of the average wage profile and the individual-specific deviation: $\mu_{it} + p_{it}$. The parameters in our model are estimated using restricted maximum likelihood (REML). In addition to being asymptotically efficient under the assumption of Gaussianality, this approach produces asymptotic standard errors and covariances for the fixed and random parameter estimates. This approach provides the best linear unbiased estimator (BLUE) for the individual-specific wage profiles.

ACKNOWLEDGMENTS

The authors thank the Russell Sage and Rockefeller Foundations for their support of this research. We are grateful to Daniel Polsky and Jay Stewart for sharing their data with us, and for comments from Peter Gottschalk and David Neumark as well as from several anonymous reviewers.

NOTES

1. By attrition we mean respondents who are permanently lost from the panel, not the proportion of respondents who miss the survey in any particular year.

2. This means that for the NLSY there is no formal definition of attrition, except through death. To make the two cohorts comparable in the use of the two-year "drop" rule, we define anyone in the NLSY cohort who missed both the 1993 and 1994 interviews as an attriter. This results in the 7.8 percent attrition rate for the NLSY.

3. The CPS employer is identified in the same way across both cohorts in all survey years: if the respondent held more than one job at the time of the survey, he was asked to focus on the one at which he worked the most hours. Our exclusive focus on the CPS employer is important to ensure comparability across cohorts, since for the recent cohort information is gathered on up to five jobs every year.

4. The reader may notice that educational attainment is actually lower in the recent cohort. CPS data show that educational attainment among men graduating from high school in the late 1970s and early 1980s fell, probably in response to the oversupply of college-educated workers in the 1970s labor market.

5. For the original cohort, end-dates for jobs are impossible to recover consistently for all years. This induces a form of censoring—that is, interval censoring with variable interval widths—that complicates the usual duration models, so we do not consider them here.

6. We model the ϕ_i as conditionally independent given the other regressors and following a mean zero Gaussian distribution. This is a generalized, linear, mixed-effects model that we fit by maximum likelihood (McCulloch 1997).

7. Many alternative specifications can be used to examine robustness. The fixed ISE specification (Topel and Ward 1992) is infeasible because we have a maximum of six observations per individual, and the conditional maximum likelihood estimator (Chamberlain 1984) does not identify the coefficients of time-invariant factors. We relaxed the assumption of independence by specifying a correlation between the ISE, tenure, and education. We also fitted a population-average logistic model using generalized estimating

equations instead of the ISE model (Hu, Goldberg, and Hedeker 1998). In neither case was the cohort effect appreciably changed.

8. We explored more complex specifications of the unemployment rate (for example, pulling out recessions), but none improved on this simple specification.

9. If we estimate model 1 without tenure, the recent cohort has even higher odds of a job change, reflecting the fact that tenure is endogenous in our model. There is no simple solution to this problem; excluding tenure altogether results in a serious misspecification, so we have decided to take the conservative route of including it.

10. The NLS data on union membership are not consistent.

11. Specifically, we include observations from individuals only after they are never enrolled in school again and their education level never increases again. Monks and Pizer's (1998) restriction of their sample to full-time workers probably serves as a rough approximation, but especially in a longitudinal survey, data on full-time work and on completion of school are not perfect substitutes.

12. Monks and Pizer (1998) estimated a probit model, while we estimated a logit model (both were fit with independent random effects). Probit and logit estimates are generally comparable, unless the probabilities being modeled are very low or very high. This is not the case here, since the majority of the probabilities of a job change are within the .3 to .6 range.

13. This means that we are now focusing only on "employer-to-employer" changes, in contrast to the earlier measure, which includes unemployment and out-of-labor-force as a destination state. Refitting the earlier models for the employer-to-employer subset, however, yields very similar results in terms of the cohort differential in instability.

14. In these graphs, statistical significance effectively ends up being a function of sample size. So, for example, in the job change panel, the gap in the early age ranges is statistically significant, and the gap among thirty-one- to thirty-three-year-olds is not: by the later ages a much smaller proportion of the samples is changing jobs.

15. As a check on our findings, we fit this same model using "permanent" wages that have been smoothed of short-term variability. (See the description of the smoothing process earlier in the chapter.) The results were quite similar, with the obvious difference that a substantially greater proportion of the variance was explained using the smoothed wages.

REFERENCES

Bartel, Ann, and George Borjas. 1981. "Wage Growth and Job Turnover." In *Studies in Labor Markets,* edited by Sherwin Rosen. Chicago: University of Chicago Press.

Berger, Mark C., and Barry T. Hirsch. 1983. "The Civilian Earnings Experience of Vietnam-Era Veterans." *Journal of Human Resources* 18: 455–79.

Bernhardt, Annette, Martina Morris, Mark Handcock, and Marc Scott. 1997.

Work and Opportunity in the Post-Industrial Labor Market. Final report to the Russell Sage and Rockefeller Foundations. Institute on Education and the Economy, Teachers College, Columbia University, New York.

Boisjoly, Johanne, Greg Duncan, and Timothy Smeeding. 1998. "The Shifting Incidence of Involuntary Job Losses from 1968 to 1992." *Industrial Relations* 37(2): 207–31.

Borjas, George, and Sherwin Rosen. 1980. "Income Prospects and Job Mobility of Younger Men." In *Research in Labor Economics,* edited by Ronald Ehrenberg. Greenwich, Conn.: JAI Press.

Brown, James, and Audrey Light. 1992. "Interpreting Panel Data on Job Tenure." *Journal of Labor Economics* 10(3): 219–57.

Center for Human Resource Research. 1995. *NLS Users' Guide 1995.* Columbus: Center for Human Resource Research, Ohio State University.

Chamberlain, Gary. 1984. "Panel Data." In *Handbook of Econometrics,* edited by Zvi Griliches and Michael D. Intriligator (vol. 2). Amsterdam: Elsevier Science Publishers.

Diebold, Francis, David Neumark, and Daniel Polsky. 1997. "Job Stability in the United States." *Journal of Labor Economics* 15(2): 206–33.

Duncan, Greg, Johanne Boisjoly, and Timothy Smeeding. 1996. "Economic Mobility of Young Workers in the 1970s and 1980s." *Demography* 33(4): 497–509.

Farber, Henry. 1997. "The Changing Face of Job Loss in the United States, 1981–1995." *Brookings Papers on Economic Activity* (microeconomics supplement): 55–142.

———. 1998. "Are Lifetime Jobs Disappearing?: Job Duration in the United States: 1973–1993." In *Labor Statistics Measurement Issues,* edited by John Haltiwanger, Marilyn Manser, and Robert Topel. Chicago: University of Chicago Press.

Gardecki, Rosella, and David Neumark. 1998. "Order from Chaos?: The Effects of Early Labor Market Experiences on Adult Labor Market Outcomes." *Industrial and Labor Relations Review* 51(2): 299–322.

Gottschalk, Peter, and Robert Moffitt. 1994. "The Growth of Earnings Instability in the U.S. Labor Market." *Brookings Papers on Economic Activity* 2: 217–72.

Haider, Steven. 1997. "Earnings Instability and Earnings Inequality of Males in the United States: 1967–1991." University of Michigan, Ann Arbor. Unpublished paper.

Handcock, Mark, and Martina Morris. 1998. "Relative Distribution Methods." *Sociological Methodology* 28: 53–97.

Heckman, James, and Burton Singer. 1984. "A Model for Minimizing the Impact of Distributional Assumptions in Econometric Models for the Analysis of Duration Data." *Econometrica* 52: 271–320.

Hu, Frank B., Jack Goldberg, Donald Hedeker. 1998. "Comparison of Population-Averaged and Subject-Specific Approaches for Analyzing Repeated Binary Outcomes." *American Journal of Epidemiology* 147: 694–703.

Levy, Frank, and Robert Murnane. 1992. "U.S. Earnings Levels and Earnings Inequality: A Review of Recent Trends and Proposed Explanations." *Journal of Economic Literature* 30(3): 1333–81.

Light, Audrey, and Kathleen McGarry. 1998. "Job Change Patterns and the Wages of Young Men." *Review of Economics and Statistics* 80(2): 276–86.

McCulloch, Charles E. 1997. "Maximum Likelihood Algorithms for Generalized Linear Mixed Models." *Journal of the American Statistical Association* 92(437): 162–70.

Monks, James, and Steven Pizer. 1998. "Trends in Voluntary and Involuntary Job Turnover." *Industrial Relations* 37(4): 440–59.

Morris, Martina, Annette Bernhardt, Mark Handcock, and Marc Scott. 1998. "The Transition to the Labor Market in the Post-Industrial Labor Market." Working paper 98–12. Pennsylvania State University, State College.

Murphy, Kevin, and Finis Welch. 1990. "Empirical Age-Earnings Profiles." *Journal of Labor Economics* 8(2): 202–29.

Polsky, Daniel. 1999. "Changing Consequences of Job Separation in the United States Economy." *Industrial and Labor Relations Review* 52(4): 565–80.

Rose, Stephen. 1995. *The Decline of Employment Stability in the 1980s.* Washington, D.C.: National Commission on Employment Policy.

Stevens, Ann Huff. 1997. "Persistent Effects of Job Displacement: The Importance of Multiple Job Losses." *Journal of Labor Economics* 15(1): 165–88.

Stewart, Jay. 1998. "Has Job Mobility Increased?: Evidence from the Current Population Survey: 1975–1995." Office of Employment Research and Program Development, Bureau of Labor Statistics, Washington, D.C.

Swinnerton, Kenneth A., and Howard Wial. 1995. "Is Job Stability Declining in the U.S. Economy?" *Industrial and Labor Relations Review* 48(2): 293–304.

Topel, Robert, and Michael Ward. 1992. "Job Mobility and the Careers of Young Men." *Quarterly Journal of Economics* 107: 439–79.

Chapter 5

Job Instability and Insecurity for Males and Females in the 1980s and 1990s

Peter Gottschalk and Robert A. Moffitt

This chapter has two objectives. The first is to measure changes in job *instability* over the 1980s and 1990s. We provide evidence on changes in short-term job turnover using a previously underutilized data source, the Survey of Income and Program Participation (SIPP), which provides monthly information on the respondent's employer.[1] The results from the SIPP are contrasted with results from the Panel Study of Income Dynamics (PSID), a more widely used data set. The second objective focuses on changes in what has been labeled job *insecurity*. The duration of jobs may not have changed, but turnover may have been accompanied by less desirable outcomes. Turnover may be more likely to be "involuntary," or turnover may lead to worse outcomes, such as an increase in the probability of an intervening spell of nonemployment or a decrease in the wage gains from changing employers. We therefore also examine several of these outcomes to see whether the perception of greater insecurity reflects changes in these events.

JOB STABILITY

REVIEW OF THE LITERATURE

There is now a sizable literature on changes in job separation rates in the United States.[2] As table 5.1 shows, the conclusions differ widely across studies. Since these studies used different data sets, samples, and measures of turnover, it is sometimes difficult to determine the underlying causes for these differences.

Almost all studies based on the various CPS supplements (Farber 1997a, 1997b; Diebold, Neumark, and Polsky 1997a, 1997b; Jaeger and Stevens, this volume) showed little change in overall separation rates through the early 1990s.[3] The exception is Swinnerton and Wial (1995), who showed substantial increases in separation rates. However, their revised estimates in Swinnerton and Wial (1996) showed much smaller increases, bringing their results closer to those of other CPS-based studies.

Although overall separation rates in the CPS may not have increased through the 1980s, a fairly consistent pattern across studies shows increases in separation rates for some subpopulations. Men showed greater changes than women, and groups that were experiencing greater declines in earnings, including the young and less educated, were also somewhat more likely to experience greater job instability through the 1980s.[4] This pattern seems to have been reversed in the 1990 to 1991 recession. Henry Farber (1998) and Francis Diebold, David Neumark, and Daniel Polsky (1997b) found that separation rates for more educated workers started increasing in the first half of the 1990s. Since these workers were experiencing increases in relative wages, this would seem to break any simple relationship between changes in the wage distribution and changes in job separation rates.

The studies based on the PSID give a much less consistent picture than those based on the CPS. Stephen Rose (1995), Johanne Boisjoly, Greg Duncan, and Timothy Smeeding (1998) and David Marcotte (1995) found rather sharp increases in job instability, while Daniel Polsky (1999) and Jaeger and Stevens (this volume) found no change.[5] Differences between the CPS and PSID could reflect constraints imposed by the two data sets. For example, the PSID questions are asked only of heads of households and wives. Unless the separation rates of heads and wives are representative of the full population, this selection affects the level of separation rates, and if the composition of the population changes over time, this selection may also affect trends. Not only is the analysis in most PSID studies limited to heads, but it is further restricted to male heads. Another inherent difference between the CPS and PSID is that the former does not provide tenure information on respondents who are not employed at the time of the interview, while the event history data in the PSID allows the full population to be analyzed.

These differences cannot be the full story since there are still major differences between PSID studies. Furthermore, differences in the variables and measures used in PSID studies may be more important than differences between the PSID and CPS; Jaeger and Stevens (this volume) find similar patterns when the PSID is used as a series of cross-sections to replicate the CPS.

The National Longitudinal Survey of Young Men (NLSYM) and of Youth (NLSY) provide other data sets with which to measure separation rates. James Monks and Steven Pizer (1998) and Annette Bernhardt and her colleagues (this volume) both found increases in separation rates for the young. The fact that these two studies give very similar results does not tell us very much about the robustness of these data, since the two studies used very similar samples and measures. Although the increase in

Table 5.1   Comparison of Studies

Study	Data Set	Sample Composition		
		Sex	Age	Self-Employed
CPS Studies[a]				
Farber (1997a)	Mobility supplement 1979 to 1996	Both	Thirty-five to sixty-four	—
Farber (1997b)	Displaced Worker Survey 1984 to 1996	Both	Twenty to sixty-four	—
Swinnerton and Wial (1995)	Job tenure supplement 1983, 1987, 1991	Both	Sixteen and older	Excluded
Diebold, Neumark, and Polsky (1996)	Job tenure supplement 1983, 1987, 1991	Both	Sixteen and older	Excluded
Diebold, Neumark, and Polsky (1997a)	Job tenure supplement 1983, 1987, 1991	Both	Sixteen and older	Excluded
Diebold, Neumark, and Polsky (1997b)	Job tenure supplement 1983, 1987, 1991 Contingent worker supplement 1995	Both	Sixteen and older	Excluded
Jaeger and Stevens (this volume)	Job tenure supplement 1973, 1978, 1981, 1983, 1987, 1991	Male reference persons	Twenty to fifty-nine	Excluded
PSID Studies				
Polsky (1999)	PSID 1976 to 1981, 1986 to 1991	Male heads	Twenty-five to fifty-four	Excluded
Jaeger and Stevens (this volume)	PSID 1976 to 1992	Household heads and wives	Twenty to fifty-nine	Excluded
Boisjoly, Duncan, and Smeeding (1998)	PSID 1968 to 1992	Male heads	Twenty-five to fifty-nine	Excluded
Rose (1995)	PSID 1970 to 1979, 1980 to 1989	Male heads	Twenty-four to forty-eight	Unknown

Other	Measure	Includes Transition to Unemployment	Findings
—	Pr(tenure more than ten years); Pr(tenure more than twenty years)	—	Decline in the proportion of males with ten or more years of tenure, especial after 1993. Increase in long-term employment of females.
—	Pr(displaced in last three years)	—	Increase in the displacement of males with high education. No change in the probability of displacement due to plant closing.
—	Pr(no exit in last four years)	—	Increase, and then decrease, in retention rates for low-seniority workers.
Nonagricultural	Four-year separation rates	—	Swinnerton and Wial (1995) overstate increase in job instability.
Nonagricultural	Four- and ten-year separation rates	—	No overall change. Some decline in stability for less educated workers.
Nonagricultural	Four- and eight-year separation rates	—	Some decline in retention in the 1991 to 1995 period, especially for more educated workers.
	Pr(tenure less than eighteen months)	—	Stability in job tenure. Blacks and low-educated workers have greater instability.
Nonagricultural, full-time	Exit if not employed or tenure in current position declines	Yes	No change in separation probabilities. Increase in involuntary separations. Lower reemployment probabilities. Larger wage loss associated with job switches.
	Tenure with employer less than eighteen months		Stability in job tenure. Greater instability for blacks and less educated workers.
Working more then one thousand hours	Pr(involuntary termination)—including plant closing and layoffs but not firings	Yes	Increase in involuntary terminations.
—	Pr(had other main employer in previous twelve months)	No	Increase in number of jobs.

(Table continues on p. 146.)

Table 5.1   *Continued*

| Study | Data Set | Sample Composition | | |
		Sex	Age	Self-Employed
Marcotte (1995)	PSID 1976 to 1978, 1985 to 1988	Male heads	Eighteen to forty-four	Excluded
NLSY Studies				
Monks and Pizer (1996)	NLSYM 1971 to 1978, NLSY 1984 to 1990	Males	Nineteen to thirty-six	
Bernhardt et al. (this volume)	NLSYM 1971 to 1978, NLSY 1984 to 1992	Males	Fourteen to thirty-seven	

ª CPS supplements that give tenure information:
1. Displaced Worker Surveys (DWS)—January 1984, 1986, 1988, 1990, 1992, and February 1994, 1996
2. Job tenure (or mobility) supplements—January 1973, 1978, 1981, 1983, 1987, 1991
3. Contingent work supplement—February 1995
4. Pension and benefit supplements—May 1979, 1983, 1988, and April 1993

separation rates for the young are substantially larger than those found in CPS data, the qualitative conclusion that turnover increased for the young is at least the same in these two data sets.

We are left with mixed evidence from these different data sets. A more direct comparison, with samples and definitions made as similar as possible, would improve our understanding of the contradictory conclusions in the literature. More work needs to be done to identify the sources of the discrepancies between the CPS, PSID, and NLSY.

Our primary contribution is to provide evidence using a new data set, the SIPP. However, in order not to introduce more noncomparabilities, we use the PSID extensively to benchmark our results against this alternative longitudinal data set, which has been used extensively in the literature. We start by comparing turnover measures from our PSID sample to previous studies using both the PSID and CPS. By showing that our PSID sample gives similar results when similar measures are used, we eliminate one potential source of discrepancy. We then use the SIPP to construct yearly separation rates that can be compared directly with those from our PSID sample. Having shown that the SIPP and PSID give similar results, we then turn to the SIPP to measure monthly turnover. This allows us to examine whether there has been an increase in short-term turnover—a particularly important question since a high proportion of jobs are of short duration (see Topel and Ward 1992). Furthermore, short-term turnover may have increased, even if yearly turnover in the PSID did not.

The evidence on turnover addresses the question of job instability. A related issue is job insecurity, which has sometimes been associated with

Other	Measure	Includes Transition to Unemployment	Findings
—	Exit if tenure declines	No	Increase in the probability of a job change, especially for blacks and less educated workers.
Full-time	Two-year separation rates	—	Increase in separation rates, especially for less educated workers. Increase in voluntary and involuntary separations.
Non-Hispanic whites	Two-year separation rates	—	Increase in separation rates.

involuntary separations. Although the longitudinal SIPP files we use do not differentiate between voluntary and involuntary terminations, they do provide information on events accompanying the turnover.[6] Were job-leavers more likely to go through a spell of nonemployment before moving to a new job? Did the duration of intervening spells of unemployment increase? Did recent job-changers experience smaller wage increases? These attributes of job exits can be used to explore whether insecurity increased even if instability (that is, turnover) did not increase.

CHANGES IN TURNOVER

PANEL STUDY OF INCOME DYNAMICS

The Panel Study of Income Dynamics (PSID) is a large, nationally representative longitudinal data set that has been used extensively to study changes in job turnover. The primary advantage of the PSID is that it covers a sufficiently long period to track long-term changes in turnover. This data set does, however, have several disadvantages. First, the tenure questions have changed over time.[7] This is particularly important for changes prior to 1984. Second, answers to questions about tenure are sometimes inconsistent. For example, cumulative tenure with an employer sometimes increases by more than the difference between interview dates. Without outside information, it is impossible to determine whether this discrepancy reflects measurement error or the respondent's return to a previous employer with which his cumulative tenure is greater than his tenure on the job he left.[8] Third, the questions are asked only of heads of household and wives. This is a particularly important drawback when examining the transition rates of the young. Fourth, the job tenure questions are not asked of self-employed heads, so it is impossible to estimate turnover for the self-employed, a group of significant size that may have substantially different dynamics.[9] Fifth, the PSID does not differentiate between first and second jobs. This not only results in some miscoding of job changes, as we discuss later, but precludes our ability to differentiate between exits to a new job and movement between simultaneously held jobs. Finally, for the period we study the PSID identifies only changes between jobs held roughly one year apart.[10] As we show in this chapter, there is considerable job turnover within a year.

Definition of Separation in the PSID

We identify a separation in the PSID if the "months with current employer" at the time of the interview is less than the difference between interview dates.[11] A separation is also identified if a person makes a transition from being employed to not being employed in the subsequent interview.

There are three potential difficulties with our definition. The first is the lack of consistent work histories for the period we study.[12] A person may cycle through several jobs during the year. Not only are durations of less than a year missed, but in some cases no separation is recorded. For example, a person may be unemployed at both interviews but may have held a short-term job in the interim. Second, some longer-term spells are miscoded.[13] Alternatively, a job switch to a job previously held is missed if the cumulative prior tenure on the new job was greater than the difference in interview dates.[14] The third potential problem involves an ambiguity in the question asked prior to 1984. Prior to that year, the question on "months with current employer" did not specify whether the respondent was to give total months across all spells with the same employer or only the most recent spell. As long as respondents answered the question consistently in all years prior to 1984, this ambiguity did not affect measures of transitions during that subperiod. (Cumulative as well as current tenure increased in each year until a transition occurred.) The change in the question in 1984 also did not lead to misclassification for persons who previously had interpreted the question as referring to cumulative tenure. However, the change in wording may have led to misclassifications for respondents who had interpreted the previous question as referring to tenure in the current spell.

Findings

Before comparing job exit rates in the PSID and SIPP, we build bridges to the previous literature by making sure that our PSID sample yields measures that are similar to those coming from PSID-CPS comparisons. In the process, we make the important distinction between longitudinal and cross-sectional measures of job exits. Since both the SIPP and PSID offer longitudinal data, we focus on longitudinal measures. For completeness we start, however, by constructing cross-sectional measures that have been used by Jaeger and Stevens (this volume) to benchmark the PSID.

The CPS is the primary data source that has been used to benchmark the PSID. Since it is a cross-sectional data set, its measure of job turnover is based on whether tenure with the current employer is less than a year. In contrast, the PSID can provide both cross-sectional measures (also based on tenure at time of interview) and the longitudinal measures discussed earlier. As we show, these two approaches to measuring job separations do not necessarily give the same picture.

The tenure supplements and the benefit supplements of the CPS ask employed respondents how many years they have worked for their current employer (see Farber 1997b).[15] The separation rate is given by the proportion of respondents who report being with their current employer for one year or less. The PSID can also be used to generate cross-sectional measures based on reported monthly tenure at the time of interview. One key issue, addressed by Jaeger and Stevens (this volume), is how to translate the *monthly* tenure in the PSID into the *yearly* tenure reported in the CPS. Jaeger and Stevens assume that respondents in the CPS round the number of months they have worked for their current employer to the nearest whole year. Following their lead, we classify any job tenure reported as eighteen months or less in the PSID as equivalent to tenure of one year or less in the CPS.

The four points in figure 5.1 labeled "CPS" show the yearly separation rates in the CPS as measured by Jaeger and Stevens. The solid line labeled "PSID Cross-sectional" identifies a transition if reported tenure is less than eighteen months. Although our sample differs slightly from that used by Jaeger and Stevens, our series is very similar to theirs.[16] In both cases, the PSID and CPS series show no upward trend in separation rates.

We contrast these cross-sectional measures with the longitudinal measure that we use in our comparison with the SIPP. A job change is assumed to have occurred if tenure with the current employer is less than the difference in interview dates. This longitudinal measure gives a different classification than the cross-sectional measure based on a single interview when reported tenure is less than or equal to eighteen months but greater than the difference in interview dates.[17] For example, if tenure is reported as one month in the first interview and thirteen months in the subsequent interview twelve months later, then the cross-sectional measure classifies this as a job change but the longitudinal measure does not. Both measures, however, miss job changes that occur when a person returns to a previously held job and reports cumulative tenure greater than eighteen months.[18] Without a full enumeration of employers, as in the SIPP, both measures miss this transition.[19]

The line labeled "PSID Longitudinal (employed)" identifies a transition when a person is employed in both interviews and tenure is less than

**Figure 5.1   Cross-Sectional and Longitudinal Estimates of Yearly Exit
Rates for Employed Male Heads of Households, Ages
Twenty to Sixty-Two, in the CPS and PSID, 1980 to 1992**

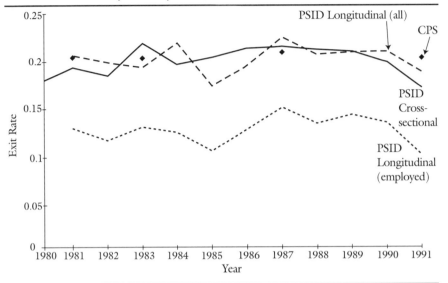

Source: CPS measures from Jaeger and Stevens (this volume). PSID measures from authors' tabulation of PSID.

the difference in interview dates. This definition leads to substantially lower
job-ending probabilities but similar patterns over time. The shift down in
the function reflects the fact that roughly 30 percent of reports of tenure of
less than eighteen months in the PSID were preceded by even lower reported tenure in the prior year. Thus, an eighteen-month definition mis-
classifies some spells with short tenure as job changes rather than a contin-
uation of a spell that began in the previous year. The time-series patterns in
the series discussed thus far, however, are very similar, confirming the conclusion that overall job separation rates did not increase.

One consequence of any procedure based on tenure with current employer is that it excludes persons who are not employed at the time of the
interview (because they are not employed, out of the labor force, or self-
employed). If the nonemployed have different separation probabilities,
then inferences cannot be made to the full population. Since the risk set
for separation rates is all persons who are employed in the base period,
we should include both persons who are employed and those who are
not employed in the subsequent period. This can be done with the SIPP
and PSID but not the CPS, since it does not ask questions about tenure
of persons who are not employed.[20] The line labeled "PSID Longitudinal
(all)" in figure 5.1 plots the proportion of persons who held jobs in the

previous interview and are either employed in another job (that is, their tenure with the current employer is less than the difference in interview dates) or not employed (unemployed, out of the labor force, or self-employed) in the subsequent interview. The large upward shift in the function indicates that excluding jobs that end in a spell of nonemployment seriously understates the amount of job transitions. The fact that this series is roughly as large as the cross-sectional measure indicates that the two previously discussed misclassifications roughly offset each other. However, this series also shows no upward trend.

In summary, comparable data from the CPS and PSID lead to the similar conclusion that separation rates did not increase. This holds even after using the longitudinal aspects of the PSID and including persons who are not employed at the time of the interview.

Although there does not seem to be an upward trend in any of the series in figure 5.1, it is possible that some demographic groups did experience an increase. To explore the possibility that the aggregate trends mask demographic-specific trends in exit rates, we estimate Cox proportional hazard models by gender, race, and education group.[21] As with all the multivariate models in this chapter, we include year, a quadratic in age, and an interaction of year and age to capture differences in trends by age within a demographic group. We do not condition on measure of labor-market tightness since we want to include the effects of secular change in labor-market tightness in the overall trend. We believe that these are the results relevant to the debate, which focuses on the gross change in instability, including instability associated with cyclical factors. However, for completeness we also estimate all models including the detrended gender-specific employment rate.[22] Results in this and the following tables are not affected by including this cyclical variable.

The sample in tables 5.2 and 5.3 includes all job beginnings during the panel for males and females, respectively. We show the exponentiated coefficients along with tests for the joint significance of the coefficients on year and the year-age interaction.[23] Separate results are shown for persons disaggregated by race and education.

The estimated equations for white males in table 5.2 indicate a statistically significant *decline* in the hazard of a job ending, with the largest decline for older workers. For white males, the coefficients indicate a decline in the hazard for all education groups, though the age interaction is significant only for college-educated workers. For nonwhite males, the coefficients on year and the year-age interaction are also jointly significant at conventional levels, though the coefficients on year and the age interaction indicate that the hazard was at first increasing with age and then decreasing. However, the bottom row of table 5.2, which shows the age at which the time derivative is equal to zero, indicates that the hazard starts to decline well before working age for all but persons with at least

Table 5.2 Cox Proportional Hazard Estimates of Job Ending for Males in the PSID

	Whites				Nonwhites			
	All	High School or Less	Some College	College or Higher	All	High School or Less	Some College	College or Higher
Year	0.938***	0.926***	0.937	0.991	1.034	1.021	1.105	1.148
	(0.017)	(0.020)	(0.039)	(0.045)	(0.030)	(0.033)	(0.082)	(0.149)
Year × age	0.999	0.999	1.000	0.998**	0.996***	0.997***	0.995**	0.993*
	(0.001)	(0.001)	(0.001)	(0.001)	(0.001)	(0.001)	(0.002)	(0.004)
Age	1.034	1.016	1.013	1.147	1.352***	1.311***	1.624**	1.730
	(0.048)	(0.058)	(0.111)	(0.127)	(0.116)	(0.128)	(0.355)	(0.668)
Age squared	1.000**	1.000	1.000	1.000**	1.000	1.000	0.999	1.000
	(0.000)	(0.000)	(0.000)	(0.000)	(0.000)	(0.000)	(0.001)	(0.001)
Some college	0.945	—	—	—	0.993	—	—	—
	(0.041)				(0.060)			
College or higher	0.799***	—	—	—	0.880	—	—	—
	(0.035)				(0.072)			
Number of jobs	4,685	2,627	1,079	979	2,414	1,721	501	192
Number of exits	3,093	1,759	731	603	1,598	1,152	318	129
Chi2(2)	284.79	182.11	45.37	62.17	114.57	93.10	14.09	8.20
Prob > chi2	0.000	0.000	0.000	0.000	0.000	0.000	0.001	0.017
Age at which ∂h/∂yr = 0	n.a.	n.a.	n.a.	n.a.	8	7	20	20

Notes: Exponentiated coefficients are shown. Robust standard errors are in parentheses. Exponentiated coefficients are significantly different from 1 at the .10(*), .05(**), and .01(***) level. "n.a." indicates that function is monotonic in year or that the coefficients on year are not jointly significant. Chi square test of joint significance of coefficients on year and year × age.

Table 5.3 Cox Proportional Hazard Estimates of Job Ending for Females in the PSID

	Whites				Nonwhites			
	All	High School or Less	Some College	College or Higher	All	High School or Less	Some College	College or Higher
Year	0.958**	0.983	0.908**	0.988	0.921***	0.926***	0.960	1.206
	(0.019)	(0.025)	(0.037)	(0.056)	(0.024)	(0.027)	(0.068)	(0.174)
Year × age	0.999**	0.998*	1.000	0.997*	1.000	1.000	0.997	0.989**
	(0.001)	(0.001)	(0.001)	(0.002)	(0.001)	(0.001)	(0.002)	(0.005)
Age	1.106*	1.143**	0.992	1.306*	0.986	0.959	1.322	2.159*
	(0.058)	(0.075)	(0.104)	(0.206)	(0.067)	(0.071)	(0.299)	(0.941)
Age squared	1.000	1.000	1.000	1.000	1.001**	1.001***	0.999	1.002
	(0.000)	(0.000)	(0.000)	(0.001)	(0.000)	(0.000)	(0.001)	(0.001)
Some college	0.963	—	—	—	0.902*	—	—	—
	(0.039)				(0.051)			
College or Higher	0.813***	—	—	—	0.774***	—	—	—
	(0.038)				(0.071)			
Number of jobs	4,676	2,619	1,220	837	2,411	1,563	672	176
Number of exits	3,020	1,704	790	530	1,537	1,031	406	101
Chi2(2)	236.25	105.07	78.79	70.84	152.26	83.80	56.90	19.30
Prob > chi2	0.000	0.000	0.000	0.000	0.000	0.000	0.000	0.000
Age at which ∂h/∂yr = 0	n.a.	n.a.	n.a.	n.a.	n.a.	n.a.	n.a.	17

Notes: Exponentiated coefficients are shown. Robust standard errors are in parentheses. Exponentiated coefficients are significantly different from 1 at the .10(*), .05(**), and .01(***) level. "n.a." indicates that function is monotonic in year or that the coefficients on year are not jointly significant. Chi square test of joint significance of coefficients on year and year × age.

some college; for them the decline starts at age twenty. The estimates for females in table 5.3 are remarkably similar to those for white males, indicating that they also experienced a decline in the hazard of leaving their jobs. From this we conclude that the duration of jobs was increasing in the PSID even within demographic groups.

The perception that jobs had become less stable may be based on the characteristics of the exits rather than their frequency. To explore this possibility, figures 5.2 and 5.3 disaggregate the overall probability of a job separation into exits to three possible exit states: exits to another non-self-employment job,[24] exits to self-employment, and exits to unemployment or out of the labor market.[25] Each series is bracketed by the 95 percent confidence interval for these estimated proportions.[26] The probability of exiting to another job increased from a low of .045 in 1982 to a high of .090 in 1987 and then declined steadily through the early 1990s.[27] In contrast, transitions to nonemployment declined during the early 1980s and then stabilized during the late 1980s and early 1990s. Females experienced very similar patterns in exit states. Thus, there is no evidence of a secular increase in the probability that a job ending would be followed by a spell of nonemployment.

Although exits to nonemployment did not increase, it is possible that a greater *proportion* of exits were to nonemployment. This would occur if exits to employment (that is, job-to-job transitions) decline faster than exits to nonemployment. To explore this possibility, tables 5.4 and 5.5 show the results of estimating trends in the conditional probability of nonemployment, given that an exit occurred.[28] Again year is interacted with age to allow trends to vary by age as well as by race and education. If a case is to be made that exits are more likely to result in nonemployment, then the case can be made only for older workers since the significant trends are all negative except for males and females in their forties.[29] And for many groups, the trend coefficients are not significant. Thus, if there was an increase in the probability that a job exit was followed by a spell of nonemployment, it was limited to a subset of older workers.

Finally, we explore the possibility, suggested by Boisjoly and his colleagues (1998), that involuntary terminations may have risen even if overall job exit rates did not. To make our work as comparable as possible to theirs, we restrict our sample to their age range (twenty-five to fifty-nine) and use the same variable to determine whether a termination was involuntary.[30] Our replication of their work also shows a significant increase in the probability of an involuntary termination in the post-1968 period that they study. However, when we limit the period to the post-1980 period, which is the focus of our study, we do not find a significant trend either for males (figure 5.4) or females (figure 5.5). We there-

**Figure 5.2   Yearly Exit Rates by Exit State for Males, Ages Twenty to Sixty-
Two, in the PSID, 1981 to 1992**

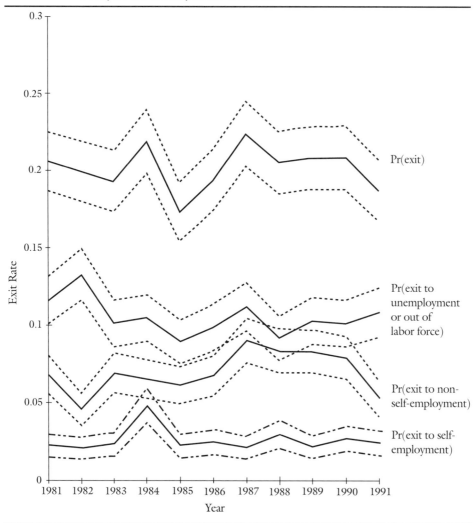

Source: Authors' tabulation of PSID. Confidence bounds are based on robust standard errors.

fore conclude that their finding of an upward trend in involuntary terminations is driven by increases in involuntary terminations from the 1970s
to the 1980s rather than by a continued increase during the 1980s.[31]

We also estimate Cox proportional hazard models of the hazard of
being involuntarily terminated (where voluntary terminations are treated
as censored spells) to see whether the hazard increased for some sub-

Figure 5.3   Yearly Exit Rates by Exit State for Females, Ages Twenty to Sixty-Two, in the PSID, 1981 to 1992

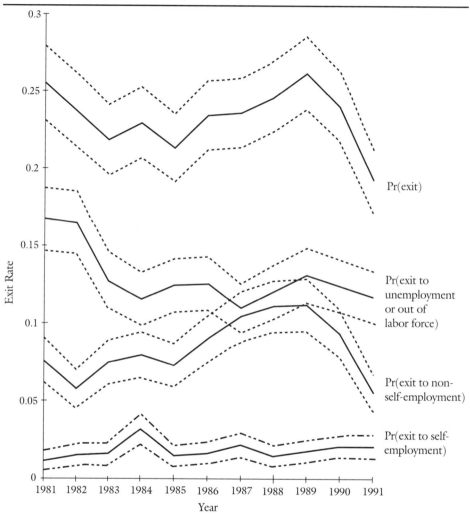

Source: Authors' tabulation of PSID. Confidence bounds are based on robust standard errors.

groups. Tables 5.6 and 5.7 indicate that over the 1980s and 1990s the hazard of involuntary terminations either did not change over time or declined for persons of working age in all demographic groups. We therefore conclude that rising involuntary terminations cannot be used to explain the perception of rising insecurity during the 1980s and early 1990s.

Table 5.4   Probit Estimates of the Probability That Exit Is to Nonemployment for Males in the PSID

	Whites				Nonwhites			
	All	High School or Less	Some College	College or Higher	All	High School or Less	Some College	College or Higher
Year	-0.039	-0.060*	-0.033	0.068	-0.122*	-0.101	-0.145	-0.370
	(0.025)	(0.032)	(0.055)	(0.063)	(0.069)	(0.081)	(0.191)	(0.245)
	[-0.015]	[-0.021]	[-0.012]	[0.027]	[-0.042]	[-0.030]	[-0.055]	[-0.147]*
Year × age	0.001	0.001	0.001	-0.002	0.003	0.001	0.006	0.012*
	(0.001)	(0.001)	(0.002)	(0.002)	(0.003)	(0.002)	(0.006)	(0.007)
	[0.000]	[0.000]	[0.000]	[-0.001]	[0.001]	[0.000]	[0.002]	[0.005]
Age	-0.127**	-0.166**	-0.081	0.096	-0.387**	-0.234	-0.812	-0.982*
	(0.061)	(0.076)	(0.141)	(0.149)	(0.188)	(0.218)	(0.566)	(0.558)
	[-0.047]	[-0.057]	[-0.030]	[0.038]	[-0.132]	[-0.069]	[-0.309]	[-0.391]
Age squared	0.001***	0.001***	0.001	0.001***	0.002***	0.002***	0.005***	0.000
	(0.000)	(0.000)	(0.000)	(0.000)	(0.001)	(0.001)	(0.001)	(0.002)
	[0.000]	[0.000]	[0.000]	[0.001]	[0.001]	[0.000]	[0.002]	[0.000]
Some college	-0.132**	—	—	—	-0.388***	—	—	—
	(0.060)				(0.151)			
	[-0.049]				[-0.132]			
College or higher	-0.517***	—	—	—	-0.681***	—	—	—
	(0.060)				(0.193)			
	[-0.193]				[-0.232]			
Chi2(2)	3.70	4.85	0.61	1.40	13.76	24.75	5.47	6.74
Prob > chi2	0.158	0.088	0.736	0.497	0.001	0.000	0.065	0.034
Number of observations	3,263	1,763	757	736	1,798	1,334	317	141
Age at which ∂Pr/∂yr = 0	39	60	33	34	41	101	24	31

Notes: Sample includes all exits. Robust standard errors are in parentheses. Derivative at the mean is in brackets. Significant at the .10(*), .05(**), and .01(***) level. "n.a." indicates that function is monotonic in year or that the coefficients on year are not jointly significant. Chi square test of joint significance of coefficients on year and year × age.

Table 5.5   Probit Estimates of the Probability That Exit Is to Nonemployment for Females in the PSID

	Whites				Nonwhites			
	All	High School or Less	Some College	College or Higher	All	High School or Less	Some College	College or Higher
Year	−0.092***	−0.110***	−0.029	−0.150**	−0.073	−0.034	−0.224	−0.005
	(0.026)	(0.033)	(0.053)	(0.065)	(0.058)	(0.070)	(0.147)	(0.305)
	[−0.035]	[−0.040]	[−0.012]	[−0.059]	[−0.026]	[−0.012]	[−0.082]	[0.002]
Year × age	0.002**	0.002**	0.000	0.004**	0.002	0.001	0.005	0.002
	(0.001)	(0.001)	(0.002)	(0.002)	(0.002)	(0.002)	(0.004)	(0.009)
	[0.001]	[0.001]	[0.000]	[0.001]	[0.001]	[0.000]	[0.002]	[0.001]
Age	−0.193***	−0.227***	−0.056	−0.299*	−0.143	−0.023	−0.553	−0.431
	(0.062)	(0.078)	(0.137)	(0.157)	(0.139)	(0.161)	(0.362)	(0.924)
	[−0.074]	[−0.083]	[−0.022]	[−0.118]	[−0.050]	[−0.008]	[−0.202]	[−0.145]
Age squared	0.001***	0.001***	0.001	0.000	0.000	0.000	0.001	0.005
	(0.000)	(0.000)	(0.000)	(0.001)	(0.000)	(0.001)	(0.001)	(0.003)
	[0.000]	[0.000]	[0.000]	[0.000]	[0.000]	[0.000]	[0.000]	[0.002]
Some college	−0.224***	—	—	—	−0.132	—	—	—
	(0.058)				(0.135)			
	[−0.085]				[−0.046]			
College or higher	−0.248***	—	—	—	−0.073	—	—	—
	(0.063)				(0.203)			
	[−0.095]				[−0.026]			
Chi2(2)	26.22	23.44	2.50	6.25	4.76	0.76	9.99	1.53
Prob > chi2	0.000	0.000	0.287	0.044	0.093	0.683	0.007	0.466
Number of observations	3,178	1,822	773	582	1,920	1,333	472	111
Age at which ∂Pr/∂yr = 0	46	55	174	38	37	34	45	n.a.

Notes: Sample includes all exits. Robust standard errors are in parentheses. Derivative at the mean is in brackets. Significant at the .10(*), .05(**), and .01(***) level. "n.a." indicates that function is monotonic in year or that the coefficients on year are not jointly significant. Chi square test of joint significance of coefficients on year and year × age.

Figure 5.4   Yearly Involuntary Exit Rates by Race for Male, Heads of Household, Ages Twenty-Five to Fifty-Nine, in the PSID, 1981 to 1991

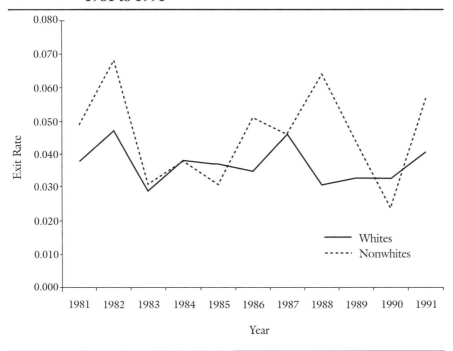

Although the probability of an involuntary termination may not have increased during the period we study, it is possible that among the exits that did take place more exits were involuntary. This would happen if the decline in the overall hazard of a job exit (documented in tables 5.2 and 5.3) declined more quickly than the hazard of involuntary terminations (as shown in tables 5.6 and 5.7). To explore this possibility, tables 5.8 and 5.9 show probit estimates of the trend in the conditional probability that an exit is involuntary. Again it is only older workers who show a statistically significant increase in the proportion of exits that are involuntary. Thus, there is some evidence of increased insecurity for older workers in the limited sense that turnover was more likely to be the result of an involuntary termination, not that turnover increased for this group.

In summary, the overall picture emerging out of our analysis of the PSID is of greater job stability, with some changes in the composition of these exits. The overall probability of a job ending did not increase during the 1980s and early 1990s. This finding holds whether we focus on all job endings or on involuntary terminations. If a case is to be made that

**Figure 5.5   Yearly Involuntary Exit Rates by Race for Female Heads of
Household and Wives, Ages Twenty-Five to Fifty-Nine, in
the PSID, 1981 to 1991**

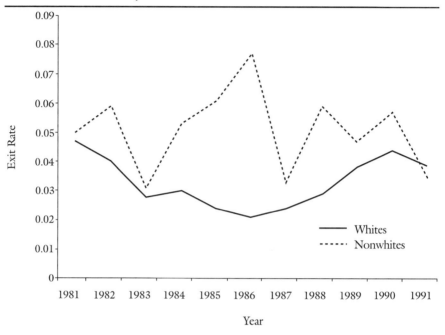

insecurity increased, then it has to be based on the changing composition
of exits for older workers. There is some evidence that exits among older
workers were more likely to be the result of involuntary terminations and
that exits were more likely to be followed by nonemployment. This
should not, however, obscure our main finding, consistent with findings
from the CPS, that job exit rates declined, both overall and across a wide
variety of demographic groups.

SURVEY OF INCOME AND PROGRAM PARTICIPATION

We now turn to the Survey of Income and Program Participation. The
availability of monthly data from this survey allows us to study short-term
dynamics as well as year-to-year turnover, as in the PSID. Within-year
turnover may have changed in ways different from yearly turnover. The
SIPP therefore adds an important dimension to the study of job instability and insecurity. The availability of job-specific monthly wage data
also allows us to examine whether the wage gains (or losses) associated

(Text continues on p. 165.)

Table 5.6   Cox Proportional Hazard Estimates of Involuntary Job Ending for Males in the PSID

	Whites				Nonwhites			
	All	High School or Less	Some College	College or Higher	All	High School or Less	Some College	College or Higher
Year	0.821***	0.806***	0.886	0.897	0.995	1.041	0.624**	1.028
	(0.029)	(0.033)	(0.070)	(0.114)	(0.054)	(0.063)	(0.121)	(0.272)
Year × age	1.003***	1.003**	1.001	1.000	0.997**	0.995**	1.011*	0.997
	(0.001)	(0.001)	(0.002)	(0.003)	(0.002)	(0.002)	(0.006)	(0.007)
Age	0.795***	0.771***	0.896	1.074	1.432**	1.588**	0.565	1.444
	(0.067)	(0.077)	(0.175)	(0.288)	(0.225)	(0.290)	(0.271)	(0.914)
Age squared	1.000	1.000	1.000	0.999	0.999**	0.999	0.994***	0.998
	(0.000)	(0.000)	(0.001)	(0.001)	(0.001)	(0.001)	(0.002)	(0.002)
Some college	0.729***	—	—	—	0.794**	—	—	—
	(0.061)				(0.794)			
College or higher	−0.392***	—	—	—	0.484***	—	—	—
	(0.042)				(0.096)			
Number of jobs	4,685	2,627	1,079	979	2,414	1,721	501	192
Number of exits	850	567	191	92	545	424	94	27
Chi2(2)	116.12	98.22	12.58	8.24	76.11	62.74	17.43	1.03
Prob > chi2	0.000	0.000	0.002	0.016	0.000	0.000	0.000	0.597
Age at which ∂h/∂yr = 0	66	72	121	238	n.a.	8	43	n.a.

Notes: Exponentiated coefficients are shown. Robust standard errors are in parentheses. Exponentiated coefficients are significantly different from 1 at the .10(*), .05(**), and .01(***) level. "n.a." indicates that function is monotonic in year or that the coefficients on year are not jointly significant. Chi square test of joint significance of coefficients on year and year × age.

Table 5.7 Cox Proportional Hazard Estimates of Involuntary Job Ending for Females in the PSID

	Whites				Nonwhites			
	All	High School or Less	Some College	College or Higher	All	High School or Less	Some College	College or Higher
Year	0.968	0.964	1.048	0.779	0.858***	0.917	0.759*	0.541
	(0.052)	(0.062)	(0.117)	(0.170)	(0.047)	(0.057)	(0.114)	(0.214)
Year × age	0.999	1.999	0.995	1.006	1.001	0.999	1.003	1.017
	(0.001)	(0.002)	(0.003)	(0.007)	(0.002)	(0.002)	(0.005)	(0.013)
Age	1.224	1.196	1.584*	0.655	0.917	1.052	0.755	0.226
	(0.166)	(0.193)	(0.432)	(0.390)	(0.130)	(0.166)	(0.333)	(0.234)
Age squared	0.999*	0.999	0.999	0.998	1.000	1.000	1.000	1.000
	(0.000)	(0.001)	(0.001)	(0.002)	(0.001)	(0.001)	(0.001)	(0.004)
Some college	0.788**	—	—	—	0.813	—	—	—
	(0.090)				(0.106)			
College or higher	0.483***	—	—	—	0.553**	—	—	—
	(0.074)				(0.140)			
Number of jobs	4,676	2,619	1,220	837	2,411	1,563	672	176
Number of exits	431	279	101	51	328	232	80	16
Chi2(2)	33.13	20.94	13.39	2.02	55.41	29.14	25.28	3.53
Prob > chi2	0.000	0.000	0.001	0.364	0.000	0.000	0.000	0.171
Age at which ∂h/∂yr = 0	n.a.	n.a.	9	n.a.	153	n.a.	92	n.a.

Notes: Exponentiated coefficients are shown. Robust standard errors are in parentheses. Exponentiated coefficients are significantly different from 1 at the .10(*), .05(**), and .01(***) level. "n.a." indicates that function is monotonic in year or that the coefficients on year are not jointly significant. Chi square test of joint significance of coefficients on year and year × age.

Table 5.8 Probit Estimates of the Probability That Exit Is Involuntary for Males in the PSID

	Whites				Nonwhites			
	All	High School or Less	Some College	College or Higher	All	High School or Less	Some College	College or Higher
Year	-0.078***	-0.079**	-0.023	-0.120	-0.157**	-0.099	-0.704***	-0.126
	(0.027)	(0.032)	(0.058)	(0.087)	(0.061)	(0.069)	(0.242)	(0.224)
	[-0.025]	[-0.028]	[-0.007]	[-0.029]	[-0.056]	[-0.038]	[-0.179]	[-0.032]
Year × age	0.002**	0.001	0.000	0.004*	0.004**	0.002	0.023**	0.004
	(0.001)	(0.001)	(0.002)	(0.002)	(0.002)	(0.002)	(0.008)	(0.006)
	[0.001]	[0.000]	[0.000]	[0.001]	[0.002]	[0.001]	[0.006]	[0.001]
Age	-0.082	-0.051	0.024	-0.197	-0.286*	-0.147	-1.783**	0.041
	(0.063)	(0.076)	(0.147)	(0.189)	(0.158)	(0.180)	(0.716)	(0.538)
	[-0.027]	[-0.018]	[0.008]	[-0.047]	[-0.101]	[-0.056]	[-0.454]	[0.010]
Age squared	-0.001***	-0.001***	0.000	-0.002***	-0.001**	-0.001	-0.003	-0.005***
	(0.000)	(0.000)	(0.000)	(0.001)	(0.001)	(0.001)	(0.002)	(0.002)
	[0.000]	[0.000]	[0.000]	[-0.001]	[-0.001]	[0.000]	[-0.001]	[-0.001]
Some college	-0.241***	—	—	—	-0.530***	—	—	—
	(0.063)				(0.149)			
	[-0.079]				[-0.188]			
College or higher	-0.561***	—	—	—	-0.617***	—	—	—
	(0.069)				(0.202)			
	[-0.184]				[-0.219]			
Chi2(2)	10.58	12.07	1.95	8.34	17.86	9.27	21.26	0.41
Prob > chi2	0.005	0.002	0.376	0.016	0.000	0.010	0.000	0.816
Number of observations	3,164	1,724	748	686	1,758	1,305	311	137
Age at which ∂Pr/∂yr = 0	39	79	n.a.	30	39	50	31	31

Notes: Sample includes all exits. Robust standard errors are in parentheses. Derivative at the mean is in brackets. Significant at the .10(*), .05(**), and .01(***) level. "n.a." indicates that function is monotonic in year or that the coefficients on year are not jointly significant. Chi square test of joint significance of coefficients on year and year × age.

Table 5.9   Probit Estimates of Probability That Exit Is Involuntary for Women in the PSID

	Whites				Nonwhites			
	All	High School or Less	Some College	College or Higher	All	High School or Less	Some College	College or Higher
Year	-0.016	-0.022	0.042	-0.202	-0.049	-0.042	-0.036	-1.021*
	(0.033)	(0.041)	(0.069)	(0.140)	(0.061)	(0.071)	(0.149)	(0.586)
	[-0.004]	[-0.006]	[0.009]	[-0.029]	[-0.015]	[-0.013]	[-0.012]	[-0.115]
Year × age	0.001	0.001	-0.001	0.006	0.001	0.001	-0.001	0.038*
	(0.001)	(0.001)	(0.002)	(0.004)	(0.002)	(0.002)	(0.004)	(0.021)
	[0.000]	[0.000]	[0.000]	[0.001]	[0.000]	[0.000]	[0.000]	[0.004]
Age	0.005	-0.015	0.117	-0.419	-0.009	-0.002	0.143	-2.741*
	(0.078)	(0.095)	(0.166)	(0.359)	(0.140)	(0.160)	(0.369)	(1.646)
	[0.001]	[-0.004]	[0.025]	[-0.060]	[-0.003]	[-0.001]	[0.047]	[-0.309]
Age squared	-0.001**	-0.001**	0.000	-0.002**	-0.001	-0.001	0.000	-0.009
	(0.000)	(0.000)	(0.001)	(0.001)	(0.000)	(0.001)	(0.001)	(0.006)
	[0.000]	[0.000]	[0.000]	[0.000]	[-0.000]	[0.000]	[0.000]	[-0.001]
Some college	-0.155**	—	—	—	0.090	—	—	—
	(0.071)				(0.142)			
	[-0.035]				[0.028]			
College or higher	-0.395***	—	—	—	-0.358	—	—	—
	(0.083)				(0.254)			
	[-0.088]				[-0.110]			
Chi2(2)	0.58	0.87	0.44	3.43	7.67	3.04	13.15	8.26
Prob > chi2	0.750	0.647	0.803	0.180	0.022	0.218	0.001	0.016
Number of observations	3,191	1,827	777	586	1,923	1,335	473	111
Age at which $\partial Pr/\partial yr = 0$	16	22	42	34	49	42	n.a.	27

Notes: Sample includes all exits. Robust standard errors are in parentheses. Derivative at the mean is in brackets. Significant at the .10(*), .05(**), and .01(***) level. "n.a." indicates that function is monotonic in year or that the coefficients on year are not jointly significant. Chi square test of joint significance of coefficients with job turnover changed during the 1980s and 1990s. Since these wage changes may be a more relevant measure of the consequences of the job changes, they offer a useful indicator of changes in job insecurity.

The Survey of Income and Program Participation consists of a series of nationally representative longitudinal surveys of nearly thirty thousand individuals who are followed for roughly two and a half years. A new panel has been started in every year (except 1989) since 1983. With recurring two-and-a-half-year panels, there is substantial overlap across panels. Individuals within each panel are interviewed every four months. These interviews, called waves, include retrospective questions on job and earnings histories that cover the previous four months.

The SIPP offers several important advantages over the PSID. First, it includes information on job histories that assign unique identifiers throughout the panel to each employer for which the respondent worked in either a primary or a secondary job.[32] The availability of full job histories for the thirty-two months covered by the typical panel is a clear advantage over the tenure questions asked in the PSID.[33] With job histories, it is possible to identify transitions without having to rely on reported measures of tenure. A second, and related, advantage of the SIPP is that it can be used to estimate the distribution of monthly duration, starting in the early 1980s. Third, the SIPP includes job histories for secondary jobs, making it possible to identify transitions in which a secondary job becomes a primary job. Finally, SIPP includes self-employment histories for all persons. This is a distinct advantage over the PSID, which does not allow us to follow nonheads or even heads who are self-employed, since the self-employed do not report tenure.

Structure of the SIPP

An important feature of the SIPP is that the sample is phased in over time. The sample is divided into four rotation groups; one group is started in each of the first four months of the panel. The four rotation groups are asked retrospective questions covering the previous four months. Since the questions cover the previous four months, each month is covered by each rotation group (other than the months at the beginning and the end of the panel). For example, the first wave of the 1990 panel was first interviewed in February 1990. Job histories and earnings histories were asked for October through January (wave 1 of rotation group 1). This first rotation group was reinterviewed in June when it provided information for February through May. The fourth rotation group, which was started in April, reported information on January through April. There is further overlap in the SIPP since new two-and-a-half-year panels have been started every year (except in 1989). Therefore, information is gathered from respondents in up to three overlapping panels at any one time.

One well-known problem with retrospective questions is that changes in status are considerably more likely to occur between interviews than within the period covered by the interview. This is known as the "seam bias" problem. For example, respondents are more likely to report the same employer in the four months covered by the survey than between surveys. This results in higher job change probabilities at the seams than between seams. Since the seams occur in different months for people in different waves, monthly job change probabilities are mixtures of the low transition rates reported between seams and the high rates at the seams. If respondents are correctly reporting the number of job changes but reallocating the timing of the change to the seams, then this mixture yields unbiased estimates of job change probabilities as long as each month has an equal probability of being at a seam.[34] We take account of seams, however, in our multivariate estimates.

Definition of Separation in the SIPP

Respondents in the SIPP are asked for the name of the employer in each primary job (job 1) and secondary job (job 2). Identification numbers are assigned to each employer so that it is possible to determine when a secondary job becomes a primary job and when an individual returns to a previously reported employer. Each individual is also asked to list self-employment businesses in which he participated in each month. These are also given unique identification numbers.

We identify transitions when the identification number of the primary employer changes.[35] This includes transitions to other employers, to self-employment, or to nonemployment. For the self-employed, we identify a transition when the individual becomes employed in a primary job, unemployed, or out of the labor force. Changes between self-employment businesses are not classified as transitions since the person continues to work for the same employer, namely himself.

Composition of the SIPP Sample

Our SIPP sample includes persons ages twenty to sixty-two with valid data on job and self-employment histories.[36] Table 5.10 shows the distribution of the sample in each year between 1983 and 1995 according to four mutually exclusive categories: the person has a primary job but no secondary job; has both a primary and secondary job; is self-employed (and not employed by someone else); or is not employed (that is, is either unemployed or out of the labor force).[37]

In 1983 only 70.2 percent of males matched the stereotype of having only one outside employer. An additional 2.8 percent had a second job, and 8.3 percent were solely self-employed. The remaining 18.7 percent were either unemployed or out of the labor force. Consistent with CPS data, the SIPP shows an increase during the second half of the 1980s in

Table 5.10   Distribution of SIPP Sample by Employment Status, 1983
             to 1995 (Averages of Monthly Proportions)

Year	Primary Job Only	Primary and Secondary Jobs	Self-Employed Only	Unemployed or Out of Labor Force
Males				
1983	70.2	2.8	8.3	18.7
1984	71.4	2.8	8.5	17.3
1985	71.5	3.1	8.8	16.6
1986	71.1	3.2	9.0	16.7
1987	71.1	3.1	9.3	16.6
1988	72.0	3.0	9.6	15.5
1989	69.4	2.8	9.2	18.6
1990	72.1	2.8	8.6	16.4
1991	70.8	2.8	8.4	18.1
1992	69.5	2.7	8.2	19.7
1993	69.5	2.7	7.9	19.9
1994	68.9	2.6	7.9	20.7
1995	62.5	2.2	7.1	28.2
Females				
1983	54.4	2.5	3.1	40.0
1984	55.7	2.4	3.2	38.8
1985	57.1	2.7	3.4	36.9
1986	58.0	2.8	3.6	35.7
1987	58.9	2.8	3.6	34.7
1988	60.2	2.9	3.7	33.2
1989	59.3	2.8	3.6	34.2
1990	60.2	3.2	3.4	33.2
1991	60.4	3.1	3.4	33.1
1992	59.7	3.1	3.5	33.7
1993	59.4	3.0	3.5	34.1
1994	59.3	3.0	3.5	34.3
1995	53.9	2.6	3.2	40.3

the proportion of males and females with multiple jobs and the proportion who were self-employed.[38] This increase in nontraditional employment was, however, reversed during the early 1990s, leaving the proportions about where they had been in the early 1980s.

Comparison of Separation Rates in the SIPP and the PSID
Before using the SIPP to explore monthly transitions, we benchmark this
data set against the PSID. The two data sets differ in the period and
sample covered, as well as in the measures of job separations. The PSID
can be used to determine whether a person was in the same job in successive interviews roughly one year apart. We therefore use the data in SIPP
to measure changes in employers one year apart. Since most interviews in

the PSID occur between March and May, we compare the reported jobs in the SIPP for these same months.[39] Because SIPP does not include a 1989 panel, it is not possible to calculate yearly transition rates between March to May 1989 and March to May 1990.[40]

To make the two data sets as comparable as possible, we also restrict the samples to employed married males. The restriction to persons employed by others is dictated by the fact that the PSID does not ask tenure questions of the solely self-employed. Since the PSID asks tenure questions only of heads of household, we must restrict the SIPP sample in the same way. However, since the SIPP does not identify heads of household, we must use other variables to make the two samples comparable. By restricting the SIPP sample to married males and the PSID to married male heads, we achieve roughly the same coverage.[41]

Although restricting the analysis to transitions between jobs a year apart for married males makes the SIPP more closely comparable to the PSID, the two data sets still differ in the underlying questions used to identify transitions. The PSID transitions are based on reported tenure, which is not asked directly in the SIPP, and the SIPP transitions are based on changes in employer identification numbers. Any differences between estimates of transitions may therefore reflect this area of continued noncomparability.

Figure 5.6 plots the estimated probability that a sample member in the

Figure 5.6   Yearly Employment Exit Rates for Employed Married Males, Ages Twenty to Sixty-Two, PSID and SIPP, 1981 and 1995

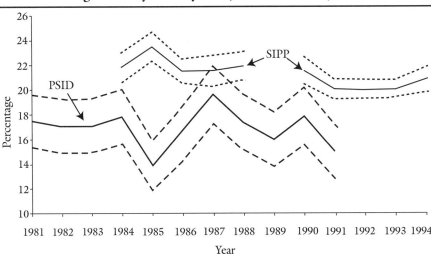

Note: Dashed lines represent 95 percent confidence intervals.

PSID or the SIPP was in a different job (or had become self-employed, unemployed, or left the labor force) roughly one year after the interview date.[42] The PSID shows transitions rates that fluctuated around 18 percent. Yearly separation rates for married males in the SIPP are somewhat higher, hovering around 22 percent; if anything, they show a downward trend.[43] Whether these differences reflect the remaining noncomparability of definitions and samples or differences in reporting is an open question. Although the levels are different, neither data set shows an increase in exit rates.[44]

We conclude that even though there are differences in these two data sets, neither shows an increase in instability. Separation rates for married males do not increase secularly in either data set; if anything, they decrease in the mid-1980s.

Monthly Transition Rates from the SIPP

Thus far we have used the SIPP to calculate the probability that a sample member would still be working for the same employer one year later. This restriction and the restriction of the sample to married males were imposed to compare the SIPP with the PSID. Having shown that the trends in yearly measures are similar in these two data sets, we now exploit the unique advantages of the SIPP by examining monthly rather than yearly transitions for persons who are self-employed as well as employed by others. The SIPP also allows us to include females and males who are not heads of households.

We determine whether each employed (or self-employed) respondent separated from his or her employer in each month (that is, had a different employer, became self-employed, or did not work in the following month).[45] Likewise, we determine whether each person who was self-employed in each month changed employment status (became employed by someone else or did not work) in the following month.

Figures 5.7 and 5.8 show the time-series patterns in the monthly separation rates for employed and self-employed males and females, disaggregated by race. Since the separation rates in each month have large sampling variability, we show the average separation rates of all person-months falling in the calendar year.[46] These data again do not show a secular increase in monthly separation rates. If anything, there was a secular decline in job exit rates between the mid-1980s and the early 1990s. Although exit rates did increase sharply for most groups in 1994, this was followed by an equally sharp decline in 1995, leaving exit rates at roughly the same level as a decade earlier. Thus, expanding the sample to include females and males who are not heads of households and using monthly separation rates (instead of separation rates based on jobs held a year apart) give further evidence that separation rates did not increase. In fact,

(Text continues on p. 173.)

Figure 5.7   Yearly Mean and Standard Errors of Monthly Job Exit Rates for Employed and Self-Employed Males, by Race, SIPP, 1983 to 1995

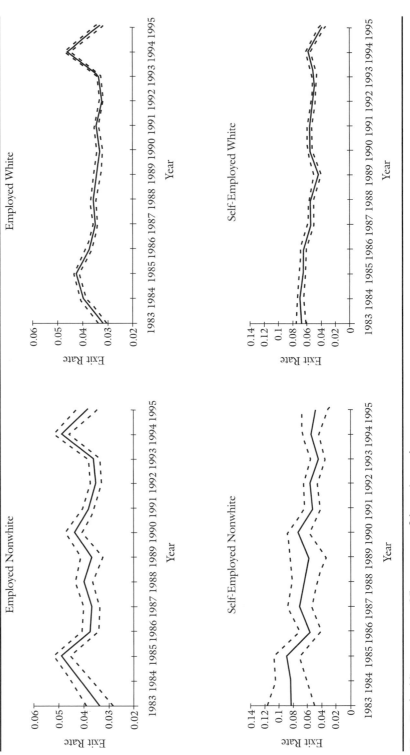

Note: Dashed lines represent 95 percent confidence intervals.

Figure 5.8   Yearly Mean and Standard Errors of Monthly Job Exit Rates for Employed and Self-Employed Females, by Race, SIPP, 1983 to 1995

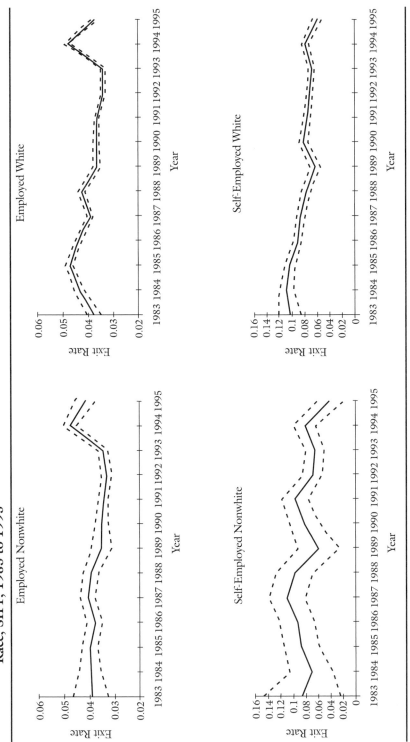

Note: Dashed lines represent 95 percent confidence intervals.

Table 5.11 Cox Proportional Hazard Estimates of Job Ending for Males in the SIPP

	Nonwhites				Whites			
	All	High School or Less	Some College	College or Higher	All	High School or Less	Some College	College or Higher
Year	0.998	1.007	0.988	0.965	0.999	0.998	.990*	1.002
	(0.008)	(0.010)	(0.016)	(0.021)	(0.003)	(0.004)	(0.006)	(0.007)
Year × age	1.000	1.000	1.000	1.001	1.000**	1.000**	1.000**	1.000
	(0.000)	(0.000)	(0.001)	(0.001)	(0.000)	(0.000)	(0.000)	(0.000)
Age	0.922***	.955*	.876***	.827***	.894***	.915***	.859***	.848***
	(0.019)	(0.025)	(0.043)	(0.046)	(0.007)	(0.009)	(0.014)	(0.015)
Age squared	1.001***	1.000***	1.001***	1.001***	1.001***	1.001***	1.001***	1.002***
	(0.000)	(0.000)	(0.000)	(0.000)	(0.000)	(0.000)	(0.000)	(0.000)
Seam	7.816***	7.236***	7.755***	10.980***	6.282***	5.974***	5.892***	7.836***
	(0.192)	(0.226)	(0.390)	(0.716)	(0.057)	(0.072)	(0.106)	(0.162)
Some college	0.811***	—	—	—	.835***	—	—	—
	(0.017)				(0.007)			
College or higher	0.727***	—	—	—	0.742***	—	—	—
	(0.017)				(0.006)			
Number of jobs	21,963	12,734	5,039	4,190	154,685	79,545	37,782	37,358
Number of exits	14,632	8,812	3,341	2,479	95,211	51,473	23,426	20,322
Chi2(2)	1.23	2.21	0.58	2.68	27.21	34.79	5.04	0.85
Prob > chi2	0.540	0.331	0.749	0.263	0.000	0.000	0.081	0.653
Age at which $\delta h/\delta yr = 0$	n.a.	n.a.	n.a.	n.a.	8	8	27	n.a.

Notes: Exponentiated coefficients are shown. Standard errors are in parentheses. Exponentiated coefficients are significantly different from 1 at the .10(*), .05(**), and .01(***) level. Year measured as year plus month divided by 12. "n.a." indicates that function is monotonic in year or that the coefficients on year are not jointly significant.

separation rates declined modestly for most groups between 1985 and 1993.

We explore whether these declines were specific to certain demographic groups by estimating Cox proportional hazard models separately by race and three education groups. Trends are again captured by year (measured in terms of months), with a time trend entered separately and interacted with age.[47] To control for the lumping of job exits at the end of an interview period, we enter a dummy variable equal to one if the risk of exit is measured in the month prior to a seam.[48] With nine panels we end up with 176,648 non-left-censored jobs for males and 154,845 for females.

The results in tables 5.11 and 5.12 indicate that the trends in exit rates are either not statistically different from zero or, when they are positive, not quantitatively important.[49] For nonwhite males and females, the coefficients on the trend terms are not significantly different from zero, indicating that the hazard of leaving a job was constant. For white males with less than a college degree, the trend coefficients are significant and indicate a mildly increasing hazard. But this is largely driven by the spike in 1994. When a dummy variable is included for this year, the trend is again insignificant. For white females, the trend in the hazard is positive for all but the middle education group. The largest trend (for college-educated white females) is, however, only 0.9 percent per year. We conclude that job separation rates were constant, or that where positive trends appeared, they largely reflected a onetime increase in 1994.

Outcomes Accompanying Exits

Again we explore the possibility that the perception of increased insecurity is more a reflection of deterioration in outcomes that accompany job endings than a reflection of an increase in the probability of a separation. To explore this, we examine whether there was an increase in the probability that a job ending was followed by a spell on nonemployment, whether that spell of nonemployment following a job loss increased in duration, and whether job changes were accompanied by smaller wage gains (or larger losses).

Figures 5.9 and 5.10 show the time trends in the probability that a job exit was followed by a nonemployment spell.[50] If anything, these probabilities decline, indicating that transitions to unemployment or out of the labor force became less common. Tables 5.13 and 5.14 explore whether the lack of a positive trend holds when we control for our standard set of characteristics. For nonwhite males and females, the probability that a job was followed by a period of nonemployment decreased over time for the young and increased for older workers, but the trends are small, even for workers in their late fifties (as indicated by the partial derivative on the age interaction).[51] The pattern for whites is less consistent, but the

Table 5.12   Cox Proportional Hazard Estimates of Job Ending for Females in the SIPP

	Nonwhites				Whites			
	All	High School or Less	Some College	College or Higher	All	High School or Less	Some College	College or Higher
Year	0.998	1.004	0.983	0.999	1.003	1.003	1.001	1.009
	(0.008)	(0.011)	(0.017)	(0.022)	(0.003)	(0.005)	(0.006)	(0.008)
Year × age	1.000	1.000	1.001	1.000	1.000	1.000	1.000	1.000**
	(0.000)	(0.000)	(0.001)	(0.001)	(0.000)	(0.000)	(0.000)	(0.000)
Age	.919***	.936**	.887**	.886**	.930***	.943***	0.922***	.902***
	(0.021)	(0.027)	(0.044)	(0.052)	(0.009)	(0.011)	(0.016)	(0.019)
Age squared	1.001***	1.001***	1.001***	1.002***	1.001***	1.000***	1.001***	1.002***
	(0.000)	(0.000)	(0.000)	(0.000)	(0.000)	(0.000)	(0.000)	(0.000)
Seam	8.002***	7.714***	8.079***	8.917***	6.017***	5.895***	5.885***	6.533***
	(0.198)	(0.252)	(0.382)	(0.560)	(0.058)	(0.079)	(0.107)	(0.138)
Some college	0.858***	—	—	—	.863***	—	—	—
	(0.017)				(0.007)			
College or higher	.776***	—	—	—	0.815***	—	—	—
	(0.018)				(0.007)			
Number of jobs	22,530	12,214	6,001	4,315	132,315	65,954	35,581	30,780
Number of exits	14,426	7,980	3,896	2,550	81,658	41,740	22,145	17,773
Chi2(2)	0.98	3.07	1.15	3.18	2.01	12.84	1.05	10.71
Prob > chi2	0.614	0.216	0.563	0.204	0.365	0.002	0.592	0.005
Age at which ∂h/∂yr = 0	n.a.	n.a.	n.a.	n.a.	n.a.	n.a.	n.a.	n.a.

Notes: Exponentiated coefficients are shown. Standard errors are in parentheses. Exponentiated coefficients are significantly different from 1 at the .10(*), .05(**), and .01(***) level. Year measured as year plus month divided by 12. "n.a." indicates that function is monotonic in year or that the coefficients on year are not jointly significant.

Figure 5.9   Probability That a Job Ending Is Followed by a Spell of Nonemployment—SIPP Males, 1983 to 1995

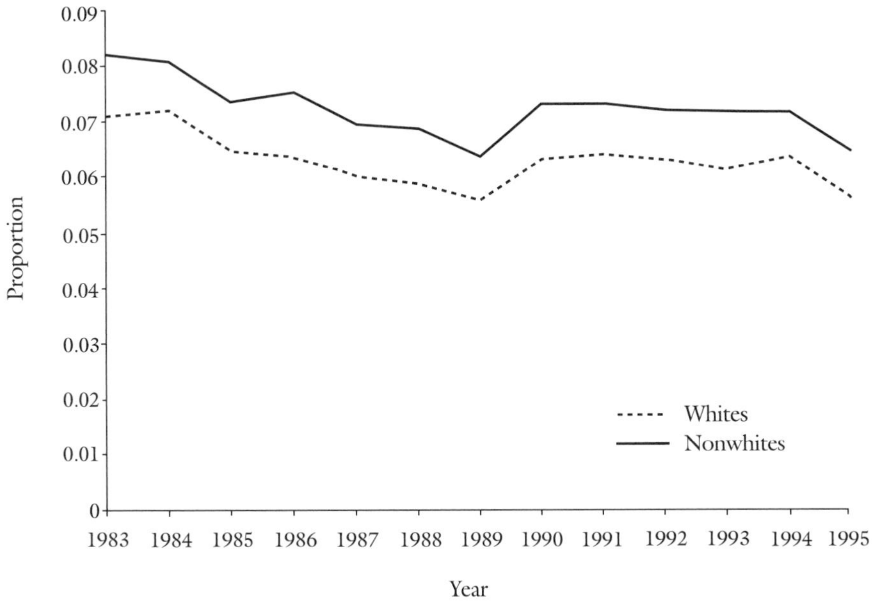

Note: Sample includes all job endings. Yearly probabilities are averages of monthly probabilities.

derivatives on year and the year-age interactions are small for all groups except white females with less than a high school degree. We conclude that (except for young females with a high school degree or less) there is little evidence that job endings were increasingly likely to be followed by a nonemployment spell.

Although the prevalence of nonemployment spells was not increasing for the vast majority of the population, the duration of these spells may have increased, leading to a perception that the consequences of job endings had worsened. Tables 5.15 and 5.16 indicate that there is some support for this perception. Most groups show no trend in the duration of nonemployment, but when the hazards of job reentry changed, they declined. White and nonwhite males with a high school degree or less had a significant decline in the hazard of reentry. For females, three out of the six race and education groups have significant declines in hazards throughout most of their working lives. Thus, there is evidence that while the prevalence of exits to nonemployment did not increase substantially, the duration of such spells did increase for some groups.

Finally, we turn to the wage changes that accompanied job changes.[52]

Figure 5.10   **Probability That a Job Ending Is Followed by a Spell of Nonemployment—SIPP Females, 1983 to 1995**

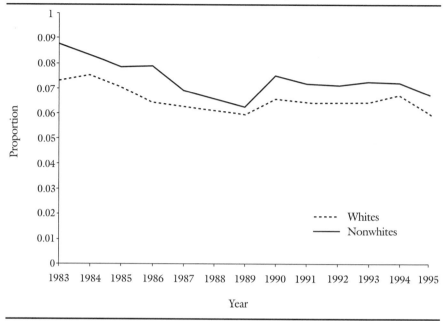

Note: Sample includes all job endings. Yearly probabilities are average of monthly probabilities.

It is well known that much of the life-cycle increases in wages occur when a person changes jobs.[53] In this section, we explore whether the resulting wage changes declined. Although we recognize that wage changes and job dynamics are clearly jointly determined, we make no attempt to model the complex causal mechanism generating these outcomes. Consistent with our general approach throughout this chapter, we provide reduced-form estimates of the net outcome of this process. Even within the context of our descriptive approach, however, we must deal with the question of the appropriate reference group against which to contrast the wage changes of job-switchers. Even if job exits were associated with increasingly small wage gains (or larger wage losses), this change would not indicate a deterioration in outcomes associated with turnover if it reflected a general decline in wages.

This can be seen by considering a very simple error components model of the association between job change and wage change. In the past literature, the major issue in estimating the effect of job change on wage change has been the possible selection bias in who moves and who does

(Text continues on p. 181.)

Table 5.13 Probit Estimates of Probability of Exit to Nonemployment for Males in the SIIP

	Nonwhites				Whites			
	All	High School or Less	Some College	College or Higher	All	High School or Less	Some College	College or Higher
Year	−.030**	−0.029	−.051*	−0.037	−0.001	.013*	−0.010	−.020*
	(0.015)	(0.019)	(0.030)	(0.038)	(0.005)	(0.007)	(0.009)	(0.011)
	[−0.011]	[−0.011]	[−0.020]	[−0.015]	[−0.000]	[0.005]	[−0.004]	[−0.008]
Year × age	.001***	.001*	.002**	0.002	.000***	0.000	.001**	.001***
	(0.000)	(0.001)	(0.001)	(0.001)	(0.000)	(0.000)	(0.000)	(0.000)
	[0.000]	[0.000]	[0.001]	[0.001]	[0.000]	[0.000]	[0.000]	[0.000]
Age	−.183***	−.159***	−.268***	−.252**	−.078***	−0.028	−.110***	−.150***
	(0.041)	(0.053)	(0.092)	(0.100)	(0.013)	(0.018)	(0.026)	(0.029)
	[−0.070]	[−0.059]	[−0.105]	[−0.100]	[−0.031]	[−0.011]	[−0.044]	[−0.060]
Age squared	.001***	.001***	.001***	.002***	.001***	.000***	.001***	.001***
	(0.000)	(0.000)	(0.000)	(0.000)	(0.000)	(0.000)	(0.000)	(0.000)
	[0.000]	[0.000]	[0.000]	[0.001]	[0.000]	[0.000]	[0.000]	[0.000]
Seam	−.187***	−.268***	−.130***	0.011	−.030***	−.082***	−0.027	.090***
	(0.031)	(0.041)	(0.062)	(0.071)	(0.011)	(0.015)	(0.020)	(0.022)
	[−0.072]	[−0.099]	[−0.051]	[0.004]	[−0.012]	[−0.032]	[−0.011]	[0.036]
Some college	−.183***	—	—	—	−.151***	—	—	—
	(0.036)				(0.013)			
	[−0.070]				[−0.060]			
College or higher	−.245***	—	—	—	−.164***	—	—	—
	(0.040)				(0.013)			
	[−0.093]				[−0.066]			
Chi2(2)	16.29	4.70	11.78	4.88	95.89	60.34	17.10	23.79
Prob > chi2	0.000	0.095	0.003	0.087	0.000	0.000	0.000	0.000
Number of observations	7,655	4,367	1,813	1,475	58,056	28,704	15,677	13,675
Age at which $\partial \Pr/\partial \mathrm{yr} = 0$	23	27	21	23	2	0	15	21

Notes: Sample includes all exits. Standard errors are in parentheses. Derivative at the mean is in brackets. Significant at the .10(*), .05(**), and .01(***) level. Year measured as year plus month divided by 12. "n.a." indicates that function is monotonic in year or that the coefficients on year are not jointly significant.

Table 5.14 Probit Estimates of Probability of Exit to Nonemployment for Females in the SIIP

	Nonwhites				Whites			
	All	High School or Less	Some College	College or Higher	All	High School or Less	Some College	College or Higher
Year	−.031**	−0.018	−0.044	−.062*	.016***	.033***	.019**	−0.016
	(0.014)	(0.020)	(0.027)	(0.036)	(0.005)	(0.008)	(0.009)	(0.011)
	[−0.012]	[−0.006]	[−0.017]	[−0.025]	[0.006]	[0.013]	[0.008]	[−0.006]
Year × age	.001**	0.000	.002**	0.001	.000**	−.001***	0.000	0.000
	(0.000)	(0.001)	(0.001)	(0.001)	(0.000)	(0.000)	(0.000)	(0.000)
	[0.000]	[0.000]	[0.001]	[0.000]	[−0.000]	[−0.000]	[−0.000]	[0.000]
Age	−.091**	−0.033	−.198**	−0.147	.030**	.059***	0.031	−0.022
	(0.039)	(0.051)	(0.080)	(0.100)	(0.014)	(0.020)	(0.026)	(0.031)
	[−0.035]	[−0.012]	[−0.078]	[−0.058]	[0.012]	[0.023]	[0.012]	[−0.009]
Age squared	.000***	0.000	.001**	.001***	.000***	.000***	.000***	0.000
	(0.000)	(0.000)	(0.000)	(0.000)	(0.000)	(0.000)	(0.000)	(0.000)
	[0.000]	[0.000]	[0.000]	[0.000]	[0.000]	[0.000]	[0.000]	[0.000]
Seam	−.103***	−.130***	−0.117**	−0.003	−.0812***	−.084***	−.073***	−.090***
	(0.029)	(0.041)	(0.055)	(0.067)	(0.011)	(0.016)	(0.020)	(0.022)
	[−0.039]	[−0.047]	[−0.046]	[−0.001]	[−0.032]	[−0.032]	[−0.029]	[−0.036]
Some college	−.221***	—	—	—	−.196***	—	—	—
	(0.033)				(0.013)			
	[−0.084]				[−0.077]			
College or higher	−.285***	—	—	—	−.245***	—	—	—
	(0.039)				(0.014)			
	[−0.108]				[−0.096]			
Chi2(2)	5.12	1.50	5.48	7.94	12.16	17.75	7.80	1.88
Prob > chi2	0.077	0.473	0.065	0.019	0.002	0.000	0.020	0.391
Number of observations	8,293	4,361	2,350	1,582	54,705	25,185	16,312	13,208
Age at which ∂Pr/∂yr = 0	39	n.a.	25	54	45	42	51	n.a.

Notes: Sample includes all exits. Standard errors are in parentheses. Derivative at the mean is in brackets. Significant at the .10(*), .05(**), and .01(***) level. Year measured as year plus month divided by 12. "n.a." indicates that function is monotonic in year or that the coefficients on year are not jointly significant.

Table 5.15 Cox Proportional Hazard Estimates of Job Reentry for Males in the SIPP

	Nonwhites				Whites			
	All	High School or Less	Some College	College or Higher	All	High School or Less	Some College	College or Higher
Year	0.974***	.958***	1.022	0.972	.990***	.975***	0.989	0.987
	(0.010)	(0.011)	(0.025)	(0.033)	(0.004)	(0.005)	(0.009)	(0.011)
Year × age	1.000	1.001*	0.999	1.001	1.000	1.000**	1.000	1.000
	(0.000)	(0.000)	(0.001)	(0.001)	(0.000)	(0.000)	(0.000)	(0.000)
Age	1.031	1.020	1.105	0.868	1.002	1.024*	.938**	.870***
	(0.028)	(0.031)	(0.082)	(0.075)	(0.010)	(0.013)	(0.024)	(0.024)
Age squared	0.999***	.999***	0.999***	1.000*	1.000***	.999***	1.000***	1.001***
	(0.000)	(0.000)	(0.000)	(0.000)	(0.000)	(0.000)	(0.000)	(0.000)
Seam	3.947***	3.711***	3.928***	6.487***	2.962***	2.728***	3.041***	3.960***
	(0.136)	(0.153)	(0.295)	(0.707)	(0.041)	(0.048)	(0.089)	(0.145)
Some college	1.972***	—	—	—	2.289***	—	—	—
	(0.056)				(0.026)			
College or higher	2.144***	—	—	—	2.228***	—	—	—
	(0.069)				(0.026)			
Number of nonemployment spells	17,890	12,992	2,936	1,962	103,722	71,331	17,004	15,387
Number of exits	8,147	5,819	1,403	925	49,886	33,969	8,796	7,121
Chi2(2)	44.94	45.34	1.06	1.12	60.42	111.58	3.36	4.09
Prob > chi2	0.000	0.000	0.590	0.571	0.000	0.000	0.186	0.129
Age at which ∂h/∂yr = 0	172	77	n.a.	n.a.	1,703	87	n.a.	n.a.

Notes: Exponentiated coefficients are shown. Standard errors are in parentheses. Exponentiated coefficients are significantly different from 1 at the .10(*), .05(**), and .01(***) level. Year measured as year plus month divided by 12. "n.a." indicates that function is monotonic in year or that the coefficients on year are not jointly significant.

Table 5.16 Cox Proportional Hazard Estimates of Job Reentry for Females in the SIPP

	Nonwhites				Whites			
	All	High School or Less	Some College	College or Higher	All	High School or Less	Some College	College or Higher
Year	.964***	.957***	0.981	0.971	.983***	.982***	.968***	.977*
	(0.010)	(0.012)	(0.023)	(0.032)	(0.004)	(0.005)	(0.009)	(0.012)
Year × age	1.000	1.001**	1.000	1.000	1.000**	1.000**	1.001**	1.001*
	(0.000)	(0.000)	(0.001)	(0.001)	(0.000)	(0.000)	(0.000)	(0.000)
Age	1.009	1.016	0.981	0.954	0.989	1.033**	0.898***	0.891***
	(0.028)	(0.033)	(0.066)	(0.084)	(0.011)	(0.014)	(0.024)	(0.029)
Age squared	.999***	.999***	1.000	1.001**	1.000***	.999***	1.000***	1.000***
	(0.000)	(0.000)	(0.000)	(0.000)	(0.000)	(0.000)	(0.000)	(0.000)
Seam	3.961***	3.703***	4.134***	5.275***	3.057***	2.857***	3.049***	3.857***
	(0.142)	(0.172)	(0.289)	(0.516)	(0.045)	(0.057)	(0.090)	(0.131)
Some college	1.924***	—	—	—	1.949***	—	—	—
	(0.051)				(0.022)			
College or higher	2.134***	—	—	—	2.334***	—	—	—
	(0.069)				(0.029)			
Number of nonemployment spells	20,400	14,325	3,874	2,201	104,999	71,314	19,545	14,140
Number of exits	8,459	5,616	1,830	1,013	46,522	30,031	9,420	7,071
Chi2(2)	52.46	25.40	2.61	15.22	36.32	20.24	14.91	3.96
Prob > chi2	0.000	0.000	0.272	0.001	0.000	0.000	0.001	0.138
Age at which ∂h/∂yr = 0	92	59	n.a.	n.a.	63	55	30	n.a.

Notes: Exponentiated coefficients are shown. Standard errors are in parentheses. Exponentiated coefficients are significantly different from 1 at the .10(*), .05(**), and .01(***) level. Year measured as year plus month divided by 12. "n.a." indicates that function is monotonic in year or that the coefficients on year are not jointly significant.

not. We do not seek to provide a new method of avoiding this bias but instead use some simple comparison groups that have been used previously but avoid bias completely only under strong assumptions.

We assume that the wage of individual i in job j with experience t is:

$$W_{ijt} = \mu_i + \alpha_{ij} + \beta_i t_i + \varepsilon_{ijt} \qquad (5.1)$$

where μ_i is an individual fixed effect, α_{ij} is a fixed effect unique to an individual-job combination, β_i is a random wage growth parameter that allows heterogeneity in age-earnings profiles across individuals but is common across jobs, and ε_{ijt} is random error for which we assume $E(\varepsilon_{ijt} | \mu_i, \alpha_{ij}, \beta_i) = 0$ in the population.[54] We add a vector of observed covariates later. Our object of interest in this model is the mean value of $\alpha_{ik} - \alpha_{ij}$ for $j \neq k$ (that is, the change in intercepts for those who change jobs between t and $t + 1$). The parameter α_{ij} is a measure of the permanent wage of a job, and hence, we seek to determine the change in that wage for those who change jobs.[55]

Let k denote the individual's job at time $t + 1$ and let D_{it} be a dummy variable indicating a job change ($D_{it} = 1$ if $j \neq k$, and $D_{it} = 0$ if $j = k$). Then

$$W_{ik,t+1} - W_{ijt} = \alpha D_{it} + \beta_i + \Delta\varepsilon_{it} \qquad (5.2)$$

where $\alpha = \alpha_{ik} - \alpha_{ij}$, which is the object of interest, and $\Delta\varepsilon_{it} = \varepsilon_{ik,t+1} - \varepsilon_{ijt}$.

We estimate equation 5.2 in two ways, by making two different identifying assumptions. The first assumption is that $\beta_i = \beta$ (no heterogeneity in slopes) and $E(\Delta\varepsilon_{it} | D_{it}) = 0$. The former rules out bias arising from a differential selection of movers and nonmovers on the basis of the value of β_i. The latter rules out differential selection of movers and nonmovers on the basis of transitory wage shocks. Under these assumptions, a simple regression of wage change on the mover dummy yields an estimate of mean α. As a sensitivity test of the potential bias associated with violation of these assumptions, we define the wage change of the comparison group (the $D_{it} = 0$ group) in one of two ways: the average wage change of the group of individuals who never moved in any of the periods we observe in our panel; and the average wage change of the group of individuals who moved during the panel, but including only wage changes in periods in which they did not change jobs. The latter comparison group, conceived by Jacob Mincer (1986), is based on the notion that the distribution of unobservables of those who move at different periods may be closer to the counterfactual distribution of movers than that of never-movers.

Our second approach to the problem of inferring the wages the person would have received had they not changed jobs drops the restriction of a homogeneous β_i but requires the use of more data. We allow individual-specific β_i, but we eliminate this component of heterogeneity by double-differencing. Let 1 be the job held at time $t = 1$, and let D_{it-1} be a dummy for whether the individual changed jobs between $t - 1$ and t. Then

$$W_{ijt} - W_{il,t-1} = \alpha' D_{i,t-1} + \beta_i + \Delta\varepsilon_{i,t-1} \qquad (5.3)$$

where $\alpha' = \alpha_{ij} - \alpha_{il}$ and $\Delta\varepsilon_{i,t-1} = \varepsilon_{ijt} - \varepsilon_{il,t-1}$. Then subtracting equation 5.3 from equation 5.2 for those who did not change jobs from $t - 1$ to t, we have

$$(W_{ik,t+1} - W_{ijt}) - (W_{ijt} - W_{ij,t-1}) = \alpha D_{it} + (\Delta\varepsilon_{it} - \Delta\varepsilon_{i,t-1}) \qquad (5.4)$$

The assumption we need for an unbiased estimate of α in this model is that $E(\Delta\varepsilon_{it} - \Delta\varepsilon_{i,t-1} | D_{it}, D_{i,t-1}) = 0$. This model simply uses the wage data from $t - 1$ to t to estimate the individual wage growth for each individual i, and then identifies α as the deviation from that wage growth between t and $t + 1$ for those who move.

We implement this second strategy in the following way. First, since equation 5.4 does not have an intercept, those who do not move from t to $t + 1$ are not needed for the estimation; the mean of the double-differenced wage of movers estimates α by itself.[56] Second, we use all wage data available for the individual's job at time t to estimate wage growth on the previous job. Specifically, in place of $(W_{ijt} - W_{ij,t-1})$ we estimate a job-specific slope, based on all years observed for the individual in that job. Third, we allow α to be a function of a vector of covariates, one important covariate being a time trend to allow us to determine whether wage gains have changed over time.

We start by showing the results of following our first approach. Figures 5.11 and 5.12 show our estimates based on the wage changes of movers and the two comparison groups described earlier: persons who changed jobs but in a different period, and persons who did not change jobs at any point in the panel.[57] Since there is substantial month-to-month variability in wage changes, we show the annual averages of the monthly changes. The first thing to notice is that the two control groups have very similar time-series patterns in wage growth. Our conclusions are therefore not sensitive to the choice between the two. Second, the time-series data do not indicate a secular decline in the gains from job changes.[58] The average wage gains for movers are generally greater than for either of the control groups, though there is substantial year-to-year variability. The series for movers, however, shows no downward drift over the full pe-

Figure 5.11   Percentage Change in Monthly Earnings of SIPP Males, Ages Twenty to Sixty-Two, by Job Change Status and Race, 1983 to 1995

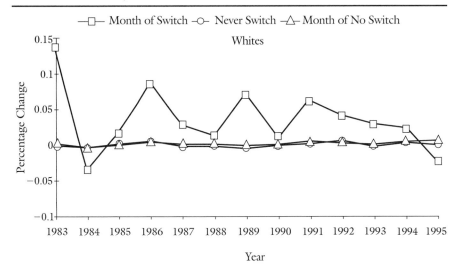

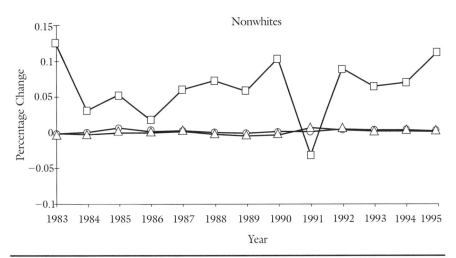

Note: Monthly earnings adjusted for age.

riod. There is, however, some downward drift after 1991 for whites; this may point to a secular trend, but only in the very recent period.

Finally, we show the results of following our second approach: using the job-changer's own prior wage growth to adjust the observed wage change for the wage growth the person would have experienced had he or she not changed jobs (as shown in equation 5.4).[59] The resulting net wage changes are the dependent variables in the descriptive linear regres-

Figure 5.12   **Percentage Change in Monthly Earnings of SIPP Females, Ages Twenty to Sixty-Two, by Job Change Status and Race, 1983 to 1995**

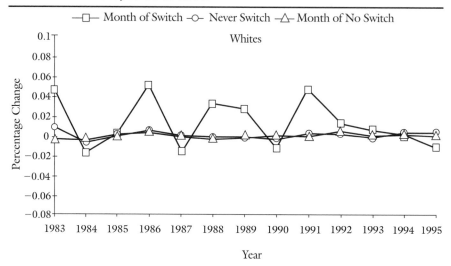

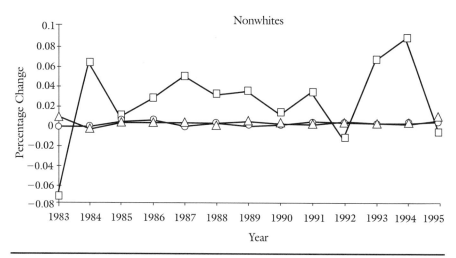

Note: Monthly earnings adjusted for age.

sions shown in tables 5.17 and 5.18.[60] The top panel shows estimates for all transitions, and the bottom panel includes only transitions with no intervening spell of nonemployment. These regressions likewise provide little evidence that job changes have been accompanied by smaller wage gains. Tests on the joint significance of the coefficients on year and the year-age interaction indicate that only one trend is significant at the 5 percent level (for older nonwhite males with some college).[61]

Table 5.17 Net Wage Changes Accompanying Job Switches for Males in the SIPP

	Nonwhites				Whites			
	All	High School or Less	Some College	College or Higher	All	High School or Less	Some College	College or Higher
All job changes								
Year	0.059	−0.003	.173**	0.207	0.011	0.013	0.005	0.004
	(0.046)	(0.050)	(0.071)	(0.188)	(0.015)	(0.022)	(0.022)	(0.036)
Year × age	−0.002	0.000	−.006***	−0.005	0.000	0.000	0.000	0.000
	(0.001)	(0.001)	(0.002)	(0.005)	(0.000)	(0.001)	(0.001)	(0.001)
Age	0.125	−0.067	.613***	0.399	−0.011	0.015	−0.043	−0.048
	(0.122)	(0.128)	(0.209)	(0.483)	(0.039)	(0.057)	(0.061)	(0.096)
Age squared	0.000	0.001	0.000	0.001	0.000***	0.000	0.001**	0.000
	(0.000)	(0.000)	(0.001)	(0.002)	(0.000)	(0.000)	(0.000)	(0.000)
Seam	−0.029	−0.061	−0.092	0.096	−0.001	−0.033	0.034	0.022
	(0.105)	(0.117)	(0.161)	(0.357)	(0.033)	(0.049)	(0.049)	(0.074)
Some college	−0.139	—	—	—	0.015	—	—	—
	(0.116)				(0.038)			
College or higher	−0.158	—	—	—	0.011	—	—	—
	(0.121)				(0.038)			
Number of observations	6,506	3,638	1,623	1,245	45,889	22,850	12,322	10,717
F-test	0.82	0.14	4.33	0.67	0.47	0.19	0.37	0.35
Probability value	0.440	0.872	0.013	0.510	0.628	0.827	0.691	0.706

(Table continues on p. 186.)

Table 5.17 *Continued*

	Nonwhites				Whites			
	All	High School or Less	Some College	College or Higher	All	High School or Less	Some College	College or Higher
Job-to-job changes								
Year	0.018	−0.013	.082**	−0.008	0.001	0.006	0.003	−0.014
	(0.017)	(0.023)	(0.034)	(0.037)	(0.006)	(0.008)	(0.010)	(0.015)
Year × age	−0.001	0.000	−.002**	0.000	0.000	0.000	0.000	0.000
	(0.000)	(0.001)	(0.001)	(0.001)	(0.000)	(0.000)	(0.000)	(0.000)
Age	0.058	−0.028	0.222**	0.019	−0.014	0.007	−0.006	−0.073*
	(0.046)	(0.061)	(0.102)	(0.097)	(0.017)	(0.022)	(0.029)	(0.042)
Age squared	0.000	0.000	0.000	0.000	0.000**	0.000	0.000	0.000***
	(0.000)	(0.000)	(0.000)	(0.000)	(0.000)	(0.000)	(0.000)	(0.000)
Seam	−0.058	−0.040	−0.078	−0.060	−0.003	−0.010	−0.004	0.009
	(0.038)	(0.054)	(0.078)	(0.069)	(0.013)	(0.019)	(0.022)	(0.029)
Some college	−0.061	—	—	—	0.012	—	—	—
	(0.040)				(0.015)			
College or higher	−0.003	—	—	—	−0.009	—	—	—
	(0.041)				(0.015)			
Number of observations	3,303	1,705	884	714	27,589	12,919	7,774	6,896
F-test	0.80	0.20	3.20	1.92	0.88	1.01	0.18	0.51
Probability value	0.449	0.816	0.041	0.147	0.414	0.363	0.837	0.601

Notes: Standard errors are in parentheses. Coefficients are significant at the .10(*), .05(**), and .01(***) level. Year measured as year plus month divided by 12.

Table 5.18 Net Wage Changes Accompanying Job Switches for Females in the SIPP

	Nonwhites				Whites			
	All	High School or Less	Some College	College or Higher	All	High School or Less	Some College	College or Higher
All job changes								
Year	-0.013	-0.042	0.033	-0.031	0.004	0.010	-0.008	-0.008
	(0.036)	(0.054)	(0.060)	(0.094)	(0.019)	(0.030)	(0.033)	(0.035)
Year × age	-0.001	0.001	-0.001	0.002	0.000	0.000	0.000	0.001
	(0.001)	(0.001)	(0.002)	(0.003)	(0.001)	(0.001)	(0.001)	(0.001)
Age	-0.050	-0.087	0.093	-0.205	-0.012	0.013	-0.004	-0.108
	(0.095)	(0.132)	(0.169)	(0.256)	(0.049)	(0.075)	(0.090)	(0.096)
Age squared	0.000	0.000	0.000	0.000	0.000	0.000	0.000	0.000
	(0.000)	(0.000)	(0.001)	(0.001)	(0.000)	(0.000)	(0.000)	(0.000)
Seam	0.063	0.102	0.047	-0.011	0.036	0.025	-0.017	0.117*
	(0.076)	(0.111)	(0.124)	(0.175)	(0.039)	(0.063)	(0.070)	(0.067)
Some college	0.071	—	—	—	-0.059	—	—	—
	(0.080)				(0.045)			
College or higher	-0.133	—	—	—	-0.018	—	—	—
	(0.089)				(0.047)			
Number of observations	6,348	3,238	1,884	1,226	38,926	17,394	11,660	9,872
F-test	0.28	0.32	0.26	1.23	0.31	0.06	0.31	3.08
Probability value	0.756	0.724	0.772	0.293	0.730	0.940	0.734	0.046

(Table continues on p. 188.)

Table 5.18 *Continued*

	Nonwhites				Whites			
	All	High School or Less	Some College	College or Higher	All	High School or Less	Some College	College or Higher
Job-to-job changes								
Year	−0.006	0.000	−0.009	−0.023	0.000	−.022**	.022**	0.001
	(0.017)	(0.023)	(0.027)	(0.058)	(0.007)	(0.010)	(0.010)	(0.017)
Year × age	0.000	0.000	0.000	0.000	0.000	0.001**	−.001**	0.000
	(0.000)	(0.001)	(0.001)	(0.002)	(0.000)	(0.000)	(0.000)	(0.001)
Age	−0.003	−0.003	0.000	−0.031	−0.004	−.051**	.063**	−0.017
	(0.046)	(0.058)	(0.077)	(0.164)	(0.018)	(0.024)	(0.030)	(0.048)
Age squared	0.000	0.000	0.000	0.000	0.000	0.000	0.000	0.000
	(0.000)	(0.000)	(0.000)	(0.000)	(0.000)	(0.000)	(0.000)	(0.000)
Seam	−0.021	0.041	−0.037	−0.127	0.003	0.023	−0.005	−0.014
	(0.034)	(0.047)	(0.053)	(0.093)	(0.014)	(0.020)	(0.022)	(0.030)
Some college	−0.030	—	—	—	−.032**	—	—	—
	(0.036)				(0.016)			
College or higher	−.092**	—	—	—	−0.016	—	—	—
	(0.039)				(0.016)			
Number of observations	3,123	1,490	950	683	22,202	9,063	7,054	6,085
F-test	0.97	0.18	0.68	0.24	0.40	2.68	3.11	0.00
Probability value	0.381	0.832	0.505	0.786	0.669	0.068	0.045	0.997

Notes: Standard errors are in parentheses. Coefficients are significant at the .10(*), .05(**), and .01(***) level. Year measured as year plus month divided by 12.

CONCLUSIONS

This chapter has provided evidence on changes in both job instability and job insecurity using two large data sets, the SIPP and PSID. On the question of instability, we find that neither data set provides evidence that yearly exit rates increased during the 1980s and 1990s. This evidence is consistent with much of the recent literature that finds little change in overall job exit rates during the period we cover. Although the evidence on earlier changes is mixed, we believe that the evidence is now strong that any increase in instability between the 1970s and 1980s that may have existed did not persist into the more recent period.

The primary contribution of this chapter is to provide evidence on changes in monthly transition rates using the SIPP. These higher-frequency data also indicate no increase in short-term job turnover. The fact that yearly and monthly measures give similar patterns suggest that the need to rely on yearly measures in previous studies has not masked offsetting changes in short-term job holding.

The second objective of this chapter has been to explore whether job insecurity has increased. The claim has been made that, even if job exits did not increase, exits were more likely to have adverse consequences. Examples of insecure jobs are those that are more likely to end involuntarily or to be followed by a spell of nonemployment or employment at a lower wage. Our evidence does not support this claim. We find no evidence of an increase in involuntary terminations during the period we study. Furthermore, we find little evidence of a greater likelihood of a job ending in a spell of nonemployment or of job changes being accompanied by wage declines.

Although there are still substantial differences across studies in results for subpopulations, we believe that a consistent picture is emerging on changes in job stability and job security in the 1980s and 1990s. Job instability does not seem to have increased, and the consequences of separating from an employer do not seem to have worsened. This holds whether we look at yearly or monthly transitions.

ACKNOWLEDGMENTS

Partial funding for this project was provided by the Henry J. Kaiser Family Foundation. Helen Connolly, Michael Hansen, and Kelly Haverstick provided outstanding assistance on this data-intensive project.

NOTES

1. John Fitzgerald (1998) has recently used the SIPP to examine job turnover of less educated workers. His focus is on twelve-month transitions, while we exploit the SIPP to estimate monthly dynamics.

2. For measures of job instability in OECD countries, see OECD (1997).

3. The following CPS supplements give information on job tenure:

   - Displaced Worker Survey (DWS)—January 1984, 1986, 1988, 1990, 1992, and February 1994 and 1996
   - Job tenure (or mobility) supplements—January 1973, 1978, 1981, 1983, 1987, and 1991
   - Contingent work supplement—February 1995.
   - Pension and benefit supplements—May 1979, 1983, 1988, and April 1993.

4. David Marcotte (1995) provided a useful comparison of studies. See OECD (1997) for a comparison of studies across OECD countries that also show greater decreases in stability among the young and less educated.

5. An early version of Gottschalk and Moffitt (1994) presented separation rates based on the PSID. Although these results are sometimes cited as showing increased instability, they were considered sufficiently unreliable because of changes in the wording of questions that they were dropped in the published version of the paper. For a summary of changes in the wording of questions in the PSID, see Polsky (1999, table A1).

6. These attributes of changes may in fact be more informative than information on whether the respondent views the separation as involuntary.

7. The appendix in Polsky (1999) provides a useful summary of these changes.

8. James Brown and Audrey Light (1992) examined this issue and concluded that if respondents were not returning to prior employers, then there is substantial inconsistency in the data. Our tabulations of the SIPP, however, indicate that many respondents do return to previous employers.

9. The question asked is: "How many years experience do you [head] have altogether with your present employer?" Self-employed individuals are coded as missing.

10. The work history files provide monthly measures of changes in employers starting in 1988, which is too late for our purposes. (Monthly changes in position are available for 1984 to 1987.)

11. An alternative would be to use "months in current position" rather than "months with current employer." This classification, however, would include changes in positions with the same employer. Polsky (1999, n. 12) uses "months in current position" rather than "months with current employer" because the latter was not asked in every year he covers in his study. Since we focus on a shorter time period, this cost is lower for us and does not warrant mixing changes across employers with changes in positions while working for the same employer.

12. Since we are interested in changes in job instability during the 1980s, we use the earliest consistent data series on tenure with the current employer; that data series is available from 1982 onward. The PSID work histories

start in 1984, but there were major changes between 1987 and 1988 (see PSID documentation, 1992 interview year, vol. 1, sec. 1, pt. 7 p. 42).

13. Even the work history files do not identify the return to an employer in a previous year, since the job histories identify only specific employers within the year (see Brown and Light 1992, n. 3).

14. If tenure were reported without error, we could identify a transition when the increase in tenure is larger than the number of months between interviews. Inspection of the data, however, indicates that the reporting error is too great to warrant this refinement.

15. Note that the CPS Displaced Worker Surveys capture only involuntary separations since questions about tenure are asked only of workers who were displaced from their jobs in the previous five years. (Starting in 1994, this has been changed to three years.)

16. Jaeger and Stevens (this volume) exclude respondents who are neither black nor white, while we include all races. They include persons twenty to fifty-nine, while our sample includes persons twenty to sixty-two.

17. Another minor difference involves the appropriate weight. If the measure of a job exit in t (that is, a change in jobs between t and t + 1) were based on truly cross-sectional data such as in the CPS, then the question on tenure would come from the interview in t + 1, so the only available weight would be for the year after the exit. Longitudinal data do not impose this restriction, so the cross-sectional measure is based on weights in t + 1 and the longitudinal measure is based on the weights in t. Weights, however, change sufficiently little to make this difference quantitatively unimportant.

18. This assumes that the difference in interview dates is less than the accumulated tenure.

19. The SIPP attaches a unique identifier to each employer the respondent works for during the panel.

20. Note that there is nothing inherent in the CPS that would preclude adding persons who had been unemployed for less than a year to both the numerator and denominator of the separation rate when estimating one-year separation rates. Since persons who were unemployed for more than a year were not in the risk set, they should not enter either the denominator or the numerator.

21. The sample includes all job beginnings during the panel.

22. These results are available from the authors.

23. For ease of interpretation, we report $e^{\hat{\beta}}$. A value below one on year implies that the hazard declines over time.

24. For convenience we use the terms "exit to a job" and "exit to a non-self-employment job" interchangeably.

25. Exits to nonemployment include both persons who are not employed at the time of the interview and persons whose tenure with the current employer is less than the difference in interview dates and who were not employed or out of the labor force during the year.

26. Note that the statistical significance of changes in exit rates cannot be read from the graph since the variance of a change includes a covariance between outcomes in the two periods being compared.

27. We refer to an exit between the job held at the interview in year t and the job held at the interview in t + 1 as an exit in t.

28. The sample is all job exits. The indicator variable is equal to one if the exit is to nonemployment.

29. The trend is zero for persons in their late thirties or early forties and gradually becomes positive for older workers.

30. We follow Boisjoly and his colleagues (1998) by defining separate samples for each pair of years. To be included in the sample of persons who are at risk of being involuntarily terminated from the job they hold at the interview in t, the respondent had to satisfy the following criteria: (1) head of household or wife aged twenty-five to fifty-nine at the interview in t; (2) not self-employed and with at least twelve months of tenure in the job held at t; and (3) worked at least one thousand hours in the year prior to t. Involuntary terminations are based on the answer to the question, "What happened with that job—did the company go out of business, were you laid off, did you quit, or what?" The major difference between our replication and their series is that they excluded firings from involuntary terminations. We would not have been able to make this exclusion even if we had wanted to, since they had to go back to the original questionnaires to identify firings. This difference, however, does not seem to affect the time-series pattern of the two series since our replication is very similar to their series. The correlation in the two series is .85.

31. A simple linear trend fit to the series in figure 1 of their paper indicates a significant positive trend over the whole period (1968 to 1991) but no significant change in the period we study. Daniel Polsky (1999) and Robert Valletta (1999) also find increases in involuntary terminations in the PSID, but their sample periods, again, start earlier than ours.

32. Codes are specific to each individual and are consistent over all interviews in the panel. For example, an employer identification number of 3 identifies the third employer observed for that individual. If the person returns to that employer later in the panel, the employer has the same code of 3. The SIPP also provides unique identifiers on each of the respondent's self-employment businesses in each month. In addition, the PSID work history file provides employer IDs that can be used to track job changes within the year. These cannot be used, however, to link employers across years since employer IDs are initialized each year.

33. The NLSY also includes job histories, but the design of the panel that follows persons aged fourteen to twenty-one in 1979 makes it difficult to separate age from period effects. Monks and Pizer (1998) and Bernhardt and her colleagues (this volume) have attempted to overcome this drawback by contrasting the job histories in the NLSY with those from a previous cohort covered by the National Longitudinal Survey of Young Men (NLSYM).

34. One-quarter of the observations are at seams wherever four rotation groups overlap (that is, except at the beginning and ends of the panels).

35. We ignore transitions between secondary jobs since the sample sizes are too small. (Less than 4 percent of the sample hold two jobs simultaneously.)

36. All valid person-months are included. We do not require valid data for all months in the panel.

37. Since there are a large number of possible combinations of primary, secondary, and self-employment, many of which would have very few observations, throughout this chapter we classify persons as self-employed if this was the only source of employment in that month. Persons with a primary job and a self-employed business are classified as having an employer and are not counted among the purely self-employed. The yearly proportions shown are the average of all person-months in each year, including persons in all panels covering the given year.

38. Katharine Abraham, James Spletzer, and Jay Stewart (1997) reported that multiple job holdings in the May CPS peaked at 6.2 percent in 1989. The peak for males in the SIPP occurred a few years earlier and is somewhat lower, though the levels are more similar when the proportion of secondary job holders in SIPP is calculated as in the CPS.

39. A person in SIPP with valid data in each of these three months in the two years provides three observations on yearly separations (March to March, April to April, and May to May). The resulting equally weighted average of the separation rates for each person in the three months is an unbiased estimator of the expected separation rates if the interview month is random. Standard errors are adjusted for repeated observations across individuals.

40. The 1988 panel covers March to May of 1988 and 1989, but not of 1990; the 1990 panel covers March to May of 1990 and 1991, but not of 1989.

41. These restrictions are imposed only for this comparison.

42. PSID interviews may not be exactly one year apart.

43. SIPP standard errors take account of the clustered nature of the data caused by our inclusion of data for up to three months in each year for each individual. The narrower confidence intervals in the SIPP than the PSID reflect the larger number of persons (or clusters).

44. Including males who were not married increases the exit rates but does not change the patterns over time.

45. The sample includes all persons ages twenty to sixty-two.

46. Overlapping panels that cover the same year therefore contribute to the separation rates shown in figures 5.7 and 5.8.

47. Year is measured in terms of months—for example, March 1990 is 90.25. Left-censored spells are excluded.

48. The large and significant coefficients on the seam variable illustrate the degree to which job turnover tends to be reported between interview periods.

49. Tests are on the joint significance of the trend and age interaction.

50. The sample includes all observed exits from jobs.

51. See the coefficients on the age interactions.

52. We do not examine this question with the PSID since the availablity of information only on annual earnings severely limits the usefulness of this data set for this question. One would have to compare earnings in the year before and the year after the job change (since earnings in the year of job change are a mixture of earnings in the two jobs).

53. For example, Topel and Ward (1992) find that roughly one-third of early career wage growth occurs at job changes.

54. Allowing β to vary across jobs as well as individuals does not alter our conclusions.

55. This statistical model is consistent with a job search model in which a set of homogeneous individuals initially located in different jobs receive draws of α_{ij} each period and accept those that are above the reservation value.

56. Put differently, the model in equation 5.4 assumes that the double-differenced wage change for nonmovers has mean zero. This could be relaxed by adding a quadratic in t to equation 5.1.

57. Since the SIPP asks respondents who are paid by the hour their "regular hourly pay rate," we use this variable whenever it is available. For others, we use earnings divided by hours. We calculate wage changes between successive jobs, whether or not there was an intervening spell of nonemployment.

58. Polsky (in press) also examines the wage consequences of job separation using the PSID. He finds larger wage losses in the late 1970s than in the late 1980s, but his results are not comparable to ours, which focus on changes during a more recent period (the 1980s and early 1990s) and use monthly data rather than annual earnings divided by hours.

59. The net wage change is the actual change in wages between jobs, ΔW, minus $\hat{\beta}_j(1 + m)$, where $\hat{\beta}_j$ is the estimated growth rate in the job the person left and m is the number of intervening months of nonemployment. Thus, for persons who went directly to a new job, the net wage change is $\Delta W - \hat{\beta}_j$.

60. Since job-leavers must have obtained a new job in order for us to observe their wage change, the sample includes all exits followed either immediately by a new job or with a completed intervening spell of nonemployment. Each observation is weighted by the inverse of the sampling variability of $\hat{\beta}_j$.

61. Again, "year" is shorthand for time measured in months.

REFERENCES

Abraham, Katharine G., James R. Spletzer, and Jay C. Stewart. 1997. "Divergent Trends in Alternative Wage Series." Washington, D.C.: U.S. Bureau of Labor Statistics (August).

Boisjoly, Johanne, Greg J. Duncan, and Timothy Smeeding. 1998. "The Shifting Incidence of Involuntary Job Losses from 1968 to 1992." *Industrial Relations* 37(2): 207–31.

Brown, James N., and Audrey Light. 1992. "Interpreting Panel Data on Job Tenure." *Journal of Labor Economics* 10(3): 219–57.

Diebold, Francis X., David Neumark, and Daniel Polsky. 1997a. "Job Stability in the United States." *Journal of Labor Economics* 15(2): 206–33.

———. 1997b. "Comment on Kenneth A. Swinnerton and Howard Wial, 'Is Job Stability Declining in the U.S. Economy?'" *Industrial and Labor Relations Review* 49(2): 348–52.

Farber, Henry S. 1997a. "Trends in Long-term Employment in the United States, 1979–1996." Working Paper 384. Princeton, N.J.: Princeton University (July).

———. 1997b. "The Changing Face of Job Loss in the United States, 1981–1995." Princeton, N.J.: Princeton University (May).

———. 1998. "Has the Rate of Job Loss Increased in the Nineties?" Working paper 394. Princeton, N.J.: Princeton University.

Fitzgerald, John. 1998. "Job Instability and Earnings and Income Consequences: Evidence from SIPP 1983–1995." Brunswick, Me.: Bowdoin College (May).

Gottschalk, Peter, and Robert Moffitt. 1994. "The Growth of Earnings Instability in the U.S. Labor Market." *Brookings Papers on Economic Activity* 2: 217–72.

Marcotte, David E. 1995. "Declining Job Stability: What We Know and What It Means." *Journal of Policy Analysis and Management* 14(4): 590–98.

Mincer, Jacob. 1986. "Wage Changes in Job Changes." *Research in Labor Economics* 8: 171–97.

Monks, James, and Steven Pizer. 1998. "Trends in Voluntary and Involuntary Job Turnover." *Industrial Relations* 37(4): 440–59.

Organization for Economic Co-operation and Development (OECD). 1997. "Is Job Insecurity on the Increase in OECD Countries?" *Employment Outlook*.

Polsky, Daniel. 1999. "Changes in the Consequences of Job Separations in the U.S. Economy." *Industrial and Labor Relations Review* 52(4): 565–80.

Rose, Stephen. 1995. "Declining Job Security and the Professionalization of Opportunity." Research report 95-04. Washington, D.C.: National Commission for Employment Policy.

Swinnerton, Kenneth A., and Howard Wial. 1995. "Is Job Stability Declining in the U.S. Economy?" *Industrial and Labor Relations Review* 48(2): 293–304.

———. 1996. "Is Job Stability Declining in the U.S. Economy?: Reply to Diebold, Neumark, and Polsky." *Industrial and Labor Relations Review* 49(2): 352–55.

Topel, Robert H., and Michael P. Ward. 1992. "Job Mobility and the Careers of Young Men." *Quarterly Journal of Economics* 107(2): 439–79.

Valletta, Robert. 1999. "Declining Job Security." *Journal of Labor Economics* 17(4): S170–S197.

Chapter 6

Has Job Stability Vanished in Large Corporations?

Steven G. Allen, Robert L. Clark, and Sylvester J. Schieber

Forget any idea of career-long employment with a big company.
Time, November 22, 1993, 37

During the past decade, the U.S. labor market has undergone considerable change, especially as increased international competition and continued technological innovation have put pressure on firms to reduce labor costs substantially. In reporting on these events, it is rare for a week to go by without headlines about plant closings, layoffs, or restructurings. The prevailing wisdom in media accounts is that many workers who had been sheltered from layoffs in earlier decades are no longer protected. Particular attention has been paid to layoffs of white-collar workers, workers employed in large corporations, and workers in the middle of their careers.[1] Media accounts focus on the plight of middle-aged and older workers, who now account for a larger share of job-losers than they did in the past.[2]

This perception also shows up in surveys of public opinion. In a *Time-CNN* poll in 1993, two-thirds thought that job security was worse than it was two years before (when the unemployment rate was the same), and 53 percent thought that this problem would last for many years (*Time,* November 22, 1993, 35).

To determine whether jobs have become less stable in the 1990s, economists have examined household data from nationally representative surveys, focusing on mobility and job tenure. For the most part, these studies find only small changes in job mobility and employment tenure. The difference between public perception, largely based on media accounts of layoffs at large companies, and statistical evidence, using representative national samples of workers, can be rationalized in two ways: either the media accounts are anecdotes that would not add up consistently when viewed from a more systematic framework (a conclusion suggested by Neumark and Polsky 1998) or the statistical studies have missed something big because they have not properly looked at some of the variables emphasized in popular discussions.

This chapter provides the first detailed analysis of job stability in large corporations in the 1990s, paying particular attention to the situation of midcareer workers. Given the public perception of rising instability in worker-firm attachments and the emphasis on large firms in media accounts, this chapter starts with a basic question: In large firms, what has happened to employer tenure and the percentage of workers in long-term jobs in the 1990s? This is a measurement issue, which we address with a data set consisting of fifty-one large firms that are clients of Watson Wyatt Worldwide. Some of the firms in this sample have been included in media accounts of downsizing. If job security for workers at the peak of their careers in large firms has become a relic of labor history, then we would expect to see noticeable changes in the tenure distribution and in the percentage of persons in long-term jobs in this sample—if not across the board, then certainly in firms that have downsized over the sample period.

This chapter begins with a brief review of recent empirical studies of tenure and mobility, followed by a theoretical discussion of why firms might have changed their decision rules for layoffs in the 1990s. The leading explanations are a change in the way the stock market reacts to layoff announcements or an increased incentive to substitute younger for older workers. The next section explains some unique features of our data set and assesses its strengths and limitations. Summary statistics are discussed in detail because they go to the very heart of the matter of what has happened to job stability in large firms in the 1990s. But such statistics can take us only so far. Simple comparisons between growing and downsizing firms are misleading if employment growth is correlated with other key determinants of job stability such as labor cost and simple comparisons, to say nothing at all about age substitution. The following section reports on regression analysis that provides more definitive results on these issues. The last section summarizes the key results and discusses some unresolved issues.

CONFLICTING PERCEPTIONS

It seems obvious: tenure is declining, jobs are riskier, retention rates are falling, and mobility is increasing. To be convinced of these trends, one need only read the newspapers (for example, *New York Times,* March 3–9, 1996), any business magazine (*Business Week,* March 11, 1996, or *Fortune,* April 1, 1996, and February 1, 1999), or some of the numerous trendy books that analyze the changing business environment in the United States (for example, Bluestone and Harrison 1986; Belous 1989; Moore 1996; and Reich 1997). Generally, these reports are based on specific instances of individual firms announcing layoffs, downsizing, or closings. Most of the firms described in these reports are very large, nationally known corporations. Most of the job-losers described in these accounts are workers in their forties and fifties who had a long-term attachment with their employer. After reading enough of these reports, it is easy to become convinced that there is a new reality in the U.S. labor market—workers must anticipate more frequent job changes, constant fear of being laid off, and the inability to retain a career job for much of their work life.

Is this perception of the U.S. labor market fact or fiction? The perception is based on news accounts of the actions of large firms; firms with fewer than ten thousand employees rarely appear on the cover of *Newsweek*. There has been no effort to aggregate systematically the experience of large firms into a general pattern of change. Instead, the accumulation of reports is taken as confirmation of the increase in instability; that is, enough media accounts presenting examples of layoffs by large employers provides a representative picture of the 1990s labor market.

To test the validity of this perception, economists have examined survey data on job duration and job changes, using data sets, such as the Current Population Survey (CPS) and the Panel Survey of Income Dynamics (PSID), that are representative of the entire labor market. These surveys include employees from firms of all size categories. Studies based on these surveys have not attempted to focus on large firms, in part because the data often do not include measures of firm size and in part because of the difficulties in making comparisons across time within firm size categories with repeated cross-sections. A brief summary of these studies is not consistent with the popular belief that employment tenure has sharply declined and job mobility has increased during the past two decades.

1. *Employer tenure:* Dan McGill and his colleagues (1996, 344) compared median years in current job for men and women by age groups between 1951 and 1991 and concluded that "disaggregation of the historical data on worker tenure does not support the general notion that workers have become inherently more job mobile in recent years." Their analysis used job tenure by age-sex group, as reported in various government publications. The data showed that the median years in current job for men in each age group were higher in 1991 than in 1966. Median years in current job for women were also higher in each age group. Subsequent tabulations of the February 1996 CPS by the U.S. Bureau of Labor Statistics (1997) indicate that median years of tenure for men declined by 0.1 years between 1991 and 1996, but median tenure for women rose by 0.3 years.

2. *Percentage of workers in long-term jobs:* Henry Farber (1997) found that the proportion of men reporting long-term jobs (tenure of more than ten years or more than twenty years) declined slightly between 1979 and 1993, and then more substantially between 1993 and 1996. In contrast, there was a small increase in the proportion of women reporting long-term employment relationships. Farber concluded: "The structure of the employment relationship in some areas may have changed toward a model with less long-term job security. However, the analysis of the data on displaced workers suggests that, to the extent that this has occurred, the mechanism may not be to target high-tenure workers for layoff but may be to structure the base employment relationship different ways earlier in jobs" (26).

3. *Mobility:* Studies comparing the distribution of employer tenure across different waves of the CPS show job mobility has remained relatively constant over the past two decades. Francis Diebold, David Neumark, and Daniel Polsky (1997) reported that retention rates declined slightly, from 0.544 in the period 1983 to 1987 to 0.530 in the period 1987 to 1991, and that when retention rates are adjusted for the business cycle, the decline in retention rates was only from 0.537 to 0.527. They reported: "The most important conclusion to emerge from our study is the approximate stability of aggregate job retention rates over the 1980s and early 1990s. . . . Taken as a whole, the evidence from 4-year job retention rates estimated over this period does not point toward a secular decline in job stability" (231). Extending this work through 1995, Neumark, Polsky, and Hansen (1997) found that the four-year retention rate for all workers was slightly higher for 1991 to 1995 (0.544) than for 1987 to 1991 and for 1983 to 1987.

Findings from research using the PSID are more diverse. Stephen Rose (1995) found increases in job turnover in the 1980s compared to the 1970s, whereas Daniel Polsky (1996), comparing the period 1976 to 1981 to the period 1986 to 1991, found no evidence of a change in the likelihood of job separation. David Jaeger and Ann Huff Stevens (this volume) and Peter Gottschalk and Robert Moffitt (this volume) carefully examine the PSID data and benchmark it against the CPS and SIPP, respectively. Their studies both conclude that there has been no trend toward decreased job stability.

None of these studies using household surveys has been able to distinguish among workers based on the size of their employers. Thus, one possible explanation for the difference in perceptions is that the press accounts have concentrated on the actions of large firms while the research studies have examined all workers. Since almost 60 percent of all workers are employed by firms with fewer than one thousand employees, this distinction could be very important in explaining the different conclusions concerning trends in job tenure and mobility. The popular perception of greater instability in large firms could be consistent with the academic findings of no overall change in stability if jobs in large (small) firms have become less (more) stable. This study provides direct evidence on job stability for large employers in the 1990s using the best possible data—firm employment records.

The measures of job duration used in this study all come from the company payroll records that are used in conjunction with their compensation systems. Payroll records are not subject to any of the sources of erroneous measurement of employer tenure found in household surveys: imperfect recall by the worker, guesstimates by other household members on behalf of the worker, and rounding errors. (For a full discussion of such errors, see Diebold, Neumark, and Polsky 1997.)

Household survey data are not well suited for examining the labor market policies of large employers. Firm size is not regularly included in household surveys, so inferences have to be drawn by comparing tenure distributions at two points in time. Comparing the number of employees with x years of tenure in year t in large firms to the number with x + n years of tenure in year t + n in large firms is problematic in a household survey for two reasons: errors in reporting employment levels, and movement of firms over and under the one-thousand-employee threshold during the n years. Employer data will provide much more accurate measures of changes in the tenure distribution.

Another big advantage of employer data is that it permits an in-depth examination of firms that are changing size. Of special interest to the current debate is the ability to focus on large firms that are shrinking and to distinguish their behavior from that of firms that are growing. Press accounts of reductions in force usually emphasize cuts in the total number of jobs. But what actually happens in large companies undergoing, say, a 10 percent reduction in force? Are firms reacting to adverse economic events by pushing more expensive, older workers out the door, or are they responding by reducing or halting the hiring of new employees? To answer this question, we must have data from employers to be able to determine retention rates by age and tenure and to calculate the cost of employing workers at various age and tenure levels.

The advantages of using employer data to examine labor market practices do not come without costs. One issue is whether the firms in any sample are representative of the large employers that have traditionally offered lifetime jobs. To address this concern, we present as much descriptive detail about the firms as possible and compare their characteristics to known values of key traits from national data. Nonetheless, the results of this study should be interpreted as a case study of fifty-one firms with almost one million employees that may or may not be generalizable across all large firms. An additional limitation of the sample used here is that the information on worker characteristics is limited to age, tenure, and compensation. Although this limitation prohibits any breakdowns by schooling, gender, or race, it should not produce any bias in our estimates; pay level can be used to control for variations in skill.

THEORETICAL FRAMEWORK

Tenure distributions and mobility decisions in each firm reflect the joint decisionmaking of the firm and its employees. A firm bases decisions about the size and composition of its labor force on demand for its product, production technology, the cost of hiring and training workers, the cost of firing workers, and the cost and substitutability of various types of labor and other inputs. In addition to comparing current and expected future costs and productivity, a firm takes into account strategic considerations, including the value of the ability to write contracts for long-term jobs. Employees base their decisions on employment opportunities elsewhere in the labor market relative to those in the firm, as well as on the perceived value of nonmarket activities.

To understand possible changes in the 1990s in long-term employment contracts, a model must be able to explain why a firm would consider reneging on such a contract *and* why employer behavior in the 1990s would differ from earlier decades. Traditionally firms have employed a combination of LIFO (last-in-first-out) layoffs and early retirement policies to reduce the number of workers. This practice is explained by a simple model of specific human capital in which the worker and the firm share the investment costs and the expected returns from increased productivity following training. (The discussion here follows closely the exposition in Lazear 1995, 1998.) During the training period, workers are paid less than the wage they are offered by competing firms (the investment cost to the worker) but more than the value of what they produce net of training costs (the investment cost to the firm). After training is completed, workers are paid less than the value of their output (firm return on investment) but more than their alternative wage (worker return on investment).

At the beginning of the employment relationship, there are no rents from training accruing to either party. As training continues, the present value of rents over time (for the worker, the firm, and both rents combined) follows a quadratic pattern. This pattern occurs because the remaining length of the investment period (a period of net costs to the worker and firm) is declining, and some investment costs have already been made and thus are now viewed as fixed costs. In addition, the length of time remaining in the training period is declining, so that the time until positive investment returns for both the worker and the firm are expected is also declining.

The present value of future rents for each party reaches a maximum at the end of the training period and then begins to decline. During this period, output is greater than compensation, which is greater than the compensation that workers could earn with their current skills at other firms. As years go by, the present value of rents for the remaining work life with the firm decline and eventually become zero at the end of the relationship.

With an adverse shock to the firm that is neutral across age and tenure categories, the entire rent profile shifts downward. The present value of future rents becomes negative at the tails of the tenure distribution. This would dictate a downsizing strategy that focuses on the most junior and most senior employees. Firms would use a combination of LIFO layoffs and buyout packages for more senior workers, with the mix depending on the shape of the tenure distribution and the size of the shock. In this framework, the only rationale for eliminating midcareer employees who generate peak rents would be a shock that is biased to be more severe for, say, the top half of the age-tenure distribution than for the bottom half.

Downsizing strategies that dictate layoffs of midcareer workers can be explained in the context of Edward Lazear's (1979) model. Even in good times, the present value of future rents is negative for all workers beyond a certain tenure level and is most negative for midcareer workers. Normally firms resist the temptation to lay off the most senior workers because they want to maintain a good reputation in the labor market—that is, they value the option of writing more such productivity-enhancing contracts in the future. Yet some decisions—such as to drop certain product lines permanently, to outsource operations, or to implement labor-saving technology—produce an endgame situation in which reputational concerns are overshadowed by the prospect of increased profitability. In such cases, layoffs of midcareer employees would be economically rational for the firm, regardless of the implicit contract. Firms would still need to address the concerns of the remaining, younger employees, and this would have to be done in a credible (and probably irreversible) manner. As a practical matter, granting stock options would be one way to offset a broken promise of lifetime employment.

This still leaves the question of why layoffs of high-tenure workers in large firms started to attract attention in the 1990s.[3] One possibility is the connection between layoff announcements, stock value, and CEO pay. *Newsweek* (February 26, 1996, 44) pasted pictures of CEOs labeled "Corporate Killers" on its cover and proclaimed: "Once upon a time, it was a mark of shame to fire your workers en masse. It meant you had messed up your business. Today, the more people a company fires, the more Wall Street loves it, and the higher the stock price goes." Theoretically the impact of such announcements on stock prices is indeterminate (Worrell, Davidson, and Sharma 1991). They could have a neutral effect if the company's problems are well known and the layoffs are expected, and a negative effect if the layoffs are not expected or are greater than expected.[4] For the reaction to be positive (the popular perception today), the market must interpret the news as a sign that the firm is no longer in denial and is making the appropriate correction.

If there has been a shift in market reactions to layoff announcements, then a corresponding change in the reward structure for CEOs would make them more inclined to downsize.[5] Firms would be willing to abrogate implicit contracts for lifetime jobs if the gains in shareholder wealth offset the losses in specific human capital and reputation in the labor market. In our data set, this would show up in a comparison of growing and downsizing firms or in a model in which turnover for workers in different tenure categories is a function of employment growth. If they were breaking implicit contracts, downsizing firms would have not only higher turnover overall but also higher turnover (relative to growing firms) across all tenure categories, including midcareer employees. The alternative possibility is that downsizing firms still rely on LIFO layoffs and early retirement buyouts, in which case turnover rates would vary at the extremes of the tenure distribution but not in the middle.

A second theory for greater job instability involves substitution of younger for older employees. In a recent story in *Fortune* titled "Finished at Forty," Munk (1999) wrote:

> Since the early 1980s big companies have been getting rid of people. For a long time, though, seniority mattered. Hierarchy was respected too. If people had to be fired, the younger, junior people were usually the first to go. That's no longer true. . . . There's no way to tell how many of these people are over 40, but this much is sure: Companies today have less and less tolerance for people they believe are earning more than their output warrants. Such intolerance, or pragmatism, hits older workers hardest. The older an employee, the more likely it is he can be replaced by someone younger who earns half as much.

Theoretically, the incentive to substitute younger for older workers is affected by the slope of the tenure-compensation profile relative to the tenure-productivity profile. Greater global competition or an increased pace of technological change dictates a need for a more flexible workforce, according to some management experts. This made young employees more attractive in the 1990s because they were supposedly more willing to relocate or to put in long hours than an older generation juggling child and elder care. The experience-productivity profile also could have flattened as a result of the increasing use of information technology, assuming that younger workers were more computer-savvy. The slope of the experience-productivity profile is not observable, so we focus empirically on the impact of the steepness of the pay profile. It is well established that wage differentials by experience widened in the 1980s and 1990s. If productivity differentials did not widen by an equal amount, this would create a rationale for substituting inexperienced for midcareer workers.

Finally, initial conditions matter. A firm with a relatively large percentage of low-tenure employees is capable of adjusting to an adverse shock through LIFO layoffs without terminating any midcareer employees. A firm with very few recent hires does not have this option. To control for this, we report data by seniority categories and control for the share of the most junior (zero to four years) and most senior (twenty-five years and up) employees in $t - 5$ in regression models of turnover.

As pointed out by Jagadeesh Gokhale, Erica Groshen, and David Neumark (1995), there also can be an interaction effect between profile steepness and initial conditions. A firm faced with a large percentage of older workers and a steep profile would obtain more cost savings through age substitution than a firm with the same percentage of older workers and a flat profile. We tested for such an effect in our data and were unable to reject the null hypothesis. To make the presentation of the empirical results more compact and easier to follow, these results are not reported.

Empirically, this study proceeds in the following fashion. First, we examine how tenure distributions have changed in our sample of firms in the 1990s. Once we get beyond the basic facts on tenure in the early and middle parts of the decade, we attempt to interpret these facts in light of the concern about rising job instability. It is difficult to draw inferences about job stability from simple comparisons of tenure distributions within a firm. An increase in mean tenure does not imply that workers are sticking around; such an increase also occurs if the firm downsizes and fires all junior employees. Similarly, a decrease in mean tenure could happen at a growing firm that has extremely low turnover accompanied by an increase in the percentage of new employees or at a firm where midcareer and senior employees have been replaced by younger workers. Accordingly, we shift attention to the retention rate of workers in different ranges of the tenure distribution. Retention in this study is measured by comparing the age and tenure distribution at two points in time; the reasons behind the observed attrition in each age-tenure cell (quits, layoffs, disability, death) are not reported. In addition to the slope of the pay profile and the initial distribution of tenure, we model retention on the following variables:

Growing versus downsizing: Worker-initiated decisions on retention are based on the difference in the expected value of opportunities within and outside the firm. Because of greater opportunities for promotions and higher-paying positions within growing firms, such firms should have fewer quits than shrinking firms. Layoffs can occur in both growing and shrinking firms but are obviously more likely in the latter. Thus, we would expect retention rates to increase with employment growth. Downsizing can be done in a variety of different ways, and this choice has important implications for retention and tenure. Firms that reduce employment through hiring freezes should have higher retention rates and a greater proportion of workers with long tenure than firms that target midcareer and senior workers for layoffs. By looking not just at overall retention rates but also at retention rates by seniority, this study is able to give a fuller accounting of what happens to job stability after downsizing.

Pay level: The level of compensation also influences decisionmaking by both workers and employers. Firms with high wages are likely to have fewer quits, holding worker alternatives constant; they also are likely to have a greater incentive for head-count reductions, holding productivity constant. Most studies of mobility do find a positive association between wages and job duration, absent controls for alternative wages and productivity.

Firm size: Company size also should influence retention rates and the incidence of long-term jobs. Even among large firms, the companies with the most employees are more likely to have greater opportunities internally, and thus greater retention of employees.

DATA AND SUMMARY STATISTICS

This study examines changes in job tenure in the 1990s using employment and compensation information on fifty-one firms. All of the firms are in the private sector, operate on a for-profit basis, and were consulting clients of Watson Wyatt Worldwide (WWW). WWW is an international benefit consulting firm that provides a variety of services associated with the development and maintenance of compensation systems to firms in all sectors of the economy. WWW markets its services to a wide range of firms; however, most of its clients tend to be firms with one thousand or more employees. Most major corporations in the United States use some of its services.

These employers are all relatively large firms ranging in size in the initial year from slightly less than one thousand employees to almost two hundred thousand employees. Each of the firms has a defined benefit pension plan, and all of the firms provide health insurance to their employees. The employers are from the manufacturing, financial, health, transportation, telecommunications, utility, and information sectors of

Figure 6.1   Log Change in Employment over Five-Year Study Period

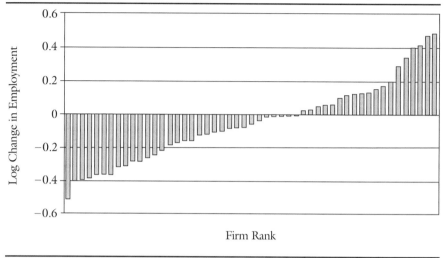

the economy. These firms do not constitute a random sample of employers, but they are a collection of firms that provide high pay, excellent benefits, and a tradition of providing long-term employment—exactly the type of firm that has been singled out in media accounts. The data set was developed by the Research and Information Center of Watson Wyatt Worldwide in an effort to help clients understand the impact of an aging labor force on individual firms. The firms included in the data represent companies for which Watson Wyatt has already conducted such an analysis and for which all relevant data were available.[6] Cases were dropped when either there were obvious inconsistencies (for example, retention rates of 125 percent) or there had been a major acquisition or sell-off that precluded a full accounting of employment in all lines of business before and after the restructuring.

The data set includes information on the number of workers employed by age and tenure for each firm for two years. In each case, the years are five years apart. The five-year period of analysis varies somewhat, however, across the firms: twenty-four firms report data for 1990 to 1995, twenty-five firms report data for 1991 to 1996, and two firms report data for 1992 to 1997. Age-tenure retention rates between the two years are provided, along with age-tenure levels of total compensation for the most recent year. In addition, the data provide age-tenure information concerning pay, health costs, pension costs, and the cost of paid leave.

Figure 6.1 shows the percentage change in employment levels for firms between the two years. Most firms (63 percent) reduced employment. Total employment among these companies contracted by 19.5

percent, from 938,105 to 755,401. The aggregate decline in employment was concentrated in the three largest firms; eliminating these three, total employment among the other forty-eight firms declined by 4.6 percent. The median percentage change in employment for these employers was −5.4 percent; the unweighted average change in employment was −2.0 percent.

Table 6.1 presents key employment data for the firms by level of employment. Generally, total employment among the smaller employers was growing, with the most rapid growth reported in the very smallest category. Employment among the largest employers was contracting, with the most significant contraction occurring among the very largest firms.

We would not expect worker characteristics in the large firms examined here to match exactly those found in household surveys. All but one of the firms in this sample have one thousand or more employees. All provide health insurance and retirement benefits. They are not evenly distributed across industries. Most of the firms are in manufacturing, transportation, communications, utilities, financial services, and health services. None are in agriculture, mining, construction, wholesale trade, or services outside of health care. With these provisos in mind, we examined the April 1993 CPS, which contains the supplemental Survey of Employee Benefits and is the only large household survey that falls within our sample period and contains information on firm size and employee benefits (availability of health insurance and retirement plans and participation in those plans). To reweight the CPS so that it resembles our sample as closely as possible, we dropped all observations in which: the respondent works in a firm with fewer than one thousand employees; the respondent is not covered by the employer's health insurance and retirement plans; and the respondent works for the government. The average age of 40.9 in the first year of the employer sample is reasonably close to the value of 40.4 in the CPS matched sample. Tenure in the employer sample in year t averaged 12.3 years, slightly higher than the value of 11.6 years in the CPS. The only dimension in which the two samples do not match up very well is in terms of pay. Pay levels in the employer sample in year t + 5 average $44,521, whereas estimated annual salary in the CPS (fifty-two times weekly salary) is $35,318. The pay discrepancy may result from differences in industry mix between the CPS and the WWW sample or from the underrepresentation of very large firms in the CPS.

To summarize, the firms in the WWW sample look very much like the type of firm that has been featured in today's headlines—high pay, generous benefits, and long job durations, at least as compared to the overall labor market. We do not maintain that this is a totally representative sample of such firms, but the sample is certainly large and diverse enough to

Table 6.1 Selected Characteristics of Sample, by Firm Size

	Under 1,500	1,500 to 2,499	2,500 to 4,999	5,000 to 9,999	10,000 to 19,999	20,000 to 79,999	80,000 or more
Number of firms	8	7	8	9	10	6	3
Number of firms with increased employment	6	4	2	4	3	0	0
Percentage change in employment	11.8	3.9	−9.8	5.8	3.1	−14.7	−32.3

be an informative "mega-case" study of employment practices in large corporations in the 1990s. As a practical matter, the type of data examined here is available only directly from the firm and is so highly sensitive that few firms are likely to be willing to respond to requests for it from academics. To get a critical mass of data points, collaborative ventures between academics and compensation experts in the private sector are currently the only way for getting this type of research done.

HAVE LONG-TERM JOBS VANISHED IN THE 1990S?

Our analysis begins by examining several key indicators of job stability, including average years of tenure, percentage of workers with ten or more years of service, percentage of workers with twenty or more years of service, and the firm's retention rate. In each case, the data are reported for the entire sample and separately by firm size. Summary statistics on the incidence of long-term jobs in the 1990s are reported in table 6.2. We report unweighted and weighted (by employment in year $t - 5$) averages for the entire sample, along with weighted averages by size class. The key findings are as follows:

1. The average duration of employee-employer matches in our sample of large firms is longer in the mid-1990s than in the early 1990s. Average tenure in the early 1990s was 12.6 years and increased by 0.8 years over the next five years.

2. The increase in tenure was far from uniform across our sample. In twelve firms, average tenure declined, and it was unchanged in one firm. Average tenure increased by two years or more in eleven firms.

3. Average tenure rose across all size categories, except for firms with fewer than 1,500 employees. The increase in average tenure was smallest in the very largest category (all three firms in this category underwent significant reductions in force) and among employers with 1,500 to 2,499 employees.

4. The percentage of workers who have been with the same employer ten or more years increased considerably in the 1990s. On average, 54.5 percent of employees had ten or more years of service in the early 1990s; this increased by 4.1 percentage points over the next five years.

5. The percentage of workers who have been with the same employer twenty or more years also increased in the 1990s. On average, 25.6 percent of employees had twenty or more years of service in the early 1990s; this increased by 0.6 percentage points over the next five years.

Table 6.2 Summary Statistics on Tenure, Age, and Retention Rates, Overall and by Firm Size

	All, no weights	All, weighted	Under 1,500	1,500 to 2,499	2,500 to 4,999	5,000 to 9,999	10,000 to 19,999	20,000 to 79,999	80,000 or more
Average age in initial year	39.9	40.7	41.2	40.5	39.7	38.2	38.6	41.2	41.5
Change in average age	1.4	1.2	1.4	1.0	1.7	1.2	1.7	1.1	1.0
Average tenure in initial year	10.4	12.6	11.2	10.5	10.8	8.5	9.1	11.3	14.6
Change in average tenure	0.9	0.8	−0.4	0.5	1.4	0.7	1.8	1.3	0.5
Percentage with ten or more years of tenure in initial year	44.7	54.5	46.8	48.6	48.1	34.5	37.6	48.7	64.4
Change in percentage with ten or more years of tenure	3.6	4.1	−1.4	−2.0	4.6	2.8	8.3	8.3	1.8
Percentage with twenty or more years of tenure in initial year	16.7	25.6	19.4	13.8	17.8	11.4	12.9	19.6	34.0
Change in percentage with twenty or more years of tenure	2.1	0.6	−1.9	2.9	5.7	0.5	4.1	1.3	−1.0
Five-year retention rate (percentage)	67.9	60.7	76.3	70.5	64.5	63.8	70.7	67.6	54.4

Note: The results in the last seven columns are all weighted by employment in the initial year.

6. About three-fifths (60.7 percent) of the workers in our sample stayed with the same employer over the entire five-year sample period.

7. The average age of workers was 40.7 in the early 1990s and increased by 1.2 years over the next five years. Average age increased by one year or more in every size category.

RETENTION RATES BY TENURE CATEGORY

The employment records indicate that average tenure and age of employees for these fifty-one large firms increased in the 1990s. As noted earlier, this does not mean that job stability has increased. We must break down retention rates by tenure category to understand whether tenure is rising because everyone is staying or because many junior and midcareer employees have been laid off. With data on employment by tenure category, we calculate retention rates by years of service to show the rate at which workers stay with the firm at different stages of their career.

As shown in table 6.3, the five-year retention rate is lowest among employees with twenty or more years of service, presumably reflecting high retirement rates among these workers. Retention rates across the entire sample rise with seniority through fifteen to nineteen years of service, a pattern that is consistent with the findings of the mobility literature and that reflects job shopping, LIFO layoffs, and perhaps up-or-out contracts. Over 70 percent of midcareer employees (ten to nineteen years of service in year t − 5) stay with the firm for another five years. In the two smallest size categories (less than 1,500 employees and 1,500 to 2,499 employees), however, retention is greatest among the most junior employees—most likely a reflection of the opportunities for advancement created by rapid growth in these firms.

An important issue in terms of job security is how the pattern of retention rates across years of service compares in growing and shrinking firms. Retention rates should be smaller for shrinking firms because of the greater odds of a layoff or an early retirement buyout. Quits might also increase if workers have opportunities elsewhere. If the implicit contract of job security for midcareer employees was abrogated in the 1990s, we would expect to see much smaller retention rates for those with ten to nineteen years of service in shrinking firms than in growing firms. On the other hand, it is conceivable that shrinking firms used the standard methods of LIFO layoffs and early retirement buyouts to downsize their workforce.

As expected, table 6.4 shows a very large difference in weighted retention rates between growing and downsizing firms—69 percent of all employees stay for five additional years in growing firms versus only 59.8

Table 6.3 Retention Rates by Tenure Category and Firm Size

Seniority	All, Weighted	Under 1,500	1,500 to 2,499	2,500 to 4,999	5,000 to 9,999	10,000 to 19,999	20,000 to 79,999	80,000 or more
Zero to four years	60.8	92.5	83.9	63.6	62.3	76.2	72.0	51.0
Five to nine years	63.7	80.4	74.7	68.5	66.7	68.2	73.7	57.7
Ten to fourteen years	70.2	78.8	62.4	74.3	70.9	73.3	78.0	66.4
Fifteen to nineteen years	71.1	76.3	61.2	70.5	70.0	73.5	74.5	69.5
Twenty years or more	48.1	56.1	49.9	55.1	52.8	59.5	50.7	42.9
All	60.7	76.3	70.5	64.5	63.8	70.7	67.6	54.4

Table 6.4 Retention Rates by Seniority and Employment Growth

Seniority	Weighted, Employment Declining	Weighted, Employment Growing	Weighted, Difference	Unweighted, Employment Declining	Unweighted, Employment Growing	Unweighted, Difference
Zero to four years	59.0	76.0	19.0	70.4	78.2	7.8
Five to nine years	63.3	67.2	3.9	69.2	72.7	3.5
Ten to fourteen years	70.4	69.0	−1.4	73.1	70.8	−1.3
Fifteen to nineteen years	71.2	70.3	−0.9	70.5	71.6	1.1
Twenty years or more	47.0	57.8	10.8	52.7	54.7	2.0
All	59.8	69.0	9.2	66.2	70.6	4.2

percent in shrinking firms. Despite this overall disparity in retention rates by employment growth, the retention rates for midcareer employees are virtually indistinguishable for growing and downsizing firms. This is true for both the weighted and unweighted tabulations. All of the difference in aggregate retention rates results from lower retention for the most recent hires and the most senior employees. *Job retention is the same for midcareer employees in downsizing companies as it is in growing companies.*

How do retention rates in the large firms in our sample compare to those for the rest of the labor market? The most straightforward comparison is with the Neumark, Polsky, and Hansen (1997) finding of an overall retention rate of 54.4 percent for 1991 to 1995. It is not especially surprising to see that the five-year retention rate for growing firms in the WWW sample is considerably higher. What may be surprising is that the *five-year* retention rate of 59.8 percent for the downsizing firms in the WWW sample is greater than the four-year retention rate for the entire labor market. From a purely statistical standpoint, a worker in the early 1990s had higher odds of staying with a large firm in the WWW sample that was going to decrease employment than he or she would have had in any job picked at random.

DETERMINANTS OF RETENTION

The data on retention imply that midcareer employees have been sheltered from downsizing in large firms in the 1990s, contrary to media accounts. A regression analysis allows us to control for other variables correlated with employment growth, especially labor costs and firm size, and it also permits a test of one dimension of the age-substitution hypothesis. The retention rate was regressed on the following variables: log employment in $t-5$; the change in log employment between $t-5$ and t; log compensation (including health care, defined benefit and defined contribution pensions, and paid time off); the steepness of the compensation profile (as measured by the log difference in compensation between those aged forty-five to forty-nine with twenty to twenty-four years of tenure and those aged twenty-five to twenty-nine with zero to four years of tenure); the percentage of workers with less than five years of service in $t-5$; and the share of workers with twenty-five or more years of service in $t-5$. To determine whether the impact of these variables varied with seniority, a separate model was estimated for five different ranges of the seniority distribution. The results are reported in table 6.5. To obtain a more in-depth view into decisionmaking by workers and firms in the context of downsizing, separate models were estimated for growing and shrinking firms; these results are reported in table 6.6.

Table 6.5 Retention Rate Regressions

	Mean (Standard Deviation)	All Workers	Tenure				
			Zero to Four Years	Five to Nine Years	Ten to Fourteen Years	Fifteen to Nineteen Years	Twenty Years or More
Constant	— —	−0.981 (0.528)	−0.154 (1.073)	−1.265 (0.958)	−3.237 (0.907)	−2.698 (1.067)	−1.298 (1.061)
Percentage with zero to four years of tenure in t − 5	0.340 (0.151)	−0.613* (0.129)	−1.089* (0.263)	−0.449 (0.235)	−0.183 (0.222)	−0.085 (0.262)	−0.025 (0.260)
Percentage with twenty-five years or more of tenure in t − 5	0.086 (0.067)	−0.284 (0.254)	−0.590 (0.517)	0.604 (0.462)	0.643 (0.437)	0.523 (0.514)	0.027 (0.511)
Log (total compensation)	10.904 (0.244)	0.193* (0.049)	0.160 (0.100)	0.203* (0.089)	0.375* (0.084)	0.318* (0.099)	0.188 (0.098)
Log compensation difference by age-seniority	0.625 (0.249)	−0.250* (0.057)	−0.317* (0.116)	−0.024 (0.103)	−0.173 (0.098)	−0.202 (0.115)	−0.262* (0.114)
$\log(L_t/L_{t-5})$	−0.048 (0.236)	0.565* (0.059)	0.775* (0.120)	0.469* (0.107)	0.396* (0.101)	0.366* (0.119)	0.298* (0.118)
$\log(L_{t-5})$	8.774 (1.335)	−0.004 (0.009)	−0.023 (0.018)	−0.012 (0.016)	0.001 (0.015)	0.008 (0.018)	−0.004 (0.018)
Mean (standard deviation) of dependent variable	— —	0.679 (0.142)	0.733 (0.236)	0.705 (0.172)	0.722 (0.166)	0.709 (0.172)	0.534 (0.157)
R^2	—	0.758	0.636	0.454	0.480	0.324	0.200
Root MSE	—	0.074	0.151	0.135	0.128	0.150	0.150
N	—	51	51	51	51	51	51

* Difference significant at .05 level or lower.

Table 6.6 Retention Rate Regressions, by Employment Growth

	All Workers	Tenure				
		Zero to Four Years	Five to Nine Years	Ten to Fourteen Years	Fifteen to Nineteen Years	Twenty Years or More
Log (total compensation)						
Growing firms	0.365*	0.309*	0.142	0.568*	0.591*	0.504*
	(0.081)	(0.154)	(0.205)	(0.175)	(0.215)	(0.191)
Shrinking firms	0.084	-0.050	0.259*	0.230*	0.160	0.058
	(0.065)	(0.147)	(0.111)	(0.114)	(0.131)	(0.139)
Log compensation difference by age and seniority						
Growing firms	-0.164	-0.100	-0.034	-0.126	-0.135	-0.124
	(0.084)	(0.158)	(0.212)	(0.180)	(0.221)	(0.197)
Shrinking firms	-0.149	-0.026	0.096	-0.060	-0.315	-0.319
	(0.096)	(0.217)	(0.164)	(0.168)	(0.194)	(0.205)
Log(L_t/L_{t-5})						
Growing firms	0.702*	0.750*	0.290	0.561	0.556	0.902*
	(0.162)	(0.307)	(0.410)	(0.349)	(0.429)	(0.381)
Shrinking firms	0.652*	0.912*	0.734*	0.661*	0.381*	0.178
	(0.086)	(0.193)	(0.146)	(0.149)	(0.173)	(0.182)

Note: Each equation is estimated over a subsample of either nineteen growing firms or thirty-two shrinking firms and includes a constant, percentage with zero to four years of tenure in t − 5, percentage with twenty-five or more years of tenure in t − 5, and log of employment in t − 5 as independent variables.

* Difference significant at .05 level or lower.

EMPLOYMENT GROWTH

As expected, retention rates increase with employment growth. A 0.1 increase in log employment growth is associated with a 5.6-percentage-point increase in the retention rate. The impact of employment growth on retention is much greater for junior than for senior employees. A 0.1 increase in log employment growth is associated with a 7.8-percentage-point increase in the retention rate of employees with zero to four years of service. In contrast, it is associated with just a 3.0-percentage-point increase in the retention rate of those with twenty or more years of service. This indicates that seniority continues to be strongly associated with firms' employment adjustment decisions.

This conclusion becomes more robust when the sample is split by employment growth. In downsizing firms, the retention rate for workers with less than five years of service is much more sensitive to employment growth than the retention rate for more senior workers. A 0.1 log decrease in employment is associated with a 9.1-percentage-point drop in the retention of workers with less than five years of service, whereas it has no effect on retention of workers with twenty or more years of service. Although this result cannot be compared to patterns in earlier decades, it has a very clear and important implication for today's debate about job security. *Most of the impact of employment adjustment is being borne by the most junior workers.*

Employment growth is also associated with higher retention rates in growing firms, but the impact is greatest at the extremes of the seniority distribution. The result for junior workers probably reflects the relatively greater internal opportunities for advancement in growing firms. The result for workers with twenty or more years of service is a bit more surprising and probably reflects the efforts of employers to delay retirement.

PAY LEVEL

Retention rates are greatest in the organizations with the highest pay levels. A 0.1 increase in log compensation is associated with a 1.9-percentage-point increase in the retention rate. Looking at the entire fifty-one-firm sample, the impact of compensation on retention appears to be greatest for midcareer employees. However, as table 6.6 indicates, compensation has much less impact on retention in shrinking than in growing firms. Among growing firms, compensation is associated with higher retention in all but one tenure category and is greatest among the most senior employees. In shrinking firms, compensation is correlated with neither overall retention rates nor retention rates for the least junior (tenure under five years) and most senior (tenure of twenty years or more) employees. In these firms, retention reflects a mix of quit and layoff decisions, making it a bit difficult to interpret the findings. The fact that compensation is associated with greater retention among workers with five to fourteen years of service could reflect some degree of "job lock" (no exits despite uncertain future prospects) or confidence in the value of a long-term relationship.

PAY DIFFERENTIALS BY AGE AND TENURE

Across the entire sample of firms, the overall retention rate is much lower in firms with the largest differentials in pay by age and seniority. A 0.1 increase in this log pay differential is associated with a 2.5-percentage-point decrease in employee retention.

Does this mean that firms are making widespread substitutions of new hires for senior workers? If this were the case, the age-seniority gap in pay would have a much greater effect on the retention of senior employees than of entry-level workers; in an extreme situation, it could even have a positive coefficient for low-tenure employees. This is clearly not the case: the results in table 6.5 show that the impact of profile steepness on retention is nearly equal for employees in the tenure categories of zero to four years and of twenty years or more. Also, if age substitution were a driving factor in today's downsizing patterns, the age-seniority gap in pay would have an impact on retention when the sample is restricted to downsizing firms. Instead, table 6.6 shows no impact of profile steepness on retention among downsizing firms.

OTHER VARIABLES

The size of the organization in t − 5 had no effect on retention. Although this finding runs counter to the prevailing wisdom that mobility should fall with size, keep in mind that all but one firm in this study had one thousand or more employees in t − 5. It could very well be that size has little to no effect beyond this threshold. Retention was much lower in firms with the largest shares of employees with less than five years of service. The firms with the largest shares of new hires in t − 5 had much lower retention in that tenure bracket, but not in any other. This suggests that some sort of up-or-out contract is used in such firms. The share of very senior employees had no effect on retention rates overall or for any particular group.

CONCLUSIONS AND CAVEATS

One possible reason for the difference between the prevailing wisdom (rising job instability, especially for midcareer workers in large corporations) and the research literature (job stability has not changed all that much) is that the latter has not focused on large firms. This is the first study to use employer data to examine job stability in the 1990s, as well as the first to make distinctions in job stability by employer size and employment growth. We have learned the following:

- Job duration in large corporations continues to be much longer than in the rest of the labor market. This is true for every measure used in this study.

- There was a 61 percent probability that a worker in one of the large firms in our sample would be with the same employer five years later. This is about seven percentage points higher than the odds for the entire labor market reported in Neumark, Polsky, and Hansen (1997). Even in large firms with shrinking employment, the odds that a worker would be with the same employer five years later were higher than the same odds for the labor market as a whole.

- There is no evidence that downsizing decisions adversely affect mid-career employees. To the contrary, retention rates for workers with ten to nineteen years of service are virtually the same in downsizing and growing firms. Retention rates in downsizing firms tend to be lowest among the most junior and most senior employees, as predicted by human capital models.

- Retention rates were much higher in firms with growing employment than in firms with shrinking employment. However, across all downsizing firms, the retention of junior employees is much more strongly affected by the degree of downsizing than the retention of senior employees.

- Firms with the largest pay differentials between younger, junior workers and older, senior workers have lower overall retention rates. However, a careful examination of how compensation profiles relate to retention in particular tenure brackets shows no evidence that such employers are substituting younger for older workers.

Even though employment declined in most of the companies in this study, the picture that emerges here is that jobs in large corporations in the 1990s continue to be much more stable than in the rest of the labor market and that this is especially true for midcareer workers.

This picture is consistent with other research by economists on job duration in that we do not find a sharp downward break during the 1990s. To reconcile our results with the prevailing wisdom is much more difficult. One possibility is that the firms in this study are not totally representative of the firms featured in media accounts: large companies with long-term job attachments and generous pay and benefits packages. Even though we have reported as much information as we can about these firms, and even though some of the firms in our sample have been featured in media accounts of downsizing, ultimately this issue can be resolved only through further research that attempts to replicate and extend the findings of this study.

Another concern is that all of our data are for the 1990s, leaving open the question of how this experience compares to earlier decades. To address this issue, we extracted data for private-sector employees aged sixteen or more from the May 1983 and April 1993 supplements to the Current Population Survey. These supplements were selected because they contain information on firm size and employee benefits. We estimated probit models of the odds of being in a long-term job (ten years or more or twenty years or more of service) and a regression of years of service and used models that included a wide range of independent variables, including indicators of firm size. We found that there was no change between 1983 and 1993 in the differential in length of service between firms with one thousand employees or more and smaller firms or in the firm-size differential in the odds of being in a long-term job. If anything, the coefficients for employers of one thousand or more workers were slightly larger in 1993 than in 1983.

One aspect of job stability that this study does not address is the consequence of mergers and sell-offs. According to data compiled by Securities Data Company reported in the *Economist* (April 18, 1998, 67–69), mergers and acquisitions were at record levels in 1997, when such deals totaled $957 billion, or 12 percent of GDP. This is well above the $138 billion level (2 percent of GDP) in 1991. Merger and acquisition activity in the intervening years ranged between 2 and 8 percent. Although this study cannot address job instability arising from restructuring, we should emphasize that much of the policy and media discussion of the issue have focused on firms that have not gone through mergers.

The other way of reconciling our results with the prevailing wisdom is to recognize that anecdotes are an imperfect substitute for data. We do not question that many individuals, families, and communities were shattered by downsizing experiences in the 1990s. What we question is whether these well-publicized events reflected a widespread shift in the incidence of long-term jobs in large corporations. So far, we have found no evidence of any such shift.

ACKNOWLEDGMENTS

Tomeka Hill, a research associate at Watson Wyatt, provided excellent research assistance in the development of this chapter, which has also been presented at seminars at North Carolina State University and the National Bureau of Economic Research.

NOTES

1. The following quote from the weeklong series "The Downsizing of America" in the *New York Times* (March 3–9, 1996) captures much of today's prevailing wisdom (italics added for emphasis): "More than 43 million jobs have been erased in the United States since 1979. . . . Many of the losses come from the normal churning as stores fail and factories move. And far more jobs have been created than lost over that period. But increasingly the jobs that are disappearing are those of *higher-paid, white-collar workers, many at large corporations,* women as well as men, *many at the peak of their careers.* Like a clicking odometer on a speeding car, the number twirls higher nearly each day. . . . What distinguishes this age are three phenomena: *white-collar workers are big victims; large corporations now account for many of the layoffs; and a large percentage of the jobs are lost to "outsourcing"*—contracting out work to another company, usually within the United States." This series is posted on the world wide web at http://www.nytimes.com/specials/downsize/glance.html.

2. The widely cited *New York Times* report includes a figure showing that the share of laid-off workers under age thirty had fallen from 40 to 25 percent between 1981 to 1983 and 1991 to 1993. The share of laid-off workers aged thirty to fifty rose from 44 to 56 percent.

3. See Cappelli (this volume) for a broader survey and an empirical analysis of which firms were most likely to downsize. His definition of downsizing is narrower than the definition used in this study. His includes firms that reduce employment *and* report no excess capacity prior to the reduction in employment.

4. Ironically, in earlier decades layoff announcements were seen as a signal of corporate distress, and this was the basis for some of the opposition to the Worker Adjustment and Retraining Notification Act (Worrell et al. 1991).

5. Kevin Hallock (1998) found small, *negative* effects of layoff announcements on share prices and no effect on CEO pay. Dan Worrell and his colleagues (1991) found that stock prices go down after layoff announcements; Wayne Cascio, Clifford Young, and James Morris (1997) found that there was no overall effect of downsizing on stock returns, but that firms combining downsizing with asset restructuring received higher returns.

6. Several studies by Watson Wyatt (Schieber and Graig 1995; McDevitt and Schieber 1996) analyze the general aging of the workforce and its implications for the cost and provision of benefits, especially retiree health benefits. The company developed an analytical model, called the Aging Diagnostic, to estimate the cost of aging on compensation costs at the individual-firm level. This tool was applied to data either as a part of routine ongoing work done for Watson Wyatt clients or to make an employer aware of issues raised in the two published reports.

REFERENCES

Belous, Richard. 1989. *The Contingent Economy: The Growth of the Temporary, Part-time, and Subcontracted Workforce.* Washington, D.C.: National Planning Association.

Bluestone, Barry, and Bennett Harrison. 1986. *The Great American Job Machine: The Proliferation of Low-Wage Employment in the American Economy.* Washington: U.S. Government Printing Office.

Cascio, Wayne F., Clifford E. Young, and James R. Morris. 1997. "Financial Consequences of Employment-Change Decisions in Major U.S. Corporations." *Academy of Management Journal* 40(5): 1175–89.

Diebold, Francis, David Neumark, and Daniel Polsky. 1997. "Job Stability in the United States." *Journal of Labor Economics* 15(2): 206–23.

Farber, Henry. 1997. "Trends in Long-term Employment in the United States, 1979–1996." Working paper 384. Princeton, N.J.: Princeton University, Industrial Relations Section.

Gokhale, Jagadeesh, Erica L. Groshen, and David Neumark. 1995. "Do Hostile Takeovers Reduce Extramarginal Wages?: An Establishment-Level Analysis." *Review of Economics and Statistics* 77(3): 470–85.

Hallock, Kevin F. 1998. "Layoffs, Top Executive Pay, and Firm Performance." *American Economic Review* 88(4): 711–23.

Lazear, Edward P. 1979. "Why Is There Mandatory Retirement?" *Journal of Political Economy* 87(6): 1261–84.

———. 1995. *Personnel Economics.* Cambridge, Mass.: MIT Press.

———. 1998. *Personnel Economics for Managers.* New York: Wiley.

McDevitt, Roland, and Sylvester Schieber. 1996. *From Baby Boom to Elder Boom: Providing Health Care for an Aging Population.* Washington, D.C.: Watson Wyatt Worldwide.

McGill, Dan, Kyle Brown, John Haley, and Sylvester Schieber. 1996. *Fundamentals of Private Pensions.* Philadelphia: University of Pennsylvania Press.

Moore, Thomas. 1996. *The Disposable Work Force: Worker Displacement and Employment Instability in America.* New York: Aldine de Gruyter.

Munk, Nina. 1999. "Finished at Forty." *Fortune* 2: 50–66.

Neumark, David, and Daniel Polsky. 1998. "Changes in Job Stability and Job Security: Anecdotes and Evidence." Paper presented at the fiftieth annual meeting of the Industrial Relations Research Association, Chicago(January 1998).

Neumark, David, Daniel Polsky, and Daniel Hansen. 1997. "Has Job Stability Declined Yet?: New Evidence for the 1990s." Working paper 6330. Cambridge, Mass.: National Bureau of Economic Research.

Polsky, Daniel. 1996. "Changes in Consequences of Job Separations in the U.S. Economy." Unpublished paper. University of Pennsylvania, Philadelphia.

Reich, Robert. 1997. *Locked in the Cabinet.* New York: Alfred A. Knopf.

Rose, Stephen. 1995. "Declining Job Security and the Professionalization of Opportunity." Report 95–04. Washington, D.C.: National Commission for Employment Policy (April).

Schieber, Sylvester, and Laurene Graig. 1995. *U.S. Retirement Policy: The Sleeping Giant Awakens.* Washington, D.C.: Watson Wyatt Worldwide.

U.S. Bureau of Labor Statistics. 1997. "Employee Tenure in the Mid-1990s."

Press release (January) posted on the world wide web at http://stats.bls.gov/news.release/tenure.nws.htm.

Worrell, Dan L., Wallace N. Davidson III, and Varinder M. Sharma. 1991. "Layoff Announcements and Stockholder Wealth." *Academy of Management Journal* 34(3): 662–78.

Part II

Job Security

Chapter 7

Declining Job Security

Robert G. Valletta

Popular concern about worker job security has been on the rise in recent years, and it became particularly acute early in the 1996 presidential election campaign. Rising media attention to this issue coincided with and was reinforced by the role of job security in monetary policy formation: Federal Reserve Chairman Alan Greenspan cited worker job security fears as a key factor holding down inflation in 1996 and rising job security as a potential inflationary factor in 1997 and 1998.

Much of the early evidence regarding job insecurity was fragmentary and anecdotal, as newspapers and other popular sources described the impact of major corporate downsizings and changes in workers' perceived job security. The first few academic papers (for example, Farber 1998a; Diebold, Neumark, and Polsky 1997; Swinnerton and Wial 1996) focused on average job tenure or job retention and found that they had been relatively constant for men since the early 1970s, a finding that some observers interpreted as inconsistent with the declining job security view.

However, recent evidence has been more supportive of the view that job security is declining. The U.S. Bureau of Labor Statistics (1997) examined average job tenure within age groups and found that it declined for men between 1983 and 1996. Although changes in the Displaced Workers Survey (DWS) limit the reliability of comparisons over time (Farber 1998b; Polivka 1998), the 1996 DWS revealed relatively high displacement rates due to slack work, abolition of position or shift, or plant closure between 1993 and 1995, particularly for skilled white-collar workers (Valletta 1997; Kletzer 1998). Using data from the Panel Study of Income Dynamics (PSID), Johanne Boisjoly, Greg Duncan, and Timothy Smeeding (1998) found an upward trend in involuntary separations for men with strong labor market attachment during the period 1968 to 1992. In my own study (Valletta 1998), I also found an upward trend in involuntary separations into unemployment during the past several decades, using aggregate time-series data from the Current Population Survey (CPS). None of this previous work, however, has provided any behavioral basis for understanding the economic implications of job

227

security. In this chapter, I provide a behavioral model that fills the gap, and I use panel data to test for declining job security during the period 1976 to 1992.

Formal analysis of changing job security requires that we define the concept in terms of standard economic models of the employment relationship and turnover decisions. Turnover costs and specific investments imply optimality of ongoing employment relationships for wide classes of workers and jobs. The efficient separations view (McLaughlin 1991) of job mobility implies that only inefficient (that is, non-surplus-producing) matches are dissolved, with the resulting turnover benefiting workers and firms. Models with costly or suppressed renegotiation of wages (Hashimoto 1981; Antel 1985; Hall and Lazear 1984; Hall 1995) imply inefficient separations in response to shocks but do not formally elucidate the underlying reasons for such rigidity vis-à-vis permanent separations. Moreover, the efficient separations view has limited implications for changes in turnover behavior and outcomes beyond those caused by productivity shocks that alter the relative value of existing job pairings.

In this chapter, I approach the issue of changing job security by defining and analyzing it in the context of implicit employment contracts designed to overcome incentive problems in the employment relationship. Early efficiency wage variants of such models implied no incentives for employer dishonesty (for example, Shapiro and Stiglitz 1984; Bulow and Summers 1986). Other models, particularly those with rising sequences of wages, include incentives for employer malfeasance but appeal to reputational constraints to eliminate employer malfeasance in equilibrium (see, for example, Lazear 1979; Bull 1987). However, employer malfeasance is not excluded under all conditions. My colleague Todd Idson and I (Idson and Valletta 1996) found evidence suggesting that involuntary separations of high-tenure workers may reflect employer breach of implicit employment arrangements in some circumstances.

For the present work, I use Garey Ramey and Joel Watson's (1997) model of bilateral incentive problems for workers and firms as my theoretical starting point. In this model, the contract is structured to overcome incentives for each party to behave opportunistically, where opportunism entails performing at levels lower than those to which the parties agreed. This situation exhibits properties akin to a "prisoner's dilemma" game: with specific investments, opportunistic behavior may occur in bad states. This causes inefficient separations even when wage renegotiation is unconstrained. Moreover, extending the model by incorporating costly monitoring of worker effort changes firms' incentives regarding opportunistic behavior toward contracted workers.

In the context of such a model, declining "job security" implies that given existing economic conditions, workers who had a reasonable expectation (presumably based on past firm behavior) of not being dismissed are being dismissed. This implies a change in the relationship between contract parameters (such as tenure and economic conditions) and the probability of being dismissed, and also the probability of voluntary quits. I look for such changes in turnover probabilities using data for male household heads and wives from the Panel Study of Income Dynamics for the years 1976 to 1993. I estimate binomial and multinomial models of job separations. The results reveal significant changes over time in the relationship between job tenure and turnover decisions by workers and firms, for male workers and skilled white-collar women. These results appear consistent with secular changes in incentives to maintain ongoing employment relationships.

IMPLICIT CONTRACT MODELS OF JOB SECURITY

CONTRACTS WITH BILATERAL INCENTIVE PROBLEMS

In a world of fully efficient job separations, job security is irrelevant: only matches that produce no joint surplus are dissolved, and their dissolution improves the well-being of both parties. Models with suppressed renegotiation imply the incidence of inefficient separations but do so through the assumption of wage rigidity (Hall 1995; Hall and Lazear 1984).

More promising are models that analyze and provide solutions to incentive problems in the employment relationship. If monitoring is imperfect, workers must be provided with incentives to exert appropriate effort on the job. This consideration motivates the literatures on efficiency wages and deferred payment contracts. Although the latter literature also recognizes the possibility of malfeasance or cheating by the firm (Lazear 1979; Bull 1987), firm and worker malfeasance are not treated in a symmetrical fashion (that is, the primary form of firm cheating is contract termination).

A recent contribution by Ramey and Watson (1997) recognized bilateral incentive problems and treated them in a symmetrical fashion. In addition to the standard worker effort constraint that must be overcome, firms face an incentive to exert a level of effort below that to which the parties agreed; both forms of noncooperation yield a short-run payoff at the expense of dissolution of the job match. Here I describe a simplified version of their model, which I use as a baseline for analyzing general changes in job security and attachment. I will then describe a modification that accounts for costly monitoring of worker behavior.

We proceed by modeling the employment relationship as a strategy game that conforms to a prisoner's dilemma under possible realizations of relevant state variables. In particular, consider the payoff matrix for a given job pairing in a single period presented in table 7.1.

Subscript f identifies employer (firm) variables, and w identifies worker

Table 7.1   Employment Payoffs

	Worker	
Firm	Cooperate	Not cooperate
Cooperate	$\tilde{z}$	y_f, x_w
Not cooperate	x_f, y_w	$0, 0$

variables. Let $\tilde{z} = z_f + z_w$ and $x = x_f + x_w$ (with x_f, $x_w > 0$). In this schema, $\tilde{z}$ is a random variable representing the net return if the worker and firm cooperate; that return is observed at the beginning of the period and divided between them according to a wage agreement. The current period payoffs to unilateral noncooperation are nonstochastic and are denoted as x_f and x_w. The benefit to the worker, x_w, can be interpreted as the utility gain from reducing effort on the job. The benefit to the firm, x_f, can be interpreted as reflecting a similar effort choice by the firm's owner or manager. Alternatively, x_f can be interpreted as the firm's gains from worker reassignment to a less desirable job, reduction of staff, capital support, or other job-related perquisites, or other employer decisions that have a short-run payoff to the firm but reduce the worker's well-being. In this setting, y_f and y_w represent the firm's and the worker's nonstochastic return when the other party does not cooperate. Assume that unilateral selfish behavior reduces joint returns below those associated with the cooperative outcome and bilateral selfish behavior:

$$\tilde{z} > 0 > (x_f + y_w), (y_f + x_w) \tag{7.1}$$

We assume that noncooperative behavior (also referred to as shirking) is detected immediately by both parties, but that cooperation cannot be enforced (even through a third party, such as the courts). Assume further that noncooperation by either party in a period results in dissolution of the relationship at the end of that period.

The key implication of this model is that given the realization of $\tilde{z}$, productive job pairings (such that $\tilde{z} > 0$) can be destroyed even with fully renegotiable wages. In particular, given sufficiently low realizations of $\tilde{z}$, the benefits of noncooperation for individual agents outweigh job rents; under these circumstances, at least one party shirks, producing a separation at the end of the period. In a single period, incentives to dissolve the relationship exist if $\tilde{z} < x_f + x_w$. Under these circumstances, either $z_f < x_f$ or $z_w < x_w$: at least one party's share of the job rents falls below its benefit from shirking. The wage agreement simply determines which party has the incentive to shirk. These basic elements of the model are not altered by extension to a multiperiod setting. Such extension mainly requires the substitution of the expected present value of return streams for the single-period returns; these streams include rents to the current and alternative employment (see Ramey and Watson 1997).

The model is similar to an efficient turnover model in terms of the separation decision; the presence of x simply implies that some separations may be inefficient. However, at this point the model provides only limited insights into the turnover process. The implications are richer—particularly in regard to job security—when we account for firm-specific investments. Assume that employers make an investment (α) in worker productivity when the contract begins; that this investment is fixed (that is, it cannot be altered once production has begun); and that the costs are borne entirely by the firm.[1] Assume further that the returns to α depend on the random realization of a good (G) or bad (B) state, with $z^G (\alpha) > z^B (\alpha) > 0$ (that is, the relationship is productive even in the bad state).

Ramey and Watson (1997) showed that under these circumstances the chosen level of investment produces either *robust* or *fragile* contracts. Under a robust contract, the level of investment and resulting productivity is high enough to preserve the job pairing in both states. Under a fragile contract, the level of investment is inadequate to preserve the job pairing when the bad state arises. Figure 7.1 illustrates the structure of the model and the distinction between robust and fragile contracts. In this figure, w represents the value of outside employment opportunities; points above the forty-five-degree line represent matches that generate a surplus ($z > w$). The investment level corresponding to outcomes G' and B' produces a robust contract, which is maintained in both the good and bad states. In contrast, the lower investment level corresponding to outcomes G and B generates a fragile contract: the employment relationship is dissolved upon realization of the bad state, despite positive rents. This outcome occurs even though there are no restrictions on wage renegotiations. It arises owing to the assumed fixity of the firm-specific investment α, which precludes the reinvestment needed to maintain positive returns in the bad state.[2]

The key point to note is that a robust contract can be interpreted as representing job conditions that entail job security. In particular, under robust contracts the relationship-specific investment is sufficiently high that workers' jobs are maintained in the face of adverse productivity shocks. In contrast, job pairings under fragile contracts are vulnerable to separations under adverse states. Such jobs are productive but not secure.

Which type of contract a firm chooses depends on features of the economic environment. In particular, Ramey and Watson (1997) showed that the incidence of fragile contracts rises as the probability of the bad state falls, increases with the value of shirking (x), and increases with the

Figure 7.1   Robust and Fragile Contracts

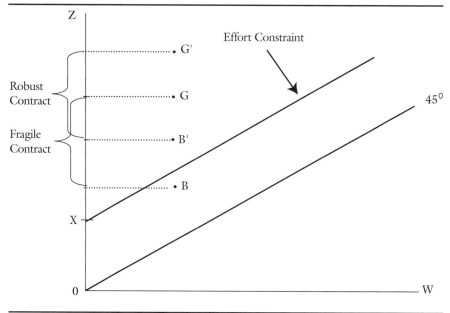

probability of finding an outside job match (which raises the relative value of outside opportunities). Each of these factors may change over time in the real economy, thereby affecting the maintenance of employment contracts. For example, if the economy undergoes a sustained expansion, employers may conclude that the probability of the bad state is low and decide to forgo the costly specific investments needed to maintain the employment relationship when the bad state arises. Such behavior may explain high layoff rates during and after the early 1990s recession, following the lengthy expansion of the 1980s. Alternatively, unexpected changes in key parameters, such as the returns to noncooperative behavior or the value of specific investments, may increase the incidence of fragile contracts.

As in a standard efficient turnover model (for example, McLaughlin 1991), in the Ramey and Watson (1997) model the determination of which party initiates the separation depends only on the rent-sharing agreement (the wage), not on any underlying economic efficiency considerations. Moreover, changes in the underlying determinants of robust and fragile contracts affect the incidence of both employer-initiated ("involuntary") and worker-initiated ("voluntary") turnover. However, the distinction between involuntary and voluntary separations is relevant to the investigation of changing job security, the perception of which is based largely on the incidence of involuntary separations. Thus, in the empirical work I separate out voluntary separations from several categories of involuntary separations. I discuss the exact empirical implications of these model features after first discussing a key extension to the Ramey and Watson model.

Costly Monitoring

An important feature of the Ramey and Watson (1997) model is the assumption that firms detect shirking by workers without cost. This assumption of costless or perfect monitoring is implausible in a wide variety of jobs. I now discuss the implications of relaxing the assumption of costless monitoring. The implications of the alternative assumption—costly monitoring—have been the focus of the efficiency wage and deferred payment contract literatures. As I discuss here, employers' responses to costly monitoring have implications for job security.

Assume that firm profits increase with worker effort, which is observed imperfectly. One scheme to solve the worker motivation problem is to promise to give the worker, near or at the end of his stay at the firm, a bonus financed by the joint value created by the pairing in all periods. This contract possesses features of a deferred payment scheme (such as Lazear 1979) without requiring up-front bonds, which George Akerlof and Lawrence Katz (1989) have argued are infeasible. Moreover, Akerlof and Katz showed that, under assumptions common to deferred payment and efficiency wage models, the optimal wage profile under imperfect monitoring pays the bonus at workers' retirement date. If the discount rate is zero and the worker is risk-neutral, this bonus equals the ratio of the worker's benefit to shirking in a period divided by the probability of detection.[3]

As with any delayed-payment contract, firms face incentives to breach their agreement to pay the bonus, perhaps by dismissing the worker prior to the time it is paid. Reputational costs are the primary constraint on such behavior: firms that promise to pay the bonus and then later refuse to do so face increased labor costs, because workers shirk more frequently or demand higher wages as insurance against such contract breach. Clive Bull (1987) demonstrated that employer commitment to a similar deferred payment scheme is part of a Nash equilibrium outcome if each worker decides whether to exert effort based on whether the firm paid the bonus to the worker immediately preceding him in the hiring sequence. More generally, in operational labor markets workers are likely to assess a firm's reliability based on the treatment of a comparison group of workers.

Because such reputational mechanisms rely on information transmission between workers hired at different times, as well as on information transmission to potential workers, the stability of the resulting equilibrium is sensitive to changes in information flow. In Bull's model, if the firm breaks its agreement with a single worker, all subsequently hired workers shirk. In operational labor markets, information regarding employer breach may be less precise (it is not known with certainty whether the firm truly cheated) but is likely to flow to a wider group of workers than in Bull's model. Under these circumstances, the decision rule regarding the perception of firm breach that workers use is less mechanical than in Bull's model, and the reputational constraints that enforce employer honesty may not always bind. For example, if there is rapid turnover in a firm's labor force owing to changing demand conditions, information about the firm's dismissal policy may be diluted sufficiently to make breach of the implicit agreement profitable for the firm (as in Idson and Valletta 1996). The employer-initiated separations caused by such opportunism raise permanent layoffs above the level required for optimal adjustment to changing demand conditions.[4]

EMPIRICAL IMPLICATIONS

The baseline bilateral incentive model (Ramey and Watson 1997) implies that productive employment relationships are fragile, or insecure, under various realizations of productivity. Moreover, imperfect monitoring of worker performance implies the use of retirement bonuses or delayed wage payments, which add incentives for opportunistic dissolution of the employment relationship by firms.

Although firm-level data might seem ideal for testing the implications of these models, the requisite information on both workers and firms is unavailable in existing firm-level data sets, so I use individual panel data (as described in the next section). I begin by making a key assumption: *In a sample of workers, the proportion of workers employed under robust contracts is higher for groups with higher tenure at their current firm.*

If the Ramey and Watson (1997) model is interpreted strictly, this assumption is tautological under the presence of adverse productivity shocks: workers who remain at the firm over multiple periods receive wage payments that eliminate joint dissolution incentives under all realizations of worker productivity over those periods.

Under this assumption, tenure reduces turnover because it proxies for contracts that have been robust to date. This by itself is not a test of the model.[5] However, we can make a set of predictions regarding interactions between tenure and other variables, the effects of aggregate and sectoral productivity shocks, and changes over time.

1. Changes over time in turnover incidence for high-tenure workers reflect secular changes in economic conditions relevant to the presence of robust and fragile contracts. In particular, a rise in voluntary and involuntary turnover among higher-tenure workers may be attributable to rising returns to noncooperative behavior (x) or increased efficiency in employment matching, both of which increase the incidence of fragile contracts. An increase in fragile contracts also may arise owing to unexpected declines in the value of existing firm-specific investments.

2. Because robust employment contracts withstand negative productivity shocks (which alter workers' value on the current job relative to alternative employment), separations of high-tenure workers should be less sensitive to negative sectoral shocks than separations of low-tenure workers if general contract incentives are maintained. Alternatively, rapid employment change in a worker's sector may relax the reputational constraints that commit firms to delayed-payment employment contracts. If so, sectoral employment decline is likely to reduce the tenure (contracting) effect on involuntary separations.

Incentive-based implicit contracts are likely to be most common among skilled white-collar workers, for whom incentives for noncooperation, obstacles to monitoring, and specific investments may be more significant than they are for lesser-skilled and blue-collar workers. Thus, we might expect to see larger changes in the effects of job security parameters among skilled white-collar workers than among other worker groups. This expectation is consistent with an upward trend in the Displaced Workers Survey since 1990 in the displacement of white-collar workers that is more pronounced than the trend for blue-collar workers (Kletzer 1998).

DATA

I use data from the Panel Study of Income Dynamics for the years 1976 to 1993, combined with March Current Population Survey data for the same and previous years. The PSID provides the requisite information concerning worker and job characteristics for household heads (married and single) for all years, and for wives for all years except 1976 through 1978; this enables the formation of pooled married-single individual samples by sex. The primary sample restriction in each survey year is to workers age twenty-one to sixty-four who are not self-employed. I excluded the Survey of Economic Opportunity low-income oversample.

The data set combines information on worker and job characteristics in survey year t (employed individuals only) with information from survey year t + 1 regarding whether the worker still works at the same firm as in year t. The observations used therefore end in survey year 1992 but incorporate job change information through 1993.

Key variables for the analysis are measures of the incidence of and reason for changing firms, and years of tenure at the current firm.[6] To measure turnover, I relied on the responses to questions concerning why respondents no longer have the job that was identified in the previous survey. For individuals who are not working for the same firm as in the previous year (excluding those on temporary layoff), the four reasons identified in the survey are: quit; permanently laid off or fired (what I term "dismissed");[7] plant closed; other reasons (mainly the ending of a temporary or seasonal job). Tenure at the current firm is measured in months, which I converted to years. As discussed by other researchers, this variable is subject to substantial error (Topel 1991; Brown and Light 1992). I corrected tenure by assuming that its value in a base year was correct and then forcing tenure to be consistent within and across the job spells identified by the job change variables.[8]

I tabulated measures of economic conditions in workers' industry or region sector using data from the March Current Population Surveys for various years. In particular, I calculated the change in sector employment levels for the ten-year periods preceding the sample frame and used it as a measure of sectoral conditions relevant to job security (as in Idson and Valletta 1996).[9] The sectors are defined by respondents' industry and the geographic location of their current residence. I use 43 detailed industry categories and 9 geographic division categories, which produces 387 sectors.[10] As a measure of aggregate economic conditions, I use the official national unemployment rate in each year.

Restriction to nonmissing values of regression model variables yields pooled samples of 24,163 for men (1976 to 1992) and 16,971 for women (1981 to 1992).[11] Table 7.2 lists descriptive statistics for the full male and female samples. Table 7.3 shows tabulations of average job tenure and turnover rates (total and by reason) for men and women in the regression samples, for selected years that span the sample period. Average job tenure was virtually constant for men over the period, with a slightly higher value in 1982. In contrast, average tenure for women increased noticeably between 1982 and 1991. These tabulations are reasonably consistent with the findings of Francis Diebold, David Neumark, and Daniel Polsky (1997) and Henry Farber (1998a).

For both men and women, table 7.3 reveals substantial year-to-year variability in turnover rates that swamps any trends over time. Quits account for the largest share of turnover incidence in general, and they demonstrate a substantial cyclical pattern, with high rates during

Table 7.2 Summary Statistics (Means and Standard Deviations) for the PSID Sample

Variable	Men, 1976 to 1992 (Household Heads)	Women, 1981 to 1992 (Wives and Single Heads)
Completed grade six, seven, or eight	0.038 (0.193)	0.018 (0.133)
Completed grade nine, ten, or eleven	0.116 (0.320)	0.087 (0.281)
Completed high school	0.222 (0.415)	0.311 (0.463)
Completed some college	0.344 (0.474)	0.347 (0.476)
College graduate	0.183 (0.386)	0.167 (0.373)
Graduate school	0.090 (0.287)	0.069 (0.253)
Years of full-time work experience since age eighteen	14.01 (10.83)	9.32 (8.75)
Government employment	0.202 (0.402)	0.245 (0.430)
Union membership	0.243 (0.429)	0.135 (0.341)
Nonwhite	0.083 (0.276)	0.103 (0.304)
Married	0.862 (0.345)	0.762 (0.426)
Number of children	1.11 (1.18)	0.963 (1.10)
MSA residence	0.680 (0.467)	0.673 (0.469)
Real hourly wage at current job (1992 dollars)	17.18 (16.60)	12.43 (16.32)
Fired	0.038 (0.191)	0.025 (0.156)
Quit	0.102 (0.302)	0.141 (0.348)
Changed job for other reasons	0.025 (0.155)	0.022 (0.148)
Plant closed	0.015 (0.121)	0.013 (0.115)
Aggregate U.S. unemployment rate	0.070 (0.013)	0.070 (0.014)
Tenure (years at current firm)	7.76 (8.44)	5.44 (5.65)
Percentage change in sector employment, previous ten years (from March CPS)	0.117 (0.356)	0.228 (0.264)
Number of observations	24,163	16,971

Note: Standard deviations in parentheses.

Table 7.3 Average Tenure and Turnover Rates, PSID Data (Selected Years)

Year	Average Tenure	Changed Jobs	Quit	Dismissed	Plant Closed	Other Reasons	Sample Size
Men (household heads)							
1976	7.766	0.150	0.081	0.026	0.015	0.028	1,408
1979	7.786	0.159	0.095	0.032	0.015	0.017	1,512
1982	8.115	0.172	0.058	0.062	0.015	0.038	1,543
1985	7.703	0.211	0.119	0.035	0.019	0.039	1,580
1988	7.632	0.178	0.123	0.032	0.014	0.010	1,614
1991	7.749	0.152	0.079	0.043	0.012	0.019	1,562
Women (wives and single household heads)							
1976	n.a.	n.a.	n.a.	n.a.	n.a.	n.a.	n.a.
1979	n.a.	n.a.	n.a.	n.a.	n.a.	n.a.	n.a.
1982	5.043	0.156	0.075	0.036	0.018	0.027	1,246
1985	5.175	0.240	0.175	0.026	0.014	0.024	1,381
1988	5.471	0.211	0.161	0.023	0.015	0.013	1,485
1991	6.045	0.174	0.118	0.026	0.011	0.019	1,516

Note: The sample is initially restricted to employed individuals, aged twenty-one to sixty-four and not self-employed in the survey year. The sample is further restricted to individuals with nonmissing values of the regression model variables (see table 7.4).

ongoing expansions (1985 and 1988) and reduced rates during recessions (1982 and 1991). Dismissals are less frequent than quits, but they appear to demonstrate a countercyclical pattern, as we might expect. The incidence of job loss due to plant closings and other reasons does not show any noticeable pattern over time or the business cycle.

EMPIRICAL ANALYSIS

FRAMEWORK

My empirical analysis consists of probit equations for the probability of dismissals (permanent layoffs and firings) and general turnover and multinomial logit models of alternative types of separation. I first focus on probit equations for the incidence of dismissals—the outcome that is most relevant to the general perception of job insecurity. I estimate the following basic probit equation for dismissal incidence D:

$$\Pr(D_{it} = 1) = H_{it}\beta + U_t^a\gamma_1 + T_{it}\gamma_2 + \Delta E_{it}^s\gamma_3 \\ + t\gamma_4 + (t \cdot T_{it})\lambda_1 + (\Delta E_{it}^s \cdot T_{it})\lambda_2 \quad (7.2)$$

In this equation, i indexes individuals, t indexes time, and the Greek letters (except Δ) denote coefficients to be estimated. The matrix H represents a relatively standard set of human capital and other control variables: educational attainment (six category dummies), years of full-time work experience since age eighteen and its square, number of children, ln(real hourly wage at the current job),[12] and dummy variables for government employment, union membership, nonwhite, marital status, and residence in a Metropolitan Statistical Area (MSA). These variables are intended to control for workers' general productivity and job prospects. The other variables are the aggregate unemployment rate U^a, job tenure T, sector employment growth ΔE^S, a time trend variable t, and tenure interacted with the time trend and with sector employment growth.[13]

The focus on dismissals is appropriate in a study of changing job security, because involuntary separations have clear implications for popular perceptions of rising job insecurity. I also estimate probit models of general turnover (job change for any reason); because job stability and retention in general have been the focus of other recent work in this area (see, for example, Diebold, Neumark, and Polsky 1997; Polsky 1999), these results provide a useful baseline for comparison. Finally, to provide more details regarding the sources of turnover, I estimate multinomial logit models using a dependent variable that takes on four values defined by the four job change categories (with no change as the omitted category) and independent variables identical to those in the dismissal and turnover probits. This model enables testing of related hypotheses regarding voluntary and involuntary turnover. In particular, although dismissal outcomes

Table 7.4 Probit Regressions for Dismissals

Variable	Men, 1976 to 1992 (Household Heads)		Women, 1981 to 1992 (Wives and Single Heads)	
	(1)	(2)	(3)	(4)
ln(real hourly wage)	−0.175**	−0.176**	−0.098*	−0.098*
	(0.035)	(0.035)	(0.045)	(0.045)
U.S. unemployment rate	5.467**	5.520**	5.654**	5.510**
	(1.309)	(1.315)	(2.027)	(2.031)
Tenure	−0.052**	−0.084**	−0.061**	−0.091**
	(0.004)	(0.010)	(0.007)	(0.024)
Time trend	0.0095*	−0.0022	0.013	0.0040
	(0.0039)	(0.0049)	(0.008)	(0.0100)
Tenure × (time trend)	—	0.0031**	—	0.0026
	—	(0.0008)	—	(0.0018)
Δln(sector employment)[a]	0.014	0.094	0.080	0.108
	(0.045)	(0.057)	(0.079)	(0.102)
Tenure × (Δln(sector employment))	—	−0.020*	—	−0.010
	—	(0.009)	—	(0.023)
Log-likelihood	−3,522.9	−3,513.9	−1,851.4	−1,850.2
Pseudo-R^2	0.094	0.097	0.063	0.064
Number of observations	24,163	24,163	16,971	16,971

Note: Standard errors in parentheses. Dependent Variable = 1 if Laid-Off-Fired; 0 Otherwise. Other variables controlled for include educational attainment (six category dummies), years of full-time work experience since age eighteen and its square, number of children, and dummy variables for government employment, union membership, nonwhite, marital status, and MSA residence.

[a] A total of 387 sectors defined by 43 industry categories and 9 geographic regions.

* Significant at the .05 level.

** Significant at the .01 level.

are most relevant for the perception of rising job insecurity, the Ramey and Watson (1997) model suggests that both voluntary and involuntary turnover will respond to changes in underlying contract parameters.

RESULTS

Table 7.4 displays results from probit analyses of dismissal incidence, using the pooled samples of men (columns 1 and 2) and women (columns 3 and 4). The estimated coefficients for the general control variables are unsurprising and therefore are omitted from the tables (with the exception of the wage variable). Columns 1 and 3 in table 7.4 list results for models without interactions; columns 2 and 4 include interactions between job tenure—which serves as a proxy for contracts—a time trend, and sector employment growth.

Turning first to the control coefficients for men and women, the hourly wage variable has a strong and consistent negative effect across the various specifications. This presumably reflects unobserved factors that enhance the productivity of individual job matches. Dismissals increase substantially with the aggregate unemployment rate, but they decline substantially with job tenure. The effects of these variables are large, particularly for job tenure. Using the coefficients for men in column 1, five additional years of tenure reduce the dismissal probability by nearly half for the typical male in the sample. By comparison, a one-standard-deviation increase in the log hourly wage or a decrease in aggregate unemployment reduces the male dismissal probability by about 20 percent.

For the male sample in columns 1 and 2, several interesting results are apparent in regard to the sensitivity of employment relationships over time. The first column reveals a significant upward time trend in the probability of dismissals. However, inclusion of the interaction between tenure and time in column 2 reveals that the upward time trend is concentrated among high-tenure workers: the coefficient on the interaction variable is significant, and its inclusion substantially reduces the size and precision of the estimated time trend effect alone. This result suggests that male workers with substantial job tenure—that is, workers whose jobs are most likely to be characterized by incentive-based, implicit employment contracts—faced rising risks of dismissal from 1976 to 1992. This reduction in the tenure effect over time is large. The coefficient on the interaction between tenure and time in column 2 implies a reduction in the tenure effect of approximately 60 percent during the sixteen years ending in 1992. This increase in the probability that high-tenure male workers will be fired is consistent with erosion over time in the incentives to maintain ongoing employment relationships.

The other key contract model variable—the interaction between tenure and the change in sector employment—also produces interesting re-

Table 7.5 Probit Regressions for Turnover, All Types

Variable	Men, 1976 to 1992 (Household Heads)		Women, 1981 to 1992 (Wives and Single Heads)	
	(1)	(2)	(3)	(4)
ln(real hourly wage)	-0.268**	-0.270**	-0.187**	-0.187**
	(0.021)	(0.022)	(0.023)	(0.023)
U.S. unemployment rate	1.365	1.510	-2.774*	-2.827*
	(0.832)	(0.835)	(1.109)	(1.110)
Tenure	-0.038**	-0.061**	-0.057**	-0.062**
	(0.002)	(0.004)	(0.003)	(0.010)
Time trend	0.0035	-0.0093**	0.0033	0.0001
	(0.0024)	(0.0030)	(0.0044)	(0.0054)
Tenure × (time trend)	—	0.0024**	—	0.0008
		(0.0003)		(0.0008)
Δln(sector employment)[a]	0.077**	0.162**	0.192**	0.262**
	(0.029)	(0.037)	(0.044)	(0.057)
Tenure × (Δln(sector employment))	—	-0.015**	—	-0.019
		(0.004)		(0.010)
Log-likelihood	-10,401.6	-10,373.3	-7,891.1	-7,888.7
Pseudo-R^2	0.085	0.087	0.075	0.075
Number of observations	24,163	24,163	16,971	16,971

Note: Standard errors in parentheses. Dependent Variable = 1 if Changed Employer; 0 Otherwise. Other variables controlled for are the same as in table 7.4.

[a] A total of 387 sectors defined by 43 industry categories and 9 geographic regions.

* Significant at the .05 level.

** Significant at the .01 level.

sults in the male sample. The effect of sector employment growth by itself essentially is zero (column 1). However, this masks variation in the effect of sector growth across workers at different tenure levels. In particular, the significant negative effect of the interaction between tenure and sector growth (column 2) implies that the negative tenure effect on dismissal probabilities is reinforced in expanding sectors. Equivalently, the negative tenure effect on dismissals is reduced in declining sectors—in other words, high-tenure (contracted) workers are more likely to be dismissed in declining sectors. Assuming that sectoral decline impedes the transmission of information regarding employer default on delayed-payment contracts, this result suggests that contracted workers face increased risk of employer default in declining industries. This finding is consistent with the results that Todd Idson and I (Idson and Valletta 1996) obtained regarding the tenure pattern in recall from temporary layoff. The magnitude of the default parameter, however, is small compared to the tenure coefficient; the tenure effect for men is reduced noticeably only in sectors that experience excessive shrinkage.[14]

In contrast to men, the results for women in panels 3 and 4 of table 7.4 reveal no apparent changes or sensitivity in employment contract conditions. In particular, no significant interaction effects between tenure and the time trend or sector employment growth are evident. This finding is consistent with the general perception that changing job security primarily is an issue for male workers. However, declining job security also may be an issue for women in skilled white-collar jobs; I return to this point later.

Table 7.5 displays results for general turnover models. These differ from the dismissal regressions in table 7.4 only in their dependent variable, which takes the value one if job change occurred for any reason and the value zero otherwise. As in the dismissal regressions, increases in job tenure and the wage significantly reduce the probability of job change. However, the effect of the aggregate unemployment rate on net turnover is insignificantly different from zero in the male sample.

No significant time trend effect on general turnover is evident for the male and female samples in columns 1 and 3 of table 7.5. This finding of no general time trend in net turnover is consistent with the job stability findings of Diebold, Neumark, and Polsky (1997). It also is largely consistent with the findings of Polsky (1999), who used PSID data but identified job-changers using information on changes in position tenure rather than the direct job change questions that I use. In column 2, the coefficient on the interaction between tenure and time indicates that the column 1 results mask a significant upward time trend in turnover among high-tenure male workers; that upward trend offsets a downward trend in turnover among low-tenure male workers. Once again, no similar trend effects are evident in the female sample. These results suggest that al-

Table 7.6   Multinomial Logit Regression by Reason for Job Change, Men 1976 to 1992

Variable	Quit	Plant Closed	Other Reason	Dismissed
ln(real hourly wage)	−0.562**	−0.423**	−0.175	−0.486**
	(0.050)	(0.119)	(0.090)	(0.081)
U.S. unemployment rate	−6.649**	2.479	21.988**	11.419**
	(1.924)	(4.534)	(3.262)	(2.839)
Tenure	−0.127**	−0.086**	−0.068**	−0.221**
	(0.012)	(0.019)	(0.020)	(0.025)
Time trend	−0.0218**	−0.0244	0.0108	−0.0084
	(0.0066)	(0.0162)	(0.0133)	(0.0105)
Tenure × (time trend)	0.0058**	0.0039*	−0.0046*	0.0077**
	(0.0009)	(0.0017)	(0.0021)	(0.0021)
Δln(sector employment)[a]	0.333**	0.459*	−0.022	0.286*
	(0.082)	(0.189)	(0.158)	(0.123)
Tenure × (Δln(sector	−0.027*	−0.053**	−0.005	−0.061**
employment))	(0.012)	(0.018)	(0.025)	(0.023)
Log-likelihood = −14929.6				
Pseudo-R^2 = 0.082				
Number of observations = 24,163				

Note: Standard errors in parentheses. Other variables controlled for are the same as in table 7.4.

[a] A total of 387 sectors defined by 43 industry categories and 9 geographic regions.

* Significant at the .05 level.

** Significant at the .01 level.

though overall job stability has not changed, high-tenure male workers became increasingly likely to change jobs between 1976 and 1992.

Table 7.6 expands on the net turnover results by presenting multinomial logit results for turnover by type, using a specification that otherwise conforms to column 2 of table 7.4; I focus on the male sample because tables 7.4 and 7.5 indicated no contract effects for women. Higher hourly wages reduce turnover, except turnover for "other reasons." Rising aggregate unemployment reduces quits and increases turnover due to dismissals and other reasons but has no effect on job loss due to plant closures. All forms of turnover decline with job tenure. The magnitudes of these effects in the quit and dismissal equations are large. For the typical man in the sample, five additional years of tenure reduce quit and dismissal probabilities by just under 25 percent and 50 percent, respectively (evaluated at the midpoint of the sample period). A standard deviation increase in log hourly wages reduces these probabilities by 20 to 25 percent, and a standard deviation decline in the unemployment rate raises quit probabilities and reduces dismissal probabilities by just under 10 percent and 15 percent, respectively.

The most interesting results in table 7.6 concern time trends in the incidence of quits and dismissals for high-tenure workers. The coefficient on the interaction between tenure and time in the dismissal column confirms that high-tenure male workers became increasingly likely to be dismissed over the sample period, with a similar result in the quit column. As with the male dismissal probit results in table 7.4, these results are consistent with rising returns to noncooperative behavior (x in the theoretical model); those rising returns, in turn, increase the incentive for workers and firms to dissolve productive employment relationships (which are indexed by tenure).

Table 7.6 also reveals significant interactions between tenure and the time trend in their effects on job loss due to plant closures and other reasons. High-tenure workers have been increasingly likely to lose their jobs due to plant closures. This suggests that the erosion of contract incentives may have affected the pattern of plant closures, perhaps through disproportionate closure of plants with a large share of high-tenure workers. The interaction effect between tenure and time is not uniform for all job change categories, however; it is negative and significant in the "other reasons" category, suggesting that the positive interaction effects in other parts of the model are not merely an odd (but consistent) artifact of the data.[15]

The coefficients on sector employment growth in table 7.6 are significant in the "quit," "plant closed," and "dismissal" segments of the multinomial logit equation. However, the underlying effect of sector employment growth is masked somewhat by its interaction with tenure. When the coefficients on sector employment growth are evaluated at the mean value of tenure, sector employment growth significantly increases quits but has no effect on the other turnover probabilities. The positive effect on quits is consistent with improving outside employment opportunities for workers employed in expanding sectors, although the negative effect of the interaction between tenure and sector employment growth suggests that high-tenure workers do not fully share in this pattern.

As I noted earlier, trends in job security stemming from changing incentives to maintain long-term employment contracts are likely to be most pronounced in skilled white-collar jobs, in which incentive and monitoring difficulties are likely to be most severe. Tables 7.7 and 7.8 present results from regressions that test this proposition, for both men and women. I excluded workers in sales and service occupations because these occupations are less likely to be characterized by the relevant model features (specific investments and costly monitoring) than are other white-collar jobs. In the first panel, the results for men are very similar to those reported for the full male sample, using a probit specification that otherwise corresponds to column 2 in table 7.4 and a multinomial logit

Table 7.7   Probit (Dismissals) and Multinomial Logit (All Turnover), Male Household Heads, White-Collar Workers Only (Excluding Sales and Service Occupations), 1976 to 1992

	Probit	Multinomial Logit			
Variable	Dismissed	Quit	Plant Closed	Other Reason	Dismissed
ln(real hourly wage)	−0.216**	−0.530**	−0.367*	−0.346*	−0.644**
	(0.060)	(0.072)	(0.176)	(0.147)	(0.143)
U.S. unemployment rate	4.120	−2.214	−2.045	27.898**	9.092
	(2.471)	(2.866)	(7.483)	(5.177)	(5.785)
Tenure	−0.107**	−0.101**	−0.096**	−0.101**	−0.289**
	(0.020)	(0.016)	(0.032)	(0.031)	(0.053)
Time trend	−0.0004	0.0037	−0.0214	−0.0166	−0.0059
	(0.0091)	(0.0103)	(0.0264)	(0.0211)	(0.0209)
Tenure × (time trend)	0.0063**	0.0035**	0.0025	−0.0002	0.0166**
	(0.0014)	(0.0013)	(0.0030)	(0.0031)	(0.0037)
Δln(sector employment)[a]	0.247*	0.435**	0.132	−0.427	0.643*
	(0.109)	(0.127)	(0.313)	(0.257)	(0.253)
Tenure × (Δln(sector employment))	−0.023	−0.043**	0.005	0.041	−0.062
	(0.014)	(0.015)	(0.036)	(0.039)	(0.033)
Log-likelihood	−1,047.3	−6,024.4			
Pseudo-R^2	0.089	0.077			
Number of observations = 11,108					

Note: Standard errors in parentheses. Other variables controlled for are the same as in table 7.4.

[a] A total of 387 sectors defined by 43 industry categories and 9 geographic regions.

*Significant at the .05 level.

**Significant at the .01 level.

specification corresponding to table 7.6. The interaction between tenure and time has a larger effect on dismissal probabilities here than it did in the full sample: the negative tenure effect on dismissals of white-collar male workers is almost completely eliminated during the sixteen years ending in 1992. In contrast to the full-sample results, however, the interaction of tenure and sector employment growth has a smaller effect on dismissal probabilities, and the coefficients on these interactions are imprecisely estimated.

In table 7.8, the coefficients on the interaction between tenure and time indicate a significant upward time trend in dismissals and quits for skilled white-collar female workers with substantial job tenure. This contrasts with the dismissal results for the full female sample in table 7.4, and it suggests that declining job security is an issue for women in skilled jobs where they have an established presence. As with the results for men, no significant interaction effects between tenure and sector employment

Table 7.8   Probit (Dismissals) and Multinomial Logit (All Turnover),
Female Wives and Single Heads, White-Collar Workers Only
(Excluding Sales and Service Occupations), 1981 to 1992

	Probit	Multinomial Logit			
Variable	Dismissed	Quit	Plant Closed	Other Reason	Dismissed
ln(real hourly	−0.170**	−0.426**	−0.124	−0.065	−0.487**
wage)	(0.060)	(0.062)	(0.176)	(0.131)	(0.148)
U.S. unemploy-	7.058**	−11.939**	1.041	16.505	14.313*
ment rate	(2.507)	(2.662)	(8.191)	(6.020)	(5.859)
Tenure	−0.156**	−0.180**	−0.085	0.006	−0.493**
	(0.034)	(0.033)	(0.093)	(0.064)	(0.098)
Time trend	0.005	−0.017	−0.013	0.043	0.001
	(0.012)	(0.013)	(0.041)	(0.030)	(0.029)
Tenure × (time	0.0072**	0.0058*	−0.0054	−0.0097	0.0228**
trend)	(0.0023)	(0.0024)	(0.0071)	(0.0052)	(0.0065)
Δln(sector employ-	0.275*	0.441**	−0.004	0.787*	0.693*
ment)[a]	(0.134)	(0.144)	(0.445)	(0.333)	(0.313)
Tenure ×	0.007	−0.026	0.071	0.079	0.028
(Δln(sector em-	(0.031)	(0.031)	(0.094)	(0.074)	(0.084)
ployment))					
Log-likelihood	−1,210.7	−7,660.3			
Pseudo-R^2	0.081	0.076			
Number of observations = 12,480					

Note: Standard errors in parentheses. Other variables controlled for are the same as in table 7.4.

[a] A total of 387 sectors defined by 43 industry categories and 9 geographic regions.

*Significant at the .05 level.

**Significant at the .01 level.

growth are evident for women. Overall, tables 7.7 and 7.8 present mixed support for the claim that changing job security parameters have been particularly important for skilled white-collar workers: they appear to face the largest erosion in basic contract incentives, but there is little evidence for greater employer contract breach despite the greater likelihood of delayed-payment wage profiles in such jobs.

SENSITIVITY TO MEASUREMENT PROBLEMS

As described earlier, my turnover variables rely on the direct information on job change available in the PSID. However, several key survey changes noted by other analysts (for example, Diebold, Neumark, and Polsky 1997; Polsky 1999; Schmidt and Svorny 1998) may bias my measurement of job change over time. First, before 1984 PSID respondents were asked the "reason for job change" question only if they indicated that they had been in their present employment position for less than twelve months. After 1984 the two questions were delinked. Thus, prior to 1984 measured job change in the PSID may be contaminated by errors in position tenure responses. Second, between 1984 and 1987, the "reason for job change" question referred to a longer reference period (since the beginning of the previous calendar year) than in all other years (since the last survey). Measured job change in the period from 1984 to 1987 may thus be inflated; the high rate of job change in 1985 displayed in table 7.3 is consistent with this interpretation.

Moreover, as discussed by Polsky (1999), up until survey year 1984 the position tenure responses exhibited substantial heaping (clumping) at multiples of six months, owing to rounding by respondents. This heaping was eliminated beginning in 1984, when the position tenure information was changed from a "months in position" basis to a "start date" basis. Because respondents were not asked the job change question if they indicated twelve or more months of position tenure prior to 1984, the tendency for responses to heap at twelve months (through rounding up) may reduce measured job change prior to 1984. Regression results may be biased in turn toward finding increasing job change over time in samples that include pre- and post-1984 data.

These data problems probably have little impact on my key results. First, although these problems are likely to affect the time trend, there is no reason why they should affect the interactions between tenure and time or tenure and sector employment growth. Second, the longer reference period for job change during survey years 1984 to 1987 (1983 to 1986 in my data) falls near the middle of my sample frame and therefore is unlikely to bias the estimated interaction effect of the time trend and tenure. Finally, the time trend alone is insignificantly different from zero in the probit regressions for all types of turnover reported in table 7.5. This result is broadly comparable to the findings of Polsky (1999), whose measure of job change is based on changes in position tenure (corrected for heaping) and therefore is not affected by the measurement problems listed earlier.

Beyond these a priori considerations, I directly investigated the sensitivity of my results to these changes over time in the measurement of turnover in the PSID. Although my job change variables can be adjusted so that they are not affected by the skip pattern prior to 1984 and the longer reference period during 1984 to 1987, the presence of heaping in the position tenure responses prior to 1984 is more problematic. Indeed, this problem cannot be corrected through any direct adjustments to the job change information in the PSID. Therefore, my key sensitivity tests are based on replicating my previous specifications using a sample restricted to the years 1983 to 1992. This sample uses job change information for survey years 1984 to 1993; during these years, the position ten-

Table 7.9   Probit Regressions for Dismissals, Years 1983 to 1992

Variable	Men, 1983 to 1992 (Household Heads)		Women, 1983 to 1992 (Wives and Single Heads)	
	(1)	(2)	(3)	(4)
ln(real hourly wage)	−0.160**	−0.156**	−0.123*	−0.123*
	(0.041)	(0.041)	(0.051)	(0.051)
U.S. unemployment rate	1.803	1.436	5.295*	5.043*
	(1.992)	(2.006)	(2.329)	(2.341)
Tenure	−0.045**	−0.061**	−0.060**	−0.083**
	(0.004)	(0.010)	(0.007)	(0.018)
Time trend	0.0043	−0.0097	0.0244*	0.0130
	(0.0085)	(0.0106)	(0.0096)	(0.0124)
Tenure × (time trend)	—	0.0032*	—	0.0034
		(0.0014)		(0.0023)
Δln(sector employment)[a]	0.043	0.223**	0.101	0.079
	(0.064)	(0.079)	(0.089)	(0.117)
Tenure × (Δln(sector employment))	—	−0.040**	—	0.008
		(0.010)		(0.027)
Log-likelihood	−2,291.6	−2,282.0	−1,502.7	−1,501.6
Pseudo-R^2	0.086	0.090	0.066	0.067
Number of observations	15,905	15,905	14,536	14,536

Note: Standard errors in parentheses. Dependent Variable = 1 if Laid-Off or Fired; 0 Otherwise. Other variables controlled for are the same as in table 7.4.

[a] A total of 387 sectors defined by 43 industry categories and 9 geographic regions.

*Significant at the .05 level.

**Significant at the .01 level.

ure and job change questions were not linked, and heaping in the position tenure responses is not an issue.[16]

Tables 7.9 and 7.10 present results for this restricted sample; besides the restriction to the years 1983 to 1992, the regressions reported in these tables are dismissal and general turnover probits that are identical to those reported in tables 7.4 and 7.5. Despite a significant negative time trend in general turnover for men (table 7.10, column 1), the key coefficients in column 2 of tables 7.9 and 7.10—on the interactions between tenure and time, and between tenure and sector employment growth—are virtually identical to those in the full male sample (column 2, tables 7.4 and 7.5). For women, the key results from this restricted sample also are similar to those from the full sample, although women on average faced an upward trend in dismissals (table 7.9, column 3) during this later period that is not evident for the full period (table 7.4, column 3). Overall, regressions using this restricted sample period suggest that my key results are not sensitive to changes in the measurement of turnover in the PSID.[17]

Table 7.10 Probit Regressions for Turnover, All Types, Years 1983 to 1992

Variable	Men, 1983 to 1992 (Household Heads)		Women, 1983 to 1992 (Wives and Single Heads)	
	(1)	(2)	(3)	(4)
ln(real hourly wage)	−0.284**	−0.283**	−0.206**	−0.206**
	(0.025)	(0.025)	(0.025)	(0.025)
U.S. unemployment rate	−1.382	−1.476	−1.792	−1.921
	(1.227)	(1.229)	(1.238)	(1.239)
Tenure	−0.034**	−0.044**	−0.056**	−0.065**
	(0.002)	(0.004)	(0.003)	(0.007)
Time trend	−0.030**	−0.044**	−0.012*	−0.021**
	(0.005)	(0.006)	(0.005)	(0.007)
Tenure × (time trend)	—	0.0024**	—	0.0020*
		(0.0006)		(0.0009)
Δln(sector employment)[a]	0.035	0.187**	0.203**	0.252**
	(0.040)	(0.051)	(0.048)	(0.063)
Tenure × (Δln(sector employment))	—	−0.025**	—	−0.013
		(0.005)		(0.011)
Log-likelihood	−7,051.6	−7,033.0	−6,855.6	−6,852.6
Pseudo-R^2	0.084	0.087	0.079	0.079
Number of observations	15,905	15,905	14,536	14,536

Note: Standard errors in parentheses. Dependent Variable = 1 if Changed Employer; 0 Otherwise. Other variables controlled for are the same as in table 7.4.

[a] A total of 387 sectors defined by 43 industry categories and 9 geographic regions.

*Significant at the .05 level.

**Significant at the .01 level.

CONCLUSIONS

I discussed the implications for changing job security of a general employment contracting framework that accounts for performance incentive problems for workers and firms, combined with imperfect monitoring of worker performance. Under these circumstances, incentives to maintain existing employment relationships may change over time and be responsive to measures of economic conditions.

Using data from the Panel Study of Income Dynamics for the years 1976 to 1993, I found evidence consistent with declining employment security—for all men, and for skilled white-collar women—in the context of such a model. In particular, the negative effect of job tenure on the probability of dismissals has weakened over time, as has the corresponding negative effect on quits. The implied increase in turnover of high-tenure male workers is consistent with the recent findings of Neumark, Polsky, and Hansen (this volume), Jaeger and Stevens (this volume), and Boisjoly, Duncan, and Smeeding (1998). Furthermore, my results for men indicate that the negative tenure effect on dismissal probabilities is reduced by employment decline in workers' current industry. I interpret this result as being consistent with employer default on delayed-payment employment contracts (as in Idson and Valletta 1996). These results are relatively insensitive to the changes in the PSID survey that have affected the measurement of job change over time.

My results do not support unambiguous conclusions regarding the source of declining job attachment. This limitation partially reflects the trade-off between model breadth and precision of empirical predictions: the model is sufficiently broad to explain a variety of changes in turnover behavior, but precise tests require better empirical analogs to the model parameters. In general, the declining attachment of high-tenure workers is broadly consistent with rising returns to noncooperative behavior in employment relationships (perhaps through rising on-the-job search) or unexpected declines in the value of job-specific investments. My results regarding interaction effects between sectoral economic conditions and tenure in the determination of dismissal probabilities suggest that employers may be breaching deferred payment compensation schemes. However, the absence of a stronger result for white-collar workers, for whom such contracts are likely to be more prevalent owing to high monitoring costs, weakens support for this view.

This chapter was primarily motivated by recent results from the Displaced Workers Survey suggesting that the rate of involuntary job loss was high during the period 1993 to 1995, and by the view of some policymakers that rising job insecurity exerted a moderating influence on wage and price inflation in 1996 (for evidence, see Aaronson and Sullivan 1998). Although constraints on available data precluded extending my model to this recent period, I identified a long-run trend toward declining job security that probably continued through 1996. Extending the analysis to later years of data should prove to be particularly interesting.

ACKNOWLEDGMENTS

I thank Randy O'Toole and Ken Fujii for indispensable research assistance, without implicating them for any mistakes. I received helpful comments from Steve Allen, David Neumark, Dan Sullivan, Tom Buchmueller, Anne Polivka, and seminar participants at the University of California at Santa Cruz, the Public Policy Institute of California, the University of California at Berkeley, and the Russell Sage Foundation Conference on Job Security and Stability. The opinions expressed in this chapter do not necessarily represent the views of the Federal Reserve Bank of San Francisco or the Federal Reserve System.

NOTES

1. Incorporating contractibility of the investment (that is, shared costs) does not change the results.

2. After adding a matching market to their model, Ramey and Watson (1997) simulate its business cycle properties and find that the impact of productivity shocks (the distribution of which is random across firms) is greatly magnified by the resulting destruction of productive employment relationships.

3. With a nonzero discount rate, this quantity increases by an amount proportional to the discount rate and the time remaining from the worker's shirk decision until retirement.

4. Similar opportunism has been discussed in other contexts. Andrei Shleifer and Lawrence Summers (1988) argued that hostile takeovers may entail opportunistic dissolution of implicit employment agreements with the targeted firm's workers. Gokhale, Groshen, and Neumark's (1995) evidence regarding the reduced employment of senior workers and flatter wage profiles in targeted firms supports the Shleifer and Summers view. Related work has found evidence consistent with breach of trust through pension fund reversion (Peterson 1992; Pontiff, Shleifer, and Weisbach 1990). In contrast, Christopher Cornwell, Stuart Dorsey, and Nasser Mehrzad (1991) found little evidence to support opportunistic dismissal of workers covered by pensions.

5. John Antel (1985) made a similar point in the context of a costly renegotiations model of employee turnover.

6. I begin the sample in 1976 because prior to that year the survey focused on position tenure and turnover (which includes intrafirm movements). As discussed by Diebold, Neumark, and Polsky (1997), Polsky (1999), and Schmidt and Svorny (1998), several measurement problems stemming from changes in the survey instrument may affect the measurement of job change over time in the PSID. In my empirical analysis here, I discuss the sensitivity of my results to these measurement issues.

7. Layoffs and firings are not separately identified in the PSID public use data files. Boisjoly, Duncan, and Smeeding (1998) hired coders to examine the original PSID questionnaire response forms and distinguish between individuals laid off owing to a decline in demand and individuals who were fired. They found that approximately 16 percent of the observations in this category involved firings, which they excluded from their measure of involuntary job loss. Distinguishing between layoffs and firings might be interesting in the context of my model; layoffs typically arise because of declining demand, but firings may be associated with shirking.

8. James Brown and Audrey Light (1992) discuss the importance of such adjustments to the PSID data. My correction proceeded as follows. I treated the reported value of tenure for the last year in an individual's first sampled job spell as correct. I counted backward to the beginning of that spell and assigned tenure based on yearly decrements. I then used the yearly job change information to identify additional spells and counted forward within

Chapter 8

Did Job Security Decline in the 1990s?

Jay Stewart

There has been a growing interest, both in the popular press and among researchers, in the question of whether job stability and security have declined in recent years.[1] The popular perception is that jobs were less stable and less secure in the 1980s than in the 1970s, and that this decline in stability and security continued into the 1990s (Neumark and Polsky 1998). So far, the evidence from academic studies indicates that job stability did not decline between the mid-1970s and the early 1990s, but that there have been changes for some groups. Job stability declined among men, primarily owing to declining stability among high school dropouts (Marcotte 1996; Farber 1998; Stewart 1998).[2] Stability decreased slightly among high tenure workers (Neumark, Polsky, and Hansen, this volume). For women with at least a high school diploma, job stability has increased significantly (Farber 1998; Stewart 1998).

However, the absence of a decline in job stability does not preclude declines in job security. Studies conducted so far have found that job loss appears to have been more common in the late 1980s and early 1990s than in the 1970s, and that the consequences may have become more severe. But as in the job stability debate, data quality has become an important issue (for a discussion of data issues in the job stability literature, see Stewart 1998).

Because the primary measure of job security is the job-loss rate, most researchers have used the Displaced Worker Supplements (DWS) to the Current Population Survey (CPS), the Panel Study of Income Dynamics (PSID), or the National Longitudinal Surveys (NLS). These data sets, in principle, measure the correct concept, but they all have breaks in series that make it difficult to generate a consistent series over a long period (and sometimes even a short period) of time. Although researchers have devised clever ways of addressing these breaks in series, we can never be sure whether observed changes are real or due to changes in the survey instruments.

I take a different approach and use the March CPS. Although the March CPS does not have a direct measure of involuntary separations, it does contain an indirect measure that is consistently defined over a long period of time. It is well known that job-losers are more likely to become unemployed and to take longer, on average, to find employment than job-leavers (Ruhm 1991; for a nice survey of the job displacement literature, see Fallick 1996). These facts suggest that I can shed additional light on the job security issue by examining trends in employment-to-unemployment (EU) transitions.

The EU transition rate is an imperfect measure of job security. Not everybody who makes an EU transition is a job-loser, and not all job-losers show up as having experienced an EU transition. Later in the chapter, however, I show that the vast majority of people who experience an EU transition are job-losers, and that nearly all of the variation in the EU transition rate, at least during the period from 1987 to 1997, is due to job loss. So even though the EU transition rate does not include all job losses, it does include the job losses that policymakers are most concerned about: those resulting in unemployment. As long as the relationship between job loss that results in unemployment and the EU transition rate remains fairly constant, the EU transition rate should be a reasonable indicator of trends in job security.

There are a number of advantages to using the March CPS. First, the series is consistently defined over a long period of time (thirty-one years), permitting longer coverage than other commonly used data sets. Since my data go through March 1998, I can also look at very recent trends. Second, because this data set is a large, nationally representative sample, it is possible to identify changes for specific demographic groups. Third, because the data are available every year, turning points can be more precisely dated.

This is not the first study to use March CPS data to examine trends in separations. In an earlier paper (Stewart 1998), I used these data to examine trends in job stability between 1975 and 1995.[3] I showed that it is possible to generate a reliable measure of job separations by combining the regular monthly labor-force data with the data from the income supplement. I compared the labor market histories generated from the 1987 March CPS to the labor market histories generated from the 1987 January Tenure Supplement and found that the histories from the two data sources were consistent nearly 90 percent of the time. Because the questions used to identify a job separation did not change, this measure is consistently defined over the period from 1975 to 1995. Using these data, I found that overall job stability remained constant over this period, although there were dramatic changes for some groups. In particular, job stability fell for men without a high school diploma and increased for women with more than a high school diploma.

PREVIOUS RESEARCH FINDINGS

Before continuing, it is useful to describe the findings of other re-searchers in the context of the data sources used and to discuss some of the advantages and disadvantages of the DWS, PSID, and NLS.

THE DISPLACED WORKERS SUPPLEMENTS

The DWS has been conducted as a supplement to the CPS every two years since 1984. It asks individuals about displacement from employers in the previous five years (1984 to 1992) or three years (1994 and later years). The DWS has the advantage of collecting information on job loss from a large, nationally representative sample. The DWS tends, however, to underestimate the incidence of job loss, for two reasons.

First, responses are subject to recall bias. David Evans and Linda Leighton (1995) showed that recall bias is severe: the DWS underesti-mates displacement by about one-third. Johanne Boisjoly, Greg Duncan, and Timothy Smeeding (1998) showed that the DWS understates job loss compared to the PSID, though part of this difference appears to be a difference in concept. When they looked only at job losses that resemble displacements, their numbers were closer to—though still larger than—numbers from the DWS. However, because the literature on job security has focused on trends in the job-loss rate, recall bias should not be a serious problem provided it has not changed over time.[4]

The second reason is that the DWS collects information on at most one job loss; as a result, it measures the number of people who experi-enced a job loss during the period in question rather than the total num-ber of job losses. Again, trends should not be affected unless the fraction of individuals with multiple job losses has changed over time.

The biggest drawback to using the DWS to look at recent trends in job security is that the main question changed in 1994 and again in 1996. Hence, uncertainty about whether changes in the job-loss rate are real or due to changes in the survey make it difficult to get a clear picture of job-loss trends in the 1990s. In 1994 the reporting window was reduced from five years to three years. To illustrate how this change affects re-sponses, consider a worker who lost a short-tenure job in 1993 and who had lost a long-tenure job in 1990. With a three-year window, this worker would report the 1993 job loss. If the window had been five years, the respondent could have reported either the 1990 or 1993 job loss. If respondents always reported the most recent job loss, researchers could make the older data comparable to the more recent data simply by counting only job losses that occurred in the last three years. To the ex-tent that respondents report the longest job lost rather than the most recent job, counting only job losses that occurred in the last three years would result in an underestimate of the incidence of job loss.

To address this break in series, Henry Farber (1997a) computed adjustment factors using individual labor market history data from the PSID and used those factors to adjust for the longer window in the earlier DWSs. Letting t be the current year, he calculated the fraction of workers who lost a job in year $t - 4$ and $t - 5$ and who subsequently lost a job in years $t - 3$ through $t - 1$. For example, among workers who lost a job in period $t - 5$, 27.05 percent also lost a job during the $t - 3$ through $t - 1$ period. (The analogous rate for $t - 4$ is 30.17 percent.) The three-year job-loss rates from the earlier data were adjusted using this formula:

$$r_{3i}^a = r_{3i} + 0.3017\, \rho_{4i} + 0.2705\, \rho_{5i}, \qquad (8.1)$$

where r_{3i}^a and r_{3i} are the adjusted and unadjusted three-year job-loss rates for group i, and ρ_{4i} and ρ_{5i} are the job-loss rates in $t - 4$ and $t - 5$ for group i.

There are several problems with Farber's adjustments. First, he assumed that all multiple job-losers reported the longest job lost. Bureau of Labor Statistics (BLS) research connected with the redesign of the DWS has found that about half of respondents report the most recent job lost, and about half report the longest. Second, using PSID to adjust DWS data is problematic because the job-loss concepts are not comparable (see Abraham 1997) and the PSID sample is not large enough to allow adjustment factors to vary by demographic group.[5]

In 1996 a subtle change in question wording appears to have led more quitters to show up as having lost a job. In 1994 the main question was: "During the last 3 calendar years, that is, January 1991 through December 1993, did [you/name] lose or leave a job because: a plant or company closed or moved, [your/his/her] position or shift was abolished, insufficient work, or another similar reason?" In 1996 the main question was: "During the last 3 calendar years, that is, January 1993 through December 1995, did [you/name] lose a job, or leave one because: [your/his/her] plant or company closed or moved, [your/his/her] position or shift was abolished, insufficient work, or another similar reason?" Both questions ask whether the individual lost or left a job, but the 1996 question places greater emphasis on leaving a job. This greater emphasis on leaving a job could have caused more job-leavers to answer yes to the main question. If the main question picked up more job-leavers in 1996, they would most likely have shown up in the "other" category. Given that the increase in the "other" category was responsible for Farber's finding of increased job loss between the 1991 to 1993 period and the

1993 to 1995 period, it is crucial to know the extent to which the change in wording affected responses.

Research at the BLS sheds some light on this question. Katharine Abraham (1997) reported that the "other" category is composed mostly of quitters. In response to this research, Farber (1997b) adjusted the DWS data to account for misreporting in the "other" category in all years and concluded that, although job loss did not increase between the 1991 to 1993 period and the 1993 to 1995 period, it almost certainly did not decrease. However, because the debriefing questions used to determine this fact were not asked in 1994, it is impossible to determine directly whether there has been a *change* in the composition of the "other" category. His correction is appropriate only if the 1996 wording change did not affect the composition of the "other" category. Later in the chapter, I present evidence that the change in wording did result in more job-leavers answering yes to the main displacement question, and that it affected the non-"other" categories.

THE PANEL STUDY OF INCOME DYNAMICS

Several studies have used PSID data (Boisjoly, Duncan, and Smeeding 1998; Polsky 1999; Valletta, this volume) to look at trends in job loss. Although the PSID collects data on job losses, it has a number of disadvantages that are worth noting. The PSID collects employment data only on household heads, so that analyses are generally restricted to male household heads. Male household heads may not be representative of all men, and they are certainly not representative of the population as a whole. The sample size is relatively small, resulting in larger standard errors than in CPS data (for a comparison, see Jaeger and Stevens, this volume). There are well-documented inconsistencies in reported tenure (see Brown and Light 1992), and the tenure and job-change questions have changed over time.

Francis Diebold, David Neumark, and Daniel Polsky (1997) examined the effect of wording changes in the PSID's job-change questions on job-separation rates. For most of the time between 1970 and 1990, the PSID asked about job separations that occurred over a twelve-month period. However, from 1984 through 1987 the reporting window was closer to a year and a half (for details, see Diebold, Neumark, and Polsky 1997; and Polsky 1999). As a result, more job separations were observed in the mid-1980s simply because the window was longer. The longer window appears to have affected Boisjoly, Duncan, and Smeeding's (1998) findings that job-loss rates were higher in the 1980s than in the 1970s, and that job losses increased more when looking at growth years than when looking at recession years.

To get around the problem of the longer reporting period, Polsky

(1999) looked at separations using the "months in current position" question. Unfortunately, this question changed in 1983. Because the earlier question resulted in considerable heaping at twelve months and separations are detected by comparing employer tenure and the time between interviews, whether a separation is observed is sensitive to the exact length of time between interviews. Taking advantage of the panel nature of the PSID, Polsky performed consistency checks to identify individuals who rounded up and those who rounded down. He then used the "reason for new position" question to distinguish between quits and job losses. Comparing the 1976 to 1981 period to the 1986 to 1991 period, he found that there was virtually no change in job separations, but that there was a large increase in the incidence of job loss conditional on a separation. Further, in comparing the late 1980s to the late 1970s, he found that job-losers had become less likely to find new jobs and earned less when they did.

Robert Valletta (this volume) looked at job security in the context of an implicit contract model. He found that, for male household heads, the job-loss rate increased over the period from 1976 to 1992, but he found no such increase for women. Interestingly, the decline in job security was largest among men with higher tenure; those in declining industries fared the worst.

THE NATIONAL LONGITUDINAL SURVEY

A paper by James Monks and Steven Pizer (1998) used the National Longitudinal Survey of Youth (NLSY) and National Longitudinal Survey Young Men (NLSYM) to examine whether job stability and job security among young men declined between the 1970s and the 1980s.[6] They found that both voluntary and involuntary separations were more common in the 1980s than in the 1970s.

Apart from the limited sample coverage, the main difficulty with using these two data sets is that their measures of separations and job loss are not necessarily comparable. The NLSYM asks whether the individual was working two years before the interview[7] and what happened to that job, whereas the NLSY collects job information using a calendar approach. The latter approach is likely to detect more jobs, and hence more job changes. Also, because the NLSYM interviews were conducted two years apart for the years used in their study, Monks and Pizer used a two-year window to analyze job separations.[8] To make the time period comparable in the NLSY, they used a two-year window for these data as well. But because the NLSY interviews were conducted annually through 1994, they had to use data from two annual interviews to determine whether a separation occurred during the two-year window of interest. It is well known that transitions are more likely to be reported between interviews than within interviews.[9] These "seam effects" imply that job separation rates should be higher in the NLSY than in the NLSYM, even if there is no actual difference between the two cohorts. Hence, it is not clear to what extent the increase in job separations from the 1970s to the 1980s found by Monks and Pizer is real and how much is due to differences in the surveys.

DATA

The data used in this study are from the 1968 through 1998 March CPS files. My sample consists of men and women aged nineteen and above in March[10] who worked at least one week in the previous year and had forty or fewer years of potential experience.[11] Because I am interested in whether job security has changed for workers in regular (postschooling) jobs, I omit individuals with less than one year of potential experience.[12] I also exclude self-employed workers[13] and people with zero earnings in the previous year. To simplify computation of standard errors and keep the data set to a manageable size, I use only the first four rotation groups; the remaining sample comprises 831,762 observations.[14]

As noted earlier, I use EU transitions as my measure of job security. It is relatively straightforward to define EU transitions in the March CPS. An individual is considered to have made an EU transition if he or she worked during the previous year and was unemployed during the reference week of March in the current year.

We know from the literature on job displacement that job-losers are more likely to become unemployed and to spend more time unemployed than workers who did not lose a job (see Ruhm 1991; Farber 1993), suggesting that a large fraction of EU transitions are due to job loss. However, for the purpose of examining trends in job security, it is more important that most of the year-to-year *variation* in the EU transition rate be due to job loss. Fortunately, I can shed some light on this issue by using more detailed data available in the 1988 through 1998 March CPS files, which contain information on the reason for unemployment.

Over the period from 1988 to 1997, most EU transitions were due to job losses. The EU transition rate averaged 4.65 percent over this period, with job loss accounting for 3.11 percentage points, quitters (job-leavers) accounting for 0.63 percentage points, and reentrants accounting for 0.91 percentage points.[15]

The next step is to determine how much of the variation in the EU transition rate is due to job loss. Figure 8.1 shows the overall EU transition rate, the EU job-loss rate (this rate is the fraction of workers who worked in the previous year and were unemployed in March because of a job loss), and the EU non-job-loss rate (this rate is the fraction of workers who worked in the previous year and were unemployed in March for

Figure 8.1   EU Transition Rates by Reason for Unemployment

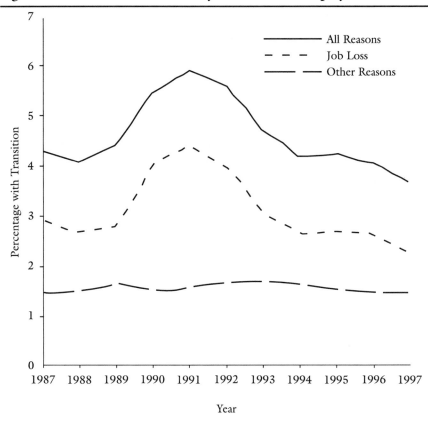

reasons other than job loss) for 1987 through 1997. It is clear from this figure that virtually all of the variation in the EU transition rate can be accounted for by variation in the EU job-loss rate.

This observation is confirmed when the eleven yearly observations are used to regress the overall EU transition rate on the EU job-loss rate. The estimated coefficient estimate on the EU job-loss rate is 0.97, which is statistically different from zero at the 1 percent level but not statistically different from one at any conventional level of significance. (The R^2 on this regression is 0.96.) Regressing the EU transition rate on the EU non-job-loss rate yields a coefficient of 0.40, which is not statistically different from zero at any conventional level of significance. (The R^2 on this regression is 0.01.)[16] These regressions imply that changes in the EU job-loss rate account for about 96 percent of the year-to-year variation in the EU transition rate over the period from 1987 to 1997 and suggest that the EU transition rate is a reasonable measure of job security.

It is important for my analysis that the relationship between job loss and EU transitions be fairly constant over time. For example, if workers have become more inclined to quit a job to become unemployed, the EU transition rate increases even if there has been no decline in job security. The assumption I maintain throughout the rest of the chapter is that this relationship was constant over the period from 1967 to 1986 as well.

POTENTIAL BREAKS IN SERIES

There have been two changes in the CPS that could lead to potential breaks in series. The first occurred in 1989 when the Census Bureau changed the CPS processing system. Beginning in 1989, the Census Bureau changed the criteria by which variables were allocated and began imputing entire Income Supplement records using a hot deck procedure. These are known as "type A" allocations and represent 8 to 10 percent of the sample. Since the type A allocated records generate a large number of spurious transitions, I omitted them from my sample.

The second change occurred in 1994, when the Basic CPS was completely overhauled and computer-assisted interviewing was introduced. The variable that is a potential problem is Employment Status Recode (ESR) from the Basic CPS (Monthly Labor Force Recode in the redesigned CPS). Research by Anne Polivka and Steven Miller (1998) has provided some guidance on how the redesign affected the ESR. They computed adjustment factors for various labor-force indicators by demographic characteristics. Although I cannot use these factors to adjust my own estimates, they do provide useful information about which groups were most affected. The redesigned CPS detects more unemployment among both men and women. However, the largest increases in the unemployment rate are for men over the age of sixty-five and for women over fifty-five. My restriction to workers with forty or fewer years of potential experience largely eliminates these older workers from my analysis. Hence, any effects of the redesign are likely to be small.

HAS JOB SECURITY DECLINED?

As noted earlier, the popular perception is that jobs were less secure in the 1980s than in the 1970s, and that the decline in job security continued into the 1990s. In this section, I examine the question of whether trends in the EU transition rate are consistent with these perceptions.

The EU transition rates in figures 8.2 through 8.8 were estimated using a two-step procedure. In the first step, I estimated a probit equation using only data for 1967 and obtained the predicted EU transition

Figure 8.2   EU Transition Rates for All Workers, for Men, and for Women

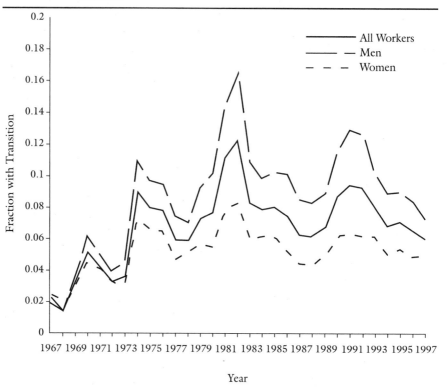

rate for 1967. I then estimated a probit on the full sample using year dummies (with 1967 as the reference year).[17] The EU transition rate for each year (1968 through 1997) was obtained by adding the marginal effect of the year dummy to the predicted 1967 transition rate obtained from the first-step probit. To derive the upper and lower bounds of the confidence interval, I took a simple average of the standard errors on the year dummies from the second-step probit and multiplied by two. These bounds were used for all years, including 1967.

Figure 8.2 shows the EU transition rates for all workers, for men, and for women. As we would expect, these series are countercyclical, with the EU transition rate for men exhibiting much wider swings. The EU transition rates for men and women were fairly close to each other in the late 1960s and early 1970s. The rate for both men and women ratcheted up during the 1970 and 1974 recessions, but the 1974 increase was much larger for men than for women. From the late 1970s through the mid- to late 1990s, the EU transition rates remained roughly constant except for cyclical variation. The behavior of these EU transition rates is consistent with the popular perception that jobs were less secure in the 1980s than in the 1970s, but it is not consistent with the perception that job security declined in the 1990s. However, topside numbers can be misleading because they mask changes in composition and within-group changes. In the next section, I present a more detailed look by demographic characteristics, with the goal of determining whether job security has declined for some groups.

EMPLOYMENT-TO-UNEMPLOYMENT TRANSITIONS BY SEX AND EDUCATION

Figure 8.3 shows the trends in the EU transition rate for men by education level.[18] As we might expect, the cyclical fluctuations are greater for high school dropouts and for high school graduates than for workers with some college and for college graduates. However, the EU transition rate for all education groups ratcheted up during the 1970 and 1974 recessions; the rates for less educated workers increased the most. Comparing high school dropouts and high school graduates, there was a slight difference in the timing of these changes. Most of the increase among high school dropouts occurred during the 1970 recession, whereas among high school graduates most of the increase occurred during the 1974 recession. From the late 1970s through the mid- to late 1990s, the EU transition rate for men of all education levels remained roughly constant except for cyclical fluctuations.

The corresponding EU transition rates for women are shown in figure 8.4. For high school dropouts and high school graduates, the patterns are similar to those for men, except that the changes are small relative to their standard errors. Like the EU transition rates for men in these education categories, the rates for women ratcheted up during the 1970 and 1974 recessions, but the increases were not as sharp. After the 1974 recession, the EU transition rate exhibited no upward or downward trend. For women with some college and college graduates, there do not appear to have been any changes over the entire period from 1967 to 1997. Again, the movements in the series are small relative to their standard errors.

In light of the debate over whether job security declined in the early 1990s, it is interesting to compare the 1982 and 1990 recessions. Although the drop in gross domestic product (GDP) was greater in the 1982 recession, the EU transition rate for male college graduates—a group that is typically insulated from cyclical job loss—was about the same in both recessions. In contrast, the EU transition rates for men in the other education groups were lower in the 1990 recession.

(Text continues on p. 276.)

Figure 8.3   EU Transition Rates for Men by Educational Level

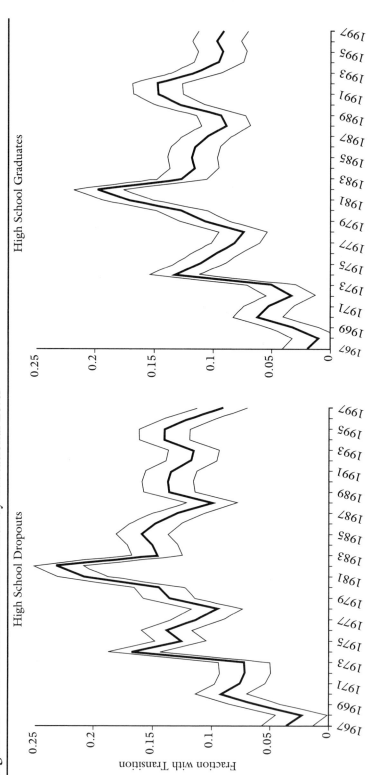

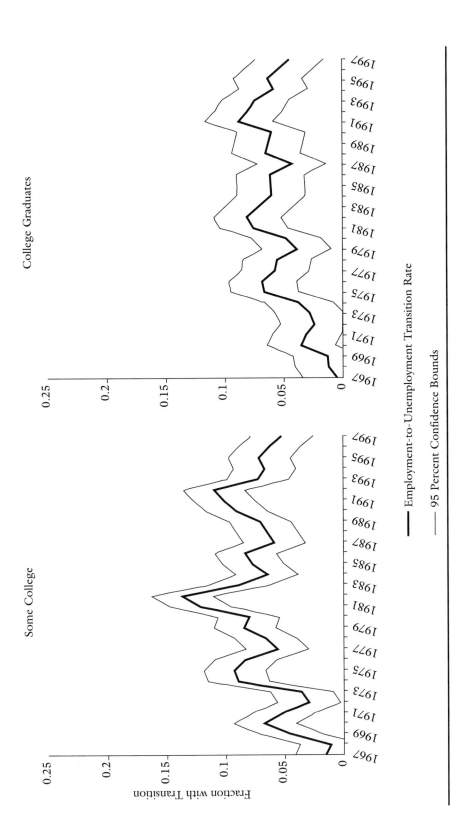

Some College

College Graduates

Fraction with Transition

0.25 0.2 0.15 0.1 0.05 0

1967 1969 1971 1973 1975 1977 1979 1981 1983 1985 1987 1989 1991 1993 1995 1997

Employment-to-Unemployment Transition Rate

95 Percent Confidence Bounds

Figure 8.4   EU Transition Rates for Women by Education Level

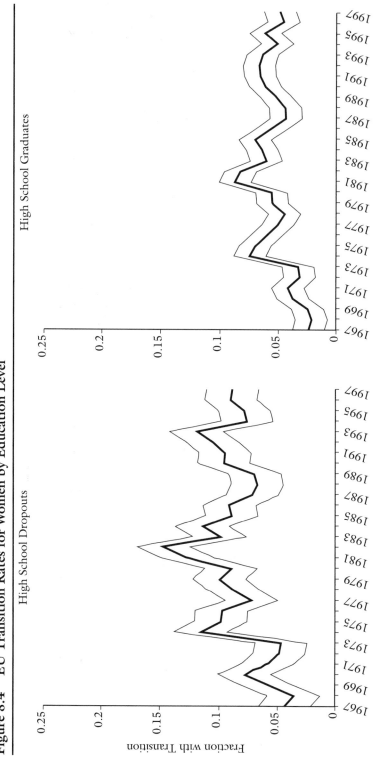

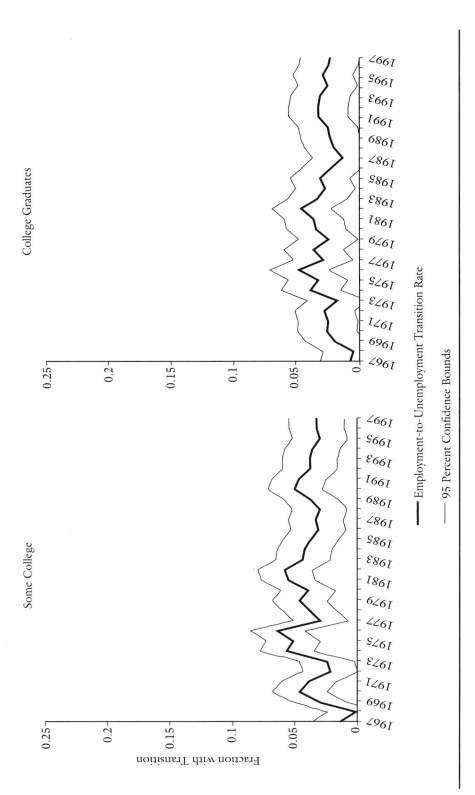

Some College

College Graduates

Fraction with Transition

— Employment-to-Unemployment Transition Rate

— 95 Percent Confidence Bounds

Figure 8.5 EU Transition Rates for Men by Years of Potential Experience

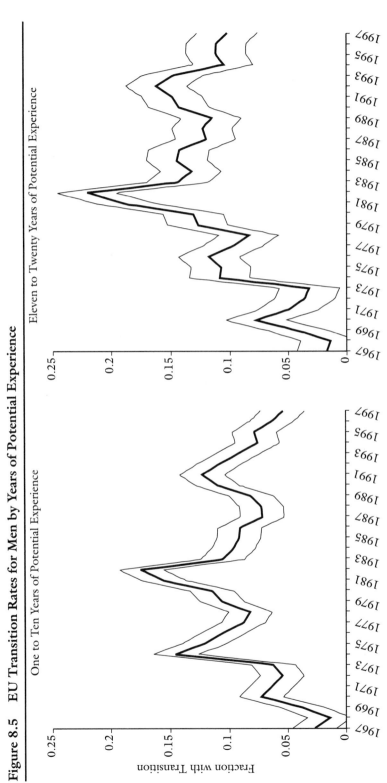

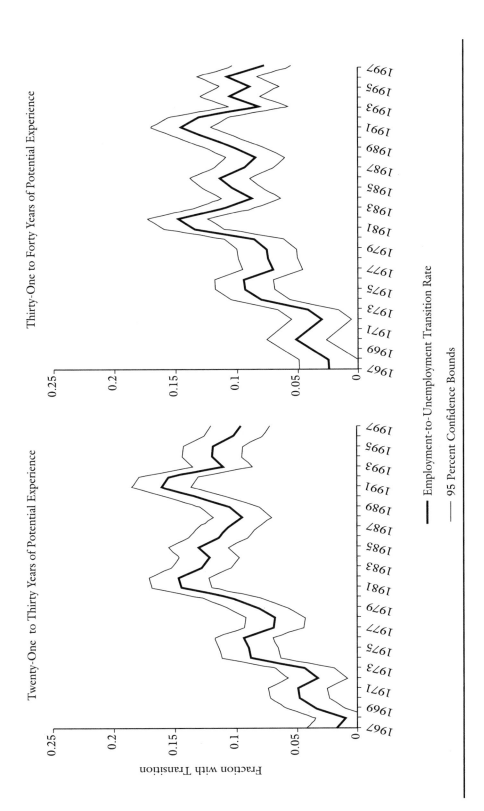

Twenty-One to Thirty Years of Potential Experience

Thirty-One to Forty Years of Potential Experience

Fraction with Transition

0.25 0.2 0.15 0.1 0.05

1967 1969 1971 1973 1975 1977 1979 1981 1983 1985 1987 1989 1991 1993 1995 1997

——— Employment-to-Unemployment Transition Rate

——— 95 Percent Confidence Bounds

Figure 8.6   EU Transition Rates for Women by Years of Potential Experience

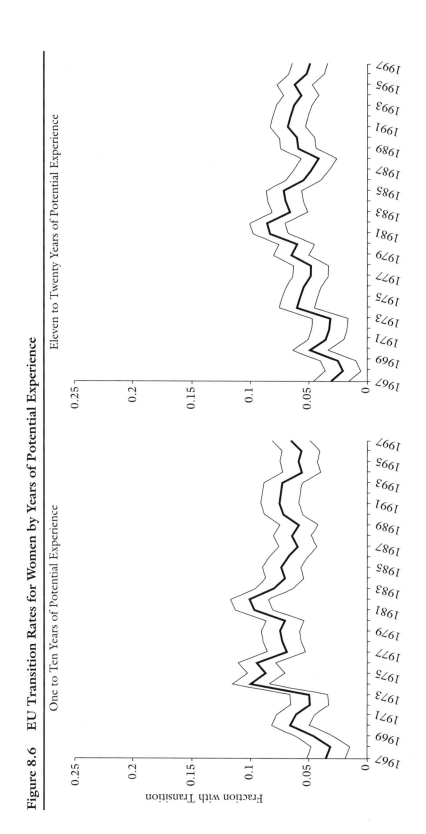

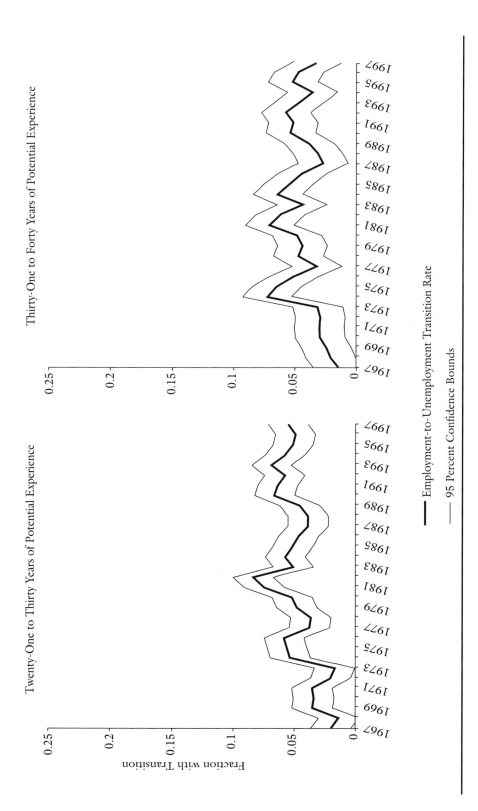

Twenty-One to Thirty Years of Potential Experience

Thirty-One to Forty Years of Potential Experience

Fraction with Transition

—— Employment-to-Unemployment Transition Rate

—— 95 Percent Confidence Bounds

EMPLOYMENT-TO-UNEMPLOYMENT TRANSITIONS BY SEX AND POTENTIAL
EXPERIENCE

The EU transition rates for men and women by years of potential experience are shown in figures 8.5 and 8.6. At all levels of experience, the rates
for women exhibit considerably less cyclical fluctuation than the rates for
men. For men and women of all experience levels, the EU transition rate
ratcheted up during the 1970 and 1974 recessions. Again, the increases
were much larger for men than for women. For men with more than ten
years of experience, the rates ratcheted up again during the 1982 recession. For all other groups, the EU transition rate remained relatively constant from about the mid-1970s through the mid to late 1990s.

Again, the 1990 recession was different from the 1982 recession for
workers who are usually insulated from cyclical job loss. For men with
twenty-one or more years of experience, the EU transition rate was as
high during the 1990 recession as it was during the 1982 recession.

EMPLOYMENT-TO-UNEMPLOYMENT TRANSITIONS BY INDUSTRY AND
OCCUPATION

Figure 8.7 shows the EU transition rates for goods-producing and services-
producing industries. Not surprisingly, the EU transition rate for goods-
producing industries exhibits much wider cyclical swings. Again, the EU
transition rate for both industry groups ratcheted up during the 1970 and
1974 recessions but remained relatively flat from the mid-1970s through
the mid- to late 1990s. Comparing the 1982 and 1990 recessions, the later
recession was less severe in goods-producing industries, but there was no
difference between the two recessions in services-producing industries.

The EU transition rates in figure 8.8 reveal some interesting patterns by
major occupation group.[19] As expected, the EU transition rate for blue-
collar workers exhibits much wider cyclical swings than the rates for the
other two groups. In all occupations, the EU transition rate ratcheted up
during the 1974 recession, with the increase being larger for blue-collar
workers. A comparison of the 1982 and 1990 recessions reveals a familiar
pattern. For blue-collar occupations, the 1990 recession was much less
severe than the 1982 recession, but for white-collar occupations there was
no difference between the two recessions.

REGRESSION RESULTS

Because business cycle effects can make it difficult to distinguish trends from
cyclical effects in these figures, I compared average EU transition rates for
the five expansions and for the four recessions covered by my data.

Table 8.1 summarizes the trends in EU transition rates for the

(Text continues on p. 283.)

Figure 8.7 EU Transitions by Major Industry Group

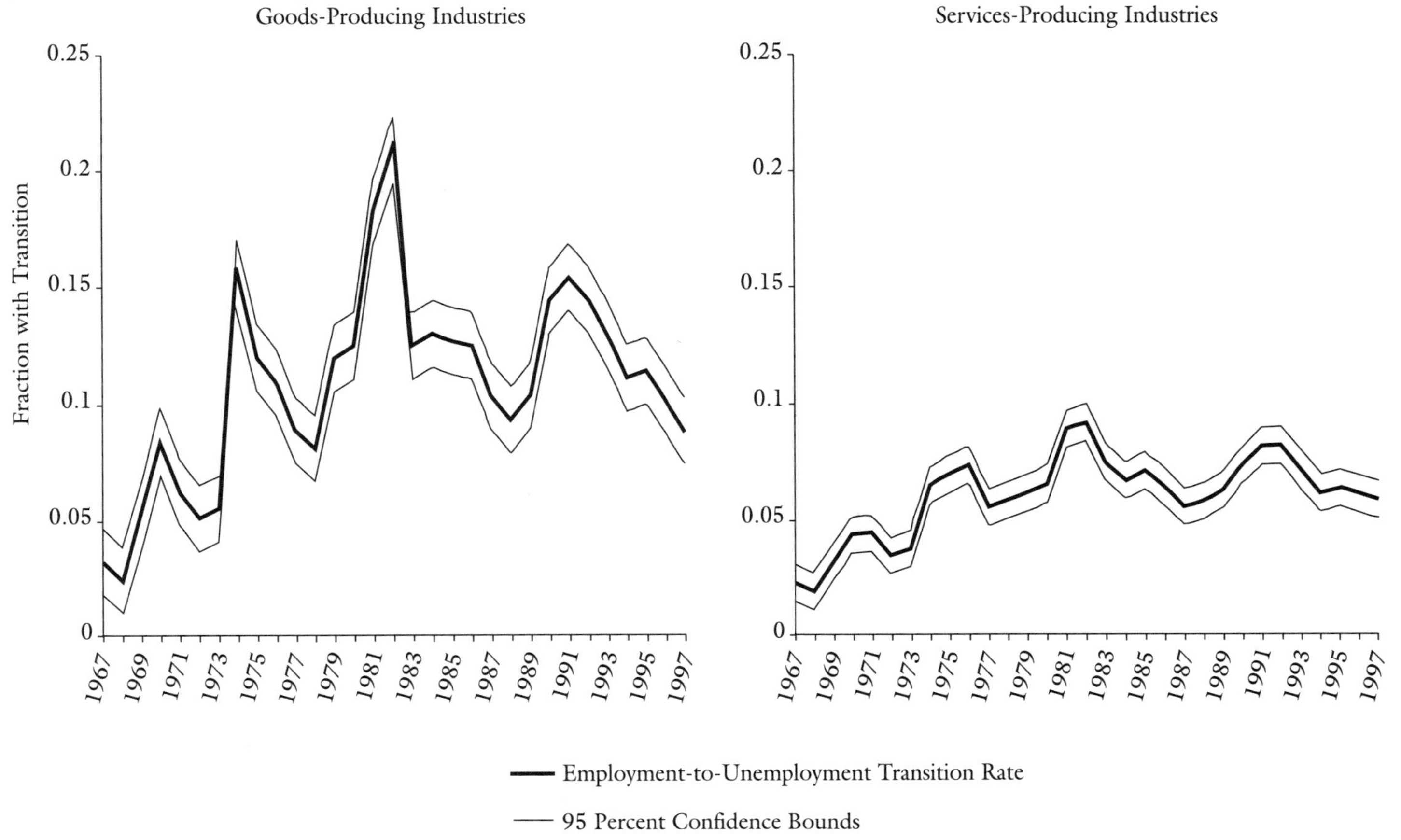
Goods-Producing Industries
Services-Producing Industries
Fraction with Transition
0.25
0.2
0.15
0.1
0.05
0
1967
1969
1971
1973
1975
1977
1979
1981
1983
1985
1987
1989
1991
1993
1995
1997
Employment-to-Unemployment Transition Rate
95 Percent Confidence Bounds

Figure 8.8 EU Transitions by Major Occupation Group

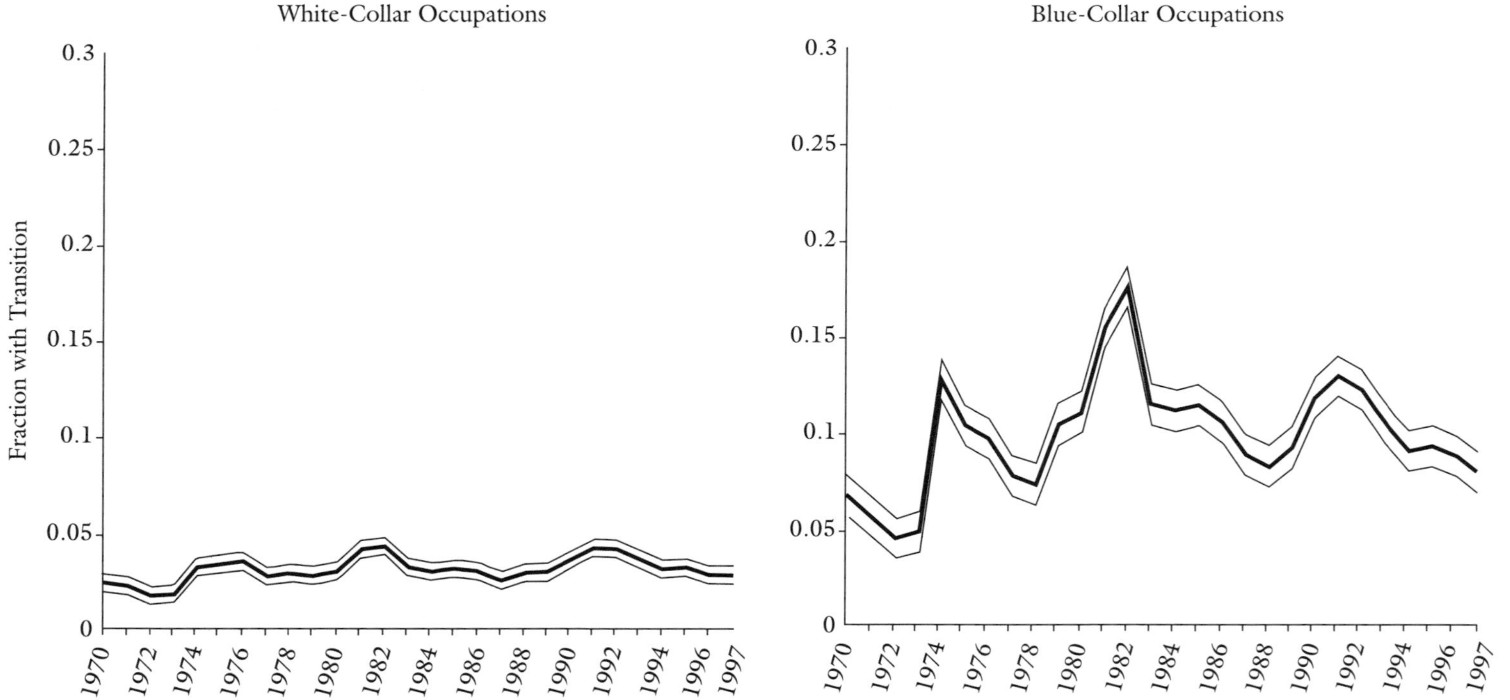

White-Collar Occupations

Blue-Collar Occupations

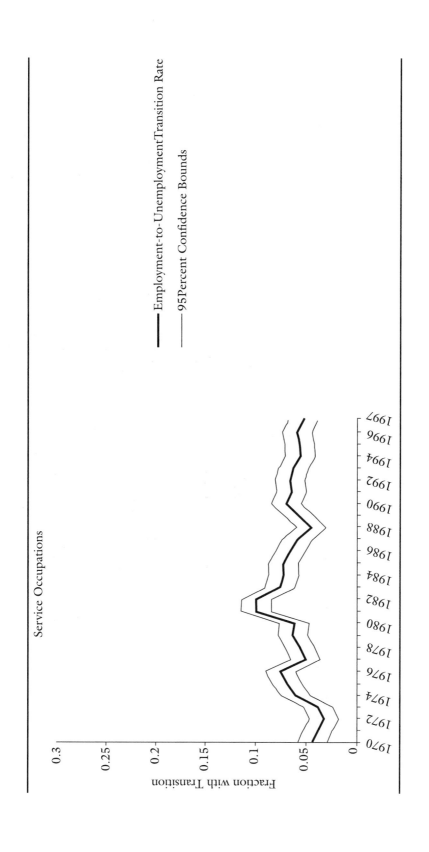

Service Occupations

——Employment-to-UnemploymentTransition Rate
——95Percent Confidence Bounds

Fraction with Transition

0.3
0.25
0.2
0.15
0.1
0.05
0

1970 1972 1974 1976 1978 1980 1982 1984 1986 1988 1990 1992 1994 1996 1997

Table 8.1 Probit Estimates of Changes in EU Transition Rates for Expansion Years and Recession Years

	Expansion Years[a]					Recession Years[a]			Observations
	1971 to 1973	1976 to 1980	1983 to 1989	1992 to 1997	1970	1974 to 1975	1981 to 1982	1990 to 1991	
All workers	0.0152*	0.0428*	0.0436*	0.0456	0.0279	0.0596*	0.0895*	0.0654*	831,762
	(0.0015)	(0.0016)	(0.0014)	(0.0016)	(0.0023)	(0.0023)	(0.0026)	(0.0023)	
Men	0.0207*	0.0564*	0.0604*	0.0623	0.0360	0.0754*	0.1226*	0.0929*	450,297
	(0.0022)	(0.0024)	(0.0022)	(0.0025)	(0.0034)	(0.0035)	(0.0040)	(0.0037)	
Women	0.0091*	0.0271*	0.0247	0.0265	0.0187	0.0415*	0.0528*	0.0354*	381,465
	(0.0020)	(0.0020)	(0.0018)	(0.0019)	(0.0030)	(0.0030)	(0.0030)	(0.0027)	
Men by education level									
High school dropouts	0.0335*	0.0792*	0.0929*	0.0870*	0.0522	0.1025*	0.1689*	0.1362*	91,969
	(0.0050)	(0.0051)	(0.0052)	(0.0062)	(0.0073)	(0.0072)	(0.0085)	(0.0091)	
High school graduates	0.0243*	0.0716*	0.0769*	0.0793	0.0414	0.1003*	0.1587*	0.1143*	157,633
	(0.0045)	(0.0048)	(0.0044)	(0.0050)	(0.0068)	(0.0070)	(0.0078)	(0.0071)	
Some college	0.0125*	0.0404*	0.0373	0.0389	0.0374	0.0572*	0.0895*	0.0613*	98,506
	(0.0049)	(0.0052)	(0.0046)	(0.0048)	(0.0083)	(0.0075)	(0.0084)	(0.0072)	
College graduates	0.0131*	0.0306*	0.0316	0.0353	0.0200	0.0331	0.0576*	0.0551	102,189
	(0.0045)	(0.0051)	(0.0043)	(0.0050)	(0.0069)	(0.0068)	(0.0082)	(0.0080)	
Women by education level									
High school dropouts	0.0056	0.0409*	0.0393	0.0456	0.0318	0.0593*	0.0872*	0.0490*	61,124
	(0.0047)	(0.0049)	(0.0049)	(0.0060)	(0.0073)	(0.0071)	(0.0082)	(0.0081)	
High school graduates	0.0124*	0.0289*	0.0307	0.0327	0.0144	0.0488*	0.0614*	0.0411*	158,721
	(0.0033)	(0.0032)	(0.0030)	(0.0034)	(0.0047)	(0.0049)	(0.0050)	(0.0046)	

Some college	0.0112* (0.0055)	0.0244* (0.0052)	0.0182* (0.0044)	0.0170 (0.0044)	0.0287 (0.0090)	0.0357 (0.0075)	0.0382 (0.0070)	0.0307 (0.0063)	88,716
College graduates	0.0102* (0.0054)	0.0191* (0.0053)	0.0107* (0.0039)	0.0137 (0.0042)	0.0125 (0.0078)	0.0219 (0.0072)	0.0289 (0.0072)	0.0183* (0.0059)	72,904
Men by years of potential experience									
One to ten years	0.0336* (0.0047)	0.0676* (0.0044)	0.0549* (0.0040)	0.0513* (0.0045)	0.0469 (0.0070)	0.1058* (0.0069)	0.1347* (0.0069)	0.0886* (0.0065)	151,281
Eleven to twenty years	0.0133* (0.0042)	0.0724* (0.0054)	0.0779* (0.0046)	0.0786 (0.0051)	0.0473 (0.0073)	0.0745* (0.0072)	0.1602* (0.0092)	0.1076* (0.0076)	127,307
Twenty-one to thirty years	0.0199* (0.0042)	0.0541* (0.0052)	0.0737* (0.0051)	0.0775 (0.0054)	0.0257 (0.0060)	0.0627* (0.0069)	0.1139* (0.0089)	0.1146 (0.0089)	97,705
Thirty-one to forty years	0.0078* (0.0038)	0.0420* (0.0049)	0.0559* (0.0051)	0.0586 (0.0059)	0.0203 (0.0059)	0.0515* (0.0065)	0.1007* (0.0090)	0.0960 (0.0096)	74,004
Women by years of potential experience									
One to ten years	0.0150* (0.0040)	0.0342* (0.0037)	0.0265* (0.0033)	0.0242 (0.0037)	0.0271 (0.0061)	0.0532* (0.0056)	0.0588 (0.0054)	0.0350* (0.0050)	132,041
Eleven to twenty years	0.0083* (0.0041)	0.0321* (0.0044)	0.0322 (0.0037)	0.0330 (0.0041)	0.0260 (0.0067)	0.0372 (0.0061)	0.0637* (0.0067)	0.0419* (0.0056)	105,272
Twenty-one to thirty years	0.0013 (0.0032)	0.0205* (0.0037)	0.0200 (0.0033)	0.0276* (0.0036)	0.0100 (0.0050)	0.0288* (0.0053)	0.0512* (0.0063)	0.0382* (0.0056)	83,869
Thirty-one to forty years	0.0095* (0.0039)	0.0204* (0.0040)	0.0203 (0.0038)	0.0206 (0.0042)	0.0087 (0.0054)	0.0419* (0.0064)	0.0385 (0.0064)	0.0269* (0.0062)	60,283

(Table continues on p. 282.)

Table 8.1 *Continued*

	Expansion Years[a]				1970	Recession Years[a]			Observations
	1971 to 1973	1976 to 1980	1983 to 1989	1992 to 1997		1974 to 1975	1981 to 1982	1990 to 1991	
All workers by industry group									
Goods-producing	0.0200*	0.0631*	0.0699*	0.0722	0.0474	0.0977*	0.1487*	0.1056*	261,885
	(0.0029)	(0.0031)	(0.0030)	(0.0034)	(0.0046)	(0.0046)	(0.0052)	(0.0050)	
Services-producing	0.0135*	0.0342*	0.0335	0.0364	0.0186	0.0409*	0.0629*	0.0509*	569,877
	(0.0017)	(0.0018)	(0.0016)	(0.0018)	(0.0025)	(0.0026)	(0.0028)	(0.0026)	
All workers by occupation group									
White-collar	—	0.0110*	0.0097	0.0133*	0.0059	0.0159*	0.0257*	0.0222	418,571
		(0.0013)	(0.0012)	(0.0013)	(0.0020)	(0.0019)	(0.0021)	(0.0020)	
Blue-collar	—	0.0476*	0.0548*	0.0511*	0.0203	0.0753*	0.1270*	0.0826*	252,949
		(0.0029)	(0.0028)	(0.0031)	(0.0041)	(0.0042)	(0.0048)	(0.0046)	
Service	—	0.0273*	0.0291	0.0247	0.0087	0.0326*	0.0694*	0.0355*	91,078
		(0.0042)	(0.0038)	(0.0040)	(0.0060)	(0.0059)	(0.0067)	(0.0057)	

Note: Each line contains the results from a separate probit equation for the indicated group. The dependent variable equals 1 if the individual made an EU transition. All coefficients are expressed as marginal effects (relative to the 1967 to 1969 period). The regressions include the following control variables (where appropriate): sex, nonwhite, a set of experience dummies, a set of education dummies, and the percentage change in real GDP.

[a]The coefficients are averages for the years listed.

*Significantly different from the *previous period of the same type* (that is, the coefficient to the left) at the .05 level. Note that the 1970 recession period is not compared to the previous recession period because the last recession is not covered by the data.

different groups. Each line contains the results from a separate probit equation and corresponds with a graph in figures 8.2 through 8.8. I divided the period from 1967 to 1997 into five expansion periods (1967 to 1969, 1971 to 1973, 1976 to 1980, 1983 to 1989, and 1992 to 1997) and four recession periods (1970, 1974 to 1975, 1981 to 1982, and 1990 to 1991) and then defined dummy variables corresponding to each of these periods. (1967 to 1969 was the omitted period.) The coefficients in the first four columns correspond to expansion years, and the coefficients in the second four columns correspond to recession years. The coefficients on these dummies are expressed as marginal effects. All equations include demographic control variables and the percentage change in real GDP.

The results in table 8.1 are consistent with figures 8.2 through 8.8. These coefficients indicate that the EU transition rate ratcheted up in the 1970 and 1974 recessions and remained high from the late 1970s through the mid- to late 1990s. For nearly every group, there were statistically significant increases in the EU transition rate between the 1967 to 1969 period and the 1971 to 1973 period, and for every group the increases were statistically significant between the 1971 to 1973 period and the 1976 to 1980 period. In the last three periods (1976 to 1980, 1983 to 1989, and 1992 to 1997), the EU transition rates remained relatively constant. Even when the EU transition rates are statistically different from each other, the differences are small in economic terms.

Overall, and for most groups, the 1982 recession was more severe than the 1990 recession. These differences are statistically significant at the 5 percent level. However, for a few groups there is no statistically significant difference between the EU transition rates during the two recessions. As noted earlier, these are groups that are normally insulated from cyclical job loss: men with college degrees, men with twenty-one or more years of experience, and white-collar workers.

Although the behavior of the EU transition rate differs somewhat by demographic characteristics, a clear picture emerges. Job security declined during the 1970s. However, most of this decline was concentrated in the early part of the decade. The EU transition rate ratcheted up during the 1970 and 1974 recessions but remained fairly constant after that. There is no evidence that job security continued to decline in the 1990s. These findings are consistent with the popular perception that jobs were more secure in the 1970s than in the 1980s, but not with the perception that job security continued to decline in the 1990s.

Part of the reason for the inconsistency between the evidence and popular perceptions may be that the 1990 recession had a differential effect on different groups. Neumark and Polsky (1998) have suggested that reporters may have written more articles about worker displacement because a relatively large fraction of their peers—managerial and professional workers—had lost jobs. The evidence presented here is consistent with that hypothesis. Groups that are usually insulated from cyclical job loss were relatively harder hit by the 1990 recession. Even though the decline in GDP was less severe in this recession than in the 1982 recession, the EU transition rate for these insulated groups was about the same in the two recessions. In contrast, the 1990 recession was far less severe for groups that are typically less insulated from cyclical job loss.

COMPARISONS TO OTHER RESEARCH

In this section, I use the March CPS data to replicate, to the extent possible, the results of three other studies: Boisjoly, Duncan, and Smeeding (1998), Farber (1997a), and Monks and Pizer (1998). I seek to determine whether the results presented earlier are consistent with these studies and to reconcile differences wherever possible.

Boisjoly, Duncan, and Smeeding (1998)

The sample used by Boisjoly, Duncan, and Smeeding consisted of male household heads age twenty-five to fifty-nine who had at least one year of tenure and worked at least one thousand hours in the previous year. I was able to impose the demographic restrictions but not the tenure and hours restrictions. Hence, the March CPS sample is composed of individuals who have a weaker labor-force attachment than those in Boisjoly, Duncan, and Smeeding's PSID sample. As a result, the job-loss rates from the PSID are lower than the EU transition rate from the March CPS.

Figure 8.9 shows the EU transition rate from the March CPS data and the job-loss rate from the PSID. The two series generally follow a very similar pattern, though they differ somewhat with respect to the timing of changes. Perhaps the most notable of these differences is that the EU transition rate fell between 1983 and 1987, whereas the job-loss rate from the PSID increased. This difference could be, at least in part, due to the longer recall period during those years.[20] Even so, their results are generally consistent with those from the March CPS.

Farber (1997a)

In replicating Farber's results with the March CPS data, the difficulty was with constructing a comparable measure of EU transitions, not with replicating the sample. I computed average three-year EU transition rates from the March CPS that are roughly comparable to Farber's three-year job-loss rates from the DWS.[21] Because Farber's job-loss rate measures the fraction of workers who experienced a job loss during each three-year period, I computed three-year EU transition rates by summing the EU transition rates for the three individual years. To replicate the effect of recall bias, I weighted the rates for each year using the implied adjust-

Figure 8.9 Comparison to Boisjoly, Duncan, and Smeeding (1998): Job Loss Rates from the PSID and EU Transition Rates from the March CPS

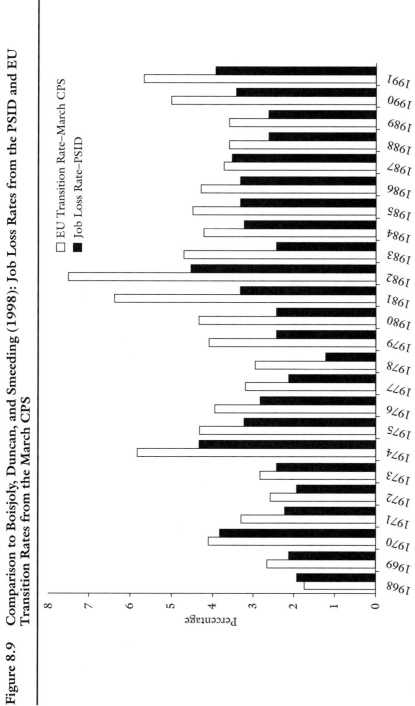

Note: The PSID data are from Boisjoly, Duncan, and Smeeding (1998).

Figure 8.10   Comparison to Farber (1997a): Job Loss Rates from the DWS and EU Transition Rates from the March CPS

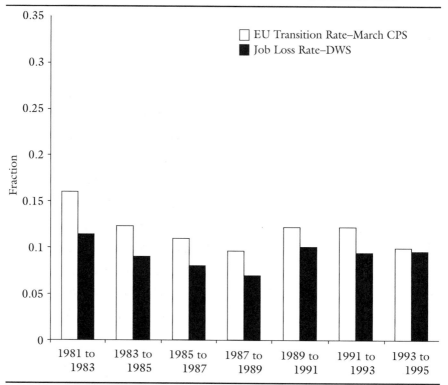

Source: The DWS data are from Farber (1997a).
Note: The rates are averages for the years listed.

ment factors in Evans and Leighton (1995).[22] I also omitted the "other" category from the DWS job-loss rates because of the problems with this category that I noted earlier. Figure 8.10 compares the three-year EU transition rates from the March CPS to the three-year job-loss rates from the DWS for all workers.[23]

The two series tell qualitatively the same story until the period from 1993 to 1995. But between the 1991 to 1993 period and the 1993 to 1995 period, the EU transition rate fell, while the job-loss rate remained roughly constant. Whether the job-loss rate fell during this period is important for determining the trend in job security in the 1990s. The natural expectation is for the job-loss rate to fall as the labor market recovers from the recession. But if, as Farber found, the job-loss rate did not fall, then that would be evidence of a more permanent decline in job security.

The divergence in the 1993 to 1995 period does not necessarily imply that the two data sources are inconsistent with each other. In particular,

Farber found that the consequences of job loss became less severe between the 1991 to 1993 period and the 1993 to 1995 period. Reemployment rates for job-losers increased, and their earnings losses fell.

The results from the DWS and the March CPS are consistent with two hypotheses. The first is that the job-loss rate did not fall, but the consequences of job loss—as reflected in reemployment rates and earnings losses—were less severe during this period. The second is that the job-loss rate did fall, but the wording change in the 1996 DWS caused more job-leavers to be classified as job-losers, even among the non-"other" categories. In that case, the milder consequences of job loss that Farber found would be due to the higher fraction of job-leavers who were misclassified as job-losers.

Recall that the main question in the 1996 DWS placed greater emphasis on leaving a job than did the 1994 question. It has been hypothesized that this wording change resulted in more job-leavers answering yes to the main question, and that it accounts for the large increase in the "other" category in the 1996 DWS. But it is possible that some job-leavers who answered yes to the main question gave a reason other than "other."

Although it is not possible to determine what reason these job-leavers might have given, the "insufficient work" category is a likely candidate because it may not be clear to respondents what the phrase means. It was intended to describe a situation in which an employee was terminated because his employer had experienced a decline in demand. But respondents may have interpreted the term to include situations in which the worker left a job voluntarily because he wanted to work more hours or there was not enough work to keep him busy.

Research associated with the redesign of the DWS has shown that a large fraction of people in the "insufficient work" category are actually job-leavers. The 1996 and 1998 DWSs included a set of debriefing questions that were designed to determine whether respondents were answering the questions correctly.[24] When they analyzed the data, BLS researchers found that 32 percent of people who gave "insufficient work" as a reason were job-leavers. Of these, only 38 percent left because they expected their job to end. Hence, a relatively large fraction—20 percent—were true job-leavers. In contrast, about 14 percent of people who said that they had lost a job owing to a "plant closing" or because their "position [was] abolished," which are less ambiguous terms, were job-leavers. Approximately two-thirds of these job-leavers said that they left because they expected their job to end, so that less than 5 percent of individuals in these two categories were true job-leavers.

However, the real issue is whether this type of misreporting became more common between the 1994 and 1996 DWSs. Unfortunately, there were no follow-up questions in the 1994 DWS, so a direct test is not possible. However, it is possible to perform a consistency check by determining whether the increase in the reemployment rate for job-losers in the DWS was large enough to be consistent with Farber's finding of no change in job-loss rates with my finding of a decline in the EU transition rate.

My strategy is to estimate a lower bound on the amount by which the reemployment rate must have increased in order for Farber's results to be consistent with mine. If the change in the reemployment rate from the DWS is less than this lower bound, it would be evidence that the 1996 DWS classified a higher fraction of job-leavers as job-losers than did the 1994 DWS. Because the reemployment rates from the DWS cover a three-year period and the EU transition rates from the March CPS cover approximately a one-year period, the levels are not comparable. Instead, I compare the percentage changes in the reemployment rates from the two surveys.

Let me begin with the following identity:

$$P_L \equiv P_{LU} + P_{LN} + P_{LE}, \qquad (8.2)$$

where P_L is the fraction of employed workers who lose a job over the course of a year, P_{LU} is the fraction who lose a job and become unemployed, P_{LN} is the fraction who lose a job and leave the labor force, and P_{LE} is the fraction who lose a job and become reemployed.

Computing the percentage change in P_{LE} from the DWS was straightforward. I used Farber's estimates of P_{LE} from the DWS to compute the percentage change between the 1991 to 1993 period and the 1993 to 1995 period.[25] As before, I excluded the "other" category from my calculations. The reemployment rate (expressed as a fraction of employment)[26] increased from 6.4 percent to 6.7 percent, an increase of 5.3 percent.

It is more difficult to compute the percentage change in P_{LE} from the March CPS data because P_{LE} cannot be estimated directly. In fact, of the variables in equation 8.2, I can directly estimate only P_{LU} (using the "reason for unemployment" question). For the other variables, it is necessary to obtain estimates from other sources or to make assumptions about their values.

For some of the variables, it is easier to make assumptions about the changes than the levels. Taking the difference between the 1991 to 1993 period and the 1993 to 1995 period yields

$$\Delta P_L \equiv \Delta P_{LU} + \Delta P_{LN} + \Delta P_{LE}. \qquad (8.3)$$

As noted earlier, I can estimate ΔP_{LU} directly from the March CPS data. By assumption, ΔP_L is close to zero. Given that $\Delta P_{LU} > 0$ (from the March CPS) and $\Delta P_{LE} > 0$ (from the DWS), the labor market must have been improving. Hence, it is reasonable to suppose that $\Delta P_{LN} < 0$. Since smaller (more negative) values of ΔP_{LN} increase the lower bound on the percentage change in P_{LE}, I take the conservative approach and assume $\Delta P_{LN} = 0$.

For both three-year periods, my estimate of P_{LU} was calculated by taking the number of people who made EU job-loss transitions and dividing by the number of people who worked at all during the previous year (2.74 percent in the 1991 to 1993 period and 2.10 percent in the 1993 to 1995 period). I adjusted my estimates of P_{LU} to account for recall bias (as described earlier) and the 1994 redesign of the CPS. For the latter adjustment, I used adjustment factors from Polivka and Miller (1998) to account for the fact that the redesigned CPS classifies a smaller fraction of the unemployed as job-losers.[27]

For my estimates of P_L, I used the job-loss rates from the DWS (9.6 percent in the 1991 to 1993 period and 9.5 percent in the 1993 to 1995 period). This is a conservative approach, because the percentage change in the reemployment rate decreases as P_L increases,[28] and the DWS job-loss rate (which is a three-year rate) is an overestimate of the average annual job-loss rate.[29] Because I had no way of estimating P_{LN}, I performed the calculations using assumed values that ranged from 0 to 2 percent (which would be about 20 percent of all job-losers). My estimate of the initial value of P_{LE} was calculated by plugging these values into equation 8.2.

The results of these calculations are presented in table 8.2. The first four columns show the values of the variables from equation 8.2, and the second four columns show the changes in these variables between the 1991 to 1993 period and the 1993 to 1995 period from equation 8.3. Using the most conservative estimate ($P_{LN} = 0$ in the 1991 to 1993 period), the reemployment rate for job-losers would had to have

Table 8.2   Estimated Lower Bounds on the Change in the Reemployment Rate for Job-Losers Between the 1991 to 1993 Period and the 1993 to 1995 Period

Initial Values (1991 to 1993)				Change Between the 1991 to 1993 and 1993 to 1995 Periods				
P_L	P_{LU}	P_{LN}	P_{LE}	ΔP_L	ΔP_{LU}	ΔP_{LN}	ΔP_{LE}	$\Delta P_{LE}/P_{LE}$
9.60	2.74	0.00	6.86	−0.10	−0.64	0.00	0.54	7.86
9.60	2.74	0.50	6.36	−0.10	−0.64	0.00	0.54	8.47
9.60	2.74	1.00	5.86	−0.10	−0.64	0.00	0.54	9.20
9.60	2.74	1.50	5.36	−0.10	−0.64	0.00	0.54	10.05
9.60	2.74	2.00	4.86	−0.10	−0.64	0.00	0.54	11.09

Note: The data have been adjusted to account for recall bias and the CPS redesign.

increased by at least 7.7 percent—compared with the actual increase of 5.3 percent in the DWS—for the small decline in the job-loss rate observed in the DWS to be consistent with the EU job-loss rate from the March CPS. If we make the more reasonable assumption that $P_{LN} = 1$ in the 1991 to 1993 period (or about 10 percent of job-losers), then the implied percentage increase in the reemployment rate is 9.2 percent, well above the DWS estimate.

Hence, these calculations support the hypothesis that the job-loss rate actually decreased between the 1991 to 1993 period and 1993 to 1995 period, and that the change in the DWS resulted in more job-leavers being classified as job-losers than in previous years.

These calculations also illustrate the potential danger of trying to examine trends when the underlying data collection instrument has changed. The raw data seem to indicate that job security fell during the mid-1990s. But further examination shows that this finding was most likely caused by a change in the questionnaire rather than by a true change in job security.

Monks and Pizer

The sample used by Monks and Pizer (1998) was restricted to young men in two NLS cohorts—one age nineteen to twenty-seven in 1971 and one age nineteen to twenty-seven in 1984—who were working full-time (at least thirty hours per week) in 1971, 1973, 1976, and 1978 (from the NLSYM) and in 1984, 1985, 1989, and 1990 (from the NLSY). I was able to impose the cohort and sample year restrictions, but not the full-time restriction.[30]

As noted earlier, Monks and Pizer determined whether a job separation occurred in the two-year period following each sample year, and whether the separation was involuntary. Because the March CPS data measure EU transitions over a fourteen-and-a-half-month window, I used data for each year of their data (plus the following year to replicate their two-year window): 1971 to 1974 and 1976 to 1979 for the NLSYM cohorts, and 1984 to 1986 and 1989 to 1991 for the NLSY cohorts.[31]

I estimated Monks and Pizer's probit equations for involuntary separations (see their table 6) using March CPS data. The main variables of interest are the set of education dummy variables interacted with a time trend variable.[32] My results were qualitatively very similar to theirs for the control variables, but there were some differences in the coefficients on the main variables of interest.

Tables 8.3 and 8.4 compare the results on the main variables of interest from the two data sets. Table 8.3 compares the coefficients from probit equations on the EU transition rate (from the March CPS) and the job-loss rate (from the NLS) for both whites and nonwhites. Both data sources indicate that there were large and statistically significant increases

Table 8.3   Comparison to Monks and Pizer (1998): Probit Equations
on Job Loss in the NLS and EU Transitions in the March
CPS

	White		Nonwhite	
	March CPS	NLS	March CPS	NLS
Time trend interacted with				
High school dropout	0.0141***	0.0182***	0.0218***	0.0135*
	(0.0028)	(0.0060)	(0.0065)	(0.0077)
High school graduate	0.0090***	0.0126**	0.0094**	0.0206***
	(0.0022)	(0.0053)	(0.0053)	(0.0076)
Some college	0.0019	0.0194***	0.0080	0.0097
	(0.0029)	(0.0063)	(0.0075)	(0.0101)
College graduate	0.0019	0.0138**	−0.0166	0.0217
	(0.0040)	(0.0063)	(0.0115)	(0.0167)
Number of observations	53,053	14,551	6,541	5,442

Note: The NLS results are from Monks and Pizer (1998). The dependent variables equal 1 if the individual made an EU transition (March CPS) or involuntarily left a job (NLS). The regressions include the following control variables: a set of education dummies, the unemployment rate, age, marital status, and industry and occupation dummies.

*Significant at the .1 level.

**Significant at the .05 level.

***Significant at the .01 level.

in the job-loss rate (NLS) and the EU transition rate (March CPS) among high school dropouts and high school graduates. Among men with some college and college graduates, the NLS data show large and statistically significant increases in the job-loss rates for whites, but not for nonwhites. In contrast, for both whites and nonwhites the March CPS data show no change in the EU transition rate among men with some college and college graduates.

To better compare the magnitude of the estimated changes, I compared the 1971 to 1991 changes implied by the point estimates. These changes, which are expressed as percentage changes to make them more comparable, are shown in table 8.4.[33]

Among whites, the two data sources tell identical stories for high school dropouts and high school graduates but differ significantly when it comes to people with more than a high school diploma. Both data sources show that the probability of a job loss (or EU transition) increased by about 75 percent among white high school dropouts and by about 50 percent among white high school graduates. In the "some college" and "college graduate" categories, the NLS shows a much larger increase in the probability of a job loss than does the March CPS. For the "some college" category, the job-loss rate increased by 100 percent in

Table 8.4 Comparison to Monks and Pizer (1998): Implied Changes in Job Loss and EU Transition Rates

	March CPS (EU Transitions)			NLS (Job Loss)		
	Probability in 1971	Change from 1971 to 1990	Percentage Change	Probability in 1971	Change from 1971 to 1990	Percentage Change
White						
Education level						
High school dropout	3.8	2.9	76	9.9	7.4	75
High school graduate	2.5	1.2	48	7.1	3.8	54
Some college	2.4	0.3	13	5.4	5.4	100
College graduate	1.8	0.2	11	5.4	3.5	65
Nonwhite						
Education level						
High school dropout	5.8	6.6	114	14.8	6.7	45
High school graduate	4.5	2.0	44	10.4	8.9	86
Some college	3.9	1.5	38	10.1	3.7	37
College graduate	5.5	−2.7	−49	3.1	4.2	135

Note: These changes were computed using the coefficients from the probit equations in table 8.3. Steve Pizer kindly provided the probabilities computed from the NLS.

the NLS, compared with a 13 percent increase in the EU transition rate in the March CPS. For college graduates, the increases were 65 percent in the NLS and 11 percent in the March CPS.

The differences between the two data sources are even greater for non-whites. For high school dropouts, the increase in the March CPS data was twice that in the NLS data, while for high school graduates the reverse was true. I hesitate to say much about the other two education categories because none of the changes are statistically significant.

It is not clear why the two surveys tell such different stories, but differences in survey design between the NLSYM and the NLSY are probably not the cause. If they were, then we would expect the NLS to indicate uniformly larger increases in probabilities between 1971 and 1990. The fact that the NLS and the March CPS produced very similar results for some education groups but not for others suggests that something else is going on.

SUMMARY AND CONCLUSIONS

The evidence presented here suggests that job security, as measured using EU transition rates, declined in the early to mid-1970s and, except for cyclical fluctuations, remained constant through the mid- to late 1990s. This finding is consistent with the popular perception that jobs were less secure in the 1980s than in the 1970s, but not with the perception that job security continued to decline in the 1990s. A more detailed look at the EU transition rate for different demographic groups does not change this conclusion, but it does shed some light on how the perception that job security declined in the 1990s may have come about.

The 1990 recession was more "white-collar" than previous recessions. Neumark and Polsky (1998) hypothesized that reporters may have written more articles about worker displacement because a relatively large fraction of their peers had lost jobs. The evidence presented here is consistent with that hypothesis. Groups that are usually insulated from cyclical job loss—such as men with college degrees, men with more labor market experience, and white-collar workers—were relatively harder hit by the 1990 recession. The EU transition rates for these groups were about the same in both the 1982 and 1990 recessions, even though the 1990 recession was far less severe in terms of the decline in GDP. In contrast, the EU transition rates for less educated men, less experienced men, and blue-collar workers were much lower in the 1990 recession than in the 1982 recession.

It is also possible that the slow recovery from the 1990 recession contributed to this perception. Even though the recession officially ended in March 1991, the labor market did not begin to recover until much later. The EU transition rate peaked in 1991 but remained high through 1992.

The unemployment rate did not peak until 1992, and job growth was sluggish through 1992.

The advantage of using March CPS data is that the series extends through 1997, so it is possible to distinguish between a slower than normal recovery from the 1990 recession and the start of a secular trend. The return of the EU transition rate to its prerecession level by 1994 implies that the higher EU transition rates in the early 1990s were not the start of a secular trend. Most other studies cannot make this distinction because the data used stop in the early 1990s. Farber's (1997a) data go through 1995, but it is problematic to make inferences about trends in the 1990s because of wording changes in the main question in the DWS.

In comparing my results to those of other researchers, I found that my results were generally consistent, though there were some differences worth noting.

I found that my results are generally consistent with those of Boisjoly, Duncan, and Smeeding (1998). Both the job-loss rate in the PSID and the EU transition rate in the March CPS show that jobs were less secure in the 1980s compared with the 1970s. Both data sources indicate that job security declined throughout the 1970s and remained constant or decreased slightly in the 1980s. However, by looking at only men, Boisjoly, Duncan, and Smeeding tended to overstate the overall decrease in job security because women did not experience as large a decline.

My results are similar to Farber's (1997a), except for the mid-1990s. The job-loss rate in the DWS data remained constant, and the EU transition rate in the March CPS data fell. I presented evidence that the DWS job-loss rate for the 1993 to 1995 period may have been affected by a subtle wording change in the main question. A consistency check indicates that it is likely that a larger fraction of job-leavers were classified as job-losers in the 1996 DWS than in previous years. Hence, it appears that job-loss rates actually fell in the mid-1990s. This finding illustrates the difficulty of trying to examine trends when the underlying data collection instrument has changed.

I was able to replicate Monks and Pizer's (1998) results for some groups but not for others. Results from the NLS and the March CPS were close for white high school dropouts and high school graduates. In the "some college" and "college graduate" categories, Monks and Pizer found a large increase in the job-loss rate, whereas I found very little change.

ACKNOWLEDGMENTS

This paper has benefited from conversations with Harley Frazis, Mark Loewenstein, Marilyn Manser, Jim Spletzer, and Rob Valletta. I thank two anonymous referees for their suggestions. I also thank Hank Farber, Larry Katz, David Neumark, and other participants in the Russell Sage Foundation's Conference on Changes in Job Stability and Job Security for their comments on an earlier version of the chapter. Héctor Rodríguez assisted in putting together the tables and figures. Any opinions expressed here are mine and do not necessarily reflect those of the Bureau of Labor Statistics.

NOTES

1. *Job stability* refers to the duration of jobs, without regard to the reasons for increasing or decreasing duration. Examples of job stability measures include retention rates (Swinnerton and Wial 1995, 1996; Marcotte 1996; Diebold, Neumark, and Polsky 1996, 1997; and Neumark, Polsky, and Hansen, this volume), job tenure (Farber 1998), the fraction of workers in new jobs (Jaeger and Stevens, this volume), and turnover (Rose 1995; Monks and Pizer 1998; Stewart 1998). *Job security* refers to the extent to which job separations are involuntary. The primary measure of job security is the job-loss rate (Polsky 1999; Farber 1997a, 1997b; Boisjoly, Duncan, and Smeeding 1998; Monks and Pizer 1998; Valletta, this volume).

2. Diebold, Neumark, and Polsky (1997) found that job stability fell among less educated workers but did not present gender breaks.

3. The shorter time period was used because a key variable for identifying job separations was not available until March 1976 (covering calendar year 1975). This variable is not required to identify EU transitions.

4. Recall bias is more of a problem if information on the year of the job loss is used to determine changes in the job-loss rate within the period covered by a single DWS. Because recent job losses are more likely to be reported, increases in the job-loss rate are overstated, while decreases are understated. However, using three-year job-loss rates (as Farber did) minimizes the impact of this bias.

5. Daniel Aaronson and Daniel Sullivan (1998) avoided the problem completely by restricting their analysis to workers with five or more years of tenure and job losses that occurred in the three years prior to the survey. They found that job-loss rates increased in the 1990s, but their analysis does not account for the 1996 change in the wording of the main question in the DWS.

6. In a similar analysis, Annette Bernhardt and her colleagues (this volume) look at job stability using NLS data.

7. More specifically, the respondent is asked whether he or she was working during a specific month and year about two years prior to the interview.

8. Interviews for the NLSYM were conducted annually from 1966 through 1971 and in 1973, 1975, 1976, 1978, 1980, 1981, 1983, and 1990. Monks and Pizer (1998) used data from 1971, 1973, 1976, and 1978 as their base years and determined whether respondents were still working at their main (CPS) job two years later.

9. Most of the research on this issue looks at Survey of Income and Program Participation (SIPP) data in the context of generating monthly gross flows

data (see, for example, Martini and Ryscavage 1991). Charles Pierret (1999) analyzed data from an NLSY test that collected data for 1992 in both the 1993 and 1994 interviews. He found that respondents were more likely to both forget and misremember events from 1992 in the 1994 interview than in the 1993 interview.

10. I use nineteen rather than eighteen as the cutoff because the age refers to the age at the time of the survey.

11. I compute potential experience as Age minus Years of Schooling Completed minus 6 if Years of Schooling is greater than 10 years, and as Age minus 16 for those with 10 or fewer Years of Schooling Completed. This definition is used in Murphy and Welch (1992). Experience is computed as of March of the previous year.

12. I use this restriction because it is not possible to identify students and recent graduates on a consistent basis for the years covered by my data.

13. I include wage and salary workers who have some self-employment income.

14. Using the full sample would result in a relatively small decline in standard errors. If the observations were independent, there would be a 40 percent reduction in the standard errors. But because each individual shows up twice (in consecutive years) in the full sample, it would be necessary to account for the covariance between observations making the actual reduction much smaller.

15. It is not clear how the reentrants should be classified. These individuals left the labor force because they lost or left a job but had reentered the labor force by March. They could be job-losers who became discouraged over their prospects of finding a new job, or they could be job-leavers who left the labor force.

    Note also that the reentrants group includes the 0.03 percent who were classified as new entrants. Presumably these new entrants were miscoded because everybody in the sample worked at some point during the previous year. For that reason (and because there are so few of them), I grouped the new entrants with the reentrants.

16. The results did not change when I looked at job-leavers and reentrants separately.

17. All of the probit equations used for figures 8.2 through 8.8 include demographic controls (dummy variables for three education levels, four experience levels, and dummy variables for race, sex, and marital status). In the probits for subgroups, the appropriate control variables are omitted.

18. Prior to 1992, the CPS used a years-of-schooling measure, whereas the 1992 and later surveys use a degree based measure. The assignment of observations to the four education categories (high school dropouts, high school graduates, some college, and college graduates) accounts for the 1992 change in the education attainment question in the CPS (see Frazis and Stewart 1999 for a description of the coding).

19. I thank Dave Macpherson for providing me with the program used to convert the 1970 Census Bureau occupation codes to 1980 codes. The graphs begin

in 1970 because the occupation codes used in the 1968 to 1970 March CPS files are not compatible with the 1970 and later Census Bureau codes.

20. Boisjoly, Duncan, and Smeeding (1998) did not adjust their data for the change in recall period noted in Diebold, Neumark, and Polsky (1997).

21. Farber used three-year intervals because the DWS measures the number of people who lost at least one job in the previous three years. Although the DWS identifies the year in which the job loss occurred, it is not designed to count the number of people who lost a job in a particular year.

22. Evans and Leighton (1995) found that respondents forgot job losses at a rate of about 17 percent per year. The exact adjustment factors are 0.908 for the previous year, 0.748 for the second year, and 0.616 for the third year. Thus, to adjust the data for the 1981 to 1982 period, the EU transition rate for 1983 was multiplied by 0.908, the EU transition rate for 1982 was multiplied by 0.748, and the EU transition rate for 1981 was multiplied by 0.616.

23. I also compared the EU transition rate and the job-loss rates by sex, by sex and education level, and by sex and age, and got qualitatively similar results.

24. The data reported here were provided by Jim Esposito of BLS. They are from the debriefing questions in the 1998 DWS. (The results are very similar to those from the 1996 DWS.)

25. The data were taken from Farber's (1997a) table 7 and appendix table 1.

26. This measure is more intuitively described as the fraction of workers who lost a job and then found a new job.

27. These adjustments do not affect the results. In fact, the calculated lower bounds were larger before making the adjustments for recall bias and the CPS redesign.

28. Actually, it is a decreasing function of P_L in the initial period. But recall that, by assumption, ΔP_L is close to zero.

29. There is the issue of recall bias, which would tend to work in the opposite direction. To check the reasonableness of using the DWS rate, I computed job-loss rates from the Basic CPS using the "reason for unemployment" variable. I computed the "monthly" job-loss rate as the number of permanent job-losers that were unemployed for four or fewer weeks divided by total employment in March. To arrive at an annual number, I multiplied by 13. The estimated annual rate of .092 is an overestimate of the relevant job-loss rate because it counts multiple job-losers more than once.

30. The required hours data are not available until the March 1976 CPS.

31. The results do not qualitatively change if only the sample years are used.

32. In addition to the main variables of interest, Monks and Pizer's equation included dummy variables for education level, the average unemployment rate, age at time of interview, marital status, and for industry and occupation. They also included a variable to account for differences in the time between the initial interview and the interview approximately two years later. I did not include this variable because this variation does not apply to the CPS.

33. Steve Pizer kindly provided the probabilities computed from the NLS.

REFERENCES

Aaronson, Daniel, and Daniel Sullivan. 1998. "The Decline of Job Security in the 1990s: Displacement, Anxiety, and Their Effect on Wage Growth." *Federal Reserve Bank of Chicago Economic Perspectives* 22(1): 17–43.

Abraham, Katharine G. 1997. "Comment on Farber 'The Changing Face of Job Loss in the United States: 1981–1995.'" *Brookings Papers on Economic Activity: Microeconomics.* 135–42.

Boisjoly, Johanne, Greg J. Duncan, and Timothy Smeeding. 1998. "The Shifting Incidence of Involuntary Job Losses from 1968 to 1992." *Industrial Relations* 37(2): 207–31.

Brown, James N., and Audrey Light. 1992. "Interpreting Panel Data on Job Tenure." *Journal of Labor Economics* 10(3): 219–57.

Diebold, Francis X., David Neumark, and Daniel Polsky. 1996. "Comment on Kenneth A. Swinnerton and Howard Wial, 'Is Job Stability Declining in the U.S. Economy?'" *Industrial and Labor Relations Review* 49(2): 348–52.

——. 1997. "Job Stability in the United States." *Journal of Labor Economics* 15(2): 206–33.

Evans, David S., and Linda S. Leighton. 1995. "Retrospective Bias in the Displaced Workers Surveys." *Journal of Human Resources* 30(2): 386–96.

Fallick, Bruce C. 1996. "A Review of the Recent Literature on Displaced Workers." *Industrial and Labor Relations Review* 50(1): 5–16.

Farber, Henry S. 1993. "The Incidence and Costs of Job Loss: 1982–1991." *Brooking Papers on Economic Activity: Microeconomics* 1: 73–132.

——. 1997a. "The Changing Face of Job Loss in the United States: 1981–1995." *Brookings Papers on Economic Activity: Microeconomics* 1: 55–128.

——. 1997b. "Has the Rate of Job Loss Increased over Time?" Unpublished paper. Princeton University (December).

——. 1998. "Are Lifetime Jobs Disappearing?: Job Duration in the United States: 1973–1993." In *Labor Statistics Measurement Issues,* edited by John Haltiwanger, Marilyn Manser, and Robert Topel. Chicago: University of Chicago Press.

Frazis, Harley, and Jay Stewart. 1999. "Tracking the Returns to Education in the 1990s: Bridging the Gap Between the New and Old Current Population Survey Education Items." *Journal of Human Resources* 34(3): 629–41.

Marcotte, David. 1996. "Has Job Stability Declined?: Evidence from the Panel Study of Income Dynamics." Unpublished paper. Northern Illinois University.

Martini, Alberto, and Paul Ryscavage. 1991. "The Impact of Survey and Questionnaire Design on Longitudinal Labor Force Measures." Unpublished paper. U.S. Department of Commerce, Bureau of the Census.

Monks, James, and Steven Pizer. 1998. "Trends in Voluntary and Involuntary Job Turnover." *Industrial Relations* 37(4): 440–59.

Murphy, Kevin M., and Finis Welch. 1992. "The Structure of Wages." *Quarterly Journal of Economics* 107(1): 285–326.

Neumark, David, and Daniel Polsky. 1998. "Changes in Job Stability and Job Security: Anecdotes and Evidence." In *Industrial Relations Research Association: Proceedings of the Fiftieth Annual Meeting,* edited by Paula B. Voos (vol.

1). Madison: Industrial Relations Research Association, University of Wisconsin.

Pierret, Charles. 1999. "Event History Data and Survey Recall: An Analysis of the NLSY Recall Experiment." Unpublished paper. U.S. Department of Labor, Bureau of Labor Statistics.

Polivka, Anne E., and Steven Miller. 1998. "The CPS After the Redesign: Refocusing the Economic Lens." In *Labor Statistics Measurement Issues,* edited by John Haltiwanger, Marilyn Manser, and Robert Topel. Chicago: University of Chicago Press.

Polsky, Daniel. 1999. "Changing Consequences of Job Separation in the United States." *Industrial and Labor Relations Review* 52(4): 565–80.

Rose, Stephen. 1995. "Declining Job Security and the Professionalization of Opportunity." Report 95–04. Washington, D.C.: National Commission for Employment Policy (April).

Ruhm, Christopher. 1991. "Are Workers Permanently Scarred by Job Displacements?" *American Economic Review* 81(1): 319–24.

Stewart, Jay. 1998. "Has Job Mobility Increased? Evidence from the Current Population Survey: 1975–1995." Working paper 308. Washington, D.C.: U.S. Bureau of Labor Statistics.

Swinnerton, Kenneth A., and Howard Wial. 1995. "Is Job Stability Declining in the U.S. Economy?" *Industrial and Labor Relations Review* 49(2): 293–304.

———. 1996. "Is Job Stability Declining in the U.S. Economy? Reply to Diebold, Neumark, and Polsky." *Industrial and Labor Relations Review* 49(2): 352–55.

Chapter 9

Job Security Beliefs in the General Social Survey: Evidence on Long-Run Trends and Comparability with Other Surveys

Stefanie R. Schmidt

In 1997 both Federal Reserve Chairman Alan Greenspan and former U.S. Secretary of Labor Robert Reich argued that the level of anxiety about job security was unusually high for an economic recovery. The *Washington Post,* the *New York Times,* the *Wall Street Journal,* and *USA Today* ran stories claiming that anxiety about job loss had increased in recent years.

Reich and other writers have argued that the decline in job security has changed the employment relationship, particularly for white-collar workers. Because workers are more anxious about losing their jobs than they were in the past, they are investing less in firm-specific human capital and are more concerned about developing general skills and a network of colleagues that will enable them to find their next job (Micklethwait and Wooldridge 1997).

In recent years, a growing literature has examined whether the alleged rise in anxiety about job loss is realistic, that is, whether jobs became less stable during the 1990s than they were in the past. Taken as a whole, the literature suggests an increase in involuntary job loss and a modest decline in job stability between the late 1980s and early 1990s (Neumark, Polsky, and Hansen, this volume).

But the literature has largely ignored the issue of what workers *believe* about their own job security. Trends in involuntary job-loss rates are indicators of the economic well-being of the minority of workers who have recently lost their jobs. However, we can learn about how changes in job stability and job loss are affecting *all* workers only by looking at data on job security perceptions. Theories about changes in the employment relationship are based on growing anxiety about job security, not simply on rising job-loss rates.

This chapter uses the 1977 to 1996 General Social Survey (GSS) to examine whether in fact workers have become more pessimistic about their own job security and whether those fears are consistent with trends in rates of involuntary job loss. It is the first study to provide an in-depth examination of long-term trends in perceptions about job security.[1] Two measures of workers' beliefs about their own job security are examined: beliefs about the likelihood that they will lose their job during the next twelve months, and beliefs about the likelihood that losing their job will be costly, that is, that job loss will result in a decline in earnings. If trends in job security beliefs diverged from trends in involuntary job loss, we could conclude that workers are overly pessimistic.

The analysis of the GSS data shows that the 1990s have been a period of relative pessimism about job security. During the economic recovery years, 1993 to 1996, workers were more pessimistic about keeping their jobs and about the chances of costly job loss than during the late 1980s, an economic recovery with comparably low unemployment. Despite the fact that the recession of 1990 to 1991 was much less severe than the recession of 1982 to 1983, workers' beliefs about their chances of job loss were quite similar during the two recessions. The pattern in overall beliefs about job security is consistent with data from the Displaced Workers Survey (DWS). Rates of involuntary job loss increased between the 1980s and 1990s, and earnings declines following involuntary job loss were more severe during most of the 1990s than they were during the previous decade (Farber 1997, 1998). The trends in job security beliefs by subgroup are largely consistent with the trends in rates of involuntary job loss for those subgroups in the DWS.

THE GENERAL SOCIAL SURVEY

This study uses the 1977 to 1996 General Social Survey, a series of cross-sectional surveys conducted by the National Opinion Research Center (NORC). The GSS, administered in February and March of each survey year, collects data from a representative sample of the U.S. adult population. For this chapter, the sample is restricted to individuals age eighteen and older who are employed full-time or part-time during the survey week. The sample size for individual cross-sections ranges from 601 to 1,364. The questionnaire asks for demographic information and opinions about a wide range of topics, and it includes two questions about job security expectations. The two questions were included in fourteen surveys between 1977 and 1996.[2]

The first question measures the beliefs of employed respondents about their chances of job loss: "Thinking about the next twelve months, how likely do you think it is that you will lose your job or be laid off—Is it very likely, fairly likely, not too likely, or not at all likely?" The second question measures workers' beliefs about their ability to find another job with similar compensation. "About how easy would it be for you to find a job with another employer with approximately the same income and fringe benefits you now have? Would you say very easy, somewhat easy, or not easy at all?"

By combining answers to the two questions, I define a variable that measures whether workers believe that they will probably suffer a pay cut or unemployment as a result of job loss in the near future. Respondents who fear costly job loss are those who said that they were very or fairly likely to lose their job in the next year, and who also said that they could not easily find another job with similar compensation.

DESCRIPTIVE STATISTICS

Figure 9.1 shows the trends in the fraction of GSS respondents who believed that job loss was very likely or fairly likely. Figure 9.2 shows the fraction who believed that they were likely to experience costly job loss. The vertical lines around each data point show the 95 percent confidence intervals.

Figures 9.1 and 9.2 show two striking patterns. First, aggregated workers' expectations about keeping their jobs and finding another have tracked the unemployment rate fairly closely. Second, during the economic recovery of 1993 to 1996, workers were more pessimistic about

Figure 9.1   Workers Who Believed That They Were Likely to Lose Their Jobs in the Next Twelve Months, 1977 to 1996 (95 Percent Confidence Intervals Shown)

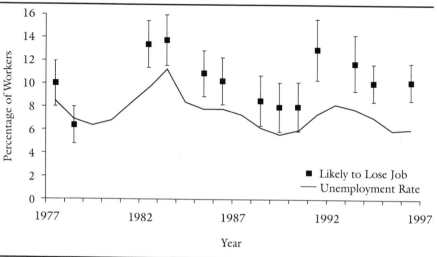

Sources: General Social Survey and U.S. Bureau of Labor Statistics.

Figure 9.2   Workers Who Believed That They Were Likely to Experience Costly Job Loss, 1977 to 1996 (95 Percent Confidence Intervals Shown)

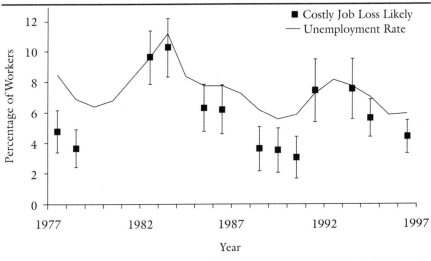

Sources: General Social Survey and U.S. Bureau of Labor Statistics.

both measures of job security than they were during previous periods of low unemployment in the late 1970s and late 1980s.

Given the relatively small sample sizes of the GSS cross-sections, t-tests lack power to detect some economically important differences in workers' beliefs across years.[3] Only two years (1982 and 1983) showed statistically significantly higher percentages of workers who believed that job loss was likely than the most recent survey in 1996. The percentages in 1982, 1983, and 1996 were 13.6, 13.8, and 9.8, respectively. One year of GSS data, 1978, showed a significantly lower share of workers (6.4 percent) who believed that job loss was likely than did 1996. The pattern for the percentage of workers who believed that costly job loss was likely was similar: 1982 and 1983 were the only years that showed significantly higher levels of job insecurity than 1996.

PROBIT MODEL RESULTS: BELIEFS ABOUT JOB SECURITY

This section uses probit models to document the trends in the two measures of job security beliefs, controlling for the profound changes in the composition of the labor force since the late 1970s. The results are similar to those shown in the descriptive statistics. During the economic recovery of the 1990s, workers were more pessimistic about their own job security than during previous economic recoveries.

Table 9.1 reports the results of probit models with two different dependent variables based on the two job security measures. Each model includes a series of dummy variables as controls: female, nonwhite, three age categories, three education categories, part-time status, two occupation categories, service-producing industry, and eight census regions. The base category consists of white male high school graduates between the ages of twenty-five and thirty-nine who worked full-time in blue-collar jobs in the manufacturing sector and lived in the mid-Atlantic region. The base year is 1988 because it was a similar point in the business cycle to 1996; both were economic recovery years several years from the depth of recessions. The reported coefficient for each year's dummy variable represents the change in the predicted value of the dependent variable due to a one-unit increase in that explanatory variable, holding constant the other explanatory variables at their mean values.

WORKERS' BELIEFS ABOUT LOSING THEIR JOBS IN THE NEAR FUTURE

If workers' beliefs were consistent with trends in involuntary job loss, we would expect workers to be more worried about keeping their jobs during the 1990s than they were in the past. Henry Farber (1998) showed that rates of involuntary job loss during the 1993 to 1997 economic recovery were higher than they were during the economic recovery of the late 1980s.[4] Controlling for the business cycle, Daniel Polsky (in press) finds a growth in involuntary job loss between the period 1976 to 1981 and the period 1986 to 1991. Rob Valletta and Randy O'Toole (1997) documented a secular increase in the share of unemployment due to involuntary job loss between 1968 and 1993. The probit model results show that workers were more concerned about keeping their jobs during the 1990s than they were in the past.

In the specifications reported in the first two columns of table 9.1, the dependent variable is equal to one for workers who believed that they were very or fairly likely to lose their jobs in the next twelve months, and zero otherwise. Column 1 does not include a control for the business cycle. Column 2 includes the regional unemployment rate.

Figure 9.3 plots the year effects from column 1 against the national unemployment rate. The coefficient for the base year, 1988, is plotted as zero. The bars show the 95 percent confidence intervals of the coefficients. Like the raw data in figure 9.1, the year effects show that concerns about job security were higher during the 1990s than during the 1980s. In 1982 and 1991, years that were at the beginning of economic downturns, the probabilities that workers believed that they were likely to lose their jobs were quite similar, despite the fact that the unemployment rate was much higher in 1982 than in 1991. The 1982 coefficient is .0563, and the 1991 coefficient is .0524. During the economic recovery years of

Table 9.1   Probit Models of Workers' Perceptions About Their Own Job
Security (General Social Survey Data)

	Dependent Variable = Likely to Lose Job		Dependent Variable = Likely to Experience Costly Job Loss	
	(1)	(2)	(3)	(4)
Regional un-employ-ment rate	—	.00631*** (.00254)	—	.00680** (.00234)
1977	.0155 (.0183)	.00502 (.02211)	.0111 (.0148)	.000718 (.01351)
1978	−.0224 (.0153)	−.0252 (.0158)	.00272 (.00147)	−.00003 (.00910)
1982	.0563*** (.0219)	.0292 (.0276)	.0759*** (.0226)	.0386*** (.0153)
1983	.0692*** (.0242)	.0290 (.0209)	.0922*** (.0255)	.0360* (.0234)
1985	.300 (.204)	.0189** (.0099)	.0368** (.0190)	.0234* (.0133)
1986	.0211 (.0189)	.0104 (.0205)	.0356** (.0181)	.0221** (.0109)
1988	base year	base year	base year	base year
1989	−.00424 (.01822)	−.00009 (.0253)	−.00237 (.01448)	.00251 (.00983)
1990	−.00269 (.01818)	−.00039 (.0245)	−.00868 (.0131)	.00619 (.0127)
1991	.0524** (.0237)	.0442 (.0312)	.0513** (.0220)	.0419*** (.0121)
1993	.0444** (.0224)	.0321** (.0161)	.0598*** (.0223)	.0438** (.0219)
1994	.0227 (.0177)	.0170 (.0185)	.0290** (.0159)	.0229* (.0143)
1996	.0255 (.0178)	.0281 (.0230)	.0142 (.0140)	.0181 (.00402)
Sample size	11,304	11,304	11,271	11,271
Log likelihood	−3,578	−3,575	−2,375	−2,370

Source: General Social Survey.

Note: Standard errors are in parentheses. Each probit model included the following dummy variables as controls: female, nonwhite, three age categories, three education categories, two occupation categories, service-producing industry, part-time worker, and eight census regions. The reported coefficient for each explanatory variable respresents the change in the predicted value of the dependent variable due to a one-unit increase in that explanatory variable, holding constant the other explanatory variables at their mean values. The heteroskedasticity robust standard errors are adjusted for the regional clustering of data.

***Significant at 99 percent level.

**Significant at 95 percent level.

*Significant at 90 percent level.

**Figure 9.3   Year Effects from "Likely to Lose Job" Probit, 1977 to 1996
(95 Percent Confidence Intervals Shown)**

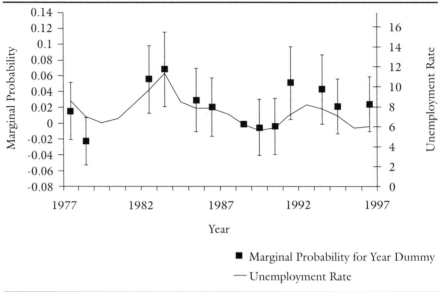

Sources: General Social Survey and U.S. Bureau of Labor Statistics.

1994 and 1996, workers were much more concerned about losing their jobs than they were during years of comparably low unemployment rates, 1978 and the 1988 to 1990 period. In 1996 workers were two and a half percentage points more likely to believe that job loss was probable than they were in 1988, and slightly more pessimistic relative to 1989 and 1990. Given that the mean of the dependent variable was .085 in 1988, the difference of two and a half percentage points between 1988 and 1996 represents nearly a 30 percent increase in the probability that workers believed that job loss was likely.

The 1994 and 1996 year dummies are not individually statistically significant, partly because of the limited power of a chi-squared test to find an effect of that size using the GSS. A chi-squared test found the 1991 to 1996 year dummies to be jointly significant at the 90 percent level. It is important to note that conclusions about the statistical significance of the year dummy coefficients in figure 9.3 are relative to the omitted year, 1988. If the economic recovery years of 1978, 1988, or 1989 were chosen as the base category of the probit model, the 1991 to 1996 year coefficients would still be jointly statistically significant. However, if a different year were chosen, the 1991 to 1996 coefficients would not be statistically significant.

The results in column 2, which includes the unemployment rate controls, are consistent with the patterns shown in figure 9.3. Relative to the recovery of the late 1980s, workers' fears about job loss were high during the period from 1991 to 1996.

BELIEFS ABOUT COSTLY JOB LOSS

If workers' beliefs about suffering a job loss that results in a decline in compensation were consistent with trends in the labor market, we would expect them to be more pessimistic during the 1990s than they were in the past. Farber (1998) found that workers who experienced involuntary job loss between 1991 and 1995 suffered larger postdisplacement earnings declines than workers who were displaced at similar points in the business cycle during the 1980s. However, the earnings consequences of job loss improved for workers displaced between 1995 and 1997. In addition, workers who were displaced from full-time jobs between 1991 and 1997 were more likely to hold part-time jobs at the survey date than workers displaced from full-time jobs. In addition, Polsky (in press) finds that the probability of reemployment following a job loss declined between the 1976 to 1981 period and the 1986 to 1991 period. The GSS probit model results show that during the 1993 to 1996 economic recovery, workers were more concerned about costly job loss than they were during the economic recoveries of the late 1970s and late 1980s.

Columns 3 and 4 of table 9.1 show the results of a probit model in which the dependent variable is equal to one for workers who believed that they were very or fairly likely to lose their jobs and that they could not easily find another job with similar compensation. Figure 9.4 plots the year effects in column 3 against the national unemployment rate. Like the raw data in figure 9.2, figure 9.4 shows that workers were more concerned about costly job loss during the economic recovery of 1993 to 1996 than during earlier recoveries. In 1996 workers were 1.4 percentage points more likely to believe that costly job loss was likely than they were in 1988, and slightly more pessimistic relative to 1989 and 1990. Given that the mean of the dependent variable was .036 in 1988, the 1.4-percentage-point difference represents nearly a 40 percent increase in the probability that workers believed that costly job loss was likely between 1988 and 1996. In 1994 workers were 2.9 percentage points more likely to believe that costly job loss was likely compared to 1988.

The 1996 coefficient was not individually statistically significant in part because of the limited power of a chi-squared test to detect an effect of that size in a sample the size of the GSS. However, a chi-squared test found the 1991 to 1996 year dummies to be jointly significant at the 99 percent level.

Figure 9.4 Year Effects from "Likely to Experience Costly Job Loss" Probit, 1977 to 1996 (95 Percent Confidence Intervals Shown)

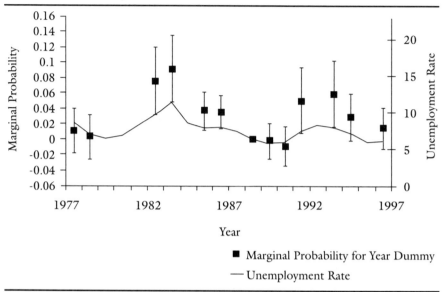

Sources: General Social Survey and U.S. Bureau of Labor Statistics.

GSS PROBIT MODEL RESULTS: TRENDS IN BELIEFS ABOUT JOB SECURITY FOR SUBGROUPS OF WORKERS

TRENDS BY OCCUPATION

If perceptions about job security were consistent with trends in involuntary job loss, we would expect to see an increase in pessimism about job loss among white-collar workers and service occupation workers. These groups of workers, who had been relatively insulated from job loss in the 1980s, experienced large increases in their rates of involuntary job loss in the 1990s (Farber 1997, 1998).

The trends in job security beliefs by occupation mirror the trends in rates of involuntary job loss. During the 1990s, white-collar workers and service occupation workers became more pessimistic about keeping their jobs, and white-collar workers became more concerned about costly job loss. Blue-collar workers became significantly more optimistic about keeping their jobs, but not about costly job loss.

Table 9.2 shows the results when the "likely to lose job" and "likely to experience costly job loss" probit models are estimated separately by occupation, education, or age subgroup. Table 9.2 reports only one coefficient from each model, the coefficient from the 1991 to 1996 year dum-

Table 9.2   Coefficients on 1991 to 1996 Dummy Variable from Probit Models Estimated Separately by Occupation, Education, or Age Subgroup

Subgroup Used to Estimate Probit Models	Dependent Variable = Likely to Lose Job	Dependent Variable = Likely to Experience Costly Job Loss	N for Subgroup
White-collar worker	.0340***	.0262***	6,509
	(.0054)	(.0032)	
Service occupation worker	.0282*	.00418	1,563
	(.0168)	(.00912)	
Blue-collar worker	− .0352*	− .0183	3,199
	(.0192)	(.0186)	
High school dropout	.00260	.0340**	1,650
	(.02462)	(.0118)	
High school graduate	.00216	− .0108	3,947
	(.0171)	(.0096)	
Some college	.0330**	.0286**	2,947
	(.0153)	(.0071)	
College graduate	.0212***	.0135**	2,727
	(.0047)	(.0030)	
Ages eighteen to twenty-four	.0183	− .0116	1,231
	(.0322)	(.0138)	
Ages twenty-five to thirty-nine	.0155	.0178**	4,962
	(.0105)	(.0092)	
Ages forty to fifty-four	.0179	.0103	3,463
	(.0116)	(.0091)	
Ages fifty-five and older	.0254**	.0272**	1,615
	(.0117)	(.0135)	

Note: Dependent variables are workers' beliefs about their chances of job loss. The probit models include the following dummy variables as controls: female, nonwhite, service-producing industry, part-time worker, eight census regions, and a control for the regional unemployment rate. The models by occupation group include controls for three education category dummy variables and three age category dummy variables. The separate models by education group include two occupation category dummy variables and three age category dummy variables. The separate models by age group include three education category dummy variables and two occupation category dummy variables. The reported coeffiicient for each explanatory variable represents the change in the predicted value of the dependent variable due to a one-unit increase in that explanatory variable, holding constant the other explanatory variables at their mean values. The heteroskedasticity robust standard errors are adjusted for the regional clustering of data.

***Significant at 99 percent level.

**Significant at 95 percent level.

*Significant at 90 percent level.

mies. The models also include a number of controls, including the regional unemployment rate. The omitted year category is the period 1982 to 1990. Therefore, the 1991 to 1996 coefficient shows how much higher fears about job loss were in the 1990s relative to the 1980s, controlling for the business cycle. Because figures 9.1 and 9.3 show an upturn in overall fears about job loss in 1991, 1990 was grouped with the 1980s.

The first three rows of table 9.2 show the results of probit models estimated separately by three broad occupational categories—white-collar workers, service occupation workers, and blue-collar workers. Service occupations include nurses, police officers, and retail clerks.

Controlling for the business cycle, the probability that white-collar workers believed that they were likely to lose their jobs was 3.40 percentage points higher in 1991 to 1996 than it was during the 1980s, and the probability that they believed in costly job loss was 2.62 percentage points higher. Those coefficients represent substantial increases over the 1980s levels. During the 1980s, 7.2 percent of white-collar workers believed that job loss was likely, and 3.9 percent believed that costly job loss was likely.

Blue-collar workers were more optimistic about keeping their jobs between 1991 and 1996 than they were during the 1980s. Between the 1980s and the 1991 to 1996 period, blue-collar workers experienced a 3.52-percentage-point decline in the probability that they believed that job loss was likely. That was a small decline relative to the percentage of blue-collar workers who believed that job loss was likely in the 1980s—19 percent.

Because white-collar workers became more pessimistic about keeping their jobs and blue-collar workers became less pessimistic, the beliefs of the two groups converged during the 1990s. Descriptive statistics illustrate this convergence. In the 1985 to 1990 period, 6.2 percent of white-collar workers believed that they were likely to lose their jobs, while the proportion of blue-collar workers was 16.5 percent. By 1996 their beliefs were very similar: 10.1 percent of white-collar workers believed that they were likely to lose their jobs compared with 9.72 percent of blue-collar workers.

Service occupation workers also experienced a statistically significant increase in their fears about keeping their jobs between the 1980s and the 1991 to 1996 period. The 2.82-percentage-point increase was substantial compared to the share of service occupation workers who believed that they were likely to lose their jobs in the 1980s—11.6 percent—but similar to the increase among white-collar workers.

TRENDS BY EDUCATION LEVEL

If trends in job security beliefs were consistent with trends in the Displaced Workers Survey, one would expect to see workers with some college and college graduates become more pessimistic about keeping their jobs and about costly job loss during the 1990s. Both groups had been relatively insulated from job loss during the 1980s and experienced increases in rates of involuntary job loss and in earnings declines following job loss during the 1990s. High school dropouts and graduates experienced little change in their rates of involuntary job loss or in the consequences of job loss (Farber 1997, 1998).

Rows 4 through 7 of table 9.2 show the results of probit models estimated separately by education category. The trends in beliefs about job loss by education level are largely consistent with trends in involuntary job loss. College graduates and those with some college became more pessimistic about losing their jobs and about costly job loss. High school dropouts and high school graduates experienced little change in their beliefs about their chances of job loss. High school dropouts became more pessimistic about their chances of costly job loss. That result is inconsistent with DWS data, which show little change in the consequences of displacement for high school dropouts during the 1990s (Farber 1997, 1998).

TRENDS BY AGE

Workers older than age forty-five experienced the largest percentage increase in involuntary job loss during the 1990s (Farber 1998). In addition, workers with more than nine years of tenure experienced the largest declines in job stability between the late 1980s and 1990s (Neumark, Polsky, and Hansen, this volume).

Rows 8 through 11 of table 9.2 show the results of probit models estimated separately by age group. As expected, workers age fifty-five and older became significantly more pessimistic, both about losing their jobs and about costly job loss, during the 1990s. But workers age forty to fifty-four did not become significantly more worried about job loss or costly job loss, despite the fact that they experienced sizable increases in rates of involuntary job loss during the 1990s. Middle-aged workers appeared to be overly optimistic about their job security during the 1990s.

ROBUSTNESS OF RESULTS:
DATA FROM OTHER PUBLIC OPINION POLLS

Public opinion research shows that respondents' answers can sometimes be greatly affected by question wording and by survey questions that precede the question of interest (Alwin and Krosnick 1991; Zaller 1992). If respondents' answers are robust to changes in question wording and ordering, then the data are more reliable indicators of public opinion.

This section compares GSS data on job security beliefs to similar data in two other public opinion data sets. Respondents' answers to questions about their own job security do not appear to be greatly affected by question wording and context. Therefore, the trends in the GSS job security data do not appear to be driven by something unique to the survey.

COMPARISON WITH PROBABILISTIC DATA FROM THE SURVEY OF ECONOMIC EXPECTATIONS

In this section, I show that trends in respondents' answers to job security questions are not greatly affected by whether the question asks for a qualitative response (for example, "50 percent chance of losing job") or probabilistic response (for example, "very likely to lose job"). The finding is important because qualitative expectations data are believed to be less reliable than probabilistic data. Jeff Dominitz and Charles Manski (1998) argued that expectations questions with probabilistic answers are preferable because qualitative answers are not comparable across individuals. In other words, the meaning of "very likely" in terms of probabilities is highly subjective.

The Survey of Economic Expectations (SEE) asks respondents for probabilistic answers to questions about their job security expectations. The SEE is a series of six cross-sectional surveys that were a module of the University of Wisconsin Survey Research Center's WISCON omnibus survey between 1994 and early 1997.

Two types of comparisons between the SEE and GSS job security questions show the robustness of the GSS results to changes in question wording. First, the trends in workers' beliefs about their chances of losing their jobs and about their chances of costly job loss were similar in the two surveys. Second, when identical probit models are estimated using the two surveys, the magnitudes of most of the coefficients are similar across the two surveys.

The SEE included two questions about job security expectations: "I would like you to think about your employment prospects over the next twelve months. What do you think is the *percent chance* that you will lose your job during the next twelve months?" The second question was, "If you were to lose your job in the next twelve months, what is the *percent chance* (or what are the chances out of 100) that the job you eventually find and accept would be at least as good as your current job in terms of wages and benefits?" (Italics added for emphasis.) Before asking the questions, the SEE gave respondents a brief tutorial about probabilities.

The second SEE question captures the respondents' beliefs about their ability to find a comparable job conditional on job loss. Therefore, trends in the answer to the SEE question about finding a comparable job should roughly correspond to trends in the measure of the likelihood of costly job loss in the GSS.

Because respondents' answers to the SEE question about job loss have reasonable distributions, comparing the trends in the SEE data and GSS

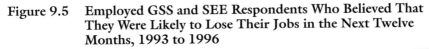

Figure 9.5   Employed GSS and SEE Respondents Who Believed That They Were Likely to Lose Their Jobs in the Next Twelve Months, 1993 to 1996

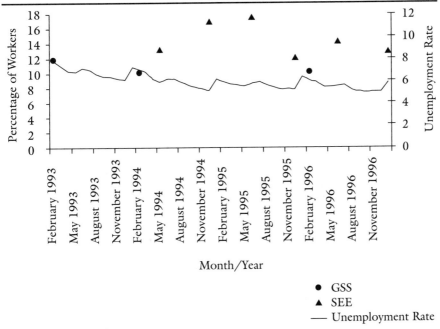

Sources: General Social Survey, Survey of Economic Expectations, and U.S. Bureau of Labor Statistics.

data is a way of validating the GSS data. Dominitz and Manski (1997) used cross-sectional data from the SEE to show that on average workers' expectations about job loss are quite accurate. Comparing the mean expected probability of job loss to the mean probability of actual job loss for various subgroups of workers, they found that for nearly all subgroups the two numbers did not differ significantly. I have confirmed Dominitz and Manski's results with longitudinal SEE data, showing that workers' beliefs about their probability of job loss predict their probability of future job loss. The results are in appendix 9B.

Figure 9.5 shows the share of respondents in each SEE survey who believed that they had a 50 percent or greater probability of losing their jobs in the next twelve months and the fraction of 1993, 1994, and 1996 GSS respondents who believed that job loss was likely.[5] In both the SEE and GSS, the share of respondents who believed that job loss was likely was roughly the same in early 1994 and early 1996. However, job-loss beliefs could have been the same in the early 1994 and early 1996 waves of the SEE owing to random fluctuations caused by the small sample size

Figure 9.6   **SEE and GSS Respondents Who Believed That They Were Likely to Experience Costly Job Loss, 1993 to 1996**

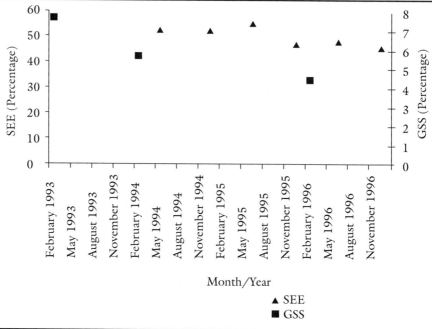

Sources: General Social Survey and Survey of Economic Expectations.

of the SEE cross-sections (between three hundred and six hundred respondents). Compared to other waves of the survey collected in 1995 and later in 1996, the early 1996 data point appears to be somewhat of an anomaly. None of the differences over time in the share of SEE respondents who believed that they had a 50 percent or greater chance of losing their jobs were statistically significant.

Figure 9.6 shows the share of SEE respondents who believed that they had a 50 percent or less probability of finding a job with similar pay after a job loss and the share of 1993, 1994, and 1996 GSS respondents who believed that they were likely to experience costly job loss. Both surveys show that workers became more optimistic about the consequences of job loss between 1994 and 1996.[6] The differences over time in the share of SEE respondents who believed they had a 50 percent or less chance of finding a comparable job were not significant. However, when I estimated a probit model using the SEE data and controlling for demographic covariates, the decline in pessimism about finding another job between 1994 and 1996 was statistically significant.

Appendix 9A shows that the probit results are robust across the SEE and GSS surveys. For each dependent variable ("likely to lose job," "likely to experience costly job loss"), parallel probit models were estimated, one using the 1994 and 1996 GSS data and a second using the SEE data. With both dependent variables, the magnitudes of most of the coefficients were similar across the two surveys.

COMPARISON WITH DATA FROM THE 1977 QUALITY
OF EMPLOYMENT SURVEY

The 1977 Quality of Employment Survey (QES), sponsored by the U.S. Department of Labor, measured respondents' job satisfaction on a variety of dimensions. The survey included a question that was identical to the GSS question about the ability to find a comparable job. However, the context of the question was quite different from the GSS.

Despite the differences in question framing, the respondents' answers to the 1977 GSS and 1977 QES questions were very similar: 41.5 percent of QES respondents and 42.1 percent of GSS respondents believed that they could not easily find another job with similar compensation.

In results reported in appendix 9A, I find that the probit results are robust across the Quality of Employment and General Social Surveys. Parallel probit models were estimated using the 1977 QES and 1977 GSS. The magnitudes of most of the coefficients were similar across the two surveys. The fact that the 1977 QES and 1977 GSS results are so similar despite the differences in the surveys' questionnaires suggests that workers' beliefs about their own job security are not influenced by question context.

The comparison of the GSS and SEE shows that answers do not appear to be greatly affected by whether the job security question is probabilistic or qualitative. The comparison of the GSS and SEE and the comparisons of the GSS and QES show that answers do not appear to be affected by other questions in the survey. Therefore, the GSS data are a reliable indicator of beliefs about job security.

CONCLUSIONS

This chapter uses 1977 to 1996 General Social Survey data to examine trends in workers' beliefs about their own job security. Two measures of job security beliefs are used. The first indicates whether respondents believed that they were likely to lose their jobs within twelve months, and the second indicates whether respondents believed that they were likely to experience a job loss that would result in a decline in compensation or a spell of unemployment.

During the economic recovery years of 1993 to 1996, workers were more concerned about keeping their jobs and about costly job loss than they were during years with comparable unemployment rates during the economic recoveries of the late 1970s and late 1980s. In addition, during the 1990 to 1991 economic recession, workers were just as worried about losing their jobs as they had been in the much more severe 1982 to 1983 recession.

Workers' beliefs about their own job security were largely consistent with trends in rates of involuntary job loss in the Displaced Workers Survey. During the economic recovery of the 1990s, rates of involuntary job loss were higher than they were during the economic recovery of the late 1980s, and the earnings declines following job loss were more severe. In addition, involuntary job loss was nearly as prevalent during the recession of the early 1990s as it had been during the recession of the early 1980s.

The results by subgroup are also largely consistent with trends in rates of involuntary job loss in the Displaced Workers Survey. During the 1990s, rates of involuntary job loss increased among white-collar workers, service occupation workers, college graduates, those with some college, and workers age fifty-five and older. During the 1990s, those groups also believed that they were more likely to lose their jobs than they were during the 1980s.

In addition, the earnings declines following job loss were more severe during the 1990s for workers with postsecondary schooling, and those workers became more pessimistic about costly job loss.

Two subgroups of workers' beliefs about job loss were not consistent with the trends in rates of involuntary job loss. Those rates increased among workers age forty to fifty-four during the 1990s, but they did not become more fearful about losing their jobs. The consequences of displacement remained roughly constant for high school dropouts between the 1980s and 1990s, yet they became more pessimistic about their chances of costly job loss.

Although rates of involuntary job loss have risen in recent years, the majority of workers still do not lose their jobs in a given year. The displacement literature is uninformative about the well-being of those workers who have not been displaced. This chapter makes an important contribution by showing that anxiety about job loss has risen among workers as a whole. It lends credence to the view that growing fears about job insecurity have changed the employment relationship.

APPENDIX 9A: TESTS FOR ROBUSTNESS OF RESULTS ACROSS SURVEYS

This appendix compares results from several public opinion polls. The comparisons are designed to test the robustness of answers to questions about job security to survey design and to question wording. The results suggest that respondents' beliefs about job security are robust and that the GSS data are reliable.

Table 9A.2   *Continued*

Independent Variables	General Social Survey (Surveys Within Six Months of Gallup Polls)	Gallup Poll (Surveys Within Six Months of GSS Surveys)	General Social Survey (1994 and 1996 Surveys)	Survey of Economic Expectations
November 1995 to January 1996	—	—	—	−.00565 (.0242)
May to July 1996	—	—	—	.0150 (.0236)
November 1996 to January 1997	—	—	—	−.00437 (.0236)
Sample size	6,753	8,860	2,656	2,753
Log likelihood	−2278	−3402	−834	−1102

Note: Standard errors are in parentheses. Dummies for eight census regions and a constant are included in all probit models. The reported coefficient for each explanatory variable represents the change in the predicted value of the dependent variable due to a one-unit increase in that explanatory variable, holding constant the other explanatory variables at their mean values.

***Significant at 1 percent level.
**Significant at 5 percent level.
*Significant at 10 percent level.

tions about job loss were not easily affected by changes in question framing and wording across surveys.

EVIDENCE FOR ROBUSTNESS OF "LIKELY TO EXPERIENCE COSTLY JOB LOSS" RESULTS

To examine the robustness of the probit results about the likelihood of experiencing costly job loss, I performed a similar exercise to compare GSS and SEE data. I estimated probit models using the 1994 and 1996 waves of the GSS and all five waves of the SEE. The GSS results are shown in column 1 of table 9A.3, while the SEE results are shown in column 2. The magnitudes of most coefficients were similar across polls. A notable exception is that fears about costly job loss were eighteen percentage points higher among forty- to fifty-four-year-olds than among twenty-five- to thirty-nine-year-olds (the base age category) in the GSS but differed only by three percentage points in the SEE. The robustness of probit results across surveys suggests that workers' expectations about costly job loss are not easily affected by question wording.

The 1977 QES did not ask about the likelihood of job loss during the next twelve months, but it did ask respondents how easily they could find another job with the same compensation. The question was identical to the one in the GSS, but the context of the question was quite different.

Table 9A.3 **Probit Model with Dependent Variable Equal to One If Workers Believed That They Were Likely to Experience Job Loss and That They Could Not Easily Find Another Job with Similar Compensation**

Independent Variables	General Social Survey (1994 and 1996 Data)	Survey of Economic Expectations
Female	.00907	−.0225
	(.0111)	(.0213)
Ages eighteen to twenty-four	−.0925**	−.0937**
	(.0385)	(.0369)
Ages forty to fifty-four	.188***	.0325
	(.0238)	(.0237)
Ages fifty-five and older	.281***	.184***
	(.0311)	(.0320)
Nonwhite	.0239***	.101**
	(.0294)	(.0321)
High school dropout	.0283*	.0934
	(.0176)	(.0530)
Some college	−.0692***	−.0681**
	(.0265)	(.0297)
College graduate	−.107***	−.130***
	(.0265)	(.0306)
Part-time worker	−.101***	−.0527**
	(.0289)	(.0265)
1996	−.0670**	—
	(.0211)	
April to July 1994	—	base wave
November 1994 to January 1995	—	−.0103
		(.0390)
May to July 1995	—	.00220
		(.0334)
November 1995 to January 1996	—	−.0582*
		(.0351)
May to July 1996	—	−.0454
		(.330)
November 1996 to January 1997	—	−.0672**
		(.0342)
Sample size	2,657	2,710

Note: Standard errors are in parentheses. Dummies for eight census regions and a constant are included in all probit models. The reported coefficient for each explanatory variable represents the change in the predicted value of the dependent variable due to a one-unit increase in that explanatory variable, holding constant the other explanatory variables at their mean values.

***Significant at 1 percent level.

**Significant at 5 percent level.

*Significant at 10 percent level.

Table 9A.4   **Probit Model: Dependent Variable Equals One if Workers Believed That They Could Not Have Easily Found Another Job with Similar Compensation (Standard Errors in Parentheses)**

Independent Variables	(1) Department of Labor Surveys (1977 Data)	(2) General Social Survey (1977 Data with DOL Hours Restrictions)
Female	.0424	.0247
	(.0320)	(.0423)
Ages eighteen to twenty-four	−.0458	−.0322
	(.0408)	(.0637)
Ages forty to fifty-four	.104***	.118***
	(.0366)	(.0457)
Ages fifty-five and older	.164***	.213***
	(.0450)	(.0164)
Nonwhite	.0580	.129**
	(.0504)	(.0603)
High school dropout	−.0382	.0684
	(.0396)	(.0514)
Some college	−.0445	−.0552
	(.0389)	(.0547)
College graduate	.0123	−.0278
	(.0446)	(.0602)
Part-time worker	−.0244	−.0660
	(.0322)	(.0726)
Service-producing industry	−.0651*	−.0600
	(.0634)	(.0480)
White-collar occupation	−.0175	−.102*
	(.408)	(.0553)
Service occupation	−.123**	−.103
	(.0502)	(.0700)
Sample size	4,170	837

Note: ***significant at 1 percent level, **significant at 5 percent level, *significant at 10 percent level. Dummies for eight census regions and a constant are included in all probit models. The reported coefficient for each explanatory variable represents the change in the predicted value of the dependent variable due to a one unit increase in that explanatory variable, holding constant the other explanatory variables at their mean values.

The GSS asks opinion questions on a wide range of topics, while the QES focused on job satisfaction.

Table 9A.4 shows the results of parallel probit models estimated with 1977 QES and 1977 GSS data, the only year in which both surveys were administered. Because the QES sample included only individuals who worked at least twenty hours per week, the GSS sample was restricted to respondents who worked at least twenty hours per week. The magnitudes of the coefficients are typically quite similar across surveys, and none of the coefficients differ significantly across surveys.

APPENDIX 9B: WORKERS' JOB SECURITY BELIEFS PREDICT FUTURE JOB TURNOVER

This appendix uses two longitudinal data sets to show that workers' beliefs about their likelihood of job loss predict what will happen to them. This study is the first to use panel data to show the accuracy of job security expectations. Dominitz and Manski (1997) used cross-sectional data from the Survey of Economic Expectations to show that on average workers' expectations about job loss are quite accurate. Dominitz and Manski compared the mean expected probability of job loss to the mean probability of actual job loss for various subgroups or workers. They found that for most subgroups the two numbers do not differ significantly. One subgroup, older workers, do have job-loss expectations that are much higher than their chances of actual job loss. The probability of job loss declines with age, but workers' expectations about job loss in the SEE do not. Workers' beliefs about job security are much more accurate than their beliefs about their chances of being victims of crimes.

Evidence from the Quality of Employment Survey

I use data from the 1973 to 1977 QES panel. The 1973 survey collected data from a representative sample of 1,426 workers who usually worked at least twenty hours per week. The 1977 panel component of the survey reinterviewed the 1973 respondents who were employed at least twenty hours per week in 1977. The survey was conducted by the Survey Research Center (SRC) at the University of Michigan and sponsored by the Employment Standards Administration at the U.S. Department of Labor and the National Institute for Occupational Safety and Health. The 1977 QES survey contained job security questions very similar to those in the GSS. The demographic, industry, and occupational characteristics of the 1977 QES and 1977 GSS samples were quite similar when I omitted GSS respondents who were employed fewer than twenty hours per week.

The 1973 QES asked respondents about their ability to find another job and about whether it was true that their job security was good. The 1973 survey did not include a question about the likelihood of job loss in the near future, but respondents' perceptions about whether their job security was good can be viewed as proxies for their expectations about their job loss in the near future. The 1977 QES did ask a question about the likelihood of job loss in the near future, as well as a question about whether job security was good. Table 9B.1 shows that answers to the

Russell Sage Foundation's Changes in Job Security and Stability Conference and from seminar attendees at the U.S. Congressional Budget Office, National Opinion Research Center, Public Policy Institute of California, the RAND/UCLA Labor and Population Workshop, the University of California at Irvine, the Urban Institute, and the U.S. Treasury Department. All remaining errors are my own. I also thank Elaine Reardon for providing the computer programs that created the occupation and industry dummy variables, and Jeff Dominitz for providing the Survey of Economic Expectations data.

NOTES

1. Daniel Aaronson and Daniel Sullivan (1998) also examined trends in job security perceptions in the General Social Survey but did not include a multivariate analysis of workers' beliefs about costly job loss or trends in job security beliefs for different groups of workers. Maria Ward Otoo (1997) compared the level of workers' anxiety about their economic future in two cross-sections of the Survey of Consumer Attitudes, but its anxiety measure cannot distinguish fears about job security from fears about changes in income.

2. GSS data for 1998 were not yet publicly available when this chapter was written.

3. Power analyses showed that a t-test could not detect a difference of less than 2.0 percentage points in the percentage of workers who believed they were likely to lose their jobs. A t-test could not detect a difference of less than 1.4 percentage points in the proportion of workers who believed that they were likely to experience costly job loss. The power analyses assumed the conventional probabilities for type I and type II errors, .05 and .20, respectively (Cohen 1977).

4. One criticism of using the DWS to measure trends in involuntary job loss is that the survey has significant recall bias (Schmidt and Svorny 1998). Some analysts (for example, Boisjoly, Duncan, and Smeeding 1997) have argued that the survey counts only the most painful and memorable job losses. The fact that workers' beliefs about their chances of job loss in the GSS track rates of involuntary job loss in the DWS results is interesting; it suggests that workers' beliefs about their chances of job loss are affected by the most painful job losses of their peers.

5. Trends in SEE respondents' beliefs do not differ when alternative cutoffs of 10, 20, 30, or 40 percent for the probability of losing a job are chosen. When cutoffs of 60 or 70 percent are chosen, fears about losing a job appear more constant over time and do not show a peak in the May-June 1995 survey.

6. Trends in SEE respondents' beliefs do not differ when alternative cutoffs of 30, 40, 60, or 70 percent for the probability of costly job loss are chosen.

7. Eleven of eighteen Gallup surveys and seven out of seventeen years of the GSS met those criteria. The Gallup polls were October 1976, January 1982, June 1982, November 1982, April 1983, July 1990, October 1990, March 1991, July 1991, December 1993, and April 1996. The GSS surveys were from 1977, 1982, 1983, 1990, 1991, 1994, and 1996. NORC conducted all GSS surveys in February and March.

8. The imputation method probably underestimates the number of job-changers. In the 1977 wave of the QES panel, respondents who were employed less than twenty hours per week were administered the short-form version of the survey and were not asked whether they had the same job in 1977 as they did in 1973. Respondents who were employed at least twenty hours per week were administered the long form and were asked whether they changed jobs. I assumed that all employed short-form respondents were with the same employer that they had in 1973.

9. The respondents were also interviewed a third time, but given the high attrition rate from the sample, I chose to restrict my analysis to the second interview.

10. Note that the interview question about the probability of future job loss was worded nearly identically to the question asked in subsequent SEE waves. The only difference was that the respondents were asked about their probability of losing their job in the next six months in the 1993 SEE and the next twelve months in 1994 to 1996 SEE.

REFERENCES

Aaronson, Daniel, and Daniel G. Sullivan. 1998. "The Decline of Job Security in the 1990s: Displacement, Anxiety, and Their Effect on Wage Growth." *Economic Perspectives* 12(1): 17–43.

Alwin, Duane F., and Jon A. Krosnick. 1991. "The Reliability of Survey Attitude Measurement: The Influence of Question and Respondent Attributes." *Sociological Methods and Research* 20(August): 139–81.

Boisjoly, Johanne, Greg J. Duncan, and Timothy Smeeding. 1997. "The Shifting Incidence of Involuntary Job Losses from 1968 to 1992." Working Paper (April).

Cohen, Jacob. 1977. *Statistical Power Analysis for the Behavioral Sciences*. Rev. ed. New York: Academic Press.

Davis, James Allan, and Tom W. Smith. 1996. *General Social Surveys, 1972–1996*. Machine-readable data file. NORC ed. Principal investigator, James A. Davis; director and coprincipal investigator, Tom W. Smith. Produced by National Opinion Research Center, Chicago. Distributed by Roper Center for Public Opinion Research, University of Connecticut, Storrs, Conn.

Dominitz, Jeff, and Charles F. Manski. 1997. "Perceptions of Economic Insecurity: Evidence from the Survey of Economic Expectations." *Public Opinion Quarterly* 61: 264–87.

Farber, Henry S. 1997. "Changing Face of Job Loss in the United States, 1981–1995." *Brookings Papers on Economic Activity* 1: Microeconomics. 55–128.

———. 1998. *Education and Job Loss in the United States: 1981–1997*. Unpublished manuscript.

Micklethwait, John, and Adrian Wooldridge. 1997. *The Witch Doctors: Making Sense of the Management Gurus*. New York: Random House.

Otoo, Maria Ward. 1997. "The Sources of Worker Anxiety: Evidence from the Michigan Survey." Federal Reserve Board Finance and Economics Discussion Series 1997–48 (September).

Polsky, Daniel. In press. "Changes in the Consequences of Job Separations in the U.S. Economy." *Industrial and Labor Relations Review*.

Schmidt, Stefanie R., and Shirley V. Svorny. 1998. "Recent Trends in Job Security and Stability." *Journal of Labor Research* 19(Fall): 647–68.

Valletta, Robert, and Randy O'Toole. 1997. "Job Security Update." *Federal Reserve Bank of San Francisco Economic Letter* 97(4, November).

Zaller, John. 1992. *The Nature and Origins of Mass Opinion*. New York: Cambridge University Press.

Part III

Understanding Behavioral Changes

Chapter 10

Long-Run Trends in Part-Time and Temporary Employment: Toward an Understanding

Alec R. Levenson

B etween the mid-1960s and the early 1980s, the rate of part-time employment in the United States increased by almost one-third, from about 13 percent to about 17 percent of all workers.[1] During the 1980s, the temporary help services industry increased in size by at least 100 percent.[2] Growth in these types of jobs, along with the perceived growth of other "alternative" employment relationships such as independent contracting, has led many observers to raise questions about the future of the traditional employment arrangement in the U.S. economy: full-time work as a permanent or indefinite (at will) employee.

Concerns over the growth in alternative employment relationships have been voiced in academic, policy, and media forums (see, for example, Tilly 1996; Economic Policy Institute 1997; *Time* 1993). These concerns center on what is perceived as the bad quality of part-time and temporary jobs. The issue has been raised against the backdrop of the worsening labor market outcomes for low-skill workers since the 1970s—a trend that has been well documented (see, for example, Murphy and Welch 1992; Katz and Murphy 1992; Juhn, Murphy, and Topel 1991; Levy and Murnane 1992; Blau and Kahn 1997; Blau 1998)—and the corporate downsizings of the 1980s and early 1990s. The typical assumption is that growth in alternative employment arrangements is part and parcel of these other trends that have made it difficult to find a "good" job. For example, Donald Barlett and James Steele (1992, 11) predicted that "workers will continue to be forced to move from jobs that once might have paid $8 to $20 an hour into jobs that will pay less. Some will be consigned to part-time employment. Some will lose all or part of fringe benefits they have long taken for granted."

A key issue addressed here is whether workers indeed are "consigned"

335

to part-time (and temporary) employment. According to this view, employers are offering only part-time and temporary jobs to people who prefer regular full-time jobs. An alternative explanation is that some of the long-run changes in part-time and temporary employment may be caused by labor supply responses to other changes in the labor market. According to this view, not all changes in part-time and temporary employment are forced on workers who would rather have full-time jobs.

I address this issue by exploiting the well-documented changes in the distribution of wages in recent decades to explain trends in part-time and temporary employment. Most of the existing literature on part-time and temporary employment uses only cross-sectional data to compare part-time and temporary jobs with other jobs. A small number of dynamic analyses have focused either on steady-state or cyclical transitions to and from part-time jobs. Yet none of these studies have analyzed the differential trends in part-time and temporary employment for workers at different levels of skill. The present study fills that gap.

The analysis finds that long-run aggregate trends in part-time and temporary employment mask marked differences between low-skill and high-skill workers. Similar to the unemployment rate, the involuntary part-time rate is higher among low-skill workers for both men and women, and it has risen faster for low-skill workers over time. Comparable patterns hold for men's voluntary part-time and temporary employment. In contrast, voluntary part-time and temporary employment are very different for women, showing no relationship with skill.

To better understand the observed trends in these series, I investigate whether a labor supply response can explain any of the changes in part-time and temporary employment. The results show that part of the long-run increase in "involuntary" part-time employment for low-skill men can be viewed as a voluntary labor supply response to falling demand for their skills. This means that some low-skill male part-time workers are misclassified as involuntary; they probably could find a full-time job at the same wage.

For women, part of the long-run increase in "involuntary" part-time employment and the decrease in "voluntary" part-time employment coincided with increased labor supply and rapidly rising employment rates. The evidence suggests that employers provided ample new job opportunities for women but slightly underprovided full-time jobs relative to what women wanted. Thus, many female involuntary part-timers face hours constraints that are probably transitory. In contrast, a labor supply response can explain only a small part of the change in temporary employment for both men and women.

CHANGES IN RETURNS TO SKILL AND TRENDS IN PART-TIME AND TEMPORARY EMPLOYMENT

A key finding of the literature on increased wage inequality during the 1980s is a marked increase in unemployment rates and nonparticipation for low-skill men that accompanied a large decline in their real wages (Juhn, Murphy, and Topel 1991; Juhn 1992). The dominant explanation for these patterns is a decline in demand for the labor supplied by low-skill men.[3] During the 1980s, women experienced skill-related shifts in demand similar to those that men experienced, with falling wages for low-skill workers and rising wages for high-skill workers. One unexplored possibility is that this decline in demand also may have increased the propensity of low-skill workers to work in part-time and temporary jobs, at least in the short run.

One reason for a possible link is that low-skill men may have increasingly turned to involuntary part-time jobs and temporary jobs to earn income while searching for increasingly scarce high-wage full-time jobs.[4] Although such part-time and temporary jobs may be viewed as inferior to full-time jobs, this perspective calls into question the notion that workers are rationed out of full-time jobs. Faced with the prospect of working full-time at a low-wage job, many workers might prefer the option of working in a part-time or temporary job.[5] Working in such jobs can be part of an optimal search strategy given the options the worker perceives to be available, particularly because unemployment is frequently viewed by prospective employers as a negative signal of worker quality.

Assuming that workers do use part-time and temporary jobs as part of a search strategy, the question addressed here is how trend changes in job opportunities over time affect the rates of part-time and temporary employment. This issue is taken up at the end of this section. First we review existing evidence on the nature of part-time and temporary jobs.

TRENDS IN PART-TIME AND TEMPORARY JOBS

Contrary to popular belief, the rate of part-time employment in the United States did not exhibit any trend increase during the 1980s and early 1990s—as I have demonstrated (Levenson 1996) for the entire workforce. As discussed later and as shown in figure 10.1, the same conclusion holds when considering a more restricted sample of prime-age (twenty-five to fifty-nine) workers. Figures 10.1 and 10.2 graph the rates of total part-time employment (voluntary plus involuntary), voluntary part-time employment,[6] involuntary part-time employment, temporary employment, and unemployment for the entire prime-age workforce (those with jobs plus those unemployed, figure 10.1), for women (figure 10.2, top panel), and for men (figure 10.2, bottom panel).

Figure 10.1 Part-Time, Temporary, and Unemployment Rates, Prime-Age Workforce, 1971 to 1996

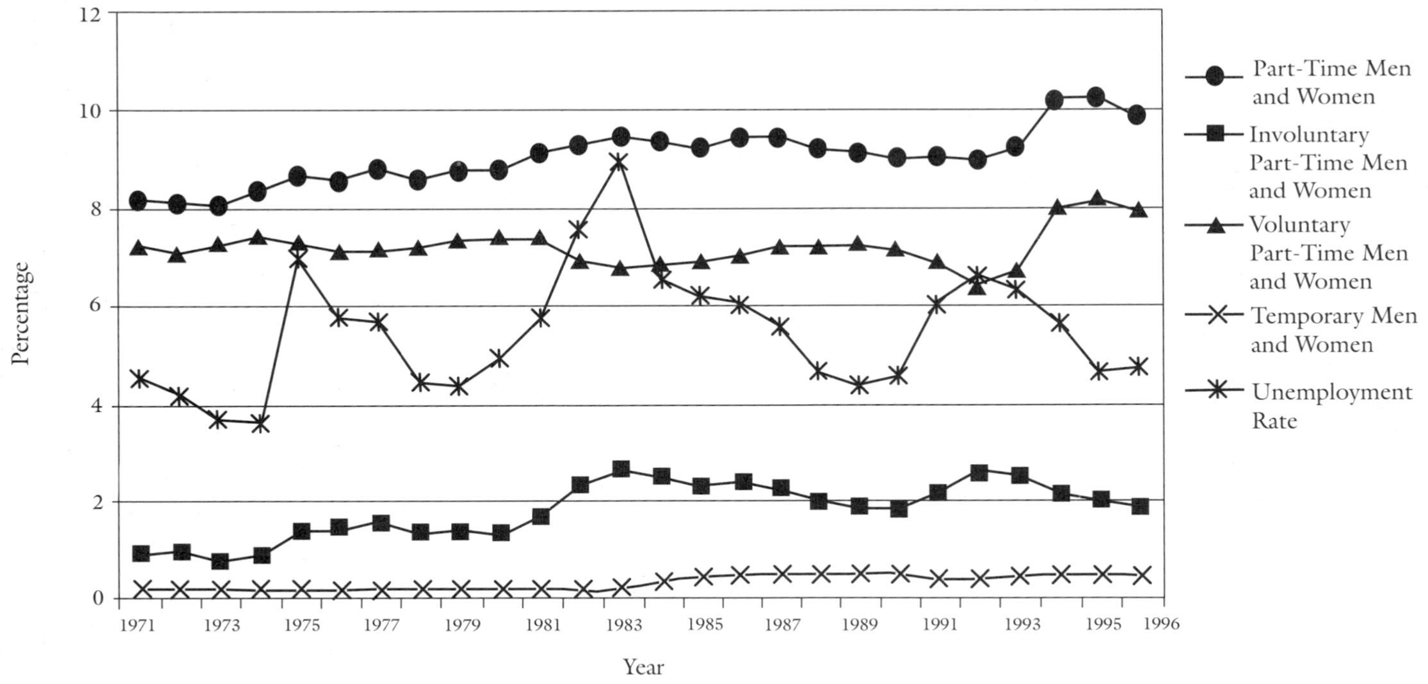

The temporary staffing industry has exhibited tremendous growth since the 1970s (Segal and Sullivan 1997), yet this growth occurred from a very small base—less than 1 percent of all workers in the 1970s, as can be seen in figure 10.3 for prime-age workers. So the total number of workers employed as temporaries by staffing agencies at any point in time was no more than 1 to 2 percent of all workers by the early 1990s (Segal and Sullivan 1997). Nevertheless, the role that temporary staffing agencies play in the labor market may extend far beyond the small fraction of workers they employ at a single point in time: many employers use agency temporaries to screen for regular workers (Houseman 1998).

Firms' increased demand for this screening role—in response to a legal environment that makes it increasingly costly to fire workers—may be one reason behind the rapid growth in temporary agency employment in recent years. Indeed, as of 1995 there were about three "direct hire" temps (that is, workers hired directly by the firm, not through a temporary staffing agency) for every one agency temp (Polivka 1996b; Houseman and Polivka, this volume). Thus, part of the growth in measured temporary agency employment may be due to firms outsourcing the hiring of temps.

However, it is doubtful that this fully explains the sharp increase in temporary agency employment. As temporary staffing agencies have grown in recent years, they have developed better techniques for matching workers to jobs, gained the ability to take advantage of economies of scale in densely populated areas, and received a lot of publicity about their "new" role in the labor market.[7] All of these factors almost certainly contributed to an expansion of the total market for temporary employees, not just a shifting of the existing placement market to temporary staffing agencies.

WAGES, TOTAL COMPENSATION, AND DURATION OF PART-TIME AND TEMPORARY JOBS

Wage differentials are a major reason for the concerns raised about the prevalence of part-time jobs: average wages for part-time jobs are lower than average wages for full-time jobs. Part-time workers are much more likely to be young, inexperienced, and lower-skilled than full-time workers. Part-time jobs also are disproportionately concentrated in low-wage industries and occupations. Controlling for differences in human capital characteristics, industry, and occupation can account for up to 80 percent of the part-time–full-time wage differential (for a review of the literature, see Blank 1990a).

Accounting further for selection into part-time work can entirely explain the voluntary part-time–full-time wage differential but cannot entirely explain the differential for involuntary part-time jobs (Blank

Figure 10.2 Part-Time, Temporary, and Unemployment Rates, Prime-Age Women and Men, 1971 to 1996

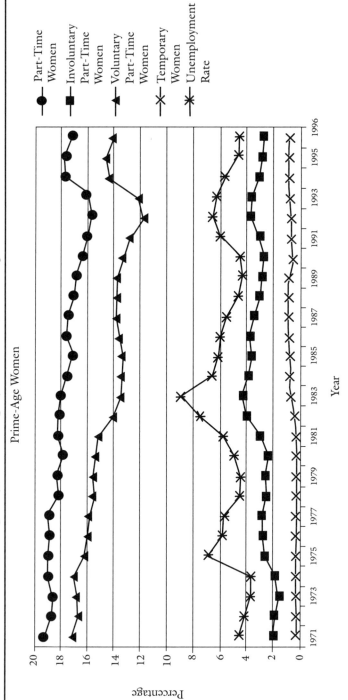

Prime-Age Women

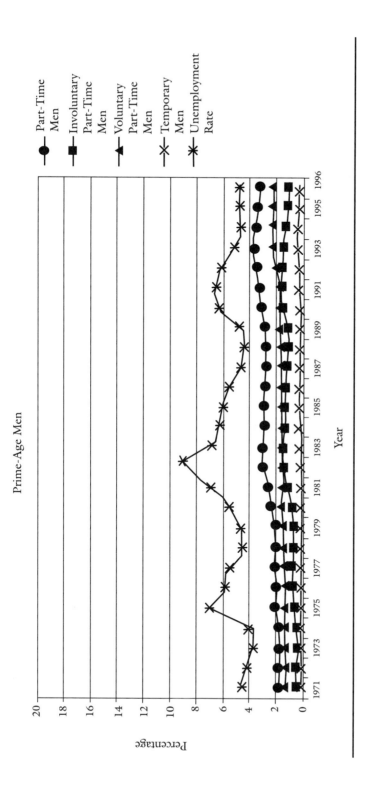

Prime-Age Men

Figure 10.3   Temporary Employment Rates, Prime-Age Workforce, 1971 to 1996

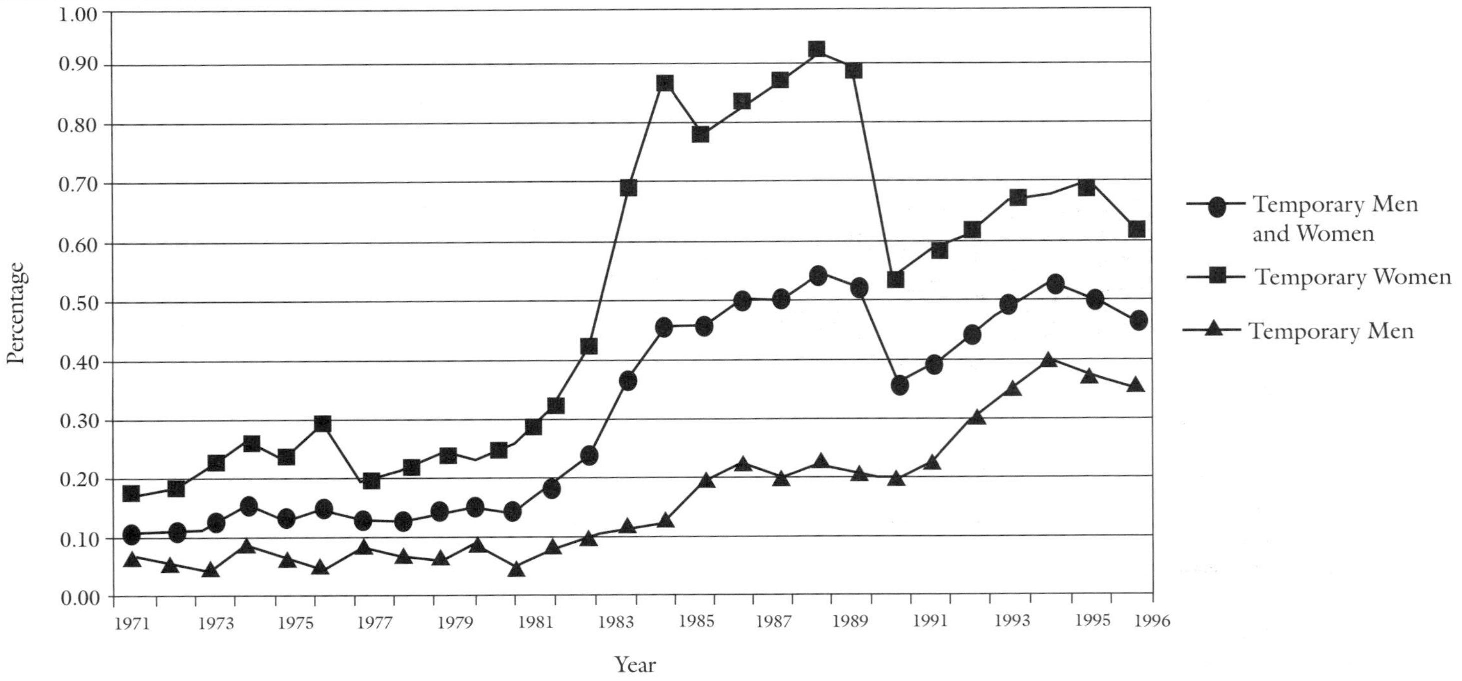

1990b). Regardless, part-time jobs are much less likely to offer fringe benefits such as health insurance and pension coverage. Total hourly compensation is thus typically even lower for part-time jobs compared to full-time jobs than the difference in hourly wage rates would imply (Blank 1998).

A similar story holds for temporary staffing industry jobs (for a review, see Segal and Sullivan 1997). On average, temporary jobs pay much less per hour than nontemporary jobs. Observable characteristics of the worker and job account for about two-thirds of the temporary—non-temporary wage differential. Further accounting for selection bias into temporary jobs by low-skill workers reduces the wage differential to about 3 percent. Moreover, the fringe benefits offered to temporary workers on average are much less generous. As a result, total hourly compensation typically is lower for temporary jobs than for nontemporary jobs.

Even though temporary jobs by definition are transitional in nature, a large minority of temp workers—about one-quarter—maintain that status from one year to the next (Segal and Sullivan 1997; Houseman and Polivka, this volume; Farber this volume). A small number of dynamic analyses have focused either on steady-state (see, for example, Blank 1994; Stratton 1996) or cyclical (Farber this volume) transitions to and from part-time jobs. These studies find that part-time jobs are more transitional in nature than full-time jobs.

VOLUNTARY VERSUS INVOLUNTARY PART-TIME WORK

At the heart of the debate over the quality of alternative employment arrangements is the question of whether those jobs are what workers really want. The voluntary versus involuntary part-time distinction plays a key role:

> The expansion in the U.S. part-time labor market actually gives us a great deal of worry. Most importantly, virtually all of the increase in the rate of part-time employment in the United States during the last two decades is due to the expansion of *involuntary* part-time employment. An involuntary part-time job is only half a job in the sense that it is only half the job the employee wants. (Tilly 1996, 2–3; italics in the original)

To determine voluntary versus involuntary part-time status, the Current Population Survey asks why the respondent worked less than thirty-five hours during the survey week. The leading reason the CPS records for involuntary part-time employment among prime-age workers is: "could only find part-time work."[8] The predominant view in the literature is that an involuntary part-time worker faces a binding hours constraint: he or she wants to work more hours at the given wage but is prevented from doing so. This view is consistent with the evidence that firms may constrain the number of hours that can be worked in some jobs (Altonji and Paxson 1988). It is also consistent with Leslie Stratton's (1996) finding that involuntary part-time workers are much more likely to make the transition to full-time jobs than voluntary part-time workers.

Evidence in favor of the hours constraint view is available from the May 1985 supplement to the CPS. All respondents were asked whether, at the given rate of pay (wage), they preferred to work the same hours (for the same earnings), fewer hours (for less earnings), or more hours (for more earnings). The vast majority of involuntary part-timers—89.2 percent of men and 77.8 percent of women—said they wanted more hours. Yet among the involuntary part-timers in the May 1985 CPS who said they could find only part-time work, 9.2 percent of men and 19.1 percent of women said they would rather work the same hours than more hours or fewer hours. If they do not want more hours, then why are they classified as involuntary part-time?

One possibility is that these workers face low wages but no hours constraints: full-time jobs at the same hourly wage as their part-time job are available. Despite this availability, they voluntarily work part-time because they require a higher hourly wage to work full-time. For these workers, "could only find part-time work" may be interpreted as "could not find a higher-hourly-wage full-time job." They voluntarily work part-time but are classified as involuntary because their hourly wages are lower than desired for full-time work and the CPS questionnaire is misinterpreted. This misclassification is likely given the popular perception that part-time is synonymous with "low wage, no benefits" and full-time with "high wage, full benefits."

In an era of falling real wages for many workers, the measured rate of involuntary part-time employment could rise because of rising dissatisfaction with the available full-time wage opportunities and without a concurrent increase in hours constraints imposed by firms. For example:

> [T]here are . . . millions more people . . . who have been thrown out of work. They are, overwhelmingly, middle income employees who are being forced into lower-paying jobs, part-time employment, premature retirement or unemployment.
>
> George Skelton, who lost his job in April 1991, is among those who can attest to plummeting wages. At Whitehall Laboratories, he earned $13.40 an hour. In his new job, he earned $7 an hour. . . . Mary Soellinger, fifty-seven, who worked at Whitehall eight years ago did not even do that well. . . . "I suppose I could probably get in at McDonald's," she said, "but I don't really feel that it is fair to push people into minimum wage jobs, because you can't live on minimum wages." (Barlett and Steele 1992, 67, 97)

workers to ensure that the vast majority had not entered retirement. Although it is beyond the scope of this study, exploring the relationship between skill and alternative employment trends for young workers and old workers is a fruitful topic for future research.

GRAPHICAL ANALYSIS

The analysis is conducted in two parts. First, in this section, each employment series is graphed for the entire period to identify the trends at each level of skill and possible explanations for those trends. Then, in the next section, regression analysis is employed to analyze more formally the role that changing wages play in explaining the trends in each series.

Much of the popular discussion of contingent work rates and trends focuses on part-time and temporary rates measured as a fraction of the workforce (all those with a job). For most of this analysis, the base used to construct the rates is the labor force (all those with a job plus those looking for a job). Using the labor force is preferable to the workforce because the unemployment, part-time, and temporary employment rates can be compared directly.

However, for women there is the added complication that rising labor-force participation rates significantly alter the base used to calculate those rates. Not accounting for those changes could lead to misinterpretation of changes in the rates over time. To guide the interpretation of those changes at each step of the analysis, table 10.1 presents each rate calculated with the population used as a base for 1971 to 1973, 1988 to 1990, and the difference.

Before presenting the descriptive analysis of part-time and temporary employment, it is useful to compare the employment and unemployment trends for the wage percentiles used here with the trends found by previous research. Throughout the discussion, wage quintile 1 refers to percentiles 1 through 20 of the predicted wage distribution, and so on.

The patterns of employment and unemployment are graphed in figures 10.5 and 10.6. In figure 10.5 only, the employment rate is equal to the employment-to-population ratio. For all other figures, the base is the labor force. Thus, the unemployment rate in figure 10.6 is equal to the fraction of the labor force (employed plus unemployed) that is unemployed. For men, there is a positive relationship between predicted wages and employment rates throughout the period 1964 to 1993 that grew stronger in the 1970s and 1980s: employment rates fell throughout the wage distribution, more so for low-wage workers. There is a comparable negative relationship between wages and unemployment rates that also grew stronger: lower-wage workers had the largest increases in unemployment. These figures show that predicting wages this way produces employment and unemployment patterns for men similar to those

Figure 10.4 Age Profile of Voluntary Part-Time Employment Rates for Women and for Men, 1964 to 1974 Versus 1983 to 1993

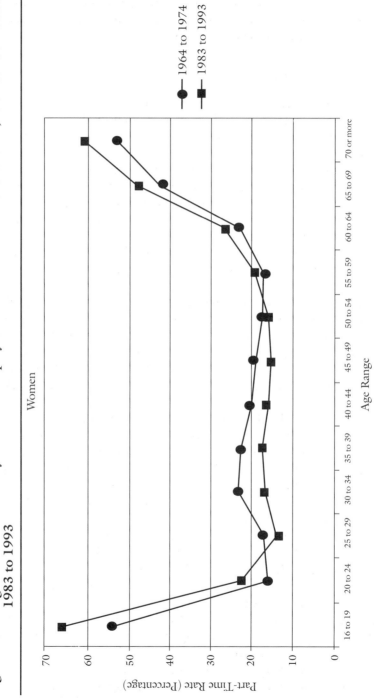

Men

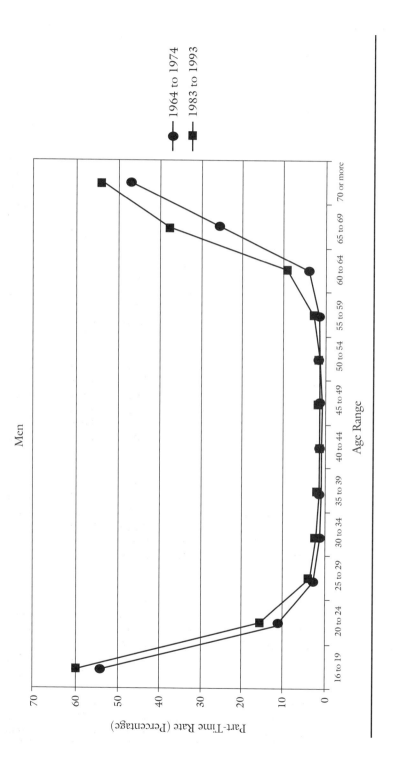

1964 to 1974
1983 to 1993

Part-Time Rate (Percentage)

70
60
50
40
30
20
10
0

16 to 19   20 to 24   25 to 29   30 to 34   35 to 39   40 to 44   45 to 49   50 to 54   55 to 59   60 to 64   65 to 69   70 or more

Age Range

Table 10.1   Employment Rates for Prime-Age Women and Men for
              1971 to 1973 and 1988 to 1990 (as a Percentage of the
              Population)

Predicted Wage Percentiles	Prime-Age Women			Prime-Age Men		
	1971 to 1973	1988 to 1990	Difference in Rates	1971 to 1973	1988 to 1990	Difference in Rates
Out of labor force						
1 to 20	59.340	45.421	−13.919	12.328	14.696	2.368
21 to 40	51.998	30.880	−21.118	7.739	10.525	2.786
41 to 60	48.991	27.349	−21.642	6.398	8.717	2.319
61 to 80	44.817	21.356	−23.461	4.958	7.324	2.367
81 to 100	40.034	17.640	−22.394	4.806	4.557	−0.249
Total	49.078	28.567	−20.510	7.255	9.186	1.931
Unemployed						
1 to 20	3.385	4.725	1.340	6.302	8.362	2.060
21 to 40	2.995	3.316	0.321	4.012	5.340	1.328
41 to 60	2.325	2.754	0.429	3.105	3.871	0.766
61 to 80	2.141	2.725	0.584	2.140	2.587	0.447
81 to 100	1.828	1.508	−0.320	1.454	1.476	0.023
Total	2.539	3.010	0.470	3.408	4.343	0.934
Temporary						
1 to 20	0.022	0.479	0.457	0.043	0.332	0.289
21 to 40	0.083	0.544	0.461	0.037	0.154	0.117
41 to 60	0.108	0.477	0.369	0.012	0.112	0.099
61 to 80	0.126	0.728	0.603	0.019	0.084	0.065
81 to 100	0.051	0.487	0.436	0.012	0.079	0.066
Total	0.078	0.543	0.465	0.025	0.153	0.128
Involuntary part-time						
1 to 20	1.580	2.862	1.282	0.885	2.244	1.359
21 to 40	0.985	2.272	1.287	0.389	1.071	0.681
41 to 60	0.667	2.208	1.541	0.357	0.723	0.366
61 to 80	0.653	1.692	1.040	0.245	0.521	0.277
81 to 100	0.573	1.012	0.438	0.099	0.379	0.280
Total	0.894	2.012	1.118	0.396	0.993	0.597
Voluntary part-time						
1 to 20	6.675	6.958	0.283	1.174	1.845	0.671
21 to 40	7.905	10.451	2.546	0.946	1.395	0.449
41 to 60	10.063	10.213	0.151	1.144	1.480	0.335
61 to 80	9.284	10.757	1.473	1.236	1.412	0.175
81 to 100	9.435	10.425	0.990	1.311	1.078	−0.234
Total	8.663	9.759	1.097	1.162	1.444	0.282
Full-time						
1 to 20	23.763	33.396	9.633	65.697	60.241	−5.456
21 to 40	30.337	44.008	13.671	71.169	66.184	4.985
41 to 60	31.715	47.597	15.882	74.322	68.324	−5.998

the changes in the employment rates can be explained as labor supply responses to changing (relative) wage opportunities driven by shifts in labor demand.

To test this hypothesis, a multinomial logit was run separately by gender for 1971 to 1973 on seven outcomes: full-time, temporary, involuntary part-time, voluntary part-time, unemployed, other (agriculture, self-employed, with a job but not at work last week), and out of the labor force (OLF). The sole regressors were the predicted weekly wage interacted with five wage quintile dummies.

This specification was chosen to focus exclusively on the labor supply response to demand-driven changes in opportunity wages, hence the exclusion of other regressors.[17] Because the predicted wage is exogenous to individuals' labor supply decisions, it is a legitimate, although imperfect, indicator of their opportunity wages in the market. A change over time in the predicted wage for a given set of human capital characteristics indicates changing market demand for the skill bundle represented by those characteristics, assuming that changes in the distribution of wages are driven primarily by shifts in labor demand. Interacting the predicted wage with a dummy for each wage quintile allows for the fact that the elasticity of labor supply with respect to demand-driven changes in opportunity wages may vary by level of skill.

Two different versions of the predicted weekly wage were used. The first version is simply the predicted wage itself. However, as discussed earlier, this version probably systematically overstates the wages available to low-wage workers because they have a lower propensity to work full-time, full-year, and so are less likely to be included in the first-stage regression of wages on human capital characteristics. Indeed, the drop in low-skill wages for men during the 1970s and 1980s calculated using this predicted wage measure was not as steep as what occurred in the actual distribution of wages.

The alternate version of the predicted wage compensated for that bias by using the predicted wage percentile ranking from the first version to assign wages from the actual full-time wage distribution. Thus, everyone in the first percentile of the predicted male (female) wage distribution was assigned the mean wage in the first percentile of the actual male (female) full-time wage distribution.[18] By doing this, the mean wage at each percentile of the predicted wage distribution is constructed to be exactly equal to the mean wage at each percentile of the actual full-time wage distribution.[19] Note that the ranking of individuals into high and low percentiles for the purpose of assigning them to a particular skill category is unaffected by this procedure.

This procedure for constructing the alternate predicted wage does not fully compensate for the potential inaccuracies necessitated by imputing wages for part-time workers and those out of the labor force, but it does

make the imputed wage for low-wage workers more accurate. This can
be seen in figure 10.10, which graphs the mean wage at each percentile
of the predicted wage distribution using both methods separately for
women (top panel) and men (bottom panel). Note that the mean predicted wage from the first method is much more compressed than the
mean wage (at each percentile) from the actual full-time distribution,
which is the same as for the alternate predicted wage: the wage from the
first method is too high at the lower tail of the distribution and too low at
the upper tail of the distribution for both men and women.

The coefficients from the multinomial regression for 1971 to 1973
were used to predict employment probabilities for each person using the
predicted wage in both 1971 to 1973 and 1988 to 1990. The regression
coefficients are reported in tables 10A.1 and 10A.2. Tables 10A.3 and
10A.4 report the actual and predicted outcomes for all states except "out
of the labor force," summarized by wage quintile and normalized so that
they total 100 percent.[20] Figures 10.11 through 10.14 summarize the
changes in actual and predicted employment rates for comparison purposes.

The model for both wage measures for women uniformly overpredicts
the increases in full-time employment for all wage quintiles and uniformly predicts decreases in all other employment states but temporary
(conditional on participating in the labor force). The changes in predicted wages do not explain any of the increases in involuntary part-time
employment (figure 10.12). The results for temporary are mixed, showing a predicted decrease using the first wage measure and essentially no
change for the alternate wage measure (figure 10.13). Changes in predicted wages explain part of the decreased propensity toward voluntary
part-time employment and unemployment, but not the increase in unemployment for the lowest wage quintile (figures 10.11 and 10.14).

The fact that this regression procedure is better able to capture long-
run trends in voluntary part-time but not involuntary part-time or temporary employment suggests fundamentally different behavioral underpin-
nings between the former and the latter for women. The findings of
Segal and Sullivan (1997) for temporary jobs and Stratton (1996) for
part-time jobs showed that voluntary part-time jobs are less transitional:
the year-to-year probability of remaining in the employment state is
much higher for voluntary part-time work, particularly for women. Combined with the regression results presented here, the implication is that
voluntary part-time employment perhaps should be viewed as more of a
stock than a flow measure, and vice versa for involuntary part-time and
temporary employment. That is, in the long run women choose among
full-time employment, voluntary part-time employment, and remaining
out of the labor force, using involuntary part-time and temporary employment as bridges between those employment states when needed

(conditional on participating in the labor force). Consistent with this view, Stratton documented a much higher transition rate from involuntary to voluntary part-time employment than from voluntary to involuntary part-time employment.

Further evidence in favor of this finding can been seen by comparing the coincident changes in full-time, voluntary part-time, and involuntary part-time employment for women at different points in the predicted wage distribution. Note that the women who realized the greatest gains in full-time employment—the lowest and middle female wage quintiles—also realized the greatest gains in involuntary part-time employment; those gains were more than offset by the greatest decreases in voluntary part-time employment (figures 10.12 and 10.14). This strongly suggests that the observed increases in involuntary part-time employment are due to a rapidly increasing supply of full-time labor that partly outpaced the available demand for full-time jobs; that is, employers were too slow to respond to the sharp increase in the supply of women's full-time labor. But the fact that these same women realized the greatest increases in full-time employment suggests that the involuntary part-time employment state is likely to be temporary for most of them.

The actual increase in women's temporary employment is undoubtedly due to the large expansion in the demand for temporary staffing industry services, an expansion which dominated the decrease in temporary employment implied by rising overall wage opportunities. The concurrent increases in involuntary part-time employment and accompanying larger decreases in voluntary part-time employment for each wage quintile could be related to these changes in the relative supply and demand of full-time jobs. Viewed this way, the increase in involuntary part-time employment was due not to a shifting of full-time to part-time jobs by employers. Rather, it was due to an increase in the supply of women looking for full-time jobs that outpaced the increase in demand by employers. That is, a rapidly rising desire to work full-time caused the increase in involuntary part-time employment and the decrease in voluntary part-time employment.

The results for men do a better job of predicting actual employment changes for low-wage than for high-wage workers. Part of the increase in unemployment and temporary, involuntary part-time, and voluntary part-time employment is explained by falling real wages (figures 10.11 through 10.14). Indeed, the alternate wage measure, which more accurately reflects falling real wages at the bottom of the wage distribution, does a better job of predicting the actual changes in employment than the first predicted wage measure. As with women, however, note that the bulk of the increase in temporary employment for all wage quintiles is undoubtedly due to the large expansion in the demand for temporary

(Text continues on p. 383.)

Figure 10.10   Mean Predicted Hourly Wages, 1988 to 1990

Prime-Age Women

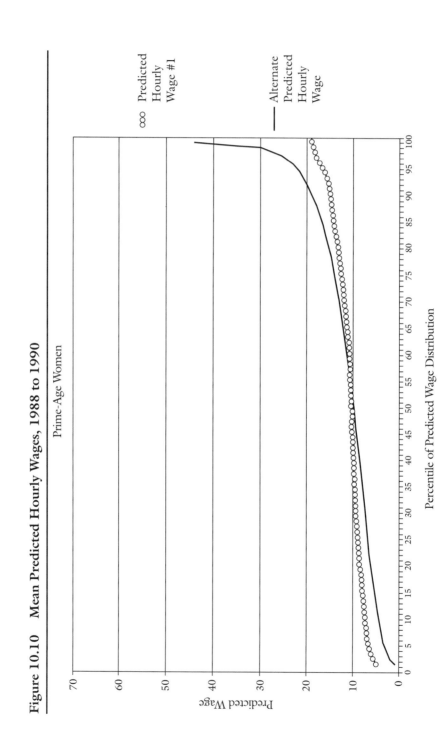

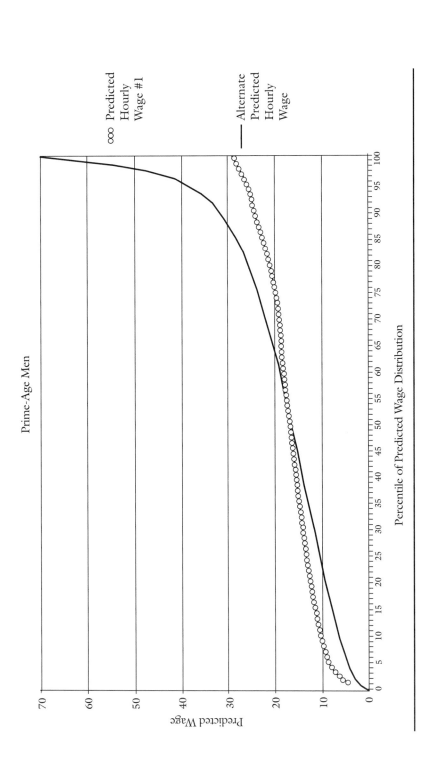

Prime-Age Men

Predicted Hourly Wage #1

Alternate Predicted Hourly Wage

Percentile of Predicted Wage Distribution

Predicted Wage

Figure 10.11   Difference in Unemployment Rates Between 1971 to 1973 and 1988 to 1990

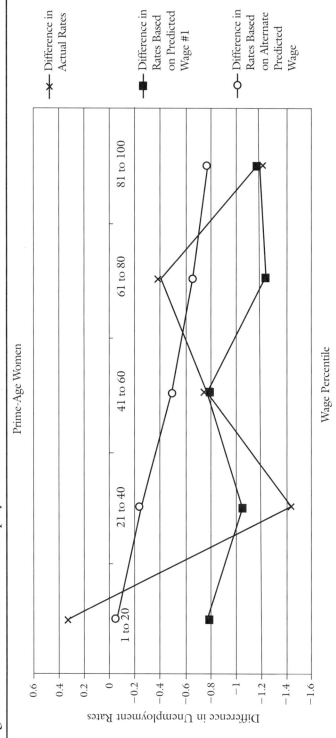

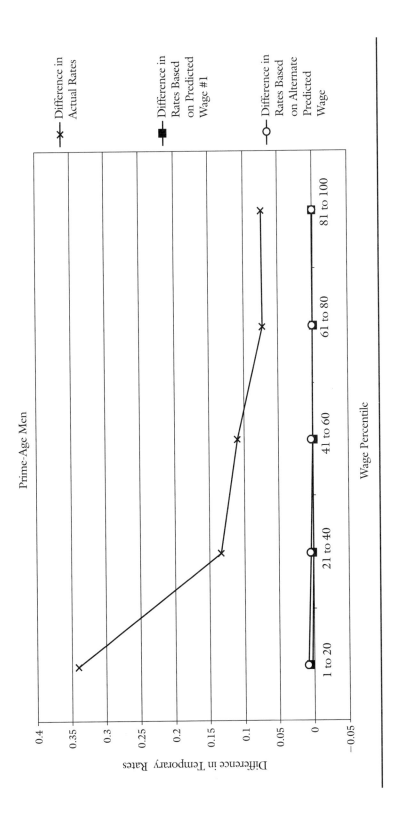

Prime-Age Men

Difference in Temporary Rates

Wage Percentile

—✕— Difference in Actual Rates

—■— Difference in Rates Based on Predicted Wage #1

—○— Difference in Rates Based on Alternate Predicted Wage

Figure 10.14 Difference in Voluntary Part-Time Rates Between 1971 to 1973 and 1988 to 1990

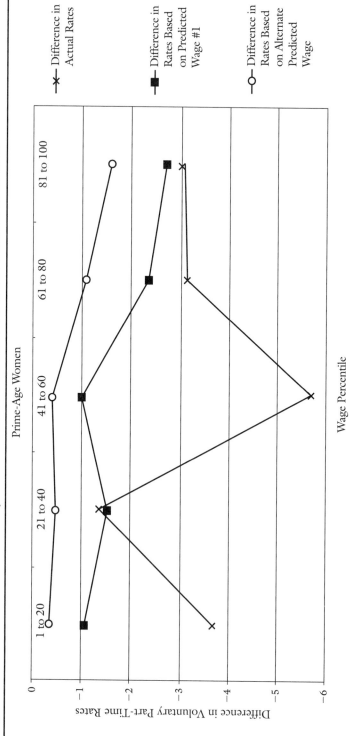

Prime-Age Women

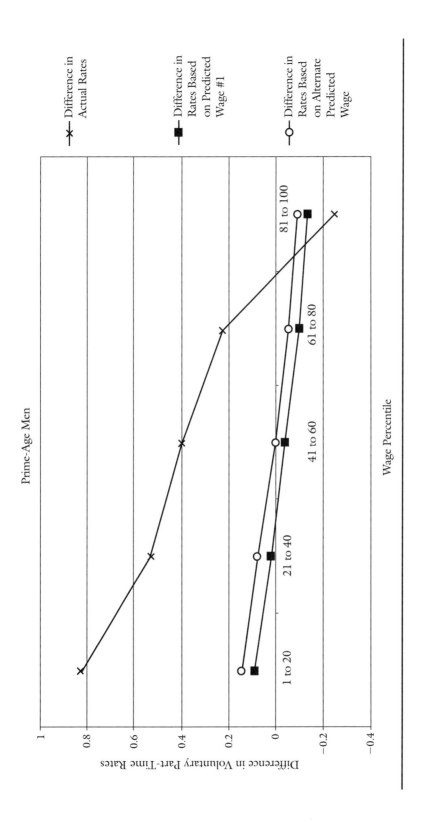

Prime-Age Men

Difference in Voluntary Part-Time Rates

Wage Percentile

1 to 20

21 to 40

41 to 60

61 to 80

81 to 100

—✕— Difference in
Actual Rates

—■— Difference in
Rates Based
on Predicted
Wage #1

—○— Difference in
Rates Based
on Alternate
Predicted
Wage

1

0.8

0.6

0.4

0.2

0

-0.2

-0.4

Table 10.3 Difference-in-Differences: Prime-Age Women

	Difference-in-Differences Actual Rates (A)	Difference-in-Differences Predicted Rates (B)	Difference-in-Differences Alternate Predicted Rates (C)	Percentage of Relative Actual Change for Low-Wage Workers Explained by Relative Change in Predicted Wages = (B)/(A)	Percentage of Relative Actual Change for Low-Wage Workers Explained by Relative Change in Alternate Predicted Wages = (C)/(A)
Unemployed					
Quintile 1 − Quintile 5	1.549	0.413	0.726	26.7	46.9
Quintile 1 − Quintile 4	0.747	0.468	0.601	62.7	80.5
Quintile 1 − Quintile 3	1.099	0.007	0.429	0.7	39.1
Quintile 1 − Quintile 2	1.774	0.276	0.188	15.6	10.6
Temporary					
Quintile 1 − Quintile 5	0.316	0.022	0.010	6.9	3.1
Quintile 1 − Quintile 4	0.125	0.060	−0.017	47.7	0
Quintile 1 − Quintile 3	0.378	0.026	−0.013	7.0	0
Quintile 1 − Quintile 2	0.208	0.032	−0.007	15.2	0
Involuntary part-time					
Quintile 1 − Quintile 5	1.086	−0.160	0.231	0	21.3
Quintile 1 − Quintile 4	0.389	−0.144	0.185	0	47.6
Quintile 1 − Quintile 3	−0.374	−0.323	0.122	86.5	0
Quintile 1 − Quintile 2	0.125	−0.068	0.055	0	44.4
Voluntary part-time					
Quintile 1 − Quintile 5	−0.591	1.623	1.257	0	0
Quintile 1 − Quintile 4	−0.521	1.278	0.739	0	0
Quintile 1 − Quintile 3	2.002	−0.045	0.038	0	1.9
Quintile 1 − Quintile 2	−2.319	0.453	0.136	0	0

Note: A zero entry indicates that the relative change in actual rates (A) is opposite in sign to the relative change in predicted rates (B) or alternate predicted rates (C).

staffing industry services, not to changes in overall wage opportunities for men.

Tables 10.3 and 10.4 use the results from figures 10.11 through 10.14 to examine how much of the change in *relative* employment outcomes for low- versus higher-skill workers can be explained by the relative change in predicted wages. The first column reports the difference-in-difference between the actual change in employment outcomes for the first wage quintile and the actual change in employment outcomes for each of the other wage quintiles. The second and third columns do the same calculation for the changes in predicted employment explained by changes in predicted wages for the two different predicted wage measures. The final two columns calculate the percentage of the relative actual change in employment explained by the relative change in predicted wages (that is, the ratio of the second column over the first column and the ratio of the third column over the first column).

The results in table 10.3 demonstrate that changes in relative wages for the lowest-wage women played a role in changing relative employment outcomes, though only for some types of employment. The relatively larger increase in unemployment for the lowest-wage workers is partly explained by the relative deterioration in their opportunity wages and is robust to the choice of predicted wage measure. In contrast, the relative increases in involuntary part-time and temporary employment for the lowest-wage workers are not well explained by relative deterioration in their predicted wages. And there is no evidence at all of a labor supply response to changing relative wages as an explanation for the relative changes in voluntary part-time employment.

The results in table 10.4 show that at least part of the disproportionate increase in all four labor market states for low-wage men was a labor supply response to demand-driven declines in wages. The patterns are robust to the choice of predicted wage measure and stronger for the alternate predicted wage measure. The unemployment patterns are consistent with the results of Juhn, Murphy, and Topel (1991). In addition, falling wages for low-wage men can explain:

- Only 2 to 3 percent of their more rapid growth in temporary employment;
- 10 to 20 percent of their more rapid growth in involuntary part-time employment;
- and 25 to 45 percent of their more rapid growth in voluntary part-time employment.

Taken together, the latter two results are most striking. They underscore a role for the misclassification hypothesis: voluntary part-time em-

Table 10.4 Difference-in-Differences: Prime-Age Men

	Difference-in-Differences Actual Rates (A)	Difference-in-Differences Predicted Rates (B)	Difference-in-Differences Alternate Predicted Rates (C)	Percentage of Relative Actual Change for Low-Wage Workers Explained by Relative Change in Predicted Wages = (B)/(A)	Percentage of Relative Actual Change for Low-Wage Workers Explained by Relative Change in Alternate Predicted Wages = (C)/(A)
Unemployed					
Quintile 1 – Quintile 5	2.595	0.655	0.976	25.2	37.6
Quintile 1 – Quintile 4	2.074	0.649	0.913	31.3	44.0
Quintile 1 – Quintile 3	1.691	0.522	0.684	30.9	40.5
Quintile 1 – Quintile 2	0.995	0.313	0.287	31.4	28.8
Temporary					
Quintile 1 – Quintile 5	0.270	0.007	0.009	2.7	3.4
Quintile 1 – Quintile 4	0.269	0.007	0.009	2.8	3.2
Quintile 1 – Quintile 3	0.230	0.006	0.007	2.4	2.9
Quintile 1 – Quintile 2	0.207	0.004	0.003	1.8	1.6
Involuntary part-time					
Quintile 1 – Quintile 5	1.328	0.121	0.234	9.1	17.6
Quintile 1 – Quintile 4	1.316	0.135	0.241	10.3	18.3
Quintile 1 – Quintile 3	1.211	0.117	0.203	9.7	16.7
Quintile 1 – Quintile 2	0.846	0.081	0.127	9.5	15.0
Voluntary part-time					
Quintile 1 – Quintile 5	1.072	0.230	0.240	21.5	22.3
Quintile 1 – Quintile 4	0.601	0.195	0.203	32.4	33.8
Quintile 1 – Quintile 3	0.425	0.133	0.148	31.3	34.9
Quintile 1 – Quintile 2	0.290	0.075	0.068	25.7	23.5

ployment is misclassified as involuntary part-time employment because of falling wages. In an era of declining real wages, when "part-time" is synonymous with "low-wage," perhaps this should not be surprising. They also show that, just as for women, voluntary part-time employment for men is probably more appropriately viewed as a stock measure of long-run labor supply than are both involuntary part-time and temporary employment, at least for low-wage men.

As an additional check on the results, the entire distribution of hours worked for 1971 to 1973 and for 1988 to 1990 was analyzed to determine whether the rise in part-time employment for low-wage men could be explained by a shift from working thirty-five hours per week to working just under thirty-five hours. In fact, the opposite occurred: the fraction of all jobs at thirty-one to thirty-four hours fell from 4.22 to 3.28 percent, while the fraction at thirty-five hours increased from 1.94 to 2.30 percent.

The results on involuntary part-time employment for men might appear to conflict with Rebecca Blank's (1998, 266) conclusion that "involuntary part-time employment is not growing much more among the less-skilled than among other male workers and cannot be the driving force behind the substantial rises in wage inequality among men." She based this conclusion on the observation that involuntary part-time employment rose by 2.8 percentage points among male workers with a high school degree or less (the "less skilled"), compared with a rise of 2.0 percentage points for other male workers. Thus, she found that less skilled male workers' involuntary part-time employment rate increased only 0.8 percentage points faster. In contrast, the results in figure 10.12 show that involuntary part-time employment among workers in the lowest prime-age male wage quintile increased 1.3 percentage points faster than among workers in the highest quintile.

Part of the discrepancy in the measured rates of involuntary part-time employment is undoubtedly due to different samples and definitions: Blank looked at all workers, not just prime-age workers; she compared changes between 1979 and 1993; she considered involuntary part-time employment as a fraction of all workers (not all workers plus the unemployed, as is done here); and her way of dividing the population into different skill groups was based solely on education.

Regardless of differences in the way the samples are constructed, however, Blank's basic conclusion is not at odds with the results presented here. In particular, Blank considered whether the causation runs from rising involuntary part-time employment to changes in the male wage distribution. This assumes that everyone indicating involuntary part-time status faces true hours constraints. The causation addressed here is the opposite: whether increases in measured involuntary part-time employment are caused by falling real wage opportunities for low-skill workers, assuming at least part of the increase is due to misclassification of voluntary part-time workers as involuntary. Viewed this way, both sets of results are consistent with each other. In particular, the partial evidence in favor of misclassification presented here makes Blank's conclusion stronger.

Finally, it is worth noting the recent debate over biases in the Consumer Price Index (CPI) (Boskin et al. 1998; Abraham, Greenlees, and Moulton 1998). If the Boskin Commission is correct that the CPI is overstated by about one percentage point per year, then average wages have grown much faster in recent years than was previously believed. However, making the Boskin Commission corrections to the CPI should not measurably change the results reported here because the steep drop in real wages for low-wage men since the 1970s was so large (calculated using the CPI).

CONCLUSIONS

Much of the concern raised over alternative employment arrangements in recent years has been motivated by deteriorating high-wage job opportunities for lower-skilled men. This analysis provides support for a link between those two phenomena. But it is important to identify properly the direction of the causation, which is at least partly from falling real wages to rising part-time employment, both voluntary and involuntary. The results suggest that some low-skill male part-time workers are misclassified as involuntary; they probably could find a full-time job at the same wage. Understanding a male worker's overall wage opportunities, not just observing his employment outcome, is important for evaluating the role of part-time employment in the labor market for men.

The same general conclusion applies for women as well. Rising involuntary part-time employment for women was probably driven at least partly by increases in female labor-force participation and the supply of full-time labor that outpaced what employers were offering: firms may have been too slow to react to the changes in female labor supply. Thus, many female involuntary part-timers face hours constraints that are probably transitory.

In contrast to involuntary part-time employment, almost none of the rise in temporary employment can be explained by overall changes in wage opportunities for either men or women. The most likely cause is a rise in demand for the services of temporary staffing industry firms.

This evidence strongly suggests that at least some of the long-run changes in part-time and temporary employment were caused by labor supply responses to other changes in the labor market, including changes in the wage distribution. In particular, a labor supply response can explain a significant portion—though no more than half—of the increase in these employment rates for lower-skill workers relative to higher-skill workers.

Voluntary part-time

1 to 20	16.415	16.489	16.740	12.748	15.406	16.384
21 to 40	16.469	16.496	16.501	15.120	14.960	16.010
41 to 60	19.727	19.755	19.774	14.058	18.717	19.380
61 to 80	16.824	16.746	16.554	13.678	14.385	15.459
81 to 100	15.734	15.710	15.692	12.658	13.003	14.080
Total	17.011	17.011	17.011	13.662	15.146	16.142

Full-time

1 to 20	58.443	58.363	58.312	61.188	61.658	58.924
21 to 40	63.199	63.182	63.199	63.668	67.571	64.331
41 to 60	62.176	62.119	62.057	65.515	65.267	63.473
61 to 80	65.678	65.791	66.052	67.198	71.729	68.540
81 to 100	69.668	69.700	69.551	69.805	76.161	73.238
Total	64.279	64.279	64.279	65.841	69.249	66.432

Other

1 to 20	12.875	12.970	12.958	11.284	12.287	12.944
21 to 40	11.867	11.880	11.868	12.341	10.795	11.705
41 to 60	12.020	12.049	12.098	12.940	11.178	11.856
61 to 80	12.208	12.170	12.080	12.581	10.505	11.698
81 to 100	10.508	10.437	10.489	13.886	8.486	9.623
Total	11.814	11.814	11.814	12.707	10.468	11.416

Note: Predicted employment rates were constructed by running a multinomial logit for 1971 to 1973 with seven outcomes: full-time, temporary, involuntary part-time, voluntary part-time, unemployed, other (agriculture, self-employed, with a job but not at work last week), and out of the labor force (OLF). The sole regressors were the predicted wage interacted with five wage quintile dummies. The coefficients from the multinomial regression from 1971 to 1973 were used to predict employment rates for 1988 to 1990. In constructing the rates reported here, only the labor force was used in the denominator.

Table 10A.4 Actual and Predicted Employment and Unemployment Rates by Percentiles of the Predicted Wage Distribution for Prime-Age Men, 1971 to 1973 and 1988 to 1990 (Percentage of the Labor Force)

Employment State and Wage Percentiles	1971 to 73 Actual	1971 to 1973 Predicted	1971 to 1973 Predicted (Alternate)	1988 to 1990 Actual	1988 to 1990 Predicted	1988 to 1990 Predicted (Alternate)
Unemployed						
1 to 20	7.188	7.213	7.090	9.803	7.607	7.768
21 to 40	4.348	4.349	4.353	5.968	4.430	4.744
41 to 60	3.318	3.312	3.312	4.206	3.184	3.306
61 to 80	2.252	2.247	2.258	2.792	1.992	2.023
81 to 100	1.527	1.509	1.588	1.547	1.247	1.289
Total	3.675	3.675	3.675	4.782	3.628	3.758
Temporary						
1 to 20	0.049	0.050	0.049	0.389	0.054	0.056
21 to 40	0.040	0.040	0.039	0.173	0.041	0.043
41 to 60	0.013	0.012	0.012	0.122	0.012	0.012
61 to 80	0.020	0.020	0.021	0.090	0.018	0.019
81 to 100	0.013	0.013	0.014	0.083	0.010	0.011
Total	0.027	0.027	0.027	0.168	0.026	0.028
Involuntary part-time						
1 to 20	1.010	1.005	0.976	2.631	1.100	1.178
21 to 40	0.422	0.426	0.431	1.197	0.440	0.507
41 to 60	0.382	0.379	0.379	0.792	0.357	0.379
61 to 80	0.258	0.261	0.266	0.563	0.221	0.228
81 to 100	0.104	0.103	0.117	0.397	0.077	0.086
Total	0.427	0.427	0.427	1.093	0.430	0.465

Voluntary part-time						
1 to 20	1.340	1.342	1.309	2.163	1.437	1.455
21 to 40	1.025	1.028	1.032	1.559	1.048	1.110
41 to 60	1.222	1.231	1.228	1.621	1.192	1.226
61 to 80	1.301	1.315	1.332	1.523	1.215	1.275
81 to 100	1.378	1.350	1.362	1.129	1.214	1.269
Total	1.253	1.253	1.253	1.590	1.220	1.266
Full-time						
1 to 20	74.935	75.165	75.749	70.620	74.531	75.506
21 to 40	77.139	77.158	77.189	73.969	77.041	77.192
41 to 60	79.402	79.400	79.420	74.849	79.627	79.410
61 to 80	80.046	80.077	80.124	75.596	80.580	80.115
81 to100	81.384	81.130	80.510	76.014	81.736	80.377
Total	78.641	78.641	78.641	74.265	78.780	78.578
Other						
1 to20	15.478	15.224	14.827	14.394	15.271	14.037
21 to 40	17.025	16.999	16.956	17.135	16.999	16.405
41 to 60	15.663	15.666	15.648	18.376	15.628	15.667
61 to 80	16.124	16.080	15.999	19.436	15.975	16.341
81 to 100	15.595	15.896	16.409	20.830	15.715	16.967
Total	15.977	15.977	15.977	18.102	15.916	15.905

Note: Predicted employment rates were constructed by running a multinomial logit for 1971 to 1973 with seven outcomes: full-time, temporary, involuntary part-time, voluntary part-time, unemployed, other (agriculture, self-employed, with a job but not at work last week), and out of the labor force (OLF). The sole regressors were the predicted wage interacted with five wage quintile dummies. The coefficients from the multinomial regression from 1971 to 1973 were used to predict employment rates for 1988 and 1990. In constructing the rates reported here, only the labor force was used in the denominator.

ACKNOWLEDGMENTS

Two anonymous referees, Michael Cragg, Susan Hosek, Lawrence Katz, Karen Lombard, Karen Needels, David Neumark, Elaine Reardon, Stefanie Schmidt, and seminar participants at the Russell Sage Foundation Conference on Changes in Job Stability and Job Security and at the Milken Institute provided very helpful comments. Claudia Hernandez, Kathryn LaBach, and, especially, Christopher Thompson provided excellent research assistance. All errors are my own.

NOTES

1. These figures are based on March CPS calculations for the nonagricultural workforce. Only people who usually work part-time are counted as part-time; those who usually work full-time but are temporarily working part-time hours during the survey week are excluded (Levenson 1996).

2. Estimates of the size of the temporary staffing industry from household- versus employer-based surveys are markedly different (Segal and Sullivan 1997).

3. Some authors have shown evidence that not all changes in the wage distribution were demand-driven. However, there is little objection to the conclusion that a large number, if not the vast majority, of the changes were demand-driven.

4. This is consistent with the general findings that part-time and temporary jobs are more transitional than full-time jobs (see discussion later in the chapter).

5. Rebecca Blank (1998) has a nice treatment of this issue in her discussion of policy options regarding part-time, temporary, and other forms of "contingent" employment.

6. Note that the jump in voluntary part-time employment for women in 1994 (figure 10.2) is the reason for the jump in voluntary part-time employment for the entire prime-age workforce (figure 10.1), and for the jump in the overall part-time employment rate for both women (figure 10.2) and the entire prime-age workforce (figure 10.1). As explained in the appendix, this increase in women's voluntary part-time employment was due to neither a sudden change in women's labor supply nor a sudden change in the types of jobs offered by employers, but to a change in the way the CPS measures employment.

7. Typical press coverage touts the fact that Manpower is the "largest employer" in the United States because it issues the largest number of W-2 tax forms per year. However, owing to the short duration of temporary assignments, the average number of temps working through Manpower (or any other staffing agency) each day is much lower than the number of W-2 forms issued at the end of the year.

8. The second-most-common reason recorded in the CPS, "slack work," is a measure of demand-driven reasons for working part-time temporarily. For those people who usually work part-time, it is likely that "slack work" is a

of these costs associated with job loss may be related to difficulty finding a conventional employment arrangement. The central goal of this study is to provide statistical evidence on the extent to which alternative employment arrangements are in fact a common response to job loss. I find that temporary employment and involuntary part-time employment are used disproportionately by job-losers, and I also investigate in some detail whether these alternative employment arrangements are a transitional experience for job-losers.

THE FEBRUARY 1995 AND FEBRUARY 1997 CAEAS DATA

The February 1995 and 1997 Contingent and Alternative Employment Arrangements Supplements to the CPS contain information on alternative employment arrangements held at the survey date. Workers in alternative employment arrangements include independent contractors, consultants, free-lance workers, other self-employed workers, temporary workers, on-call workers, and contract workers. To focus the analysis, I combine these into three categories. The first, which I call "independent contractors," consists of independent contractors, consultants, and free-lance workers. The second is composed of other self-employed workers ("other self-employed"). The third, which I call "temporary workers," consists of temporary, on-call, and contract workers.[5]

To place workers in these categories, I use data from the basic CPS questionnaire as well as from the CAEAS. Specifically, a worker is classified as an independent contractor if he or she is employed at the survey date, is classified as self-employed in the basic CPS, and responds affirmatively in the CAEAS that he or she is "self-employed as an independent contractor, independent consultant, free-lance worker, or something else." A worker is classified as "other self-employed" if he or she is employed at the survey date, is classified as self-employed in the basic CPS, and is *not* classified as an independent contractor as defined here.[6] A worker is classified as a temporary worker if he or she is employed at the survey date, is not classified as either type of self-employed worker, and responds affirmatively that he or she is in a temporary job, works for a temporary work agency, is an on-call worker, is a day laborer, or is a contract employee. All other workers (including part-time) are classified as "regular" workers.

The first four columns of table 11.1 contain weighted breakdowns of employment arrangements for 102,318 individuals in the February 1995 and 1997 CAEASs ages twenty to sixty-six who are employed at the survey date.[7] The first row of the table contains the breakdown for the entire

Table 11.1 Employed Workers, Ages Twenty to Sixty-Six, in Alternative Employment Arrangements: February 1995 and 1997 CAEAS

Group	Regular	Contractor	Other Self-Employment	Temporary	Full-Time	Voluntary Part-Time	Involuntary Part-Time
All	0.825 (.001)	0.059 (0.001)	0.054 (0.001)	0.062 (0.001)	0.847 (0.001)	0.108 (0.001)	0.045 (0.001)
Sex							
Male	0.802 (.002)	0.076 (0.001)	0.061 (0.001)	0.061 (0.001)	0.918 (0.002)	0.045 (0.001)	0.036 (0.001)
Female	0.851 (0.002)	0.039 (0.001)	0.046 (0.001)	0.064 (0.001)	0.765 (0.002)	0.180 (0.001)	0.055 (0.001)
Education							
Less than twelve years	0.823 (0.004)	0.053 (0.002)	0.047 (0.002)	0.077 (0.003)	0.818 (0.004)	0.087 (0.003)	0.094 (0.002)
Twelve years	0.841 (0.002)	0.054 (0.001)	0.052 (0.001)	0.053 (0.001)	0.853 (0.002)	0.097 (0.002)	0.050 (0.001)
Thirteen to fifteen years	0.828 (0.002)	0.054 (0.001)	0.049 (0.001)	0.069 (0.001)	0.810 (0.002)	0.148 (0.002)	0.042 (0.001)
Sixteen years or more	0.803 (0.002)	0.071 (0.001)	0.064 (0.001)	0.062 (0.001)	0.890 (0.002)	0.084 (0.002)	0.026 (0.001)
Age							
Twenty to twenty-four	0.851 (0.004)	0.012 (0.002)	0.014 (0.002)	0.123 (0.002)	0.705 (0.003)	0.226 (0.003)	0.070 (0.002)
Twenty-five to thirty-four	0.853 (0.002)	0.042 (0.001)	0.035 (0.001)	0.070 (0.001)	0.868 (0.002)	0.088 (0.002)	0.044 (0.001)
Thirty-five to forty-four	0.826 (0.002)	0.066 (0.001)	0.057 (0.001)	0.052 (0.001)	0.871 (0.002)	0.090 (0.002)	0.039 (0.001)
Forty-five to fifty-four	0.810 (0.003)	0.076 (0.002)	0.072 (0.002)	0.043 (0.002)	0.885 (0.002)	0.075 (0.002)	0.040 (0.001)
Fifty-five to sixty-four	0.767 (0.004)	0.088 (0.002)	0.095 (0.002)	0.050 (0.002)	0.812 (0.003)	0.139 (0.003)	0.049 (0.002)

sample and shows 82.5 percent in regular employment relationships, 5.9 percent as independent contractors, 5.4 percent as other self-employed, and 6.2 percent as temporary workers.

The last three columns of table 11.1 contain weighted breakdowns of full and part-time status for the same sample. The full- and part-time distinction is made using data from the basic CPS information on hours of work. Part-time workers are those whose total hours on all jobs are less than thirty-five per week.[8] Those part-time workers who report a preference for working full-time and who report being part-time for economic reasons (slack work, can't find a full-time job, seasonal work) are classified as "involuntary part-time." The remainder are classified as "voluntary part-time." The first row of the table contains the breakdown for the entire sample and shows 84.7 percent in full-time employment relationships, 10.8 percent as working voluntary part-time, and 4.5 percent as working involuntarily part-time.

The remainder of table 11.1 contains breakdowns of employed workers by type of employment and full-part-time status separately by sex, education level, and age.[9] A significantly larger fraction of females than males (85.1 percent versus 80.2 percent) are in regular employment relationships, owing to the fact that females are significantly less likely than males (8.5 percent versus 13.8 percent) to be self-employed (either type). There is only a small difference by sex in the rate of temporary employment. Despite being more likely to be in regular employment arrangements, females are substantially more likely than males to be employed part-time. The overall differential of 15.3 percentage points is accounted for largely by a 13.5-percentage-point differential in the rate of voluntary part-time employment, which is supplemented by a 1.9-percentage-point differential in the rate of involuntary part-time employment. These differences are likely to reflect systematic differences in labor supply between men and women.

There is not a strictly monotonic relationship between education category and the incidence of regular employment relationships, but the most obvious pattern is that workers with at least sixteen years of education have lower rates (by two to four percentage points) of regular employment than do workers with less education. This is accounted for by higher rates of self-employment (both types) among workers in the highest education category. With respect to part-time employment, the most striking difference is that workers in the highest education category have substantially higher full-time employment rates than do workers with less education. Workers with twelve years of education have an intermediate rate of full-time employment. The fact that the involuntary part-time rate is monotonically declining with education accounts for these findings (along with the unusually high voluntary part-time rate for workers with thirteen to fifteen years of education).

Table 11.2　Part-Time Status of Workers Ages Twenty to Sixty-Six, by
　　　　　　　Employment Arrangement: February 1995 and 1997
　　　　　　　CAEAS (Row Fractions)

Group	Full-Time	Voluntary Part-Time	Involuntary Part-Time
Regular	0.874	0.092	0.034
Contractor	0.756	0.148	0.097
Other self-employment	0.781	0.151	0.069
Temporary	0.638	0.244	0.119
All	0.847	0.108	0.045

Note: N = 102,318.

The fraction of workers in regular employment relationships declines monotonically with age. This results from an increase with age in the proportion of workers who are self-employed (both types) and a decrease with age in the fraction of workers who are in temporary jobs. The temporary job rate is particularly high for workers in the youngest age category. Full-time employment rates are lowest for workers in the youngest and oldest age categories, primarily owing to high voluntary part-time rates among workers in these two age categories. These lower rates may reflect part-time work while enrolled in school (for the youngest workers) and a decrease in the labor supply of workers approaching retirement (for the oldest workers).

Note that the type of employment arrangements and full-part-time status are not independent. Table 11.2 contains a cross-tabulation of employment arrangements with part-time status for the 102,318 workers in the combined February 1995 and February 1997 samples used in table 11.1.[10] Regular workers are substantially more likely to be full-time and less likely to be in either part-time category than are workers in the other employment arrangements. At the other extreme, temporary workers are least likely to be full-time and most likely to be in either part-time category. Fully 24.4 percent of temporary workers are voluntarily part-time, and 11.9 percent of temporary workers are involuntarily part-time. This compares with 9.2 percent of regular workers in voluntary part-time jobs and 3.4 percent of regular workers in involuntary part-time jobs. The self-employed categories are intermediate in their full- or part-time status.

MATCHING THE FEBRUARY DWS AND FEBRUARY CAEAS DATA

The first step in matching the February 1994 and 1996 DWS with the February 1995 and 1997 CAEAS, respectively, is to define the pool of individuals eligible to be matched from the DWS. To be eligible to be in the CPS in both the DWS and CAEAS in the subsequent year, a household must be in one of its first four months in the sample in the DWS. Such a household is then eligible to be in the sample in the CAEAS in the subsequent year (in one of its four months back in the sample after an eight-month hiatus). But because addresses rather than specific households or individuals are sampled and surveyed, only individuals who have not moved in the intervening year are eligible to be matched. Information contained in the CPS since 1994 is meant to allow an exact match of individuals across CPSs, but to reduce the likelihood of coding errors leading to inappropriate matches, I also match on a set of demographic characteristics (age, sex, and race).

I restrict my analysis to individuals age twenty to sixty-four in the February DWS (1994 and 1996). There are 39,841 individuals in this age group in rotation groups 1 through 4 in February 1994, and there are 34,689 individuals in this age group in rotation groups 1 through 4 in February 1996. Thus, 74,530 individuals are eligible to be matched with individuals in the CAEAS in the subsequent year (February 1995 or February 1997). Of these, I am able to match 50,620, for a match rate of 67.9 percent. A problem is that the match rate depends centrally on whether individuals have changed residence between the survey dates. Not surprisingly, workers who lose jobs (defined precisely later in this section) are more likely to change residence. The match rate among job-losers is 65.4 percent, compared with a 69.1 percent match rate among non-job-losers. The lower match rate among job-losers is particularly unfortunate given the focus of this study, but there is no obvious solution to this problem.

It might be expected that the distribution of type of employment in the CAEAS in the subsequent year would be related to the probability of matching, and that those in alternative employment relationships would be less likely to be matched. It turns out that there are generally small differences in the distributions of employment arrangements by whether the observation was matched. Specifically, recall that 82.5 percent of the overall sample from the CAEAS (including all eight rotation groups) were employed in regular jobs. Among those matched, 82.9 percent were employed in regular jobs. The comparisons for the other categories are fairly close: independent contractors (5.9 percent overall versus 5.6 percent matched), other self-employed (5.4 percent overall versus 6.8 percent matched), and temporary (6.2 percent overall versus 4.7 percent matched). The fact that other self-employed are more likely to be matched may reflect the fact that, based on the algorithm that defines this category, it includes independent business owners, whose businesses are not likely to be geographically mobile. On the other hand, temporary workers are less likely to be matched. Although nothing can be done about this problem, it is important to note these differences in match rates.

Job Loss as Defined by the Displaced Workers Survey

The February 1994 and 1996 Displaced Workers Survey asks whether they were displaced from a job at any time in the preceding three-year period (1991 to 1993 and 1994 to 1996, respectively). Other events, including quits and being fired for cause, are not considered displacement. Thus, the supplement is designed to focus on the loss of specific jobs that result from business decisions of firms unrelated to the performance of particular workers.

The central purpose of using the DWS in this study is to identify individuals who have lost a job in the relevant intervals. Although job loss as measured by the DWS almost certainly does not represent all job loss which we ought to be concerned, it does represent the best available source of data on job loss. (For a detailed discussion of the definition and limitations of the measure of job loss from the DWS, see Farber 1997a.) Overall, 6,637 individuals age twenty to sixty-four reported in the February 1994 DWS that they had lost a job in the 1991 to 1993 period. Similarly, 6,459 individuals age twenty to sixty-four reported in the February 1996 DWS that they had lost a job in the 1994 to 1996 period.[11] Of these 13,096 job-losers, 6,733 were in rotation groups 1 through 4 and hence are potentially matchable to the subsequent CPSs with the CAEAS.

The Final Match

Of the 50,620 individuals age twenty to sixty-four in the February 1994 and 1996 CPS who were successfully matched to the February 1995 and 1997 CPS, 2,145 were not interviewed for the Displaced Workers Survey, so that there is no information on job loss for these workers. These individuals are dropped from the analysis. Although only the employed were eligible to be interviewed for the CAEAS, I am interested in all employment-related outcomes for displaced workers. Thus, for now I retain those who are not employed at the CAEAS date. But 3,412 employed individuals were not administered the CAEAS. When these nonrespondents are eliminated from the sample, there are 45,063 individuals, including 4,102 job-losers, left in the matched sample, and they form the core of the analysis using the matched data. There is complete information for this sample on job loss in the three-year period prior to the DWS and on employment arrangements in the subsequent CAEAS. Of the 45,063 individuals in the sample, 33,296 are employed at the relevant CAEAS date.

JOB LOSS AND ALTERNATIVE EMPLOYMENT ARRANGEMENTS: THE MATCHED DATA

Table 11.3 contains a breakdown of employment arrangements at the CAEAS date by whether the individual reported a job loss in the three years prior to the relevant DWS. The sample contains all individuals, whether employed at the CAEAS date or not. In particular, it shows the fraction of the sample separately for job-losers and non-job-losers who are in each type of employment (or nonemployment) arrangement. I also present the difference between the rates for non-job-losers and the rates for job-losers, and I call this difference the job-loss differential.

These data include individuals who are not employed in order to highlight two issues. First, individuals who lost jobs in the three years prior to the DWS are more likely than non-job-losers (by 6.2 percentage points) to report being unemployed a year after the DWS date.[12] Second, job-losers are less likely than non-job-losers (by 6.8 percentage points) to be out of the labor force (OLF) a year after the DWS date because, in order to have lost a job, workers must have been employed at some point in the three years prior to the DWS. Many of the workers who were not job-losers have been out of the labor force for a long period of time (or were never in the labor force).

It would be most appropriate to omit workers with no long-term attachment to the labor force from the analysis because they are not (to a first approximation) affected by job loss, but it is not possible to identify these workers. I proceed by analyzing the employment status of the sample of workers who are employed at the CAEAS date. Since a substantial fraction of job-losers are not employed (25.6 percent in table 11.3), this analysis errs in excluding individuals who were affected by job loss. Nonetheless, it gives the clearest picture of the distribution of employment arrangements subsequent to job loss and of how this distribution is related to a history of job loss.

Table 11.4 is organized identically to table 11.3 with the difference that the breakdown in table 11.4 recomputes the fraction of workers in each type of employment relationship excluding those who are not employed. The results show that employed job-losers have a smaller probability than non-job-losers of being in a regular job. The job-loss differential for temporary work is positive, suggesting that job-losers who find work are substantially more likely than non-job-losers (by 5.7 percentage points) to be in temporary jobs. Another difference is that job-losers are less likely (by 3.1 percentage points) to be "other self-employed," but there is not a significant job-loss differential in the probability of being an independent contractor. The analysis in table 11.3 which includes those not employed, yields the same qualitative results.

A word is required on the interpretation of the two self-employed cat-

Table 11.3 Workers Ages Twenty to Sixty-Four (in DWS) in Specific Alternative Employment Arrangements, by Job-Loss Status: Matched DWS-CAEAS Data

Group	Regular	Contractor	Other Self-Employment	Temporary	Unemployed	Out of Labor Force
Non-job-losers	0.613	0.047	0.044	0.035	0.028	0.234
	(0.002)	(0.001)	(0.001)	(0.001)	(0.001)	(0.002)
Job-losers	0.599	0.046	0.021	0.078	0.090	0.166
	(0.007)	(0.003)	(0.003)	(0.003)	(0.003)	(0.006)
Difference	−0.014	−0.001	−0.023	0.043	0.062	−0.068
	(0.008)	(0.003)	(0.003)	(0.003)	(0.003)	(0.007)

Note: Based on tabulations from the matched February 1994 and 1996 DWS with the February 1995 and 1997 CAEAS, respectively. Workers are classified as unemployed and out of the labor force according to the standard CPS definitions. All fractions are weighted by CPS sampling weights. The numbers in parentheses are standard errors. $N = 45,063$.

Table 11.4   Workers Ages Twenty to Sixty-Four (at DWS Date) in Specific Alternative Employment Arrangements, by Job-Loss Status: Matched DWS-CAEAS Data

Group	Regular	Contractor	Other Self-Employment	Temporary
Non-job-losers	0.830	0.063	0.060	0.047
	(0.002)	(0.001)	(0.001)	(0.001)
Job-losers	0.805	0.062	0.029	0.105
	(0.007)	(0.004)	(0.004)	(0.004)
Difference	−0.025	−0.001	−0.031	0.057
	(0.007)	(0.005)	(0.004)	(0.004)

Note: Based on tabulations from the matched February 1994 and 1996 DWS to the CPS with the February 1995 and 1997 CAEAS to the CPS, respectively. All fractions are weighted by CPS sampling weights. The numbers in parentheses are standard errors. $N = 33,296$.

egories. The "independent contractor" category includes self-employed workers who say that they are independent contractors, independent consultants, free-lance workers, or something else. This appears to be the category that captures the sort of self-employment arrangements that individuals find themselves in after leaving a company and perhaps performing the same function for their old employer on a contract basis or starting a "consulting" business selling their services. The "other self-employed" category is the residual category and probably captures owners of small businesses. As such, the "contractor" category is more likely to be used by job-losers than "other/self-employed." This is consistent with the tabulations in tables 11.3 and 11.4.

The next step is to carry out multivariate analyses of the probability of employment by type in order to estimate the job-loss differentials in employment probabilities controlling for demographic characteristics. Given the similarity of the relationship between job loss and type of employment found in the analysis that includes those not employed and the analysis that focuses on those employed, I continue using only the sample composed of those employed at the CAEAS survey date. I estimate simple probit models of the probability of employment of the various types as a function of job-loss status, age, education, sex, marital status, the interaction of sex and marital status, and race.[13]

The key variable for the purposes of this study is the job-loss indicator. Its normalized coefficient measures the adjusted (for demographic characteristics) job-loss differential in the probability of employment of the indicated type controlling for the observable demographic characteristics.[14] The differences in the structure of employment relationships across demographic groups implicit in the probit estimates are as noted in the raw tabulations in table 11.1 from the February 1995 and 1997 CAEAS;

for this reason, the estimates of the coefficients of the demographic variables are not presented here.

The first row of table 11.5 contains the adjusted job-loss differentials for the overall sample of 33,095 workers. The results are similar to the unadjusted differences found in table 11.4. Job-losers are about 2.8 percentage points less likely than non-job-losers to be in regular jobs. There is no difference by job-loss status in the probability of being an independent contractor, but job-losers are significantly less likely than non-job-losers (by 3.1 percentage points) to be in "other self-employed" jobs. Job-losers are significantly more likely to be in temporary jobs (by 4.1 percentage points).

The job-loss differentials in the first row of table 11.5 control for observable differences across workers, but they constrain the job-loss differential in the employment outcomes to be the same for all types of workers. I relax this restriction by estimating separate probit models for various categories of workers. Each of these probit models contains the same set of variables as the overall model (omitting the set of variables on which the particular subsample is stratified). The remaining rows of table 11.5 contain the normalized probit coefficients of the job-loss dummy variable from each of these models for (1) separate models by sex and marital status, (2) separate models by educational category, and (3) separate models by age category.

The adjusted job-loss differentials estimated from separate probit models by sex and marital status are not very different. The adjusted job-loss differentials show lower probabilities of regular employment and other-self-employment for job-losers, and these differentials are largest for unmarried workers of both sexes. This is offset largely by higher probabilities of temporary work for job-losers. Single females who lose jobs also show a higher probability of being an independent contractor.

The adjusted job-loss differentials estimated from separate probit models by educational category suggest that there is a contrast in the job-loss differentials between workers with less than sixteen years of education and workers with sixteen or more years of education. Although job-losers with less than sixteen years of education are about one percentage point less likely than non-job-losers to be employed in a regular job, job-losers with at least sixteen years of education are fully six percentage points less likely than non-job-losers to be employed in regular jobs. This difference across education groups appears to be accounted for largely by a higher adjusted job-loss differential in the probability of being an independent contractor (about 1.8 percentage points for highly educated workers compared with zero for less educated workers), and by a higher adjusted job-loss differential in the probability of being a temporary worker (about 5.1 percentage points for highly educated workers compared with 3.5 to 4.0 percentage points for less educated workers). Job-

Table 11.5   Job-Loss Differential in Probability of Employment of
Workers (Employed at CAEAS Date) Ages Twenty to
Sixty-Four (at DWS Date), by Type: Normalized Probit
Estimates Using Matched DWS-CAEAS Data

Group	Regular	Contractor	Other Self-Employment	Temporary
All	−0.0277	0.0010	−0.0313	0.0414
	(0.0068)	(0.0042)	(0.0049)	(0.0033)
Sex-marital status				
Single male	−0.0339	−0.0073	−0.0242	0.0514
	(0.0168)	(0.0107)	(0.0101)	(0.0096)
Married male	−0.0132	−0.0039	−0.0548	0.0416
	(0.0119)	(0.0085)	(0.0095)	(0.0046)
Single female	−0.0529	0.0133	0.0080	0.0266
	(0.0126)	(0.0052)	(0.0055)	(0.0090)
Married female	−0.0259	−0.0001	−0.0410	0.0439
	(0.0132)	(0.0080)	(0.0106)	(0.0065)
Education				
Less than twelve years	−0.0105	−0.0066	−0.0314	0.0354
	(0.0252)	(0.0147)	(0.0174)	(0.0137)
Twelve years	−0.0196	−0.0149	−0.0308	0.0422
	(0.0116)	(0.0076)	(0.0084)	(0.0052)
Thirteen to fifteen years	−0.0123	0.0011	−0.0317	0.0332
	(0.0118)	(0.0069)	(0.0079)	(0.0064)
Sixteen years or more	−0.0614	0.0183	−0.0311	0.0514
	(0.0116)	(0.0076)	(0.0084)	(0.0052)
Age				
Twenty to twenty-four	−0.0156	0.0079	−0.0042	0.0055
	(0.0251)	(0.0056)	(0.0084)	(0.0229)
Twenty-five to thirty-four	−0.0189	0.0027	−0.0121	0.0254
	(0.0122)	(0.0071)	(0.0071)	(0.0076)
Thirty-five to forty-four	−0.0378	−0.0089	−0.0463	0.0564
	(0.0118)	(0.0081)	(0.0092)	(0.0052)
Forty-five to fifty-four	−0.0346	0.0161	−0.0343	0.0342
	(0.0143)	(0.0090)	(0.0113)	(0.0057)
Fifty-five to sixty-four	0.0014	−0.0305	−0.0632	0.0569
	(0.0248)	(0.0166)	(0.0200)	(0.0100)

Note: The estimates are the normalized coefficients on the job-loss dummy variable from separate probit models where the dependent variable is the indicator variable for the type of employment in each column. Other variables included in the probit model include, where appropriate, a constant, three dummy variables for education category, four dummy variables for age category, and dummy variables for sex, marital status, the interaction of sex and marital status, and race. The estimates are based on the matched February 1994 and 1996 DWS with the February 1995 and 1997 CAEAS, respectively. The normalized asymptotic standard errors are in parentheses. All analyses are weighted by CPS sampling weights from 1994 or 1996.

losers in all educational categories are about 3.0 percentage points less likely than non-job-losers to be in the "other self-employed" category.

The remainder of table 11.5 contains the adjusted job-loss differentials estimated from separate probit models by age category. It appears that the largest job-loss differential in the probability of regular employment is for middle-aged workers (thirty-five to fifty-four years of age). The positive job-loss differential in the rate of temporary employment is shared by workers in all age categories except the youngest. The negative relationship between job loss and the rate of other self-employment is stronger among older workers.

To summarize, employed job-losers are more likely to be in alternative employment arrangements, broadly defined, than are non-job-losers. The largest consistent differences are that job-losers are more likely than non-job-losers to be in temporary jobs, and job-losers are less likely than non-job-losers to be "other self-employed" workers. There is also some evidence that highly educated job-losers are more likely to be independent contractors relative to similarly educated non-job-losers.

IS TEMPORARY EMPLOYMENT SUBSEQUENT TO JOB LOSS A TRANSITIONAL EXPERIENCE?

There are at least two interpretations of the finding that workers who have lost jobs are more likely to be in temporary jobs. The first is that temporary employment relationships are used by some workers in a transition period following job loss owing to difficulty in finding regular employment. Following this transition period, displaced workers find regular employment. The second interpretation is that the relationships between job loss and temporary employment are the result of unmeasured heterogeneity across workers so that workers who tend to be employed in temporary jobs are also workers who are more likely to lose jobs regardless of the type of job they are holding.

Although the data do not allow me to make a definitive determination of the relative importance of these two explanations, there is some evidence available that can shed some light on this issue. The first explanation (alternative employment as a transition phase) implies that the probability that a worker holds a temporary job declines with time since displacement. The second explanation (unmeasured heterogeneity) has no such implication.

I investigate this implication directly using the matched sample and information available in the DWS reporting the year of job loss. Unfortunately, the design of the 1994 and 1996 DWS was such that the year of job loss was asked only of individuals who reported losing a job for a subset of the allowed reasons. Specifically, individuals who reported losing a job owing to a plant being closed, slack work, or a position or shift

Table 11.6   Employment Arrangements of Workers (Employed at
CAEAS Date) Ages Twenty to Sixty-Four (at DWS Date),
by Years Since Job Loss: Matched DWS-CAEAS Data

Years Since Loss	Regular	Contractor	Other Self-Employment	Temporary
Two years	0.795	0.055	0.032	0.118
	(0.013)	(0.008)	(0.008)	(0.007)
Three years	0.816	0.058	0.029	0.097
	(0.015)	(0.010)	(0.009)	(0.009)
Four years	0.829	0.074	0.019	0.078
	(0.015)	(0.010)	(0.009)	(0.009)
No loss	0.830	0.063	0.060	0.047
	(0.002)	(0.001)	(0.001)	(0.001)

Note: Based on tabulations from the merged February 1994 and 1996 DWS with the February 1995 and 1997 CAEAS, respectively. All fractions are weighted by CPS sampling weights from 1994 or 1996. The numbers in parentheses are standard errors. $N = 32,321$, including 2,056 job-losers.

being abolished were asked follow-up questions, including the year of job loss. Individuals who reported losing a job for other reasons were not asked the follow-up questions. Thus, information on the year of job loss is available for only 2,056 of the 3,031 workers who reported a job loss in February 1994 or 1996, were matched to an observation in February 1995 or 1997, and were employed at the survey date in February 1995 or 1997. I computed the number of years since job loss for these 2,056 workers. Given that job loss occurred in the three years prior to the DWS date, years since job loss range from two to four years at the CAEAS date. Of the 2,056 workers in the sample, 851 reported a loss two years earlier, 612 reported a loss three years earlier, and 593 reported a loss four years earlier.[15]

Table 11.6 contains a breakdown of employment arrangements by years since job loss, and it confirms that the likelihood of regular employment increases with time since job loss (by 3.4 percentage points from two to four years, p-value $= 0.043$). In fact, at four years since job loss (three years prior to the DWS date, four years prior to the CAEAS date), the fraction of job-losers employed in regular jobs is virtually identical to the fraction of non-job-losers in regular jobs. This can be accounted for by a decline in the likelihood of temporary employment with time since job loss (by 4.0 percentage points from two to four years, p-value $=$ 0.00023), although the likelihood of temporary employment among job-losers still substantially exceeds the likelihood of temporary employment among non-job-losers, even after four years. There are also offsetting movements with time since job loss in the likelihood of being in the two self-employment categories. However, these movements are not statistically significant at conventional levels. The movements with time since job loss in the likelihood of regular and temporary employment provide support for the view that temporary employment is used by some workers as a transition to regular employment.[16]

BRIEF COMMENTS ON THE RESULTS ON ALTERNATIVE EMPLOYMENT ARRANGEMENTS

The advantage of using the matched DWS-CAEAS data is that detailed information on employment arrangements allows the identification of alternative employment arrangements made subsequent to job loss. But there are at least two disadvantages. First, the sample size is relatively small, owing to the relatively small fraction of workers who report a job loss in the DWS, the relatively small fraction of individuals who report being in an alternative employment arrangement in the CAEAS, and the inability to match a substantial number of individuals across the two surveys. The second disadvantage is that the information on alternative work arrangements refers to a point in time substantially after the time of job loss (at least fourteen months later at best, and up to four years at worst). To the extent that alternative employment arrangements as a response to job loss are part of a transitory phase, these matched data might substantially understate the use of alternative employment arrangements as a response to job loss.[17]

Although I cannot address these issues directly owing to data limitation, I now turn to analysis of part-time employment and its relationship with job loss. I do this for three reasons. First, part-time employment, particularly involuntary part-time employment, may be experienced by job-losers in a transition period. Second, information on part-time employment is available as part of the basic CPS questionnaire and so is available at the DWS date (one year more proximate to the job loss) as well as at the CAEAS date. Third, because observations on part-time status are available at two points in time in the matched data (three points in time for job-losers), I can address directly the question of the transitory nature of part-time employment subsequent to job loss.

JOB LOSS AND PART-TIME EMPLOYMENT

I begin the analysis of job loss and part-time employment by carrying out an analysis of part-time employment using the matched DWS-CAEAS data that parallels the analysis presented earlier for alternative employment arrangements. The matched data have measures of part-time employment at two points in time: the DWS date and the CAEAS date.[18] Since the DWS date is more proximate to the date of job loss (one to three years) than the CAEAS date (two to four years), a comparison of the part-time rates at the two dates, as well as measures of the transition

Table 11.7 Employed Workers Ages Twenty to Sixty-Four (at DWS Date) in Specific Full- and Part-Time Employment Arrangements, by Job-Loss Status: Matched DWS-CAEAS Data

Group	Full-Time at DWS	Voluntary Part-Time at DWS	Involuntary Part-Time at DWS	Full-Time at CAEAS	Voluntary Part-Time at CAEAS	Involuntary Part-Time at CAEAS
Non-job-loser	0.850	0.109	0.041	0.854	0.107	0.039
	(0.002)	(0.002)	(0.001)	(0.002)	(0.002)	(0.001)
Job-loser	0.794	0.116	0.090	0.842	0.104	.054
	(0.007)	(0.006)	(0.004)	(0.006)	(0.005)	(0.004)
Difference	−0.056	0.008	0.049	−0.011	−0.003	0.015
	(0.007)	(0.006)	(0.004)	(0.007)	(0.006)	(0.004)

Note: Based on tabulations from the matched February 1994 and 1996 DWS with the February 1995 and 1997 CAEAS, respectively. All fractions are weighted by CPS sampling weights from 1994 or 1996. The numbers in parentheses are standard errors. $N = 33,705$ at DWS date, and $N = 33,296$ at CAEAS date.

rates from part-time to full-time employment, can shed some light on the extent to which part-time employment is used as a transition strategy after job loss.

Table 11.7 provides strong evidence that involuntary part-time employment is an important transition strategy for job-losers. The first three columns of the table contain the full-time, voluntary part-time, and involuntary part-time rates for non-job-losers and for job-losers measured at the DWS date. Also presented is the job-loss differential in these rates. The full-time employment rate is 5.6 percentage points lower for job-losers than for non-job-losers. This is almost entirely accounted for by a 4.9-percentage-point higher involuntary part-time rate for job-losers relative to non-job-losers. The important contrast is with the tabulations in the last three columns of table 11.8, which provide the same breakdown for part-time employment status at the CAEAS date. Here there is no significant difference in the full-time rate between job-losers and non-job-losers, and only a 1.5-percentage-point higher involuntary part-time rate for job-losers relative to non-job-losers.

As before, the next step is to carry out multivariate analyses of the probability of the three full- and part-time categories in order to estimate the job-loss differentials in employment probabilities controlling for demographic characteristics. The first row of table 11.8 contains estimates of the adjusted job-loss differentials from simple probit models of the probability of employment of the various types as a function of job-loss status, age, education, sex, marital status, the interaction of sex and marital status, and race.[19] The estimates in the first three columns of table 11.8 use the subset of the matched sample consisting of those individuals who are employed at the DWS date, while the estimates in the last three

Table 11.8　Job-Loss Differential in Full- and Part-Time Status of Workers (Employed at CAEAS Date) Ages Twenty to Sixty-Four (at DWS Date): Normalized Probit Estimates Using Matched DWS-CAEAS Data

Group	Full-Time at DWS	Voluntary Part-Time at DWS	Involuntary Part-Time at DWS	Full-Time at CAEAS	Voluntary Part-Time at CAEAS	Involuntary Part-Time at CAEAS
All	−0.0613	0.0168	0.0354	−0.0219	0.0075	0.0130
	(0.0060)	(0.0049)	(0.0030)	(0.0059)	(0.0047)	(0.0032)
Sex-marital status						
Single male	−0.0445	0.0069	0.0355	−0.0124	0.0049	0.0073
	(0.0145)	(0.0105)	(0.0091)	(0.0137)	(0.0098)	(0.0091)
Married male	−0.0394	0.0104	0.0263	−0.0225	0.0115	0.0095
	(0.0053)	(0.0037)	(0.0036)	(0.0052)	(0.0032)	(0.0038)
Single female	−0.0744	0.0164	0.0480	−0.0099	−0.0004	0.0097
	(0.0164)	(0.0138)	(0.0089)	(0.0158)	(0.0128)	(0.0091)
Married female	−0.0920	0.0413	0.0410	−0.0293	0.0012	0.0239
	(0.0161)	(0.0151)	(0.0066)	(0.0160)	(0.0152)	(0.0068)
Education						
Less than twelve years	−0.0775	−0.0056	0.0667	−0.0093	−0.0276	0.0277
	(0.0243)	(0.0183)	(0.0162)	(0.0255)	(0.0176)	(0.0173)
Twelve years	−0.0666	0.0279	0.0334	−0.0422	0.0282	0.0122
	(0.0106)	(0.0080)	(0.0062)	(0.0103)	(0.0077)	(0.0062)
Thirteen to fifteen years	−0.0666	0.0279	0.0334	−0.0422	0.0282	0.0122
	(0.0106)	(0.0080)	(0.0062)	(0.0103)	(0.0077)	(0.0062)
Sixteen years or more	−0.0497	0.0036	0.0348	0.0016	−0.0108	0.0093
	(0.0114)	(0.0099)	(0.0052)	(0.0112)	(0.0095)	(0.0054)
Age						
Twenty to twenty-four	0.0276	−0.0700	0.0306	0.0409	−0.0338	−0.0021
	(0.0385)	(0.0361)	(0.0197)	(0.0338)	(0.0309)	(0.0165)
Twenty-five to thirty-four	−0.0580	0.0233	0.0271	−0.0206	0.0118	0.0076
	(0.0108)	(0.0087)	(0.0056)	(0.0111)	(0.0086)	(0.0062)
Thirty-five to forty-four	−0.0582	0.0095	0.0371	−0.0177	0.0060	0.0099
	(0.0099)	(0.0077)	(0.0049)	(0.0096)	(0.0072)	(0.0050)
Forty-five to fifty-four	−0.0676	0.0257	0.0340	−0.0209	0.0015	0.0173
	(0.0104)	(0.0080)	(0.0056)	(0.0106)	(0.0080)	(0.0060)
Fifty-five to sixty-four	−0.1150	0.0561	0.0492	−0.0897	0.0538	0.0316
	(0.0221)	(0.0189)	(0.0117)	(0.0221)	(0.0192)	(0.0112)

Note: The estimates are the normalized coefficients on the job-loss dummy variable from separate probit models where the dependent variable is the indicator variable for the type of full- and part-time status in each column. Other variables included in the probit model include, where appropriate, a constant, three dummy variables for education category, four dummy variables for age category, and dummy variables for sex, marital status, the interaction of sex and marital status, and race. The estimates are based on the matched February 1994 and 1996 DWS with the February 1995 and 1997 CAEAS, respectively. Normalized asymptotic standard errors are in parentheses. All analyses are weighted by CPS sampling weights from 1994 or 1996.

second and third rows report the postdisplacement full- and part-time employment status of full-time job-losers and part-time job-losers, respectively. The first three columns report the fraction in each full- and part-time status at the DWS date, and the last three columns report the fraction in each full- and part-time status at the CAEAS date.

Among those employed at the relevant survey date, there is a sharp contrast between the full-time job-losers and the part-time job-losers. By the DWS survey date, the fraction of full-time job-losers who are working full-time is virtually identical to the fraction of non-job-losers who are working full-time (84.3 percent versus 85.0 percent), and by the CAEAS date, the fraction of full-time job-losers who are working full-time is significantly larger than the fraction of non-job-losers who are working full-time (88.3 percent versus 85.4 percent, p-value of difference < 0.00005). It is also the case that full-time job-losers are less likely than non-job-losers to be voluntarily part-time and more likely than non-job-losers to be involuntarily part-time at the DWS date. By the CAEAS date, the gap in the voluntary part-time rates increases and the gap in the involuntary part-time rate decreases. This pattern is a result of the fact that the pool of non-job-losers contains a core of individuals who are voluntarily part-time as a result of labor supply choices and that the full-time job-losers have shown evidence of a commitment to full-time work. This interpretation of the evidence is further supported by the postdisplacement full or part-time status of the part-time job-losers, who are substantially less likely than full-time job-losers to be employed full-time at either the DWS date or the CAEAS date.

Transitions in Full- and Part-Time Status Between the DWS Date and the CAEAS Date

The preceding analysis strongly suggests that there is heterogeneity among the workforce in general, and among job-losers in particular, in preferences for full-time work. There may also be further heterogeneity in the ability to find and hold a full-time job. Implicit in the earlier discussion is the idea that full-time workers are committed to full-time work, but it is surely the case that some full-time workers move to part-time work, and vice versa, even without a job loss. This presumably reflects changes in individual constraints and in market conditions over time. In this section, I examine individual transitions in full- and part-time status between the DWS date and the CAEAS date separately for non-job-losers and for full-time and part-time job-losers.

Conditioning on full- and part-time status at the DWS date, I use the non-job-losers as a "control group," and I measure their transition rates to full-time, voluntary part-time, and involuntary part-time employment by the CAEAS date. These are, in a sense, the "natural" rates of transi-

Table 11.10 Employed Workers Ages Twenty to Sixty-Four (at DWS Date) by Full- and Part-Time Employment Arrangement at CAEAS Date and by Job-Loss Status and Full- or Part-Time Status on Lost Job and Job at DWS Date: Matched DWS-CAEAS Data (Row Fractions)

Group	Full-Time at CAEAS	Voluntary Part-Time at CAEAS	Involuntary Part-Time at CAEAS
Full-time at DWS			
Non-job-loser	0.954	0.026	0.020
	(0.001)	(0.001)	(0.001)
Full-time job-loser	0.961	0.015	0.024
	(0.006)	(0.004)	(0.004)
Part-time job-loser	0.926	0.027	0.047
	(0.023)	(0.017)	(0.015)
Voluntary part-time at DWS			
Non-job-loser	0.265	0.654	0.081
	(0.008)	(0.009)	(0.005)
Full-time job-loser	0.481	0.388	0.131
	(0.040)	(0.043)	(0.025)
Part-time job-loser	0.217	0.711	0.072
	(0.056)	(0.060)	(0.035)
Involuntary part-time at DWS			
Non-job-loser	0.558	0.208	0.234
	(0.015)	(0.012)	(0.013)
Full-time job-loser	0.676	0.138	0.186
	(0.046)	(0.037)	(0.039)
Part-time job-loser	0.540	0.170	0.290
	(0.101)	(0.082)	(0.086)

Note: Based on tabulations from the merged February 1994 and 1996 DWS with the February 1995 and 1997 CAEAS, respectively. Only those individuals employed at both dates are included in the analysis. All fractions are weighted by CPS sampling weights from 1994 or 1996. The numbers in parentheses are standard errors. $N = 30,383$.

tion. I then contrast these transition rates with the transition rates for full- and part-time job-losers. These analyses provide further information on the incidence and persistence of part-time employment subsequent to job loss.

Table 11.10 contains the core of this analysis. The first panel contains the transition rates of workers who were working full-time at the DWS date. In the control group of non-job-losers, 95.4 percent remained employed full-time a year later, 2.6 percent moved to voluntary part-time status, and 2.0 percent moved to involuntary part-time status. Think of these as the natural transition rates. The picture is not far different for losers of full-time jobs who were employed full-time at the DWS date. However, part-time job losers who are employed full-time at the DWS date are less likely to remain in full-time employment (92.6 percent) and more likely to move to involuntary part-time status (4.7 percent).[23]

The second and third panels of table 11.10 contain the transition rates of workers who had voluntary and involuntary part-time status, respectively, at the DWS date. The key finding is that a substantially higher fraction of full-time job-losers (relative to either non-job-losers or part-time job-losers) moved from part-time jobs to full-time jobs between the DWS date and the CAEAS date. This is further evidence that full-time job-losers find themselves in part-time employment as a transition to re-employment full-time.

THE INTERACTION OF ALTERNATIVE EMPLOYMENT ARRANGEMENTS AND FULL- OR PART-TIME STATUS

I have established that temporary and part-time employment, particularly involuntary part-time employment, are important transitional outcomes for displaced workers. Further, the breakdowns in table 11.2 clearly show that temporary workers are the least likely of all groups to be in full-time jobs. Temporary workers are more likely than other workers to be both voluntarily and involuntarily part-time. In this section, I briefly investigate how the interactions between alternative employment arrangements and full- or part-time status generally, and between temporary work and part-time status specifically, are related to job loss.

Table 11.11 contains breakdowns, using the merged data, of full- and part-time status by employment status at the CAEAS date separately for non-job-losers and job-losers. The top panel of the table uses the merged data to reproduce the breakdowns in table 11.2 (which used the entire 1995 and 1997 CAEASs), and the results are very similar. This finding verifies that the merged sample is not substantially different in these dimensions from the overall sample. The second panel of table 11.11 contains the same breakdowns for non-job-losers. It is not surprising that these breakdowns are very close to those for the overall sample given that only a small fraction of the sample consists of job-losers. The third panel of the table contains the breakdowns for all employed job-losers, and there are some important differences here. A significantly higher fraction of temporary workers who lost jobs are employed full-time at the CAEAS date relative to non-job-losers (12.0 percentage points, p-value $<$ 0.0000001). This is entirely accounted for by an 11.8-percentage-point difference in the voluntary part-time rate between non-job-losers and job-losers (p-value $<$ 0.0000001).

The contrast between non-job-losers and job-losers is even more striking when considering only full-time job-losers. The bottom panel of table 11.11 contains breakdowns for 1,772 full-time job-losers who are employed at the CAEAS date. Full-time job-losers who are employed in

Table 11.11   Part-Time Status of Workers Ages Twenty to Sixty-Four
(at DWS Date), by Employment Arrangement at CAEAS
Date: Merged DWS-CAEAS Data (Row Fractions)

Group	Full-Time	Voluntary Part-Time	Involuntary Part-Time
All workers			
Regular	0.879	0.091	0.030
	(0.002)	(0.002)	(0.001)
Contractor	0.745	0.153	0.101
	(0.008)	(0.007)	(0.004)
Other self-employment	0.784	0.154	0.062
	(0.008)	(0.007)	(0.004)
Temporary	0.638	0.254	0.107
	(0.008)	(0.007)	(0.005)
Non-job-losers			
Regular	0.880	0.091	0.029
	(0.002)	(0.002)	(0.001)
Contractor	0.744	0.151	0.105
	(0.008)	(0.007)	(0.004)
Other self-employment	0.790	0.150	0.059
	(0.008)	(0.007)	(0.005)
Temporary	0.616	0.277	0.108
	(0.009)	(0.008)	(0.005)
All job-losers			
Regular	0.869	0.087	0.044
	(0.007)	(0.006)	(0.005)
Contractor	0.754	0.179	0.066
	(0.026)	(0.022)	(0.016)
Other self-employment	0.651	0.232	0.117
	(0.039)	(0.032)	(0.024)
Temporary	0.736	0.159	0.105
	(0.020)	(0.017)	(0.013)
Full-time job-losers			
Regular	0.911	0.052	0.037
	(0.008)	(0.006)	(0.006)
Contractor	0.754	0.147	0.099
	(0.031)	(0.024)	(0.021)
Other self-employment	0.729	0.143	0.128
	(0.047)	(0.037)	(0.033)
Temporary	0.768	0.109	0.124
	(0.024)	(0.019)	(0.017)

Note: Based on tabulations from the merged February 1994 and 1996 DWS with the February 1995 and 1997 CAEAS, respectively. Only individuals employed at the CAEAS date are included in the analysis. All fractions are weighted by CPS sampling weights from 1994 or 1996. The numbers in parentheses are standard errors. $N = 33{,}296$.

temporary jobs at the CAEAS date are even more likely to be in full-time jobs (76.8 percent) and even less likely to be in voluntary part-time jobs (10.9 percent).

These results imply that temporary jobs are often taken by workers who have a preference for part-time work. It may be that temporary employment arrangements are efficient for these workers. However, it is clear that among job-losers, particularly those who lost full-time jobs, temporary jobs are transitional outcomes that are more likely than the usual temporary job to be characterized by full-time hours.

CONCLUSIONS

It is clear that alternative employment arrangements are an important feature of the U.S. labor market. Tabulation of the February 1995 and 1997 CAEAS showed that 17.5 percent of workers were self-employed or in temporary jobs. Additionally, 15.3 percent of workers in these same surveys were employed part-time (10.8 percent voluntary, 4.5 percent involuntary). My analysis of the matched DWS-CAEAS data shows that job-losers are more likely than non-job-losers to use alternative and part-time employment arrangements. I find that job-losers are significantly more likely than non-job-losers to be in temporary jobs (including on-call work and contract work) and that job-losers are significantly more likely than non-job-losers to be employed involuntarily part-time.

I also find that the likelihood of temporary and involuntary part-time employment falls with time since job loss. Thus, it appears that these alternative employment arrangements are often part of a transitional process subsequent to job loss leading to regular full-time permanent employment. In this respect, temporary employment by job-losers is of a different character than temporary employment by non-job-losers. Job-losers who find employment in temporary jobs are more likely to be working full-time, and non-job-losers who are employed in temporary jobs are more likely to be working voluntarily part-time.

ACKNOWLEDGMENTS

Support for this research was provided by the Office of the Assistant Secretary of Labor for Policy, U.S. Department of Labor, under Purchase Order B9462164, and by the Industrial Relations Section at Princeton University. Karen Conneely and Harry Krashinsky provided able research assistance. Susan Houseman, David Neumark, and two anonymous referees provided useful comments on earlier drafts.

NOTES

1. Civilian employment was 89.9 million in January 1977 and had risen to 128.6 million by January 1997, for an average annual increase of almost 2 million jobs per year. These statistics are taken from U.S. Bureau of Labor Statistics Series ID LFS11000000. This is the seasonally adjusted civilian employment level derived from the CPS for workers age sixteen and older.

2. See Farber (1997c) for a brief review of and references to the literature on job quality and for an analysis of the quality of new jobs. Farber and Levy (1999) present an analysis of the decline in employer-provided health insurance that focuses on workers in new jobs and on part-time workers.

3. The most recently available data show elevated rates of job loss in the 1993 to 1995 period (Farber 1997a) and a reduction between 1993 and 1996 in the fraction of the workforce who have been in their jobs for long periods of time (Farber 1997b). For further analyses of job loss and its consequences, see Farber (1993), Gardner (1995), Kletzer (1989), Neal (1995), Parent (1995), Podgursky and Swaim (1987), and Topel (1990).

4. See, for example, Abraham (1990), Abraham and Taylor (1996), Belous (1989), Blank (1990b), Golden and Applebaum (1992), Houseman (1997), and Howe (1986) for discussions of the incidence of and motivations for alternative employment arrangements.

5. Another way to identify temporary workers is to classify those workers who report their industry of employment as personnel supply services (Census Industry Code 731). However, most workers who actually work for personnel supply firms apparently report themselves as employed in the industry to which they are assigned. Evidence for this is that the Current Employment Survey (CES) data, which are based on information collected from employers, shows that 2.2 percent of nonfarm employment was in the personnel supply services industry (SIC 736) in 1997 (based on BLS series EEU00000001 and EEU8073601). In contrast, my tabulations from the February 1997 CPS show that 0.76 percent of employment was in the personnel supply services industry (CIC 731). Additionally, the personnel supply services industry includes an unknown number of workers who are not temporary workers. Thus, use of this industry classification to identify temporary workers in the CPS is not likely to be very useful here. See Segal and Sullivan (1997) for an analysis that does use this method to identify temporary workers. See also Polivka (1996).

6. Many of these workers are likely to be owners of small businesses.

7. This age range was selected to match individuals who were twenty to sixty-four in the February 1994 DWS. These percentages and other statistics presented in this study are weighted by the CPS final sampling weights. The CAEAS is distributed with special supplement weights to account for nonresponse to the supplement. These are based on differential response rates by demographic group, and they are highly correlated with the final sampling weights (correlation = 0.9988). Thus, although my use of the final sampling weights would understate overall population counts relative to

those derived by using the special supplement weights, both weights yield similar results with regard to computation of means and proportions.

8. The algorithm for assigning part-time status to workers has several steps: (1) a worker is considered part-time if his or her usual total hours are less than thirty-five per week; (2) when usual total hours are missing, a worker is considered full-time if his or her usual hours on the main job are at least thirty-five per week; (3) when part-time status remains unassigned, actual total hours during the reference week are used; (4) an indicator in the basic CPS for "usually full-time" is used to resolve the remaining cases.

9. Although not presented here, I also carried out multivariate probit analyses of the probability of being in employment relationships of each type. These probit models controlled for race as well as for sex, education, and age, and they show the same relationships of the likelihood of alternative arrangements as the simple breakdowns in table 11.1.

10. A Pearson chi-squared text of independence in table 11.2 yields a test statistic of 3,586.5 distributed as $\chi^2(6)$ and clearly rejects independence (p-value < 0.000001).

11. These represent 8.6 and 10.6 percent (weighted) of the total samples, respectively. However, these are not good estimates of the job-loss rates because many of those sampled had not worked and hence were not at risk to lose a job.

12. That unemployment rates are higher among displaced workers is well known from the literature on job displacement (see, for example, Podgursky and Swaim 1987).

13. Note that I am not estimating a multinomial choice model of employment type, such as multinomial logit or probit. What I am interested in here is data description and summary rather than estimates of some structural choice model. The ease of interpretation of the estimates from the binomial probit models makes them a preferred method for this purpose.

14. The coefficients are normalized to represent the derivative of the probability of the outcome with respect to a change in the particular explanatory variable evaluated at the means of the explanatory variables. The normalization factor is $\phi(\bar{X}\hat{\beta})$, so that the normalized coefficient is computed as $\hat{\beta}\,\phi(\bar{X}\hat{\beta})$ where $\hat{\beta}$ is the vector of estimated parameters of the probit model, $\bar{X}$ is the vector of means of the explanatory variables, and ϕ is the standard normal probability density function. The standard errors are also normalized by $\phi(\bar{X}\hat{\beta})$, but they do not take into account the fact that the normalization itself is a random variable.

15. I have repeated the analyses of adjusted job-loss differentials using only non-job-losers and this restricted sample of job-losers, and the results are very similar. The declining number of job-losers with time since the survey probably reflects recall bias. Such bias makes it more likely that recent events and more salient events are recalled (Topel 1990).

16. Although not presented here, probit models of the probability of employment of the various types that control for age, education, sex, race, marital

status, and the interaction of sex and marital status, along with time since job loss, do not change these findings.

17. For example, the estimates suggest that the likelihood of temporary employment arrangements falls by about two percentage points with each year since job loss. Simple (weighted) tabulation of the data show that 11.9 percent of those employed at the CAEAS date who had lost jobs in the year prior to the relevant DWS (two years prior to the CAEAS) were in temporary jobs at the CAEAS date. If the point estimate is taken seriously (admittedly a stretch given the out-of-sample nature of this calculation), then about 14 percent of those displaced in the year prior to the CAEAS would be predicted to be in temporary jobs at the CAEAS date.

18. The DWS also has information on full- and part-time status on the lost job. I use this information later in this section.

19. These differentials are the coefficients on the job-loss variable in the probit models normalized to represent the derivative of the probability of the outcome with respect to a change in job-loss status. See note 14 for details.

20. Although the full estimates of the probit model are not presented here, the estimates based on both samples verify the common finding that married females are substantially less likely to be employed full-time, a fact that is largely accounted for by a substantially higher probability of being employed voluntarily in a part-time job. The results also support the common finding that the probability of involuntary part-time employment falls monotonically with education.

21. Of the 2,598 job-losers for whom we have information on the full- and part-time status of the lost job, 10.9 percent (weighted) reported losing a part-time job. In contrast, 15.0 percent (weighted) of those workers who did not lose a job were employed part-time at the DWS survey date. Thus, the job-loss rate on full-time jobs appears to be higher than the job-loss rate on part-time jobs.

22. Tabulations of the February 1994 and 1996 CPS data yield the result that 68.1 percent of part-time workers are part-time for voluntary reasons.

23. There are relatively few part-time job-losers in the sample used for this analysis (173 total), and even fewer who are employed full-time at the DWS date (92). As a result, the standard errors on the transition rates for part-time job-losers are relatively large and the differences between these transition rates and those for other groups are not generally statistically significant at conventional levels.

REFERENCES

Abraham, Katharine G. 1990. "Restructuring the Employment Relationship: The Growth of Market-Mediated Work Arrangements." In *New Developments in the Labor Market: Toward a New Institutional Paradigm*, edited by Katharine G. Abraham and Robert B. McKersie. Cambridge, Mass.: MIT Press.

Abraham, Katharine G., and Susan K. Taylor. 1996. "Firms' Use of Outside Contractors: Theory and Evidence." *Journal of Labor Economics* 14(July): 394–424.

Belous, Richard S. 1989. *The Contingent Economy.* Washington, D.C.: National Planning Association.

Blank, Rebecca M. 1989. "The Role of Part-time Work in Women's Labor Market Choices over Time." *American Economic Review* 79(May): 295–99.

———. 1990a. "Are Part-time Jobs Bad Jobs?" In *A Future of Lousy Jobs?*, edited by Gary Burtless. Washington, D.C.: Brookings Institution.

———. 1990b. "Understanding Part-Time Work." In *Research in Labor Economics*, edited by Laurie J. Bassi and David L. Crawford (vol. 11). Greenwich, Conn.: JAI Press.

Farber, Henry S. 1993. "The Incidence and Costs of Job Loss: 1982–1991." *Brookings Papers on Economic Activity: Microeconomics* 1:73–119.

———. 1997a. "The Changing Face of Job Loss in the United States: 1981–1995." *Brookings Papers on Economic Activity: Microeconomics* 1:55–128.

———. 1997b. "Trends in Long-term Employment in the United States, 1979–1996." Working Paper 384. Princeton, N.J.: Industrial Relations Section, Princeton University (July).

———. 1997c. "Job Creation in the United States: Good Jobs or Bad?" Working Paper 385. Princeton, N.J.: Industrial Relations Section, Princeton University.

Farber, Henry S., and Helen Levy. 1999. "Recent Trends in Employer-Sponsored Health Insurance: Are Bad Jobs Getting Worse?" *Journal of Health Economics* 19(1): 93–119.

Ferber, Marianne, and Jane Waldfogel. 1996. "'Contingent' Work: Blessing and/or Curse?" Radcliffe Public Policy Institute, Cambridge, Mass. Unpublished paper.

Gardner, Jennifer M. 1995. "Worker Displacement: A Decade of Change." *Monthly Labor Review* 118(April): 45–57.

Golden, Lonnie, and Eileen Appelbaum. 1992. "What Was Driving the 1982–1988 Boom in Temporary Employment?" *American Journal of Economics and Sociology* 51(October): 473–93.

Houseman, Susan N. 1997. "Temporary, Part-time, and Contract Employment in the United States: New Evidence from an Employer Survey." W. E. Upjohn Institute for Employment Research, Kalamazoo, Mich. Unpublished paper (February).

Howe, Wayne J. 1986. "Temporary Help Workers: Who They Are, What Jobs They Hold." *Monthly Labor Review* 109(November): 45–47.

Kletzer, Lori G. 1989. "Returns to Seniority After Permanent Job Loss." *American Economic Review* 79(June): 536–43.

Montgomery, Mark, and James Cosgrove. 1993. "The Effect of Employee Benefits on the Demand for Part-time Workers." *Industrial and Labor Relations Review* 47(October): 87–98.

Neal, Derek. 1995. "Industry-Specific Capital: Evidence from Displaced Workers." *Journal of Labor Economics* 13(October): 653–77.

Parent, Daniel. 1995. "Industry-Specific Capital: Evidence from the NLSY and the PSID." Working Paper 350. Princeton, N.J.: Industrial Relations Section, Princeton University (November).

Podgursky, Michael, and Paul Swaim. 1987. "Job Displacement Earnings Loss: Evidence from the Displaced Workers Survey." *Industrial and Labor Relations Review* 41(October): 17–29.

Polivka, Anne. 1996. "Are Temporary Help Agency Workers Substitutes for Direct Hire Temps? Searching for an Alternative Explanation for Growth in the Temporary Help Industry." U.S. Bureau of Labor Statistics, Washington, D.C. Unpublished paper (May).

Segal, Lewis M., and Daniel G. Sullivan. 1997. "The Growth of Temporary Services Work." *Journal of Economic Perspectives* 11(1997): 117–36.

Tilly, Chris. 1991. "Reasons for the Continuing Growth of Part-time Employment." *Monthly Labor Review* 114(March): 10–18.

Topel, Robert. 1990. "Specific Capital and Unemployment: Measuring the Costs and Consequences of Job Loss." *Carnegie Rochester Conference Series on Public Policy* 33: 181–214.

Chapter 12

The Implications of Flexible Staffing Arrangements for Job Stability

Susan N. Houseman and Anne E. Polivka

There is a widespread perception that the nature of the employment relationship is fundamentally changing, resulting in less attachment between workers and firms and a decline in the stability of jobs (Schmidt, this volume). For many, flexible staffing arrangements—including temporary, contract, and part-time work—epitomize unstable jobs, and recent growth in some of these arrangements is viewed as evidence of a broader decline in job stability (Belous 1989; Castro 1993).

However, there is little evidence on whether jobs in various flexible staffing arrangements are in fact less stable. Although some studies have examined the labor market dynamics of female part-time workers (Blank 1994) and workers in the temporary help industry (Segal and Sullivan 1997a, 1997b), lack of data has hampered the examination of such issues for individuals in other, quantitatively important arrangements, such as on-call workers, temporary workers hired directly by the company, contract company workers, and independent contractors.

The purpose of this chapter is to shed light on the job stability of workers in a wide range of flexible staffing arrangements using two new sources of data: a nationwide employer survey on flexible staffing arrangements conducted by the Upjohn Institute for Employment Research and the February 1995 Contingent and Alternative Employment Arrangements Supplement (CAEAS) to the Current Population Survey (CPS). The Upjohn Institute Employer Survey on Flexible Staffing Arrangements provides evidence on why employers use various flexible staffing arrangements and the extent to which employers move workers in these positions into regular jobs within their organization. The survey results reveal that employers' reasons for using flexible staffing arrangements vary considerably by type of arrangement—a finding that suggests that the consequences for job stability differ across arrangements.

The February 1995 supplement to the CPS represented the first attempt in government statistics to provide a comprehensive count of workers in a wide variety of employment arrangements. Exploiting the longitudinal component of the CPS, we compare the subsequent labor market status of individuals in flexible work arrangements and those holding regular full-time positions in February 1995. We find that workers in most flexible staffing arrangements have less job stability than workers in regular full-time positions in the sense that they are more likely to switch employers, become unemployed, or drop out of the labor force within a year. However, consistent with the Upjohn Institute survey results, we find that the degree of job stability varies considerably across arrangements.

Finally, we extend our analysis of the CPS data to examine the effects of the growth in flexible staffing arrangements on aggregate job stability, as measured by one-year transition rates to a different employer, to unemployment, and out of the labor force. We conclude that growth in certain types of flexible staffing arrangements could have translated into small declines in job stability and can account for a substantial share of the modest increase in job switching observed over the last decade.

FLEXIBLE WORK ARRANGEMENTS: DEFINITIONS AND PREVALENCE

Using the February 1995 CPS data, we classified workers into eight mutually exclusive categories: agency temporaries, on-call workers, contract company workers, direct-hire temporary workers, independent contractors, regular self-employed (who are not independent contractors), regular part-time workers, and regular full-time workers. We do not distinguish between those who work part-time and full-time hours in the first six categories of employment. The categories "regular part-time" and "regular full-time" comprise those workers who are not classified in one of the other arrangements; regular part-time workers are regular employees who usually work less than thirty-five hours per week. Our temporary help agency category includes all of those who state that they are paid by a temporary help agency. Thus, it includes the permanent staff of these agencies, though they represent a relatively small percentage of those employed in this industry.[1] On-call workers are hired directly by the organization but work only when needed. Examples of on-call workers include substitute teachers and many types of hospital employees. We classified individuals as contract company workers if they work for a company that contracts out their services, they generally work at the customer's work site, and they are usually assigned to just one customer. In the February 1995 CPS, a small number of individuals were classified as both on-call and contract company workers. We classified these individuals as on-call workers.

The category "direct-hire temporaries" comprises temporaries hired

Table 12.1   Employment by Work Arrangement

	Percentage of All Workers	Percentage with Tenure of One Year or Less	Percentage of All Workers with Tenure of One Year or Less
Agency temporaries	1.0	74.9	2.7
On-call workers	1.7	47.2	3.0
Direct-hire temporaries	2.8	57.7	6.0
Contract workers	0.5	49.8	0.9
Independent contractors	6.7	17.3	4.3
Regular self-employed	5.9	12.2	2.6
Regular part-time	13.6	46.3	23.9
Regular full-time	67.8	22.0	56.6

Source: Authors' tabulations using the February 1995 CPS. Unpaid workers and those in the armed forces are excluded from tabulations. All tabulations were weighted using the CPS supplement weight.

directly by the company rather than through a staffing agency. The CPS does not include a specific question classifying individuals as direct-hire temporaries. We constructed this category based on a series of questions in the February supplement. Specifically, we classified individuals as direct-hire temporaries if they indicated that their job is temporary or that they cannot stay in their job as long as they wish for any of the following reasons: they are working only until a specific project is completed, they are temporarily replacing another worker, they were hired for a fixed period of time, their job is seasonal, or they expect to work for less than a year because their job is temporary.

The category "independent contractor" includes those stating that they work as an independent contractor, an independent consultant, or a free-lancer. Thus, the category comprises a large and, no doubt, diverse group of workers. The vast majority of independent contractors (85 percent) report being self-employed.[2]

Table 12.1 reports the distribution of employment by arrangement according to data from the February 1995 CPS. Together, agency temporary, on-call, direct-hire temporary, contract company, independent contract, and regular part-time workers account for 26.3 percent of total employment. Despite the media attention given agency temporaries, it is interesting to note that on-call, direct-hire temporary, contract company, and independent contractor employment are all quantitatively as important or more important than temporary help agency employment.[3]

Workers in flexible arrangements generally have much shorter job tenure than regular full-time workers. As shown in table 12.1, the share of workers with job tenure of one year or less is much higher for most flexible arrangements than it is for regular full-time arrangements. The exception is independent contracting, which, like regular self-employment, has a smaller proportion of workers with one year of tenure or less. Although workers in flexible arrangements comprise 26.3 percent of the workforce, they account for 40.8 percent of those with job tenures of one year or less. Lower job tenure in flexible staffing arrangements could partly reflect either greater growth of new jobs in these arrangements or a tendency of new entrants to hold these jobs. Even so, lower tenure is consistent with the hypothesis that any shift in employment toward flexible staffing arrangements results in less stability.

WHY EMPLOYERS USE FLEXIBLE STAFFING ARRANGEMENTS

Understanding why employers use flexible staffing arrangements can provide useful insights into whether these jobs are less stable. If employers are using these arrangements primarily in response to a temporary need for additional workers, then the jobs are intrinsically less stable than regular positions. If, however, employers are using workers in flexible staffing arrangements to accommodate predictable and stable fluctuations in their workload over the day and week or to accommodate employee desires for more flexible schedules or shorter hours, there is little reason to believe these arrangements would result in less job stability.

The implications for job stability are ambiguous if firms are using these arrangements as a way to screen workers for regular jobs. On the one hand, using flexible arrangements to screen workers for permanent jobs should facilitate better job matches and may even increase job stability. This outcome is particularly likely if flexible workers are hired through third parties, like temporary help agencies, and if these organizations have a comparative advantage in screening workers and can make better initial matches than firms would make hiring on their own. On the other hand, screening workers for permanent positions by trying them out in flexible arrangements arguably lowers the costs of dismissing workers who demonstrate low productivity and may result in lower job stability. For instance, if the workers are hired through a third party, employers need not maintain records on workers they decide not to hire, and the chance that workers will take legal action in the event of dismissal is probably not as great. The dismissal of low-productivity workers also would not increase a firm's unemployment insurance rating if they were hired through a third-party intermediary. Given these potential cost savings, employers may try out more workers for any given position than they would if hiring on their own, resulting in a decline in job stability. Still, the consequences for job stability are likely to be less adverse if employers are using flexible staffing arrangements to screen workers for permanent positions than if they are using them to fill temporary slots.

Evidence from the Upjohn Institute Employer Survey on Flexible Staffing Arrangements

The Upjohn Institute Employer Survey on Flexible Staffing Arrangements, conducted in 1996, provides evidence on why employers use flexible staffing arrangements. In that survey, employers from a stratified random sample of 550 private-sector establishments with five or more employees were interviewed on their use of five types of flexible work arrangements: temporary help agency, direct-hire temporary, regular part-time, on-call, and contract workers. If a company used agency temporaries, direct-hire temporaries, on-call workers, or regular part-time workers, they were asked a detailed set of questions on why they used the particular arrangement. In addition, employers who stated that since 1990 they had increased employment in a particular flexible staffing arrangement relative to regular employment were asked why they had increased their use.[4] The latter question reveals why, on the margin, employers may be increasing their use of flexible arrangements and is particularly relevant for assessing the probable effects of any increase in the use of flexible staffing arrangements on job security.

The reasons most commonly cited by employers for using agency temporaries, direct-hire temporaries, and on-call workers had to do with the need to accommodate fluctuations in their workload or in their regular staff. For example, 47 percent of employers using agency temporaries cited as important the need to fill a vacancy until a regular employee was hired; 47 percent using agency temporaries and 69 percent using on-call workers cited the need to fill in for an absent regular employee; 55 percent using direct-hire temporaries cited seasonal needs; and 52 percent using agency temporaries and 51 percent using on-call workers cited the need for assistance at times of unexpected increases in business. These reasons indicate that these jobs are often temporary and thus are likely to be less stable than regular jobs.

Employers primarily said that they use part-time workers to provide needed assistance during peak-time hours of the day or week (cited by 62 percent); cover for hours not covered by full-time shifts (cited by 49 percent); and accommodate employees' wishes for part-time hours (cited by 54 percent). These responses have no obvious implications for the stability of part-time jobs.

As noted earlier, flexible staffing arrangements could be associated with greater job stability if employers are using them to screen workers for permanent positions. However, screening workers for permanent jobs appears to be an important factor only in employers' use of agency temporaries and, to a lesser extent, regular part-time workers. Twenty-one percent of employers using agency temporaries and 15 percent using regular part-time workers cited screening for permanent jobs as an important reason for using these arrangements. Among employers who increased their relative use of agency temporaries since 1990, about half explained the increase by citing greater use of agency temporaries to screen workers for regular positions or difficulty finding qualified workers on their own.

Besides asking employers whether they used flexible staffing arrangements to screen workers for regular positions, the Upjohn Institute survey asked them to evaluate the extent to which they actually moved workers in flexible arrangements into regular positions. Specifically, employers using agency temporaries, direct-hire temporaries, regular part-time workers, or on-call workers were asked whether their organization moved each type of worker into regular positions often, occasionally or sometimes, seldom, or never. Responses to these questions are reported in table 12.2. Only a small minority of employers stated that they often moved workers in flexible arrangements into regular positions, although a substantially greater percentage reported occasionally or sometimes moving them. Along with the reasons employers gave for using flexible staffing arrangements, these responses suggest that although many employers use flexible arrangements—particularly agency temporaries—to screen workers for permanent positions, other factors are generally more important in determining employer use.

Moreover, though certainly some employers do move workers in flexible arrangements into regular positions, there is concern that companies also do just the opposite: move workers from regular positions into flexible arrangements. Questions in the February 1997 supplement to the CPS shed some light on the prevalence of this phenomenon.[5] Specifically, individuals who were identified in the February 1997 CPS as agency temporaries, on-call workers, contract company workers, or independent contractors were asked whether they had always been in their present arrangement at the place they were currently working. Nine percent of all

Table 12.2   Mobility of Workers in Flexible Arrangements into Regular Positions

	Often	Occasionally-Sometimes	Seldom	Never	Don't Know	Sample Size
Agency temporaries	11.5	31.3	19.0	36.8	1.6	253
On-call workers	9.3	26.7	27.3	32.7	4.0	150
Direct-hire temporaries	9.0	34.3	17.1	38.6	1.0	210
Regular part-time workers	14.7	39.6	16.0	28.9	0.8	394

Source: Upjohn Institute Employer Survey on Flexible Staffing Arrangements.

agency temporaries, 11.5 percent of contract company workers, 15.9 percent of on-call workers, and 8.5 percent of independent contractors reported working at the same place in another type of work arrangement. These workers were not directly asked the type of arrangement in which they were previously working, but they were asked how long they had worked there prior to being switched. Among agency temporaries, 39.5 percent had worked a year or more and 22.5 percent had worked three or more years prior to being switched; among on-call workers, 76.8 percent had worked a year or more prior to being switched and 51.2 percent had worked three or more years prior to being switched; and among independent contractors, 84.2 percent had worked three or more years prior to switching arrangements. These tenure distributions imply that, with the possible exception of agency temporaries, the majority of workers who were switched were not in a short-term arrangement. This fact, coupled with evidence presented later in the chapter that most flexible arrangements are associated with less job stability, suggests that most of those who were switched probably were initially in "regular permanent" positions.

In sum, the evidence collected in the Upjohn Institute survey on why employers use flexible staffing arrangements indicates that the effect on job stability of these arrangements varies with the type of arrangement. Employers' reports that they primarily use agency temporaries, on-call workers, and direct-hire temporaries to fill temporary positions suggest that, on average, these positions would be associated with less job stability than regular full-time positions. This adverse effect on job stability may be mitigated by some employers' use of these arrangements to screen workers for permanent positions. However, only for agency temporaries do we find substantial numbers of employers reporting that they use or are increasing their use of these workers to screen for permanent positions. Moreover, data from the February 1997 CPS supplement indicate that some employers are switching workers from regular positions into flexible arrangements. The reasons employers give for hiring regular part-time workers do not suggest any strong relationship between part-time employment and job stability.[6]

JOB STABILITY: EVIDENCE FROM THE CURRENT POPULATION SURVEY

In this section, we exploit the longitudinal component of the CPS to examine more directly the implications of flexible staffing arrangements on job stability. Specifically, we track workers who were in flexible arrangements in February 1995 and compare their labor market status over time with the labor market studies of those who were in regular full-time jobs in February 1995.

DATA

Households in the CPS are in the sample for four months, out of the sample for eight months, and back in the sample for four months. From one month to the next, a maximum of three-fourths of the sample can be matched; in months exactly one year apart, a maximum of one-half of the sample can be matched. In practice, given that the CPS sample is based on addresses, the proportion of individuals who are the same across months is lower because some individuals move each month and some refuse to continue cooperating. We matched individuals from the February 1995 CPS with those from the March 1995 CPS and February 1996 CPS.

The proportion of workers we were able to match was slightly lower for those in flexible arrangements in February 1995 than for those in regular full-time positions, suggesting that workers in flexible arrangements are somewhat more inclined to move. Assuming that changing jobs or becoming unemployed is an important reason why individuals move, our analysis may understate the extent to which workers in flexible arrangements change jobs and become unemployed relative to regular full-time workers. Although we believe that any bias in the data is minimal, we weighted the tabulations of the raw data to help account for differences in attrition from our sample. Specifically, our weights maintain the same distribution across eight gender-age-race groups in March 1995 and February 1996 as in February 1995.[7]

Our matched data allow us to follow the labor market status of workers in flexible arrangements one month and one year later and compare their outcomes with the outcomes of those who began in regular full-time jobs. Specifically, from the March 1995 and February 1996 data, we can determine whether an individual is employed with the same employer, employed with a different employer, unemployed, or not in the labor force.[8] A drawback of the CPS data is that we know the individual's type of work arrangement only in February 1995. Thus, for example, we do not know if a direct-hire temporary worker who changed employers between February 1995 and March 1995 holds another temporary position or is in a regular permanent job.

Determining whether agency temporary and contract company workers have changed employers between periods is complicated by the fact that many misreport their employer as the client firm. In the basic CPS each month, the respondents are asked to give or verify the name of their employers. In the February 1995 supplement, individuals identified as working for a temporary help agency or for a company that contracts out their services were then asked whether the employer listed for them in the basic CPS was the temporary help agency or contract company or the business for which they were doing the work. In February 1995, 57 percent of agency temporaries and 17 percent of contract company workers had incorrectly given the client firm as their employer. In the analysis later in the chapter, we exclude individuals who misreported their employer as the client firm in the February 1995 data. Although these exclusions increase the accuracy of our classification as to whether the individual has the same or a different employer, they substantially reduce the sample sizes, particularly for agency temporaries.

DESCRIPTIVE STATISTICS

Tables 12.3 and 12.4 show the labor-force status in March 1995 and February 1996 of workers by their employment arrangement in February 1995. In the next section, we present results of multivariate analyses that test for differences in labor-force transitions by initial employment arrangement, controlling for individual and job characteristics.

According to the figures in tables 12.3 and 12.4, the subsequent labor-force outcomes of workers who were in flexible arrangements in February 1995 are markedly different from those for workers who were in regular full-time positions. Agency temporaries, on-call workers, direct-hire temporaries, and contract company workers are much more likely to switch employers within a month and a year, and regular part-time workers are much more likely to change employers within a year compared to regular full-time workers. In addition, workers in all flexible arrangements are less likely to be employed one month and one year later compared to regular full-time workers. The differences in employment rates are particularly dramatic for agency temporaries, on-call workers, and direct-hire temporaries after both one month and one year, and for contract company workers and regular part-time workers after one year. Their lower employment rates may be ascribed to both higher unemployment rates and lower labor-force participation rates. Agency temporary, on-call, direct-hire temporary, contract company, and part-time workers are also more likely to drop out of the labor force but express a desire to still work.[9] We use the term "involuntarily out of the labor force" to denote this status. The pattern for independent contractors and regular self-employed is quite different. Their lower employment rates after one month and one year may be attributed, for the most part, to a greater propensity to drop out of the labor force voluntarily.

Some might suspect that workers in flexible arrangements are more likely to become unemployed because they are more inclined to quit their jobs voluntarily. Questions on the March 1995 CPS specifically asked the unemployed whether they held a job prior to becoming unemployed and, if so, whether they lost or left that job. About 80 percent of those who were regular full-time workers in February 1995 and who were unemployed the following month reported losing their job. This

Table 12.3 Labor-Force Status in March 1995 by Work Arrangement in February 1995

	Proportion in March 1995										
	Employed				Unemployed		Not in Labor Force				
Status in February 1995	Total	Difference Between Arrangement and Full-Time	Different Employer	Difference Between Arrangement and Full-Time	Total	Difference Between Arrangement and Full-Time	Total	Difference Between Arrangement and Full-Time	Want to Be in Labor Force	Difference Between Arrangement and Full-Time	Number of Observations
Agency temporary[a]	0.869	-0.114	0.090	0.070	0.098	0.089	0.034	0.025	0.000	-0.002	145
On-call worker	0.840	-0.143	0.062	0.041	0.071	0.063	0.089	0.080	0.023	0.021	672
Direct hire temporary	0.886	-0.097	0.057	0.037	0.045	0.036	0.069	0.061	0.022	0.020	1,173
Contract worker[a]	0.981	-0.001	0.063	0.043	0.010	0.001	0.009	0.001	0.009	0.007	147
Independent contractor	0.948	-0.035	0.032	0.011	0.015	0.007	0.037	0.028	0.010	0.008	2,854
Regular self-employed	0.947	-0.036	0.025	0.004	0.007	-0.002	0.046	0.037	0.006	0.004	2,573
Regular part-time	0.936	-0.047	0.031	0.011	0.020	0.011	0.045	0.036	0.012	0.010	5,758
Regular full-time	0.983	—	0.020	—	0.009	—	0.009	—	0.002	—	27,952

Note: The figures in these tables are based on weighted tabulations. The appendix describes the construction of these weights.

[a] Excludes individuals misreporting their employer in the basic February 1995 CPS.

Table 12.4 Labor-Force Status in February 1996 by Work Arrangement in February 1995

| | Proportion in February 1996 | | | | | | | | | | |
| | Employed | | | | Unemployed | | Not in Labor Force | | | | Number of |
Status in February 1995	Total	Difference Between Arrangement and Full-Time	Different Employer	Difference Between Arrangement and Full-Time	Total	Difference Between Arrangement and Full-Time	Total	Difference Between Arrangement and Full-Time	Want to Be in Labor Force	Difference Between Arrangement and Full-Time	Observations
Agency temporary[a]	0.810	−0.123	0.515	0.414	0.123	0.098	0.067	0.025	0.016	0.008	44
On-call worker	0.734	−0.199	0.214	0.112	0.107	0.083	0.159	0.117	0.034	0.026	320
Direct hire temporary	0.768	−0.166	0.244	0.143	0.062	0.037	0.171	0.128	0.028	0.020	451
Contract worker[a]	0.821	−0.112	0.219	0.118	0.062	0.037	0.117	0.075	0.077	0.069	69
Independent contractor	0.906	−0.027	0.086	−0.016	0.014	−0.010	0.079	0.037	0.012	0.004	1346
Regular self-employed	0.870	−0.063	0.069	−0.033	0.011	−0.014	0.119	0.077	0.004	−0.004	1252
Regular part-time	0.773	−0.161	0.185	0.084	0.045	0.020	0.183	0.141	0.027	0.019	2381
Regular full-time	0.933	—	0.101	—	0.024	—	0.042	—	0.008	—	12070

Note: The figures in these tables are based on weighted tabulations. The appendix describes the construction of these weights.

[a] Excludes individuals misreporting their employer in the basic February 1995 CPS.

figure is the same or higher for all categories of flexible arrangements, although the sample sizes are small in some cases. Thus, it appears that the higher incidence of unemployment among workers in flexible arrangements cannot simply be ascribed to a higher propensity on the part of those workers to quit their jobs.

RESULTS FROM MULTINOMIAL LOGIT MODELS

The different labor market outcomes experienced by workers in flexible arrangements relative to those in regular full-time jobs may result from the nature of the arrangements themselves. Alternatively, they may stem from differences in the average personal and job characteristics of individuals in those arrangements. To control for personal and job characteristics, we estimated multinomial logit models using the February 1995 to March 1995 matched data and the February 1995 to February 1996 matched data. In the models estimated, there are four possible labor market outcomes: employed, same employer (E_s); employed, different employer (E_d); unemployed (U); and not in the labor force (N). To identify the model, the coefficients for one outcome must be set equal to zero. We used employed-same employer as the base group in our models. The probability of each outcome is as follows:

$$Pr(E_s = 1) = \frac{1}{1 + e^{X\beta(E_d)} + e^{X\beta(U)} + e^{X\beta(N)}}$$

$$Pr(I = 1) = \frac{e^{X\beta(I)}}{1 + e^{X\beta(E_d)} + e^{X\beta(U)} + e^{X\beta(N)}} \tag{12.1}$$

$$I = E_d, U, \text{ or } N$$

where X is a vector of control variables measuring personal and job characteristics and ß is a vector of coefficient estimates.[10]

In each set of specifications, we controlled for age, age squared, gender, race, level of education, industry (nineteen categories), occupation (twelve categories), region of the country, whether the individual was from a central city or a rural area, whether the individual lived in a poverty area, marital status, marital status interacted with gender, tenure on the job, and tenure squared. All of these variables were taken from the February 1995 CPS. We included dummy variables for each flexible work arrangement; the excluded category is regular full-time workers.

Unmeasured personal characteristics are potentially important in explaining any lower job stability among those in flexible arrangements. Our data set contains many measures of job history that arguably control for such unobserved characteristics by capturing an individual's predisposition to change employers, experience spells of unemployment, or drop out of the labor force. In the February 1995 supplement, those who had three or fewer years of tenure in their current arrangement were asked a series of questions about what they were doing prior to their current arrangement. We included controls for whether, just prior to their current job, these individuals held another job, lost a job, and were unemployed.[11] We also included controls for the number of employers individuals had in 1994, the number of weeks they were unemployed in 1994, and the number of weeks they were out of the labor force in 1994. These variables come from the March 1995 CPS Income Supplement.

Finally, we included the logarithm of the hourly wage. The wage variable may be correlated with unmeasured characteristics affecting worker quality and stability in the workforce. Alternatively, workers earning low wages relative to their education, tenure, and job characteristics may be more inclined to quit and find a new job, quit and become unemployed, or drop out of the labor force. The hourly wage measure was constructed from 1994 earnings data, which were collected in the March 1995 CPS Income Supplement.[12]

Selected coefficient estimates for the multinomial logit models predicting labor-force status in March 1995 and February 1996 are reported in tables 12.5 and 12.6, respectively. The marginal effects on the probability of switching employers, being unemployed, or dropping out of the labor force are reported in brackets below the coefficient estimates.[13] For instance, in table 12.5, column 1, being an agency temporary versus a full-time regular worker increases the probability of switching employers by 4.4 percentage points.

The coefficient estimates for the control variables in the multinomial logit models have the expected signs, and many are statistically significant. For example, workers who had another job immediately prior to their current one are more likely to change employers within a month or a year. Those who lost a job immediately prior to their current one are also more likely to be unemployed one month and one year later. The number of employers an individual had in 1994 is positively associated with switching employers and becoming unemployed. The number of weeks a worker was unemployed in 1994 and the number of weeks the worker was out of the labor force in 1994 are positively related to the probability that the individual will switch employers, be unemployed, or drop out of the labor force both in one month and in one year. The logarithm of a worker's hourly wage is inversely related to the probability that the individual will be unemployed after one month and drop out of the labor force after one year.

Although the inclusion of controls for individual and job characteristics, employment history, and wage levels reduces the magnitude of some coefficients on the flexible arrangement dummy variables, most of these

Table 12.5 Multinomial Logit Models Predicting Labor-Force Status in March 1995

	Employed, Different Employer			
	(1)	(2)	(3)	(4)
Agency temporary	1.325***	1.313***	1.111***	1.211***
	[0.044]	[0.043]	[0.043]	[0.040]
On-call worker	1.085***	1.118***	0.943***	0.798***
	[0.029]	[0.031]	[0.025]	[0.020]
Direct-hire temporary	0.844***	0.865***	0.731***	0.708***
	[0.021]	[0.022]	[0.018]	[0.017]
Contract worker	0.856**	0.862**	0.729*	0.775**
	[0.025]	[0.025]	[0.020]	[0.022]
Independent contractor	0.555***	0.575***	0.547***	0.629***
	[0.013]	[0.013]	[0.013]	[0.016]
Regular self-employed	0.264*	0.294*	0.293*	0.247
	[0.005]	[0.005]	[0.006]	[0.005]
Regular part-time	0.156	0.185*	0.126	0.022
	[0.003]	[0.003]	[0.002]	[0.000]
Another job before	—	0.354***	0.345***	0.253*
		[0.008]	[0.007]	[0.005]
Unemployed before	—	0.401***	0.343**	0.319*
		[0.010]	[0.009]	[0.008]
Lost job before	—	0.083	0.021	0.076
		[0.002]	[0.000]	[0.002]
Number of employers in 1994	—	—	0.328***	0.384***
			[0.007]	[0.008]
Weeks unemployed in 1994	—	—	0.019***	0.018***
			[0.000]	[0.000]
Weeks not in labor force in 1994	—	—	0.013***	0.009**
			[0.000]	[0.000]
ln(wage)	—	—	—	−0.074
				[−0.001]

Note: All models also include an intercept term and control for age, age squared, gender, race, education, tenure, tenure squared, tenure less than three years, occupation, industry, region, central city and rural locations, marital status, and marital status interacted with gender. The marginal effect on the probability of being employed with a different employer, unemployed, or not in the labor force is reported in brackets.
*Denotes significance of the coefficient estimate at .10 level.
**Denotes significance of the coefficient estimate at .05 level.
***Denotes significance of the coefficient estimate at .01 level.

coefficients remain statistically significant with large implied effects on the probability of switching employers, becoming unemployed, or dropping out of the labor force. In our models, being an agency temporary, an on-call worker, a direct-hire temporary, or a contract company worker increases the probability that the individual will switch employers within a month and within a year; being an independent contractor increases

	Unemployed		
(1)	(2)	(3)	(4)
1.807***	1.761***	1.490***	1.154***
[0.036]	[0.034]	[0.026]	[0.016]
1.874***	1.867***	1.535***	1.483***
[0.037]	[0.037]	[0.026]	[0.024]
1.524***	1.504***	1.240***	1.251***
[0.026]	[0.025]	[0.019]	[0.019]
−0.604	−0.617	−0.891	−0.797
[−0.004]	[−0.004]	[−0.006]	[−0.005]
0.348*	0.371*	0.233	0.118
[0.003]	[0.003]	[0.002]	[0.000]
0.123	0.155	0.059	−0.277
[0.001]	[0.001]	[0.000]	[−0.002]
0.442***	0.453***	0.286**	0.157
[0.004]	[0.005]	[0.003]	[0.001]
—	0.229	0.538***	0.533***
	[0.003]	[0.006]	[0.005]
—	0.480**	0.283	0.253
	[0.007]	[0.004]	[0.003]
—	0.367***	0.200	0.229
	[0.005]	[0.002]	[0.002]
—	—	0.092	0.144*
		[0.001]	[0.001]
—	—	0.054***	0.054***
		[0.001]	[0.001]
—	—	0.034***	0.033***
		[0.000]	[0.000]
—	—	—	−0.195**
			[−0.002]

(Table continues on p. 442.)

the probability that the individual will change employers within a month; and being a regular part-time worker increases the probability that the individual will change employers within a year. The implied effects of being in a flexible staffing arrangement on the probability of switching employers is often quite large. For example, estimates from table 12.6, model 4, indicate that being an agency temporary increases the probability of switching employers within a year by 21.3 percentage points relative to regular full-time workers; being an on-call worker, a direct-hire temporary, or a contract company worker increases the probability of switching employers by 8.7, 7.5, and 7.9 percentage points, respectively.

One caveat to these findings is that employers may be using flexible staffing arrangements to screen workers for regular positions. Agency

Table 12.5   *Continued*

	Not in Labor Force			
	(1)	(2)	(3)	(4)
Agency temporary	1.448***	1.447***	0.718	0.617
	[0.025]	[0.026]	[0.009]	[0.004]
On-call worker	2.162***	2.045***	1.354***	1.521***
	[0.057]	[0.052]	[0.024]	[0.019]
Direct-hire temporary	1.785***	1.708***	0.986***	1.096***
	[0.039]	[0.037]	[0.015]	[0.011]
Contract worker	0.430	0.355	0.299	0.762
	[0.005]	[0.004]	[0.004]	[0.007]
Independent contractor	1.479***	1.423***	0.940***	1.287***
	[0.029]	[0.028]	[0.015]	[0.015]
Regular self-employed	1.546***	1.477***	0.855***	1.219***
	[0.032]	[0.030]	[0.014]	[0.014]
Regular part-time	0.952***	0.868***	0.428***	0.556***
	[0.014]	[0.013]	[0.006]	[0.005]
Another job before	—	−0.733***	0.257**	0.103
		[−0.013]	[0.004]	[0.001]
Unemployed before	—	−0.280**	−0.331**	−0.359
		[−0.005]	[−0.005]	[−0.003]
Lost job before	—	0.130	−0.022	0.089
		[0.002]	[−0.000]	[0.001]
Number of employers in 1994	—	—	−0.207***	0.009
			[−0.004]	[−0.000]
Weeks unemployed in 1994	—	—	0.049***	0.037***
			[0.001]	[0.000]
Weeks not in labor force in 1994	—	—	0.077***	0.070***
			[0.001]	[0.001]
ln(wage)	—	—	—	−0.050
				[−0.000]

temporaries, contract company workers, and independent contractors—who are not employees of the client firm—in theory are classified in the data as switching employers when they are being hired into a regular position by the client company. This possibility complicates the interpretation of the estimates of the probability of switching employers. However, data from the Upjohn Institute employer survey, cited earlier, suggest that this is unlikely to be a significant problem for any flexible staffing arrangement—save perhaps agency temporaries.

It is also interesting to compare differences between the proportions of workers in flexible arrangements and of regular full-time workers who switch employers in the raw data (reported in tables 12.3 and 12.4) with the estimated marginal effects of being in flexible staffing arrangements after controlling for individual and job characteristics (reported in tables

12.5 and 12.6). For instance, as shown in table 12.4, the percentage of on-call workers who switch employers in a year is 11.2 percentage points higher than the percentage of regular full-time workers who switch. Estimates from model 4 in table 12.6 (which includes the most control variables) indicate that being an on-call worker increases the probability of switching employers in a year by 8.7 percentage points compared to a regular full-time worker. Therefore, in this as in other cases, differences in individual and job characteristics account for some, but by no means all, of the differences in labor market outcomes of workers in flexible staffing arrangements, according to our models.

In general, workers who were agency temporaries, on-call workers, direct-hire temporaries, or regular part-time workers in February 1995 also were significantly more likely to be unemployed in March 1995 and February 1996 compared to regular full-time workers. For example, estimates from model 4 in table 12.6 indicate that being in one of these four flexible staffing arrangements increases the probability of entering unemployment from 1.0 percentage point (for part-time workers) to 4.5 percentage points (for on-call workers).

In addition, those in most flexible staffing arrangements in February 1995 were more likely than regular full-time workers to be out of the labor force in March 1995 and February 1996. These results are difficult to interpret by themselves. On the one hand, certain flexible arrangements may be amenable to balancing family and work responsibilities or may make good bridge jobs to retirement, and therefore a larger proportion of workers in these arrangements may voluntarily drop out of the labor force over the course of the year. On the other hand, workers in flexible arrangements may be more likely to lose their job and drop out of the labor force even though they would prefer to work. To address this issue we used the February 1995 to February 1996 matched data to estimate multinomial logit models with four possible labor-status outcomes: employed; unemployed; not in the labor force, don't want to be; and not in the labor force, want to be. Selected results from these models, reported in table 12.7, show that on-call workers, direct-hire temporaries, regular part-time workers, and, in most specifications, contract company workers are significantly more likely to drop out of the labor force involuntarily than are regular full-time workers.[14]

One of the most interesting findings from our analysis is that independent contractors do not appear to experience less job stability over the course of a year than regular full-time employees. Once controls for individual characteristics are included, independent contractors are not more likely to switch employers and generally are significantly less likely to become unemployed than are regular full-time workers. In addition, although independent contractors are more likely to drop out of the labor force, their change in labor market status appears largely voluntary. These

Table 12.6   Multinomial Logit Models Predicting Labor-Force Status in
              February 1996

	Employed, Different Employer			
	(1)	(2)	(3)	(4)
Agency temporary	1.992***	2.000***	1.883***	1.805***
	[0.221]	[0.220]	[0.220]	[0.213]
On-call worker	1.007***	1.031***	0.925***	1.003***
	[0.075]	[0.081]	[0.075]	[0.087]
Direct-hire temporary	0.994***	1.018***	0.988***	0.948***
	[0.072]	[0.078]	[0.077]	[0.075]
Contract worker	0.912***	0.918***	0.949***	0.950**
	[0.076]	[0.078]	[0.079]	[0.079]
Independent contractor	0.162	0.169	0.095	0.115
	[0.012]	[0.013]	[0.008]	[0.010]
Regular self-employed	−0.016	−0.002	−0.072	−0.182
	[−0.006]	[−0.004]	[−0.010]	[−0.017]
Regular part-time	0.310***	0.333***	0.304***	0.278***
	[0.017]	[0.020]	[0.016]	[0.015]
Another job before	—	0.181**	0.211*	0.185
		[0.022]	[0.020]	[0.017]
Unemployed before	—	0.064	−0.021	−0.122
		[0.005]	[−0.001]	[−0.009]
Lost job before	—	0.009	0.062	0.108
		[−0.003]	[0.003]	[0.006]
Number of employers in 1994	—	—	0.298***	0.328***
			[0.025]	[0.026]
Weeks unemployed in 1994	—	—	0.019***	0.016***
			[0.001]	[0.001]
Weeks not in labor force in 1994	—	—	0.019***	0.016***
			[0.001]	[0.001]
ln(wage)	—	—	—	−0.145**
				[−0.011]

Note: All models also include an intercept term and control for age, age squared, gender, race, education, tenure, tenure squared, tenure less than three years, occupation, industry, region, central city and rural locations, marital status, and marital status interacted with gender. The marginal effect on the probability of being employed with a different employer, unemployed, or not in the labor force is reported in brackets.
*Denotes significance of the coefficient estimate at .10 level.
**Denotes significance of the coefficient estimate at .05 level.
***Denotes significance of the coefficient estimate at .01 level.

findings are subject to the caveat that in the BLS data independent contractors are a large and diverse group of workers who label themselves
independent contractors, independent consultants, or free-lancers and
who may or may not work at the client's work site. It is possible that
certain types of independent contractors experience less job stability than
regular full-time workers.

Our conclusion that most flexible staffing arrangements are associated

	Unemployed		
(1)	(2)	(3)	(4)
2.185***	2.201***	1.912***	1.339*
[0.077]	[0.079]	[0.056]	[0.024]
1.599***	1.586***	1.275***	1.499***
[0.054]	[0.054]	[0.035]	[0.045]
1.466***	1.422***	1.190***	1.252***
[0.044]	[0.042]	[0.027]	[0.030]
1.205**	1.150**	1.129*	1.200**
[0.035]	[0.032]	[0.027]	[0.029]
−0.640**	−0.634**	−0.702**	−0.528
[−0.012]	[−0.012]	[−0.012]	[−0.009]
−0.589**	−0.556*	−0.200	−0.092
[−0.011]	[−0.011]	[−0.005]	[−0.002]
0.471***	0.457***	0.476***	0.506**
[0.009]	[0.009]	[0.009]	[0.010]
—	−0.004	0.350	0.292
	[0.001]	[0.008]	[0.007]
—	0.615***	0.469	0.439
	[0.020]	[0.014]	[0.013]
—	0.497***	0.429**	0.506**
	[0.014]	[0.011]	[0.012]
—	—	0.280***	0.266**
		[0.005]	[0.005]
—	—	0.051***	0.051***
		[0.001]	[0.001]
—	—	0.031***	0.024***
		[0.001]	[0.000]
—	—	—	0.026
			[0.001]

(Table continues on p. 446.)

with less job stability is subject to the qualification that unobserved personal characteristics may still account for the remaining differences. However, earlier we argued that we included many controls for past work history and for wages, which should be correlated with unobserved characteristics that result in less job stability. Moreover, work by Segal and Sullivan (1997b) suggests that controlling for individual fixed effects has almost no impact on estimates of the job stability of workers in the temporary help industry. Using longitudinal data from administrative records, they found that workers in the temporary help industry are much more likely than other workers to experience short employment spells.[15]

Finally, the pattern of coefficient estimates in the models reported in tables 12.5, 12.6, and 12.7 is consistent with evidence from the Upjohn

Table 12.6 *Continued*

| | Not in Labor Force | | | |
	(1)	(2)	(3)	(4)
Agency temporary	1.235*	1.260*	0.496	0.760
	[0.036]	[0.038]	[−0.002]	[0.016]
On-call worker	1.401***	1.291***	0.956***	0.692***
	[0.079]	[0.069]	[0.045]	[0.023]
Direct-hire temporary	1.550***	1.476***	1.358***	1.232***
	[0.096]	[0.090]	[0.081]	[0.066]
Contract worker	1.044**	1.021**	1.022**	1.059**
	[0.051]	[0.050]	[0.051]	[0.051]
Independent contractor	0.450***	0.413***	0.166	0.123
	[0.023]	[0.021]	[0.008]	[0.005]
Regular self-employed	0.744***	0.708***	0.671***	0.643***
	[0.045]	[0.043]	[0.041]	[0.037]
Regular part-time	0.971***	0.902***	0.836***	0.799***
	[0.058]	[0.053]	[0.048]	[0.043]
Another job before	—	−0.662***	−0.348***	−0.353**
		[−0.037]	[−0.022]	[−0.019]
Unemployed before	—	−0.281**	−0.382**	−0.343*
		[−0.017]	[−0.020]	[−0.016]
Lost job before	—	0.166	0.060	0.037
		[0.008]	[0.002]	[0.000]
Number of employers in 1994	—	—	−0.102	−0.061
			[−0.009]	[−0.006]
Weeks unemployed in 1994	—	—	0.031***	0.024***
			[0.001]	[0.001]
Weeks not in labor force in 1994	—	—	0.034***	0.031***
			[0.002]	[0.001]
ln(wage)	—	—	—	−0.132*
				[−0.006]

Institute employer survey and accords well with our intuition. Workers in arrangements that are explicitly temporary (agency temporaries, direct-hire temporaries) or quite likely to be temporary in nature (on-call, contract company)[16] are the most likely to change employers and become unemployed. Tests show that regular part-time workers, while significantly more likely to change employers and become unemployed than regular full-time workers, are significantly less likely to switch employers and become unemployed than are workers in these four arrangements.

TRENDS IN FLEXIBLE STAFFING ARRANGEMENTS AND THE IMPLICATIONS FOR JOB STABILITY IN THE AGGREGATE

The question of whether aggregate job stability has declined in the United States in recent years is a subject of much debate. Some studies have found a significant decline in job stability among men. Although other studies have found little or no decline in overall job stability, they have generally found significant declines in the job stability of certain subgroups (for example, blacks, youth, men with long tenure, and less educated workers).[17] In addition, several studies that found negligible declines in job stability in the 1980s uncovered larger declines in the 1990s (Jaeger and Stevens, this volume; Neumark, Polsky, and Hansen, this volume; U.S. Bureau of Labor Statistics 1997, 1998). There also is evidence that the rate of involuntary job loss increased, particularly in the 1990s (Boisjoly, Duncan, and Smeeding 1998; Farber 1997, 1998; Polsky 1999; Valletta, this volume).

To conclude the chapter, we examine the effect of changes in the share of workers in flexible staffing arrangements on job stability in the aggregate. Using our multinomial logit estimates from the previous section, we simulate the effects of changes in the composition of employment across work arrangements on one-year labor market transition rates. We then compare the magnitude and pattern of our predicted effects to actual changes in the one-year labor market transition rates.

To develop a trend measure of aggregate job stability comparable to the measure of job stability used in the analysis in this chapter, we matched individuals in the January 1986 CPS and the January 1987 CPS. The availability of tenure data in the January 1987 CPS supplement allowed us to construct one-year labor market transitions, as was done for the 1995 to 1996 data reported earlier. We then compared one-year labor market transitions for 1986 to 1987 to labor market transitions for 1995 to 1996. The results of this comparison, shown in table 12.8, are consistent with other findings of a modest decline in job stability in recent years. According to these tabulations, the number of workers remaining with the same employer one year later was 0.6 percentage points lower in the 1995 to 1996 period compared to the 1986 to 1987 period.

Interestingly, all of the decline in one-year job retention rates may be attributed to an increase in the proportion changing employers. The proportion entering unemployment actually declined between the two time periods (a finding consistent with the fact that aggregate unemployment also declined); the proportion dropping out of the labor force remained the same; and the proportion switching employers rose by one percentage point.

How much of the decline in job stability may be attributed to a growth in flexible staffing arrangements? Examination of this issue is hampered by the paucity of time-series data on employment by flexible staffing arrangement. Statistics for on-call, direct-hire temporary, contract company, and independent contract workers were first collected in the February 1995 supplement to the CPS.[18] Although time-series data for part-time employment are available from the CPS, the measurement

Table 12.7 Multinomial Logit Models Predicting Labor-Force Status in February 1996

	Unemployed			
	(1)	(2)	(3)	(4)
On-call worker	1.330***	1.313***	1.065***	1.263***
	[0.047]	[0.046]	[0.031]	[0.039]
Direct-hire temporary	1.195***	1.164***	0.909***	1.001***
	[0.038]	[0.037]	[0.023]	[0.026]
Contract worker	1.091**	1.034*	1.045*	1.086*
	[0.035]	[0.032]	[0.029]	[0.030]
Independent contractor	−0.675***	−0.668***	−0.703**	−0.540
	[−0.011]	[−0.011]	[−0.010]	[−0.008]
Regular self-employed	−0.612**	−0.581**	−0.204	−0.089
	[−0.010]	[−0.010]	[−0.004]	[−0.002]
Regular part-time	0.404***	0.392***	0.432**	0.455**
	[0.008]	[0.008]	[0.008]	[0.009]

Note: All models also include an intercept term and control for age, age squared, gender, race, education, tenure, tenure squared, tenure less than three years, occupation, industry, region, central city and rural locations, marital status, and marital status interacted with gender. The marginal effect on the probability of being employed with a different employer, unemployed, or not in the labor force is reported in brackets.

*Denotes significance of the coefficient estimate at .10 level.

**Denotes significance of the coefficient estimate at .05 level.

***Denotes significance of the coefficient estimate at .01 level.

of part-time work was changed with the redesign of the CPS in 1994, resulting in a break in the series. Self-employment data for both incorporated and unincorporated individuals are available only beginning in 1989; the measurement of self-employment was also affected by the redesign of the CPS in 1994. Adjusting for the breaks in the series, Anne Polivka and Stephen Miller (1998) argued that both part-time and self-employment declined in the 1990s.[19] However, even use of adjusted figures is problematic because the categories "part-time" and "self-employment" in the CPS differ from the categories "regular part-time" and "regular self-employment" used in this chapter. In particular, time-series data on part-time employment include agency temporaries, on-call workers, direct-hire temporaries, contract company workers, and independent contractors classified as employees who work fewer than thirty-five hours per week. Self-employment figures include both regular self-employed and self-employed independent contractors.

"Agency temporaries" is the only flexible staffing category for which a relatively clean time series is available. The Current Employment Statistics (CES) provide information on employment in the help supply services industry (SIC 7363), which is comprised primarily of temporary help agencies. According to these figures, employment in temporary help agencies grew dramatically in the 1980s and 1990s. From 1982 (the first

Not in Labor Force, Don't Want to Be			
(1)	(2)	(3)	(4)
1.146***	1.042***	0.722***	0.410
[0.056]	[0.049]	[0.031]	[0.013]
1.302***	1.235***	1.086***	0.986***
[0.069]	[0.065]	[0.057]	[0.046]
0.608	0.593	0.654	0.853
[0.022]	[0.022]	[0.026]	[0.037]
0.446***	0.406***	0.176	0.131
[0.018]	[0.017]	[0.007]	[0.005]
0.852***	0.807***	0.773***	0.742***
[0.042]	[0.040]	[0.039]	[0.034]
0.949***	0.882***	0.783***	0.738***
[0.046]	[0.042]	[0.037]	[0.032]

(Table continues on p. 450.)

year for which data are available) to 1997, the share of total employment in help supply services rose sharply from 0.4 percent to 2.0 percent. For the 1986 to 1987 subperiod to the period from 1995 to 1996, the share of total employment in help supply services increased from 0.8 to 1.7 percent.[20]

Table 12.8 reports on a simulation of the effects of the increase in agency temporaries over the period from 1986 to 1987 to the 1995 to 1996 period on the one-year labor market transition rates. We used the estimates in table 12.6, model 4, which contains the greatest number of control variables, as the basis for our simulations. In calculating the marginal effects of the growth in temporary help employment, we assumed that the distribution of characteristics of individuals joining temporary help agencies during the period was the same as the distribution of characteristics among those who currently are agency temporaries.[21] We also assumed that, in the absence of growth in temporary employment, workers would be employed in regular part-time and regular full-time jobs in proportion to the number of agency temporaries actually working part-time and full-time hours.

Our estimates suggest that the growth in agency temporaries over the period from 1986 to 1987 to the 1995 to 1996 period would have increased the number of workers switching employers (where the employer is defined as the agency) within a year by .30 percentage point. With a labor force of over 129 million in 1997, this would translate into an increase of about 387,000 workers changing employers in a year. The effects on unemployment are more modest: the growth in agency tempor-

Table 12.7 *Continued*

| | Not in Labor Force, Want to Be | | | |
	(1)	(2)	(3)	(4)
On-call worker	1.284***	1.194***	1.079**	1.133**
	[0.014]	[0.012]	[0.010]	[0.010]
Direct-hire temporary	1.278***	1.190***	1.041***	1.186***
	[0.013]	[0.012]	[0.009]	[0.010]
Contract worker	1.547**	1.518**	1.557*	1.193
	[0.022]	[0.021]	[0.020]	[0.011]
Independent contractor	0.360	0.343	0.154	−0.046
	[0.003]	[0.003]	[0.001]	[−0.000]
Regular self-employed	−0.144	−0.120	−0.076	−0.027
	[−0.001]	[−0.001]	[−0.001]	[−0.000]
Regular part-time	0.741***	0.684***	0.847***	0.976***
	[0.006]	[0.006]	[0.007]	[0.008]

aries would be expected to increase the number who are unemployed by only 0.03 percentage point, or about 39,000.

Most interesting is the fact that the predicted effect from the growth in agency temporaries on labor market transitions mirrors the pattern observed between the period from 1986 to 1987 and the period from 1995 to 1996. In particular, according to our simulations, the principal effect of the growth in agency temporaries was to increase the proportion of workers switching employers, a finding that accords with the fact that the decline in aggregate job stability resulted entirely from an increase in employer switching. The estimates presented in table 12.8 suggest that about 30 percent of the growth in employer switching may be attributed to the increase in agency temporary employment.[22]

These simulations reflect only the effects of the growth of agency temporary employment over the 1986 to 1996 period. The share of employment accounted for by agency temporaries also grew rapidly prior to 1986 and after 1996. The simulated effects on aggregate job stability over the 1982 to 1997 period are over 60 percent greater than those for the subperiod 1986 to 1996. In particular, over the 1982 to 1997 period our simulations indicate that the growth in agency temporary employment increased the number of workers changing employers by 0.5 percentage point.

The next two rows of table 12.8 simulate the effects of the decline in part-time and self-employment. We make the assumption that all of the decline occurred in regular part-time employment and regular self-employment.[23] According to the simulations, the decline in part-time employment would have almost no effect on the probability of switching employers and becoming unemployed, and a very small effect on the

Table 12.8   Effects of Growth in Flexible Staffing Arrangements on Job Stability, 1986 to 1996—Labor Force Status One Year Later

	Employed, Different Employer	Unemployed	Not in Labor Force	Employed, Same Employer
1. One-year labor-market transitions, 1986 to 1987	0.1038	0.0338	0.0759	0.7864
2. One-year labor-market transitions, 1995 to 1996	0.1139	0.0291	0.0763	0.7807
3. Actual changes 1986–1987 to 1995–1996 (2 − 1)	0.0101	− 0.0047	0.0004	− 0.0057
4. Predicted changes from growth in agency temporaries	0.0030	0.0003	0.0000	− 0.0033
5. Predicted changes from decline in part-time employment	− 0.0001	− 0.0000	− 0.0003	0.0004
6. Predicted changes from decline in self-employment	—	—	− 0.0004	0.0004
7. Predicted changes assuming on-call, contract company, and direct-hire temps have doubled as percentage of workforce	0.0022	0.0012	0.0018	− 0.0051

Note: Details of the data and the methodology for the simulations are provided in the appendix.

probability of exiting the labor force. Because we estimated no significant effect from being in regular self-employment on the probability of switching arrangements or becoming unemployed, the simulations for the decline in self-employment are limited to estimating the effect on the probability of exiting the labor force. These simulations also suggest a very small decline in the number of individuals exiting the labor force from the decline in self-employment. Although these estimates are admittedly rough, they nonetheless illustrate an important point: declines in part-time and self-employment are unlikely to offset the strong effects of the growth in temporary employment on the probability of switching employers.

The simulations in rows 4 to 6 of table 12.8 arguably represent a lower-bound estimate of the effects of changes in flexible staffing arrangements on aggregate job stability. Although our multinomial logit models suggest that any increase in independent contractors would have little effect on aggregate job stability, growth in the other arrangements—on-call workers, direct-hire temporaries, and contract company workers—would have a more substantial impact. And although no statistics are available on trends in these arrangements, qualitative evidence from employer surveys indicates that there has been some growth in these arrangements in the 1980s and 1990s. For instance, in a Conference Board (Axel 1995) survey, one-fourth to one-third of member companies reported sizable growth in their use of direct-hire temporaries in the preceding five years and expected sizable growth in the coming five years. Data from BLS Industry Wage Surveys in 1986 and 1987 show growth in the contracting out of services in thirteen manufacturing industries between 1979 and the period from 1986 to 1987 (Abraham and Taylor 1996). In a survey of members of the Bureau of National Affairs, a larger percentage of employers reported an increase than reported a decrease between 1980 and 1985 in their use of direct-hire temporaries, on-call workers, administrative or business support contracts, and production subcontracting relative to regular workers (Abraham 1990). In the Upjohn Institute Employer Survey on Flexible Staffing Arrangements, a much larger percentage reported contracting out work previously done in-house than reported bringing work back in-house since 1990. Moreover, two-thirds of respondents to the Upjohn Institute survey predicted that organizations in their industry would increase their use of flexible staffing arrangements in the coming five years. Thus, it is reasonable to assume that there has been some growth recently in other types of flexible staffing arrangements, though the amount by which they have grown is unknown.

The last row of table 12.8 presents the results of a hypothetical simulation that assumes that on-call, contract company, and direct-hire temporary employment each doubled as a percentage of the workforce over the 1986 to 1996 period. This simulation illustrates that, as with agency temporaries, the largest effect of any growth in these other flexible staffing arrangements would be an increase in the proportion of workers switching employers. Although the percentage growth assumed for these categories is slightly less than that actually experienced by agency temporaries, employment in these arrangements is unlikely to have increased as much as twofold. Thus, the simulation in row 7, combined with the other simulations, probably represents an upper-bound estimate of the effects of the growth in flexible staffing arrangements on job stability. Summing the effects of rows 4 through 7 of table 12.8, growth in flexible staffing arrangements could result in a 0.51-percentage-point increase in the percentage of workers switching employers. This figure represents about half of the net growth in employer switching over the period.[24]

CONCLUSIONS

We set out in this chapter to examine whether workers in a wide variety of flexible work arrangements experience less job stability as a consequence of those arrangements. Although our evidence suggests that they generally do, it is important to distinguish between types of arrangements.

Evidence of lower job stability is clearest for agency temporaries, on-call workers, direct-hire temporaries, and contract company workers. Results from the Upjohn Institute survey show that employers primarily use agency temporaries, on-call workers, and direct-hire temporaries for temporary assignments. Only for agency temporaries do a substantial proportion of employers report using the arrangement to screen workers for permanent positions, and even then it is not the primary reason that employers report for using them. Moreover, our analysis of CPS data shows that compared to regular full-time workers, agency temporaries, on-call workers, direct-hire temporaries, and contract company workers are more likely to change employers, become unemployed, or, in the case of on-call workers and direct-hire temporaries, involuntarily drop out of the labor force after one month and/or one year. These results hold up even after controlling for individual and job characteristics, job histories, and wages.

We also find considerable evidence of job instability for those in regular part-time jobs. Regular part-time workers are more likely than regular full-time workers to change employers, become unemployed, or involuntarily drop out of the labor force, particularly over the course of a year. Although regular part-time work is less stable than regular full-time work, it is more stable than agency temporary, on-call, direct-hire temporary, and contract company work.

We find little evidence that the employment of independent contractors is less stable than that of regular full-time workers. Although independent contractors display some increased tendency to drop out of the labor force, this change in labor-force status appears largely voluntary.

Our simulations indicate that the recent rapid growth in agency temporaries resulted in a modest decline in job stability primarily because agency temporaries are much more likely than workers in regular full-time and regular part-time positions to switch employers. According to our simulation results, the growth in agency temporaries over the periods from 1986 to 1987 to the period from 1995 to 1996 increased the number of workers switching jobs over the course of a year by 0.30 percentage point, which represents about 30 percent of the increase in employer switching evidenced in the CPS data. The decline in part-time and self-employment over the period would not have offset the increase in job switching caused by the growth in agency temporaries. Given qualitative evidence of growth in other forms of flexible staffing arrangements, this probably represents a lower-bound estimate of the effects of the growth in flexible staffing arrangements on job stability. Thus, although the decline in aggregate job stability is itself modest, our results indicate that the growth in agency temporaries and other flexible staffing arrangements can account for a substantial part of the decline.

Future CPS supplements on contingent and alternative work arrangements will supply better time-series data on employment in flexible staffing arrangements. The results we present in this chapter suggest that continued growth in agency temporaries and other types of flexible staffing arrangements would bear watching for their effects on job stability.

APPENDIX

LONGITUDINAL MATCHING AND WEIGHTING WITH THE CURRENT POPULATION SURVEY

Households in the CPS are interviewed for four consecutive months, not interviewed for the next eight months, then interviewed for four more consecutive months. In each calendar month of the year, a new group of households is administered its first monthly interview. Given this structure, it is theoretically possible to match 75 percent of the households in consecutive calendar months and 50 percent of the households in months one year apart. The actual percentage that can be matched is lower because some individuals refuse to continue participating and because the sample is address-based and some individuals move. In addition, starting in January 1996, the sample of both new and continuing households in the CPS was reduced by approximately 12 percent, resulting in a lower match rate for the February 1995 to February 1996 matched sample. Of those who were not in their fourth or eighth interview and were employed in February 1995, 96.3 percent had a valid record to which they could be matched in March 1995. Of those who were in the first half of their interviewing rotations (interviews one through four) and who were employed in February 1995, 67.1 percent were matched to a valid record in February 1996.

Because a new area sample was phased in, household identifications on the public use tapes were generated such that households could not be matched forward starting in May 1995. All longitudinal data reported in this chapter were constructed using internal BLS data containing household identification numbers and unique personal identification numbers for individuals within a household.

The tabulations reported in tables 12.3 and 12.4 were weighted to account for the reduction in observations caused by the rotation pattern of interviewing, attrition, and the overall reduction in the CPS sample instituted in January 1996. We constructed weights to preserve the February 1995 age, race, and gender distribution of workers in the matched February 1995–March 1995 data and in the matched February 1995–February 1996 data. To do this, we multiplied the individual February 1995 supplement weights by a ratio that captures the attrition in each individual's age-race-gender group. We calculated ratios for eight age-race-gender groups (male, white, more than twenty-five years old; male, nonwhite, more than twenty-five years old; and so on). Specifically, the ratio equals the weighted number of individuals in that particular group in February 1995 to the weighted number of individuals in the same group in the matched sample, where the weight was the February 1995 supplement weight.

DEFINITION OF SELECTED VARIABLES

Living in a Poverty Area
A poverty area is defined as a census tract in which more than 20 percent of the households had incomes below the poverty level in 1990.

Job Tenure
Job tenure in February 1995 for those who were agency temporaries, contract company workers, or on-call workers is defined as how long the individual had worked for the temporary help agency or contract company or had been an on-call worker rather than how long the individual had been at a particular assignment. Independent contractors and the self-employed were asked how long they had been in these arrangements. In the February 1996 tenure supplement, wage and salary workers were asked how long they had worked for the employer identified as their current and main employer in the monthly CPS. The self-employed were asked how long they had been self-employed.

Earnings
Hourly earnings were constructed using data from the March Income Supplement, which inquires about earnings in the previous year. Using data on 1994 earnings from the March 1995 CPS has the drawback that we must exclude those who worked in February 1995 but report no earnings the previous year. Inclusion of the March earnings variable, however, generally has little effect on the size and significance of the other coefficients in the model.

BEING SWITCHED TO A FLEXIBLE WORK ARRANGEMENT AT THE CURRENT PLACE OF WORK

Agency temporaries, on-call workers, and contract company workers were asked whether they had always worked at the place where they were currently working in this arrangement. In February 1995, only independent contractors who were identified as wage and salary workers were asked about their previous status. In addition, in February 1997 independent contractors identified as self-employed were asked, "Have you ever worked for one of your clients as something other than an independent contractor?" The proportion of independent contractors reporting to have been switched in 1995 was higher than in 1997. However, this is almost entirely attributable to the fact that only wage and salary independent contractors were asked about their previous status. The percentage of workers in the other three flexible work arrangements who said that their work arrangements had changed was higher or about the same in 1995 as in 1997.

Agency temporaries, on-call workers, contract company workers, and wage and salary independent contractors who had previously worked in another arrangement at their current workplace were asked directly in both 1995 and 1997 how long they had worked in that previous arrangement before being switched. Tenure prior to being switched for independent contractors identified as self-employed was less precisely derived from a series of questions asked of those who had been independent contractors for no more than three years. In these questions, independent contractors who stated that they had been employed directly prior to becoming an independent contractor were asked how long they had worked in this other job.

CONSTRUCTING TRENDS IN AGGREGATE JOB STABILITY FROM THE CURRENT POPULATION SURVEY

Aggregate job stability measures were constructed by matching those who were in the first half of their interviewing rotations and were employed in either January 1986 or February 1995 to their individual records a year later. January 1987 and February 1996 were chosen because in each of these months a tenure supplement for those who were employed at the time of the survey was conducted in conjunction with the monthly CPS. Individuals were defined as being employed with the same employer if they were reported to have been employed in January 1987 or February 1995 and their tenure in January 1987 or February 1996 was greater than or equal to a year. Individuals were classified as being employed with a different employer if they had been employed one year earlier and their tenure was less than one year in January 1987 or February 1996. Those employed in January 1986 or February 1995 were classified as going from employment to unemployment, or from employment to not being in the labor force, if they were unemployed or not in the labor force, respectively, in January 1987 or February 1996.

Individuals observed in February 1995 were matched to their February 1996 data using household identification numbers and unique personal identification numbers for individuals within a household, as described earlier. Individuals observed in January 1986 were matched to their data in January 1987 also by using household and personal identification numbers. However, because identification numbers were somewhat less likely to be consistent month to month in 1986 than in 1995, we also required that an individual's gender, race, and age (or age plus one) be the same between 1986 and 1987 in order for a match to be considered valid. The match rate for those who were employed in January 1986 was 68.4 percent. Nonresponse and attrition from the sample were accounted for when estimating the job stability measures in both 1986 to 1987 and 1995 to 1996 by adjusting the weights as described in the discussion on weighting.

METHODOLOGY FOR SIMULATIONS

The estimated effect of a change in the employment share of a particular work arrangement on the one-year labor market transition rates was calculated as

$$\Delta S \times ME_{fsa\text{-}pt} \times \rho + \Delta S \times ME_{fsa\text{-}ft}[1 - \rho],$$

where ΔS is the change in the flexible staffing arrangement share; $ME_{fsa\text{-}pt}$ is the marginal effect of being in a particular flexible staffing arrangement relative to being in a regular part-time arrangement on labor market transitions (employed with the same employer, employed with a different employer, unemployed, or not in the labor force); $ME_{fsa\text{-}ft}$ is the marginal effect of being in a particular flexible staffing arrangement relative to being in a regular full-time arrangement on labor market transitions; and ρ is the proportion of workers in that flexible staffing arrangement who work part-time hours. The marginal effects were based on table 12.6, model 4, which contains the greatest number of control variables, and were calculated as the average of the marginal effects for individuals who were in that particular flexible staffing arrangement in February 1995. The individual marginal effects were calculated as the difference between the predicted probability assuming the individual was a regular part-time worker (or a regular full-time worker) and the predicted probability assuming the individual was in the particular flexible arrangement (agency temporary, on-call worker, and so on). By taking the average of the individual marginal effects only across those in the flexible staffing arrangements, we are implicitly assuming that the distribution of characteristics of workers joining (or leaving) a particular arrangement reflects the distribution among workers in that arrangement in February 1995. For example, we assume that the growth in temporary employment was drawn disproportionately from young, female, and minority workers. Calculating the marginal effects, however, as the average across all workers (as reported in tables 12.5, 12.6, and 12.7) produces qualitatively similar results.

ACKNOWLEDGMENTS

We thank Alec Levenson, David Neumark, Stephen Miller, Charles Pierret, and two anonymous referees for helpful suggestions. We are grateful to Lillian Vesic-Petrovic for outstanding research assistance and to Claire Black and Nancy Mack for assistance in preparing the document. The views expressed in this chapter are those of the authors and do not necessarily reflect the policies of the Bureau of Labor Statistics or the views of other BLS staff members.

NOTES

1. A 1989 Industry Wage Survey indicated that permanent full-time staff constituted 3.2 percent of employment in "help supply services."

2. A further explanation of the variables in the Contingent and Alternative Employment Arrangements Supplement is contained in the appendix to this chapter and in Polivka (1996).

3. Agency temporaries, as measured in the February CPS supplement, account for only about 1 percent of total employment. They account for over 2 percent of employment in the Current Employment Statistics (CES), the Bureau of Labor Statistics' establishment survey. Although the CES somewhat overstates the number of employees of temporary help agencies, it is generally presumed that the CPS somewhat understates the number of agency temporaries. For a discussion of the differences between CPS and CES statistics on temporary help agency workers, see Polivka (1996).

4. Employers were not asked why they contracted out work but only why, if pertinent, they had changed their use of contract workers since 1990. The concept of contract workers in the Upjohn survey differs from the concept of contract company workers and independent contractors in the 1995 CPS supplement, and results on contract workers from the Upjohn survey are not discussed in this chapter. Susan Houseman (1997) provides a detailed discussion of the Upjohn survey.

5. The Contingent and Alternative Employment Arrangements Supplement to the CPS was repeated in February 1997. We report the 1997 figures here because, as a result of a questionnaire error in 1995, very few independent contractors were asked whether they had previously worked for their employer or client in another arrangement. This problem was corrected in the 1997 survey.

6. The Upjohn Institute employer survey does not provide evidence on job stability for contract company workers and independent contractors.

7. Details on the construction of these weights along with other variables are provided in the appendix.

8. A question on the basic March 1995 survey explicitly asks individuals who are employed whether their employer is the same as in the previous month. We determined whether individuals held the same job in February 1996 as they did one year earlier using data on job tenure from the February 1996 supplement to the CPS.

9. As noted earlier, the results for agency temporaries exclude those who mis-reported their client as their employer in the February 1995 basic CPS. These agency temporaries displayed a pattern of labor market transition rates similar to that of agency temporaries who correctly reported the agency as their employer. Their exclusion from the tabulations and the mul-tivariate analysis reported here does not affect the qualitative nature of our findings.

10. The multinomial logit model assumes that the ratio of the probability of one state to the probability of another state, or the odds ratio, is indepen-dent of the other alternatives. We performed a Hausman specification test on this independence of irrelevant alternatives assumption, and it was ac-cepted. (For a discussion of this test, see Greene 1997, 920–21.)

11. Because these three variables are defined only for individuals with three or fewer years of tenure, we also included a dummy variable set equal to one if the individual had three or fewer years of tenure on the job.

12. We also have run models using a wage measure based on reported hourly earnings from the February 1995 CPS. The results from these models are almost identical to the results from those reported here, in which wages are calculated from annual earnings. Although reported hourly earnings from the February 1995 survey are likely to be more accurate, we cannot include any of the variables from the March 1995 CPS in regressions with the Feb-ruary 1995 wage measure because February 1995 wage data for regular part-time and regular full-time workers were collected only for the outgoing rotations. For this reason, we report regression models with the hourly wage calculated from annual 1994 earnings.

13. The reported marginal effects were calculated as the average of the marginal effects for each individual in the sample. For continuous variables, the marginal effect of variable x_i on the probability of being in state j, P_j, is $P_j(B_{ij} - \overline{B}_i)$. For binary variables, the individual marginal effects were calcu-lated as the difference in the predicted probability, first assuming a value of zero and then a value of one. For the flexible staffing dummy variables, the individual marginal effects were calculated as the difference between the predicted probability assuming the individual was a regular full-time worker and the predicted probability assuming the individual was in the particular flexible arrangement (agency temporary, on-call worker, and so on) (see Greene 1997, 876–78, 916).

14. These results included the same set of control variables as the equations reported in table 12.6. Agency temporaries were excluded from the models because none were in the category "not in the labor force, want to be." Similarly, because there were no individuals in the category "not in the labor force, want to be" for certain work arrangements in March 1995, these models could not be run on the February 1995 to March 1995 matched data. We also estimated a specification with the interaction of the work ar-rangement dummy variables with gender. These interactions were almost always insignificantly different from zero. In addition, the estimates from a model in which the sample was restricted to those between the ages of twenty and sixty-four were qualitatively similar to those reported here. We

do find, however, that among workers forty-five and older the proportion who report being in retirement in February 1996 is much higher among those in most flexible staffing arrangements than among those in regular full-time arrangements in February 1995. Thus, there is some evidence to suggest that flexible staffing arrangements are often bridges to retirement for older workers.

15. Because individuals' work arrangements are recorded only at one point in time in our data, we cannot adopt an empirical strategy similar to that used in Segal and Sullivan (1997b).

16. Recall that, following the BLS definition of contract company workers, we restrict the category to those who work primarily for one client at the client's work site.

17. For reviews of this literature, see Schmidt and Svorny (1998), Gottschalk and Moffitt (this volume), or Bansak and Raphael (1998).

18. The CAEAS was repeated as a supplement to the February 1997 CPS; between 1995 and 1997, the percentage of workers in these arrangements remained roughly constant.

19. Adjusting for the redesign, the percentage of workers in part-time employment declined from 19.1 percent in 1986 to 18.3 percent in 1996. Self-employment (both incorporated and unincorporated) declined from 12.5 percent in 1989 to 11.5 percent in 1996.

20. The CES includes only data for paid employees in nonfarm industries. We calculated agency temporaries as a share of total employment by adding figures on self-employment and farm employment from the CPS to total paid employment figures from the CES. We averaged the share of temporary employment in the years 1986 and 1987 and in the years 1995 and 1996.

21. Our results were not particularly sensitive to this assumption. See the appendix for a further explanation of the simulations.

22. We noted earlier that some of the employer switching associated with temporary agency employment may occur when agency temporaries are hired by their client firm. Nevertheless, such transitions would also be recorded as employer switches in the CPS figures that we are trying to explain.

23. We have already taken into account a shift from regular part-time employment to agency temporary part-time employment in the simulation for agency temporary employment. The decline in self-employment is measured over the 1989 to 1996 period. All calculations were based on estimates that accounted for the effect of the redesign of the CPS in 1994. Other details concerning the simulations are provided in the appendix.

24. It should be pointed out that our simulations capture only permanent changes to one-year labor market transition rates from changes in the composition of employment arrangements; the aggregate data, however, measure both these permanent changes and changes that result from one-time changes in the composition of employment arrangements. For instance, if, during the period, individuals were shifting from being in regular jobs to being independent contractors, there would be a one-time increase in job

switching owing to the growth in the number of independent contractors, even though, according to our estimates, independent contractors are no more likely to switch jobs than regular full-time workers. Our simulations probably understate the extent to which growth in flexible staffing arrangements has contributed to a decline in job stability, but the understatement is likely to be slight because we measure job stability over a relatively short time horizon (one year). However, the contribution of such one-time shifts to changes in job stability in the 1980s and 1990s will be more important when job stability is measured over a longer time horizon, as it is done in most studies.

REFERENCES

Abraham, Katharine G. 1990. "Restructuring the Employment Relationship: The Growth of Market-Mediated Work Arrangements." In *New Developments in the Labor Market: Toward a New Institutional Paradigm*, edited by Katharine Abraham and Robert McKersie. Cambridge, Mass.: MIT Press.

Abraham, Katharine G., and Susan K. Taylor. 1996. "Firms' Use of Outside Contractors: Theory and Evidence." *Journal of Labor Economics* 14(3): 394–424.

Axel, Helen. 1995. *HR Executive Review: Contingent Employment,* vol. 3, no. 2. New York: Conference Board.

Bansak, Cynthia, and Steven Raphael. 1998. "Have Employment Relationships in the United States Become Less Stable?" Discussion Paper 98–15. San Diego: University of California, Department of Economics.

Belous, Richard. 1989. *The Contingent Economy: The Growth of the Temporary, Part-time, and Subcontracted Workforce.* Washington, D.C.: National Planning Association.

Blank, Rebecca M. 1994. "The Dynamics of Part-time Work." Working Paper 4911. Cambridge, Mass.: National Bureau of Economic Research.

Boisjoly, Johanne, Greg J. Duncan, and Timothy Smeeding. 1998. "The Shifting Incidence of Involuntary Job Losses from 1968 to 1992." *Industrial Relations* 37(2): 207–31.

Castro, Janice. 1993. "Disposable Workers." *Time,* March 29, 1993.

Farber, Henry S. 1997. "The Changing Face of Job Loss in the Unites States, 1981–1995." *Brookings Papers on Economic Activity: Microeconomics* 1: 55–128.

———. 1998. "Has the Rate of Job Loss Increased in the Nineties?" *Industrial Relations Research Association Series Proceedings of the Fiftieth Annual Meeting* 1: 88–97.

Greene, William H. 1997. *Econometric Analysis.* 3rd ed. Upper Saddle River, N.J.: Prentice-Hall.

Houseman, Susan N. 1997. "Temporary, Part-time, and Contract Employment in the United States: A Report on the W. E. Upjohn Institute's Employer Survey on Flexible Staffing Policies." Final report. Prepared by the W. E. Upjohn Institute for the U.S. Department of Labor.

Polivka, Anne E. 1996. "Contingent and Alternative Work Arrangements, Defined." *Monthly Labor Review* 119(10): 3–9.

Polivka, Anne E., and Stephen M. Miller. 1998. "The CPS After the Redesign:

Refocusing the Economic Lens." In *Labor Statistics Measurement Issues,* edited by John Haltiwanger, Marilyn Manser, and Robert Topel. Chicago: University of Chicago Press.

Polsky, Daniel. 1999. "Changing Consequences of Job Separation in the United States." Industrial and Labor Relations Review 52(4): 565—80.

Segal, Lewis M., and Daniel G. Sullivan. 1997a. "The Growth of Temporary Services Work." *Journal of Economic Perspectives* 11(2): 117–36.

———. 1997b. "The Nature of Temporary Services Employment: Evidence from State UI Data." Federal Reserve Bank of Chicago. Unpublished paper.

Schmidt, Stefanie R., and Shirley V. Svorny. 1998. "Recent Trends in Job Security and Stability." *Journal of Labor Research* 19(4): 647–68.

U.S. Bureau of Labor Statistics. 1997. *Employer Tenure in the Mid-1990s.* U.S. Department of Labor News Release 97–25 (January 30).

———. 1998. *Employee Tenure in 1998.* U.S. Department of Labor News Release 98–387 (September 23).

Chapter 13

Examining the Incidence of Downsizing and Its Effect on Establishment Performance

Peter Cappelli

cademic research and casual observation before the early 1980s suggested that employment levels were derived in a straightforward way from the demand for a firm's product or services. Most layoffs were seen as driven by business cycles: they were temporary in that employees were rehired when product demand returned, and production workers were most often affected. The exceptions were typically limited to industry-specific market changes—the long-term decline of an industry, such as coal mining, or the movement of an industry, such as textiles, overseas. Thus, virtually all of the public policy attention given to unemployment assumed that job losses were driven by cyclical or structural declines in product demand.

After the 1980s, however, this assumption no longer seemed valid. Layoffs were more likely to be permanent, and although business cycles still drove unemployment rates, they did not neatly explain corporate layoff announcements, now labeled "downsizing." The term "downsizing" was introduced to describe the contemporary practice of permanently cutting jobs in an effort to improve operating efficiency, not necessarily in response to declines in business. (For further discussion of downsizing, see, for example, Cascio 1993; Cappelli et al. 1997.) Downsizing has received a great deal of attention, especially in the business press, in part because it represents something of an enigma. As noted later in this chapter, the companies engaged in downsizing have not necessarily appeared to be in financial distress. The perception that even successful companies can improve their financial performance by downsizing has led to a series of studies of the financial consequences of downsizing decisions.

This chapter focuses on the main empirical question about downsizing: What are the factors that cause it? There have been no prior studies of the determinants of downsizing and only a handful on related topics such as plant closings. The most important empirical challenge facing such investigations is defining and then measuring downsizing. The studies of the *consequences* of downsizing rely either on self-identifications by firms themselves when they have had a downsizing or on media announcements. I take a different approach and define downsizing as reductions in jobs driven by the desire to improve operating efficiencies, and I distinguish it from the layoffs typically associated with shortfalls in demand. One might think of downsizing, therefore, as driven by developments inside the firm, in its production function, rather than by changes in the product market and product demand. I can identify such situations indirectly by controlling for cases in which firms experience shortfalls in demand as well as for cases that involve other unrelated sources of job loss such as outsourcing. I define job losses in the remaining cases as downsizing. I examine the factors that explain both general job losses and downsizing across a national probability sample of firms, using hypotheses associated with management practices, most commonly as they relate to incentives to cut the use of labor. Finally, I contribute to the growing literature on the consequences of job losses for firms by relating job losses and downsizing to the subsequent performance of the firms.

THE DOWNSIZING CONSTRUCT

Downsizing represents for many the most obvious manifestation of a perceived decline in the nature of the employment relationship as it relates to job security. In particular, the perception that even profitable companies can raise the price of their stock by making downsizing announcements seems to have stood on its head the conventional wisdom that layoffs are a sign of trouble for a firm, something that happens only when its business is failing. As Kevin Hallock (1998) observed, the belief that companies reward those CEOs who downsize their operations has fed the perception that downsizing is good for companies. (Whether these perceptions are justified is another matter, as discussed later.)

Much of the concern and interest in downsizing has focused on large corporations, which have been perceived until relatively recently as places where most employees, especially managers, could expect lifetime jobs, subject to adequate performance (see, for example, Kanter 1977). Finding systematic evidence of the change in practice, however, can be difficult. Job security in most companies has been an implicit policy that was never spelled out in the employee handbook. It is difficult, therefore, to use changes in explicit policies as a measure of the change in job security. But there is anecdotal evidence of changes in policies associated with employment security. The authors of *The One Hundred Best Companies to Work for in America,* for example, found that ten of those companies had an explicit no-layoff policy in the 1980s but that only two of them still had such a policy in 1997, and one of those was privately held (Levering and Moskowitz 1993; see also *Mother Jones,* July 17, 1997, 5). A benchmark study of leading companies conducted by the Corporate Leadership Council (1995) discovered an important change in their expectations about career development from the 1980s to the 1990s: companies were now explicitly expecting managerial incumbents to stay with the company for an average of three to four years, and to leave sometime during that time period, rather than to remain with the company until they retired. A recent survey of large employers conducted by the Conference Board (1997) reported that 69 percent of those companies had abandoned job security policies for their employees; only 3 percent said that they still had such policies. This finding in particular suggests that an important change has taken place, but in the absence of a representative sample, it is difficult to interpret its significance.

The concept of downsizing appeared after the recession of 1981 to 1983. The layoffs were initially driven by sharp declines in business and were seen as traditional, temporary layoffs. Sixty-one percent of the human resource executives surveyed by the Conference Board thought that by 1984 the downsizing trend was losing its momentum (Gorlin 1985). In 1991, in contrast, a similar Conference Board survey found that more than half of the surveyed executives believed that downsizing would continue to be necessary indefinitely to maintain competitive firms (Johnson and Linden 1992). That year other surveys reported that 22 percent of surveyed companies were planning to make cuts in their workforce. In fact, twice as many of those companies, 46 percent, ended up cutting workers (Ehrbar 1993).

The American Management Association (AMA) has surveyed approximately one thousand of its member companies about downsizing every year since 1990. Although AMA members are no doubt different from the population of all employers—different even from the average large employer by virtue of their membership in that organization—the trends in their experience over time may be instructive. The AMA surveys found that the incidence of downsizing increased every year until 1996, when 48.9 percent of companies reported having at least one downsizing wave, only a trivial decline from 50 percent the year before. (The AMA survey essentially counts every layoff as a downsizing and in that sense measures the occurrence more than the intensity of job loss.) Downsizing therefore increased across companies even as the economy expanded following the 1991 recession. Hallock's (1998) calculations of layoff announcements (not necessarily downsizing per se) found that they increased in the 1990s as compared to the 1980s.

The causes of downsizing as reported in the AMA annual surveys also changed. In the early 1990s, virtually all respondents cited overall economic conditions as an important cause of downsizing. By 1996, however, most were citing restructuring (66 percent) as the cause, and most of the companies reporting cuts were now profitable in the year they were cutting (American Management Association 1996). In more recent years, firms have been hiring at the same time that they have been downsizing. In 1996, 31 percent of firms in the AMA survey were adding workers even as they reported job cuts, and the average firm reporting a downsizing in fact was growing by 6 percent.

EVIDENCE FROM DATA ON INDIVIDUALS

The firm-level data cited earlier are suggestive of interesting and potentially new relationships with job loss. But because the surveys from which they are derived are proprietary and typically use nonrepresentative sampling frames, it is difficult to use these data as the basis for conclusions about the economy as a whole. In contrast, a considerable literature has developed on the labor market experience of individuals to examine questions related to downsizing. Although it is only suggestive of employer practices, this literature has the advantage of being based on representative samples. Many studies find increases in job losses of a kind associated with changes in the nature of employment security and in the factors shaping it. James Medoff (1993) found that the proportion of prime-age male workers (ages thirty-five to fifty-four) who were permanently (as opposed to temporarily) displaced from their jobs almost doubled between the 1970s and the early 1990s. Henry Farber (1997, 1998) concluded that the overall rate at which workers were permanently displaced decreased a bit during the late 1980s from the peak of the 1981 to 1982 recession, but then rose again—despite the economic recovery—and jumped sharply through 1995 (Farber 1997; for concerns about data problems that may have inflated more recent figures, see Polivka 1998). The rate at which workers were thrown out of their jobs was almost as great from 1993 to 1995, a period of significant economic expansion and prosperity in the economy as a whole, as it had been from 1981 to 1983, the worst recession period since the Depression. And economic or companywide reasons, such as downturns in business or plant closings, were no longer the sole or primary cause of the job losses. More and more often, particular positions were being eliminated.

Another feature of changing layoff practices has been the susceptibility to downsizing of white-collar and management employees, whose jobs were traditionally the most protected. The data on the experiences of individual workers suggest that the rate of displacement was actually higher for managers and white-collar workers in the 1980s than for other occupations, controlling for other characteristics (Cappelli 1992; Kletzer 1998). It rose sharply through the early 1990s but appears to have declined somewhat from 1993 to 1995 (Farber 1997). Older and more educated workers, the kind we would expect to find in the "better" jobs buffered by the organization from market pressures, seem to have been more likely to be displaced in the early 1990s as compared to earlier periods (Gustman, Mitchell, and Steinmeyer 1995; Farber 1997). The increases in job losses for these groups have also been attributed to internal restructuring (for example, "position abolished") rather than external economic conditions (Farber 1997).

Also contributing to our understanding of changing employment relationships are the studies of changes in average employee tenure, a measure driven by the combination of voluntary and involuntary employee turnover. Turnover for the average employee seems quite stable over time (although not for all demographic groups), as estimated by data from both the Current Population Survey (CPS) and the Panel Study of Income Dynamics (PSID) (see, for example, Jaeger and Stevens, this volume). David Neumark, Daniel Polsky, and Daniel Hansen (this volume) find that overall turnover, though stable in the 1980s, appears to have risen somewhat in the mid-1990s, even for managerial employees who have traditionally been seen as having significant job security. The more relevant question for downsizing and job security generally, however, is whether involuntary or employer-initiated turnover has increased. The answer appears to be yes. Polsky (forthcoming) examines whether there has been an increase in employer-initiated job loss, such as layoffs, using the Panel Study of Income Dynamics. He compares the 1976 to 1981 period to the 1986 to 1991 period and finds that the overall rate of employee turnover was similar, but that involuntary job losses were greater, especially for older employees and those with more tenure with the employer, the group traditionally associated with internal labor markets. Johanne Boisjoly, Greg Duncan, and Timothy Smeeding (1998) found similar results with the same data. Robert Valletta (1996) reported that the proportion of the unemployed accounted for by permanent dismissals (technically, non-layoff job-losers) rose through the 1980s and early 1990s.

Together, both the limited descriptive data on employer layoff decisions and the more representative studies of employee job loss and turnover suggest that the factors driving contemporary job loss may be different than in the past. Those factors appear to be related less to downturns in product demand and more to internal factors associated with management decisions.

RESEARCH ON DOWNSIZING

Despite the popular attention given to downsizing and the continuing stream of studies about job security for individual workers, there has been essentially no research directed at the causes of downsizing. A growing body of research on the consequences of downsizing addresses the perception that firms can improve their financial performance by downsizing. Although these studies do not relate to the central question here—What factors explain employer downsizing?—they may shed light on how to conceptualize and measure downsizing. These studies include Abowd, Milkovich, and Hannon (1990), Caves and Krepps (1993), and Worrell, Davidson, and Sharma (1991), all of whom found that, on average, financial performance as measured by stock prices seems to decline after a downsizing (for similar results, see DeMeuse, Vanderheiden, and Bergmann 1994; Iqbal and Shetty 1995; and, for Canadian firms, Gunderson, Verma, and Verma 1997). At least some part of the negative performance of downsizing firms can be traced to a wide range of adverse effects on the workforce (see, for example, Brockner 1992; for surveys, see Cameron 1994).

But some studies also find that performance improves after downsizing for firms with certain characteristics. Worrell, Davidson, and Sharma (1991) found that firms with restructuring plans as part of their downsizing effort show an improvement in stock prices after a downsizing. Wayne Cascio, Clifford Young, and James Morris (1997) took a longer time perspective in examining several different model specifications and found some positive relationships between reductions in employment and financial performance, although the relationship was generally negative. A study of the positive effects on performance associated with downsizing at General Dynamics suggested that the restructuring of firm operations and management that presumably drove much of that company's improved performance both led to and was facilitated by downsizing (Dial and Murphy 1995).

The central analytic problem facing studies of downsizing is to define it and to differentiate the cutting of jobs because a firm already has financial problems from the cutting of jobs to seek new efficiencies. The data outlined later in the chapter make it possible to address this issue and to contribute to the literature on the relationship between downsizing and performance effects.

There is also a body of research on firm financial performance and plant closings, which are not identical to downsizings but may be similar enough to shed some light on how to conceptualize downsizing. David Blackwell, Wayne Marr, and Michael Spivey (1990) observed early on that negative relationships between plant closings and firm financial performance may be spurious because such decisions are associated with, and difficult to untangle from, the overall competitiveness of firms. Michael Gombola and George Tsetsekos (1992) found that plant-closing decisions in general hurt share prices, but not for firms that are financially secure. These results appear to be consistent with the view in the downsizing studies that cuts in struggling firms help identify those firms that are already declining while cuts in more successful firms may proxy efforts to restructure and reposition operations. Rajiv Kalra, Glenn Henderson, and Michael Walker (1994) made a similar finding: plant closings may be associated with improved performance when firms are restructuring.

One of the drawbacks with these studies is that, because they use stock prices as a dependent variable, they are limited to publicly held companies. Moreover, the unit of analysis must be the entire corporate entity, which is often far removed from where employment decisions are made; a massive company like General Electric, with its hundreds of divisions and facilities, is counted as a single observation because it has a single stock price. Martin Baily, Eric Bartelsman, and John Haltiwanger (1996) took a different approach and examined the effects of job reductions on plant productivity using plant-level data from the U.S. Census Bureau. From a range of results they concluded that downsizing plants have only slightly more productivity growth than do plants that are increasing employment.

The more fundamental complication illustrated by all of these studies is the problem of defining and then measuring what counts as a downsizing. The studies of downsizing announcements rely on firms to self-identify through their public announcements that they are implementing a downsizing and to define it consistently.[1] Not all reductions in employment merit public announcements, firms differ in what type of job cuts they define as downsizing, and as noted earlier, actual cuts often do not seem closely related to planned cuts. Studies of downsizing announcements may thus measure something that differs systematically from actual job losses—perhaps something about the effects of public statements, or the unobserved characteristics associated with the type of changes that merit such announcements. To illustrate, Hallock's (1998) study of layoff announcements found that the initial positive relationship between layoffs and CEO pay (presumably motivated by the perception that layoffs improve firm performance) in fact appears to be driven by firm characteristics associated both with CEO pay and with the layoff decision. When one controls for those characteristics, the relationship between layoff announcements and pay disappears.

The study by Baily and his colleagues (1996) took the simpler approach of examining actual employment changes, and Cascio and his colleagues (1997) defined "employment downsizers" as companies that cut employment more than they cut plant and equipment. The latter study attempts to differentiate job cuts associated with declines in business activity from what might be thought of as "true" downsizing—job cuts designed to increase efficiency by operating with proportionately fewer employees.

MODELING THE DOWNSIZING DECISION

In an attempt to define downsizing clearly and consistently, I define downsizing as job cuts driven by pressures for increased efficiency in the use of labor rather than by declines in demand. We can therefore begin to conceptualize downsizing by thinking about the factors that drive reductions in jobs—essentially reductions in labor demand—and then differentiate the factors that are consistent with the drive for improved efficiency. The demand for labor is typically seen as derived from the demand for the final product or service produced by the firm through a production function that represents how labor and capital are combined to produce final products (see, for example, Hamermesh 1993). Reductions in the level of demand for the product or service lead to reductions in the demand for labor of the kind traditionally associated with layoffs: especially if the firm is a price taker in its factor markets and cannot cut wages and other factor prices, it will respond to a decline in product demand by attempting to reduce inputs and laying off employees. A wide range of forces and developments might be responsible for a decline in the demand for a firm's final products, such as general business cycle conditions, changes in import penetration, or other industry- and firm-specific effects. For the purposes of estimation, they operate by reducing effective product demand and creating excess capacity.

Factor Prices

Changes in the input mix within a given production function are the other main cause of reductions in the demand for labor, the kind associated with the concept of downsizing as I define it. Such changes represent perhaps the best-known conceptual illustration of developments within a given production function that would lead to reductions in the demand for labor: employers substitute other, cheaper factors for labor and reduce their use of labor in the process. Wage rates and changes in the price of various factors that substitute for labor, such as technology or even management practices that might economize on the use of labor, are examples of these factor prices. (Of course, changes in factor prices may also affect product prices and, in turn, product demand and the derived demand for labor.)

Employment practices may affect the ability to substitute other factors for labor by changing the costs of laying off employees. Severance payments and employer pension obligations may be the clearest examples. The presence of unions and collective bargaining agreements can also restrict management's ability to adjust employment. The use of part-time and temporary employees, in contrast, may provide a substitute for downsizing by making it easier to adjust the total hours of work: contract work can be reduced without cutting employees.

Efficiency Parameter

The other explanation for downsizing relates to the general efficiency parameters in production function models. They represent the technology, broadly defined, for combining labor and other factors into final products. The typical assumption is that efficiency parameters are fixed in a given production function, although no doubt employers have some choice of practices within a given production function (see discussion later in the chapter). Firms may have choices *between* production functions, however, and essentially between different efficiency parameters.

One basic choice that is likely to affect the basic operation and production function of a firm is business strategy. The traditional concept of business strategy is competitive strategy—how a firm positions itself against competitors in a given product market. The notion behind competitive strategy is that firms have choices and discretion in selecting niches within markets. Michael Porter's (1985) framework describing the competitive strategy choices of firms is the best known. He argued that each strategy choice has implications for the internal structure of the firm, including employment practices. These practices, in turn, have implications for job security and downsizing.

Practices and Incentives

The distinction between substitution of other factors for labor within a given production function and the shift to different production functions that use less labor is easier to establish in theory than in practice. For example, whether the automation of a production operation represents only substitution of capital for labor within a production function or a move to a new production function altogether may be difficult to distinguish empirically. Doing so would require, among other things, estimates of the firm's production frontier.

It is possible to identify some changes in practices that are directly associated with shifts within or between production functions. It may be easier to identify managers' different incentives to pursue more efficient operations that reduce the use of labor and relate them to downsizing. The classic argument about the operation of modern, publicly held firms is that managers pursue their own interests and do not necessarily maximize efficiency because their interests are not aligned with those of the shareholders (Berle and Means 1932). Arrangements that align the interests of the managers who operate the companies with those of the shareholders are thought to change the operation of firms in fundamental ways, such as reducing excess jobs (Lichtenberg and Siegel 1992; Matsusaka 1993). Programs such as stock options for managers are perhaps the most obvious attempts to change the way a firm operates by creating these incentives for managers to act like stockholders as they execute their responsibilities.

In a typical production function like the well-known Cobb-Douglas form, where $Y = AK^\delta L^{1-\delta}$, these arguments about the practices that may affect the overall efficiency of the function relate to the general efficiency parameter A. Changes in the distribution parameter δ reflect general technological changes as well as changes in employment practices that affect the ability to substitute other factors for labor. The general cost of labor and the employment practices that influence these costs relate directly to the incentives to substitute capital (as well as other factors) for labor. The cost of labor relates directly to the incentives to substitute capital and other factors for labor. Changes in the demand for the output Y are the basis of the derived demand for labor. Reductions in that demand are behind traditional capacity-related layoffs. Changes in factor prices, the distribution parameter, and the efficiency parameter, in contrast, are associated with the more contemporary phenomenon of downsizing as defined earlier.

The analyses that follow examine the extent to which variables associated with the potential substitution of other factors for labor and with the shift to more efficient production regimes explain the incidence of more general job reductions and then the specific case of downsizing.

DATA AND ANALYSES: THE EQW NATIONAL EMPLOYER SURVEY

To examine the causes of downsizing, we need data about changes in employment, about product demand and related firm characteristics, and about management practices at the establishment level where downsizing decisions take place, a combination that has been difficult to find in the same data set. A recent establishment-level survey of employment practices conducted by the U.S. Census Bureau for the National Center on the Educational Quality of the Workforce (EQW) (1994) contains such data and allows us to address some of these questions.

The EQW National Employers Survey was administered as a telephone survey in August and September 1994 to a nationally representative sample of private establishments with more than twenty employees. It is structured to provide information on all categories of incumbent workers, not just new hires or those in core occupations.

The survey oversampled establishments in the manufacturing sector and establishments with more than one hundred employees. Public-sector employees, nonprofit institutions, and corporate headquarters were excluded from the sample. Although the survey excluded establishments with fewer than twenty employees (which represent approximately 85 percent of all establishments in the United States), the sampling frame represents establishments that employ approximately 75 percent of all workers, since most establishments are small (fewer than five employees) but most workers are employed in larger establishments. The survey concentrates on those establishments with the most employees. The target respondent in the manufacturing sector was the plant manager and, in the nonmanufacturing sector, the local business site manager.

The sampling frame for the survey was the Census Bureau (Standard Statistical Establishment List [SSEL]) file, one of the most comprehensive and up-to-date listings of establishments in the United States. Of the 4,633 eligible establishments contacted by the Census Bureau, 1,275 refused to participate in the survey. This represents a 72 percent response rate, which is substantially higher than that of similar establishment surveys.[2] The usual reason employers gave for not participating in the survey was either that they did not participate in voluntary surveys or that they were too busy to participate. Probit analysis conducted by Lisa Lynch and Susan Black (1996) of the characteristics of nonrespondents indicates that there was no significant pattern at the two-digit industry level in the likelihood that an establishment would participate in the survey. The only differentiating characteristic was that manufacturing establishments with more than 1,000 employees, 0.1 percent of the sample, were less likely to participate in the survey. Of the 3,358 establishments that participated in the survey, not all respondents completed all parts of the survey by the interview cutoff date of October 1, 1994. Completing all parts of the survey were 1,621 establishments in the manufacturing sector and 1,324 establishments in the nonmanufacturing sector—a "completed" survey response rate of 64 percent overall. For the analyses in this chapter, we restricted the sample to establishments that reported usable data for all questions used in any of the regressions to ensure that differences across specifications or across different dependent variables do not reflect changes in the sample.

The questionnaire was designed to allow for multiple respondents. Establishments that kept financial information in a separate office, such as corporate headquarters for multi-establishment enterprises, could have that information reported directly. Computer-assisted telephone interviewing (CATI) was used to administer each survey, which took approximately twenty-eight minutes to complete.

The survey was repeated again in August 1997 (NES II) and administered by the Census Bureau through CATI. The sampling frame was again drawn from the SSEL, targeting business establishments throughout the United States and excluding those with fewer than twenty employees. The survey oversampled the nation's largest establishments and those in the manufacturing sector. The sample for the NES II has three components: an oversampling of states involved in particular educational reform efforts (2,000 completed interviews in California, Kentucky, Michigan, Maryland, and Pennsylvania); approximately 2,500 completed interviews that make up a representative sample of the rest of the United

Table 13.1 Employment Changes for All Plants, 1991 to 1994

			All Plants			
			Percentage Change in Employment			
	N	Share as Percentage of Worker Population	Un-weighted Mean	(Standard Deviation)	Worker-Population Weighted Mean	(Standard Deviation)
Total	2,689	100.0	4.9	(35.7)	5.3	(37.4)
By operating level versus capacity in 1994						
Below	901	30.1	−1.2	(32.3)	0.7	(25.4)
At	1,523	60.6	6.7	(33.3)	1.5	(31.1)
Above	265	9.3	15.3	(52.6)	45.2	(70.2)
By plant size						
Less than 50	458	10.3	1.5	(23.7)	5.6	(20.6)
50 to 99	405	10.7	9.5	(50.9)	7.1	(43.0)
100 to 249	522	14.0	4.8	(31.1)	4.9	(26.3)
250 to 499	453	10.7	6.8	(40.5)	3.7	(57.1)
500 to 999	286	10.3	7.0	(38.6)	8.1	(33.7)
1,000 or more	565	44.0	1.8	(27.5)	4.7	(36.8)
By industry						
All manufacturing	1,510	25.5	4.4	(36.6)	7.6	(46.5)
Food, tobacco	123	2.1	10.6	(60.8)	16.9	(85.7)
Textile, apparel	115	1.8	10.6	(61.8)	11.9	(72.0)
Lumber, paper	171	2.8	4.1	(28.8)	4.6	(27.7)
Printing, publishing	139	1.9	2.3	(16.4)	3.1	(15.5)
Chemical, petroleum	148	2.2	−0.1	(17.7)	1.6	(14.2)
Primary metals	169	1.0	3.3	(31.8)	4.2	(29.0)
Fabricated metals	140	1.5	0.5	(22.9)	4.6	(22.8)
Machinery, instruments	171	7.0	3.9	(41.6)	12.7	(52.1)
Transportation equipment	161	1.9	6.6	(44.0)	1.4	(52.5)
Miscellaneous manufacturing	173	3.2	3.8	(16.8)	4.1	(17.1)
All nonmanufacturing	1,179	74.5	5.6	(34.4)	4.5	(33.8)
Construction	132	3.3	1.3	(26.2)	21.3	(57.4)
Transportation services	107	5.1	8.7	(43.2)	4.6	(26.9)
Communications	64	8.0	1.8	(22.9)	−8.5	(11.0)
Utilities	112	2.5	−3.5	(12.4)	−3.2	(8.0)
Wholesale trade	131	13.7	4.1	(26.6)	−4.1	(28.1)
Retail trade	100	17.1	2.5	(13.5)	−4.3	(19.2)
Finance	107	3.9	17.7	(61.2)	16.5	(48.0)
Insurance, real estate	99	2.3	4.6	(30.7)	2.9	(20.1)
Hotels	134	1.6	2.0	(15.5)	2.1	(14.8)
Business services	103	8.2	19.7	(59.1)	38.9	(55.1)
Health services	90	8.8	3.9	(14.6)	6.3	(14.8)

Note: Worker-population weights are calculated as sampling probability weights times total employment in 1994. Below the first row, worker-population weighted shares have been renormalized to sum to 100 by "versus capacity," "size," or "industry," as appropriate.

States (45 states plus the District of Columbia); and a longitudinal component of about 900 completed interviews with business establishments that had participated in the initial National Employer Survey, the component of interest for this study. A total of 5,465 establishments responded to NES II, for a response rate of 78 percent. The longitudinal component elicited 915 responses, for a response rate of 88 percent. Excluding

1994. Table 13.3 presents the statistics for all plants. Table 13.4 repeats the descriptions presented in table 13.1 using data for the period 1994 to 1997, and table 13.5 repeats the descriptions offered in table 13.2 for establishments operating at or below capacity in 1994 using employment change data for 1994 to 1997.

JOB LOSS AND DOWNSIZING VARIABLES

The creation of the downsizing variable begins with the more general measure of employment change over time, from 1991 to 1994 in the NES and from 1994 to 1997 in the NES II. This measure is then converted into a measure of job reduction: zero if employment was unchanged or increased, the percentage change if it decreased. The resulting variable contains more information than would a simple dummy variable for whether jobs declined. But the variable is truncated at zero, suggesting the need for estimation techniques associated with limited variables such as Tobit procedures.

The measure of downsizing needs to differentiate the reductions in employment that are associated with declines in business—more traditional layoffs—from those associated with production function changes that correspond to the notion of downsizing. The NES 1994 includes a question that captures whether the establishment is experiencing a shortfall in demand. It asks whether the establishment is operating below capacity (one if operating below capacity; zero if at or above capacity). Establishments operating below capacity may not have enough business to keep the current workforce employed and may be expected to implement traditional layoffs. Establishments that cut jobs even when they are at or above their normal operating capacity, in contrast, fit the notion of downsizing defined as job cuts driven by the changes in the production function in pursuit of improved efficiency.

The most straightforward way to incorporate this measure of excess capacity into a measure of downsizing is to include in the analysis of downsizing only those establishments that are operating at or above capacity. The middle column in tables 13.2 (for 1991 to 1994) and 13.4 (for 1994 to 1997) presents statistics for those establishments that meet the definition set out here for downsizing—operating at or above capacity and having decreased employment during the period. Establishments that fit the downsizing definition tend to be somewhat larger and less concentrated in manufacturing than the average establishment for the 1991 to 1994 period. These differences are less pronounced for the 1994 to 1997 period.

It is also important to distinguish job reductions associated with outsourcing from downsizing. For example, an employer who contracts out some function such as janitorial service to an outside vendor would expe-

Table 13.2 **Employment Changes of Plants at or Above Capacity in 1994 and 1991 to 1994**

			All Plants			
			Percentage Change in Employment			
	N	Share as Percentage of Worker Population	Un-weighted Mean	(Standard Deviation)	Worker-Population Weighted Mean	(Standard Deviation)
Total	1,788	69.9 of all	8.0	(36.9)	7.3	(41.4)
By plant size						
Less than 50	266	8.7	5.0	(21.1)	8.4	(17.7)
50 to 99	247	9.2	13.3	(56.6)	11.4	(49.0)
100 to 249	354	13.3	8.1	(33.1)	7.6	(27.8)
250 to 499	307	11.3	10.3	(44.4)	3.9	(64.5)
500 to 999	201	10.6	8.1	(31.7)	5.8	(28.6)
1,000 or more	413	46.9	4.8	(27.9)	7.4	(41.4)
By industry						
All manufacturing	997	24.6	8.2	(38.9)	11.7	(50.5)
Food, tobacco	85	2.1	16.5	(71.6)	24.2	(99.2)
Textile, apparel	91	2.0	10.9	(65.7)	13.0	(78.1)
Lumber, paper	122	3.1	3.6	(24.5)	2.5	(22.9)
Printing, publishing	97	1.7	3.7	(16.8)	6.3	(15.8)
Chemical, petroleum	102	2.4	1.8	(14.9)	3.5	(12.0)
Primary metals	114	1.0	6.6	(34.3)	7.3	(30.8)
Fabricated metals	70	1.1	7.9	(19.1)	11.9	(21.9)
Machinery, instruments	98	6.4	12.6	(43.7)	17.9	(55.5)
Transportation equipment	95	1.4	16.3	(42.6)	20.0	(50.4)
Miscellaneous manufacturing	123	3.3	6.2	(15.4)	6.1	(15.3)
All nonmanufacturing	791	75.4	7.6	(34.2)	5.8	(37.8)
Construction	81	3.0	6.0	(27.1)	33.4	(67.9)
Transportation services	76	3.0	11.5	(49.7)	10.7	(40.6)
Communications	49	11.3	3.6	(24.0)	−8.5	(10.8)
Utilities	75	3.0	−4.0	(10.9)	−3.8	(6.2)
Wholesale trade	90	16.9	7.9	(26.3)	−4.1	(29.0)
Retail trade	60	12.3	2.8	(14.6)	−8.8	(24.4)
Finance	83	4.4	16.3	(60.1)	16.8	(47.0)
Insurance, real estate	74	2.6	5.4	(23.3)	4.8	(19.1)
Hotels	72	1.4	2.6	(15.7)	3.4	(15.5)
Business services	60	7.0	25.8	(52.2)	60.0	(56.3)
Health services	71	10.4	5.7	(13.8)	7.2	(13.8)

Note: Worker-population weights are calculated as sampling probability weights times total employment in 1994. Below the first row, worker-population weighted shares have been renormalized to sum to 100 by size or industry, as appropriate.

rience a reduction in its total "employment" even though the total number of workers performing tasks for the enterprise has not changed. The variable measuring the total value of goods and services other than labor used in production includes contracts for materials and services that have been outsourced and should help control for these situations.[3]

The decision to examine employment declines per se, as opposed to looking more generally at all changes in employment, may seem obvious given the interest in understanding the factors driving downsizing and

| | | Plants with Decreasing Employment | | | |
| | | Percentage Change in Employment | | | |
N	Share as Percentage of Worker Population	Un-weighted Mean	(Standard Deviation)	Worker-Population Weighted Mean	(Standard Deviation)
429	35.6 of at/ above capacity	−15.5	(13.9)	−18.2	(17.2)
48	2.0	−19.4	(17.4)	−15.6	(12.7)
47	5.6	−17.7	(16.5)	−13.7	(12.2)
72	5.6	−16.9	(14.5)	−15.1	(11.3)
71	11.2	−16.6	(13.8)	−38.6	(17.7)
55	11.2	−11.4	(11.0)	−11.2	(8.2)
136	64.3	−13.8	(11.7)	−16.6	(16.6)
231	15.7	−15.9	(15.0)	−14.7	(13.1)
12	1.2	−15.8	(14.8)	−16.5	(11.8)
19	1.6	−19.9	(20.9)	−22.1	(17.9)
45	1.6	−11.1	(8.9)	−16.2	(12.2)
22	0.8	−14.8	(18.8)	−12.9	(14.7)
32	1.6	−12.7	(9.5)	−12.2	(7.7)
31	0.8	−17.3	(15.6)	−12.6	(10.3)
11	0.4	−13.9	(12.7)	−10.7	(12.0)
22	5.2	−22.0	(19.6)	−13.0	(13.3)
12	0.4	−29.1	(16.4)	−23.8	(14.4)
25	2.0	−14.1	(11.4)	−13.3	(8.6)
198	84.3	−15.1	(12.4)	−18.8	(17.7)
16	1.2	−21.8	(11.9)	−15.6	(12.0)
16	1.6	−18.8	(9.8)	−16.1	(6.6)
16	29.7	−15.6	(15.9)	−10.5	(2.6)
39	6.8	−11.2	(9.3)	−5.2	(5.4)
23	20.1	−15.1	(14.2)	−28.6	(22.9)
13	12.4	−15.4	(13.0)	−35.4	(18.9)
21	2.4	−17.6	(16.2)	−22.5	(20.7)
21	1.6	−17.1	(14.4)	−18.2	(11.9)
18	0.8	−10.9	(6.0)	−10.7	(6.1)
n.a.	n.a.	n.a.	n.a.	n.a.	n.a.
13	6.8	−12.1	(7.7)	−11.5	(4.8)

(Table continues on p. 480.)

not job change more generally. But to do so we must assume that the factors driving reductions in employment are different from those that drive employment increases—that downsizing is more than just a special case of job change. If one believes that increases in jobs are explained by the same factors as decreases, then it could be difficult to argue that downsizing merits examination on its own. If, on the other hand, one believes that the factors driving downsizing are different from those behind job growth, then a separate examination of downsizing is war-

Table 13.2 *Continued*

	N	Share as Percentage of Worker Population	Plants with Increasing Employment Un-weighted Mean	(Standard Deviation)	Worker-Population Weighted Mean	(Standard Deviation)
Total	876	43.3 of at/ above capacity	23.8	(46.1)	31.8	(50.6)
By plant size						
Less than 50	112	9.2	20.2	(20.5)	21.2	(17.9)
50 to 99	127	9.9	32.3	(73.0)	30.5	(65.5)
100 to 249	177	14.9	23.1	(40.0)	20.4	(34.3)
250 to 499	178	13.2	24.4	(52.9)	34.7	(75.8)
500 to 999	94	11.9	23.9	(39.7)	20.4	(34.2)
1,000 or more	188	40.6	20.5	(33.4)	41.2	(48.0)
By industry						
All manufacturing	510	28.7	23.3	(48.3)	29.9	(65.4)
Food, tobacco	49	3.0	32.5	(90.9)	45.3	(123.5)
Textile, apparel	48	2.3	28.5	(85.6)	38.9	(104.5)
Lumber, paper	42	1.3	22.2	(33.0)	28.7	(37.4)
Printing, publishing	47	2.0	14.5	(11.6)	15.6	(11.9)
Chemical, petroleum	46	3.3	12.7	(12.7)	10.2	(9.2)
Primary metals	60	1.0	21.4	(39.8)	23.8	(37.0)
Fabricated metals	35	1.3	20.1	(18.5)	23.7	(21.8)
Machinery, instruments	52	7.3	33.0	(49.5)	43.0	(68.7)
Transportation equipment	62	2.3	30.6	(45.2)	34.5	(55.1)
Miscellaneous manufacturing	69	4.3	16.1	(10.6)	16.1	(11.7)
All nonmanufacturing	366	71.3	24.6	(42.9)	32.6	(43.2)
Construction	40	4.3	20.9	(29.8)	57.2	(76.5)
Transportation services	46	5.0	25.5	(59.2)	19.3	(45.4)
Communications	21	1.3	20.2	(24.5)	28.9	(30.9)
Utilities	16	0.3	8.6	(6.4)	8.1	(5.3)
Wholesale trade	42	14.9	25.3	(27.4)	21.5	(16.9)
Retail trade	22	7.3	16.8	(9.3)	16.1	(8.5)
Finance	40	5.9	43.2	(77.2)	37.2	(51.4)
Insurance, real estate	38	3.3	19.9	(21.0)	16.2	(14.9)
Hotels	23	1.3	16.8	(19.9)	15.4	(18.4)
Business services	38	13.9	41.6	(60.3)	71.3	(54.2)
Health services	40	14.5	14.1	(11.5)	16.4	(8.8)

ranted. The suggestion that management practices, such as those that increase fixed labor costs, have distinctive effects on downsizing points to different causes. There is also empirical evidence for that view. Studies like Davis and Haltiwanger's (1992), for example, have found that the factors driving job loss are different from those driving job creation. The analyses that follow test whether reductions in employment should be examined separately from increases in jobs.

INDEPENDENT VARIABLES

The independent variables used in the analyses are described in table 13.6. The basic model predicting job loss and downsizing includes control variables describing important aspects of establishments such as their size, age, and capital structure. Including controls for industry presumably helps control for some of the industry-specific product market conditions that drive demand-related job reductions, but excluding industry controls makes it possible to identify the effects of the sources of downsizing associated with variation across industries. Additional analyses, available on request, indicate that industry control variables are jointly insignificant predictors of both employment losses and downsizing as defined here. In virtually all cases, they are individually insignificant as well and have little substantive effect on any of the results examined by the hypotheses. They are therefore not included in the analyses presented here.

The analysis begins with variables that might capture factor price changes that create incentives to reduce the use of labor. The first of these is compensation levels. An important issue with wages is the extent to which they are above market levels, a calculation that requires standardizing for job requirements, worker characteristics, and local labor markets. The alternative used in these data is simply to ask respondents whether they believe that their establishment's compensation for each of five different occupational groups is high or low (with one level the omitted category) compared to their competitors. The associated share of the workforce accounted for by each occupation is included to differentiate the effect of having more highly compensated employees as a result of using more expensive employees such as managers.

The next set of variables examining possible substitution effects includes the presence of a union, associated with wage premiums and work rule restrictions that raise labor costs. Union contracts may contain restrictions on layoffs that raise the costs of downsizing (see, for example, Allen 1986; Rees 1989) and thus mitigate the job-cutting incentive created by higher costs. Severance pay obviously raises the costs of downsizing (Lazear 1990), as do pensions, at least some of which are defined benefit plans stipulating that the employer's obligations to vested employees do not end when employment is terminated. (Even if the pension plan is fully funded for vested employees, the employer nevertheless loses in this scenario by having to pay out pension benefits for former employees while not having their productive work and possibly needing also to replace them with new hires whose pensions must be funded. The data unfortunately do not provide information on the type of pension plan.) The presence of temporary help may also reduce the extent of downsiz-

Table 13.3 Employment Changes for All Plants, 1994 to 1997

			All Plants			
			Percentage Change in Employment			
	N	Share as Percentage of Worker Population	Un-weighted Mean	(Standard Deviation)	Worker-Population Weighted Mean	(Standard Deviation)
Total	4,125	100.0	7.0	(41.1)	13.5	(50.8)
By plant size						
Less than 50	786	15.6	4.2	(34.8)	5.9	(22.6)
50 to 99	618	13.1	6.6	(41.4)	8.4	(51.2)
100 to 249	881	19.0	9.4	(61.6)	9.2	(72.8)
250 to 499	793	13.6	7.0	(29.5)	19.5	(61.1)
500 to 999	481	12.2	10.0	(28.5)	30.7	(57.5)
1,000 or more	566	26.5	5.2	(30.6)	12.4	(26.3)
By industry						
All manufacturing	2,396	27.4	5.9	(42.7)	8.8	(62.4)
Food, tobacco	241	2.9	4.0	(18.2)	5.0	(17.2)
Textile, apparel	190	2.1	−0.2	(28.8)	1.1	(24.9)
Lumber, paper	244	2.1	2.3	(17.6)	5.5	(17.6)
Printing, publishing	212	2.0	2.2	(15.3)	−0.1	(17.6)
Chemical, petroleum	216	1.7	4.9	(46.2)	6.5	(35.5)
Primary metals	255	1.0	8.3	(30.9)	9.2	(29.9)
Fabricated metals	256	2.2	6.3	(29.3)	12.6	(28.9)
Machinery, instruments	278	6.0	11.9	(92.5)	17.1	(123.6)
Transportation equipment	223	2.3	11.9	(48.6)	6.4	(45.1)
Miscellaneous manufacturing	281	5.1	4.9	(23.9)	9.5	(18.7)
All nonmanufacturing	1,729	72.6	8.6	(38.7)	15.2	(45.6)
Construction	229	4.5	7.8	(25.6)	11.1	(25.1)
Transportation services	156	2.8	11.2	(34.2)	14.8	(29.5)
Communications	72	1.4	7.5	(25.8)	16.5	(28.4)
Utilities	145	1.3	−2.9	(21.5)	−3.0	(20.8)
Wholesale trade	176	9.6	6.9	(24.5)	16.4	(21.5)
Retail trade	144	17.9	7.2	(47.2)	7.8	(26.6)
Finance	122	4.7	11.1	(44.8)	24.3	(54.8)
Insurance, real estate	130	2.6	3.5	(23.0)	2.7	(22.8)
Hotels	172	2.0	8.3	(36.1)	7.1	(17.3)
Business services	173	12.3	24.5	(50.4)	37.3	(75.3)
Health services	210	13.4	7.1	(57.1)	7.5	(48.3)

Note: Worker-population weights are calculated as sampling probability weights times total employment in 1997. Below the first row, worker-population weighted shares have been renormalized to sum to 100 by "versus capacity," "size," or "industry," as appropriate. In contrast to 1994, the 1997 NES survey asked for the 1994 to 1997 percentage change in employment of *permanent* workers.

ing by providing a substitute for it: employers can easily reduce hours of work by cutting back on temps without having to downsize. Part-time workers may also be easier to cut than other workers because they may have a more casual relationship with the employer and fewer severance-related benefits. But because they count as part of the workforce in calculating downsizing in these data, they should be associated with increased use of downsizing.

The final set of variables relates more directly to changes in the efficiency of production functions or shifts to new production functions that use less labor. Some management practices may reduce the need for em-

		Plants with Decreasing Employment			
			Percentage Change in Employment		
N	Share as Percentage of Worker Population	Un-weighted Mean	(Standard Deviation)	Worker-Population Weighted Mean	(Standard Deviation)
903	15.1	− 20.2	(17.3)	− 19.0	(15.3)
157	13.2	− 29.4	(23.3)	− 25.0	(16.9)
130	12.6	− 21.0	(17.8)	− 21.6	(18.7)
170	20.5	− 21.7	(16.8)	− 23.3	(16.2)
182	13.9	− 16.9	(13.4)	− 15.1	(11.5)
104	10.6	− 15.0	(13.1)	− 15.3	(12.9)
160	29.1	− 15.8	(12.8)	− 15.4	(12.5)
565	35.8	− 20.2	(17.1)	− 19.5	(14.6)
51	4.0	− 14.1	(14.2)	− 12.8	(10.9)
60	3.3	− 27.2	(20.8)	− 27.6	(17.8)
58	2.0	− 17.0	(12.5)	− 17.2	(12.2)
52	4.0	− 14.5	(12.2)	− 19.4	(15.4)
73	2.6	− 15.6	(12.6)	− 14.5	(11.3)
49	1.3	− 17.6	(14.3)	− 14.8	(11.3)
50	1.3	− 28.2	(21.2)	− 27.3	(17.3)
62	7.9	− 19.2	(13.6)	− 19.5	(12.6)
48	5.3	− 27.5	(21.4)	− 23.1	(14.5)
62	3.3	− 22.4	(18.7)	− 18.0	(14.9)
338	64.2	− 20.1	(17.7)	− 18.7	(15.6)
37	3.3	− 24.7	(20.4)	− 19.6	(11.2)
25	2.6	− 24.1	(18.0)	− 20.0	(13.2)
16	1.3	− 20.8	(19.1)	− 16.8	(12.4)
64	4.6	− 15.4	(13.1)	− 14.1	(9.6)
34	6.6	− 21.9	(19.2)	− 16.9	(14.3)
28	15.2	− 22.1	(22.4)	− 23.1	(17.4)
19	3.3	− 27.2	(25.4)	− 19.6	(12.2)
40	4.0	− 18.6	(14.7)	− 27.2	(18.3)
14	1.3	− 9.6	(5.1)	− 8.5	(4.0)
19	5.3	− 29.1	(17.1)	− 15.1	(16.4)
42	15.2	− 15.4	(13.7)	− 16.1	(15.5)

(Table continues on p. 484.)

ployees. The variables measuring efforts to restructure the firm include whether the number of levels in the organizational hierarchy or chart has changed in the past three years. Flattening the organizational chart does not automatically imply a reduction in jobs, since positions are typically retitled in the process. But they may well go together, and reducing the organizational chart may also proxy other changes that eliminate jobs, such as decentralizing authority. The percentage of employees in self-managed teams, for example, reduces the need for supervisors and associated management support. Ideally, we would want to know when this practice was introduced (information that is not available), because potential reductions in employment presumably occur as a result of their introduction. There is some evidence that these practices are a relatively

Table 13.3 *Continued*

			Plants with Increasing Employment			
				Percentage Change in Employment		
	N	Share as Percentage of Worker Population	Un-weighted Mean	(Standard Deviation)	Worker-Population Weighted Mean	(Standard Deviation)
Total	1,782	53.2	26.4	(54.5)	30.7	(63.9)
By plant size						
Less than 50	269	11.5	29.3	(43.7)	23.1	(23.5)
50 to 99	262	10.2	26.1	(55.7)	27.8	(73.8)
100 to 249	415	16.5	28.8	(84.3)	28.4	(103.0)
250 to 499	359	13.2	24.0	(34.9)	42.2	(77.8)
500 to 999	239	14.8	26.6	(30.9)	50.2	(62.7)
1,000 or more	238	33.8	22.9	(38.6)	22.1	(25.8)
By industry						
All manufacturing	1,014	24.8	25.1	(58.1)	26.3	(85.6)
Food, tobacco	101	2.6	16.7	(18.8)	15.6	(17.3)
Textile, apparel	60	1.3	26.6	(27.6)	23.5	(21.1)
Lumber, paper	86	1.7	17.9	(16.6)	19.3	(15.8)
Printing, publishing	85	1.5	14.3	(13.2)	14.4	(12.4)
Chemical, petroleum	75	1.3	29.2	(70.8)	23.9	(47.8)
Primary metals	115	0.9	26.0	(37.1)	26.4	(35.9)
Fabricated metals	118	2.3	25.6	(27.7)	28.1	(28.1)
Machinery, instruments	136	5.6	33.1	(128.4)	41.3	(168.9)
Transportation equipment	114	2.1	34.8	(56.4)	30.3	(55.6)
Miscellaneous manufacturing	124	5.3	22.3	(20.8)	20.2	(16.8)
All nonmanufacturing	768	75.4	28.2	(49.3)	32.1	(54.8)
Construction	111	3.9	24.3	(23.4)	28.7	(25.7)
Transportation services	87	3.4	27.0	(36.5)	26.9	(29.3)
Communications	33	1.5	26.4	(22.3)	31.7	(26.4)
Utilities	30	0.6	18.6	(32.9)	22.9	(30.9)
Wholesale trade	83	12.2	23.7	(21.8)	26.9	(16.6)
Retail trade	50	12.4	33.0	(70.7)	29.3	(30.5)
Finance	54	5.5	34.7	(56.2)	42.9	(62.1)
Insurance, real estate	58	2.4	20.6	(20.0)	18.8	(13.9)
Hotels	62	1.5	25.1	(56.4)	20.1	(20.9)
Business services	107	17.1	44.8	(53.6)	51.8	(82.7)
Health services	93	14.7	22.9	(82.4)	17.7	(60.3)

recent innovation that is not likely to have been put in place before the 1990s (see, for example, Osterman 1994). Moreover, it may take some time for their effects to play out after they are introduced.

Other variables help capture both the incentives and opportunities to shift toward more efficient operations using less labor. Competitive strategy is measured by four questions representing Porter's (1985) generic strategies: "competing on price," "competing on innovation," and "competing by tailoring products to customer needs," with "competing on quality" as the omitted variable. Each strategy choice, as noted earlier, has been associated with distinctive employment policies. Raymond Miles and Charles Snow (1978), among others, have articulated how different employment practices are associated with different business strategies, and how those strategies create continuing incentives to change employment levels. In particular, the "competing on quality" dimension (the omitted category) is thought to require long-term, stable employment relationships, first because secure, committed workers are more likely to care about quality, and second because long tenure may be required to understand jobs and products well enough to improve quality continuously. The "competing on price" dimension requires low cost, thus creating incentives to cut jobs and costs where possible. "Competing on innovative products" and "tailoring products to specific customer needs," the other two dimensions, have a somewhat more ambiguous relationship with downsizing. They may demand flexibility that requires firms to restructure, possibly shedding workers in the process. Innovative firms in particular may find better methods that use less labor.

Total quality management (TQM) programs involve employees and the entire organization in problem-solving exercises designed to reveal opportunities for improvements in quality and efficiency. Most of the formal TQM programs require that employees be protected from any layoffs that new efficiencies might produce (see, for example, Walton 1986), even though the process may well reveal opportunities for cutting jobs. Whether the establishment has a research and development (R&D) function and, if so, how important it is to the organization may indicate something about the level of continuing technological innovation in the establishment. Innovation may suggest a greater use of new methods and efficiencies. But establishments with important R&D priorities may also be ones where seeking cost-efficiencies in production is less important than other goals. The use of computers may proxy the extent to which the establishment is involved in substituting capital for labor. Again, it would be useful to know about the introduction of computers as well as the level of use. As with the self-managed team variable cited earlier, computer use may also reduce the need for labor not only after it was introduced but for some time thereafter.

Variables measuring the compensation structure for managers and employees help capture the employers' incentives to make improvements in efficiency that might lead to reductions in employment. Extending stock options to managers, for example, creates incentives for them to act like stockholders—cutting costs, including excess employees, in order to increase the value of their shares. Profit-sharing may do something similar, especially for managers who can make decisions about the use of labor. Profit-sharing for other employee groups may be associated with participative programs that empower employees, creating both the incentive and the ability to reduce jobs (possibly through attrition) in order to increase profits. Variables measure whether the establishment offers stock options and profit-sharing, the latter measured for each of the five occupational categories. Here again, it would be interesting to have data on

Table 13.4   1994 to 1997 Employment Changes for All NES Panel Plants

		All Plants				
			Mean Change in Employment			
		Share as Percentage of Worker Population	Unweighted Mean	(Standard Deviation)	Worker-Population Weighted Mean	(Standard Deviation)
	N					
Total	842	100.0	3.6	(27.2)	6.8	(22.2)
By operating level versus capacity in 1994						
Below	303	40.1	1.0	(21.6)	4.0	(20.2)
At	462	49.9	4.7	(31.4)	8.7	(24.9)
Above	77	9.9	7.3	(17.2)	8.3	(12.2)
By plant size						
Less than 50	114	16.8	0.5	(21.4)	3.3	(11.5)
50 to 99	125	11.7	6.5	(21.8)	12.7	(24.0)
100 to 249	174	21.1	6.4	(45.3)	3.7	(32.7)
250 to 499	150	16.6	1.3	(16.9)	6.6	(15.8)
500 to 999	113	13.9	4.5	(20.9)	9.2	(18.9)
1,000 or more	166	19.9	2.1	(19.0)	8.0	(19.8)
By industry						
All manufacturing	593	45.9	2.6	(29.2)	6.9	(27.2)
Food, tobacco	55	4.5	2.2	(18.7)	4.1	(15.3)
Textile, apparel	37	2.6	−1.6	(25.7)	2.4	(24.6)
Lumber, paper	88	4.0	−0.5	(13.7)	3.7	(13.3)
Printing, publishing	51	3.1	−0.5	(15.3)	−1.2	(15.1)
Chemical, petroleum	51	3.2	2.7	(20.3)	9.1	(17.8)
Primary metals	73	2.0	3.0	(16.9)	1.2	(15.3)
Fabricated metals	53	2.8	−0.5	(21.7)	3.6	(15.6)
Machinery, instruments	55	9.9	4.2	(25.1)	7.3	(28.9)
Transportation equipment	59	3.3	13.3	(70.6)	14.7	(70.4)
Miscellaneous manufacturing	71	10.7	3.0	(22.5)	11.0	(15.1)
All nonmanufacturing	249	54.1	5.9	(21.6)	6.7	(16.9)
Construction	50	6.7	8.1	(23.5)	15.0	(22.9)
Transportation services	23	3.0	7.0	(14.7)	10.8	(17.0)
Communications	12	1.2	−1.1	(20.5)	8.7	(21.7)
Utilities	32	1.6	−0.6	(11.2)	0.5	(12.5)
Wholesale trade	28	6.9	2.5	(17.1)	0.1	(11.8)
Retail trade	14	13.6	−4.3	(11.4)	−2.8	(12.2)
Finance	12	1.8	17.8	(46.6)	4.8	(11.8)
Insurance, real estate	15	1.7	3.1	(22.0)	3.4	(10.9)
Hotels	21	1.7	5.8	(9.4)	6.4	(9.1)
Business services	21	6.9	18.6	(31.8)	19.3	(16.2)
Health services	21	8.8	7.9	(13.1)	10.7	(12.7)

Note: Worker-population weights are calculated as sampling probability weight times 1997 employment.

the introduction of these practices; that information is unfortunately not available. But these practices clearly create incentives to seek efficiencies in the use of labor that continue as long as they are in place.

We can better understand the strengths and limitations of the data used in this analysis by looking at table 13.7, which outlines the sources and time periods of that data.

Job losses are measured over a period of time; the other variables, especially operating capacity, are measured only at a point in time.[4] It is arguably better to have the measure of operating capacity at the begin-

| | | Plants with Decreasing Employment | | | |
| | | Mean Change in Employment | | | |
N	Share as Percentage of Worker Population	Un-weighted Mean	(Standard Deviation)	Worker-Population Weighted Mean	(Standard Deviation)
218	17.4	−17.7	(14.9)	−16.6	(12.7)
89	52.3	−20.5	(16.1)	−19.1	(13.6)
114	43.1	−16.2	(13.9)	−14.3	(11.1)
15	5.2	−12.5	(12.8)	−9.7	(8.6)
27	8.0	−21.8	(19.9)	−16.9	(15.0)
25	10.3	−16.7	(14.6)	−11.6	(6.9)
40	23.0	−20.7	(13.9)	−24.7	(14.4)
45	18.4	−16.4	(14.8)	−14.4	(11.1)
27	14.9	−17.8	(17.7)	−13.1	(12.8)
54	25.3	−15.0	(10.9)	−14.7	(9.1)
171	55.7	−17.9	(15.1)	−17.0	(12.7)
13	4.6	−16.0	(12.3)	−15.5	(10.2)
14	4.6	−25.1	(16.9)	−23.7	(14.3)
26	4.6	−14.4	(11.5)	−12.0	(8.4)
18	6.3	−13.8	(8.3)	−15.8	(8.7)
20	2.9	−13.0	(7.3)	−12.5	(6.1)
17	3.4	−15.9	(12.4)	−15.0	(9.6)
16	2.9	−23.5	(21.7)	−19.2	(12.2)
16	16.7	−19.7	(15.7)	−17.6	(13.3)
15	5.7	−17.2	(13.6)	−16.6	(12.0)
16	4.0	−25.2	(24.0)	−19.4	(20.5)
47	44.3	−16.9	(14.4)	−16.1	(12.6)
6	1.1	−27.7	(24.1)	−24.2	(17.5)
n.a.	n.a.	n.a.	n.a.	n.a.	n.a.
5	2.3	−19.1	(11.7)	−16.1	(9.7)
10	4.0	−12.1	(9.3)	−9.9	(6.4)
6	10.9	−17.0	(17.3)	−12.9	(8.2)
5	16.1	−14.1	(14.7)	−20.6	(15.9)
n.a.	n.a.	n.a.	n.a.	n.a.	n.a.
5	1.7	−14.6	(11.8)	−10.1	(10.0)
0	—	—	—	—	—
n.a.	n.a.	n.a.	n.a.	n.a.	n.a.
n.a.	n.a.	n.a.	n.a.	n.a.	n.a.

(Table continues on p. 488.)

ning of the period over which job loss is measured rather than at the end. It is certainly possible that the characteristics measured by the independent variables were the same at the end of the period measuring employment changes as at the beginning. But the causal relationship is obviously easier to establish if the independent variables precede the dependent variables in time.[5] Particularly with the capacity measure, the ideal situation might be to have measures of capacity throughout the period and measures of job reductions in each period as well. Similar arguments could be made about relationships with the other independent variables

Table 13.4 *Continued*

		Plants with Increasing Employment				
				Mean Change in Employment		
		Share as Percentage of Worker Population	Un-weighted Mean	(Standard Deviation)	Worker-Population Weighted Mean	(Standard Deviation)
	N					
Total	339	50.0	20.3	(33.3)	19.3	(23.5)
By operating level versus capacity in 1994						
Below	110	32.6	19.3	(19.0)	20.6	(17.9)
At	188	54.0	21.4	(41.8)	20.0	(28.1)
Above	41	13.4	18.3	(14.4)	13.5	(10.9)
By plant size						
Less than 50	31	11.0	20.9	(22.4)	14.4	(9.7)
50 to 99	58	13.4	21.3	(21.2)	25.1	(24.5)
100 to 249	74	16.0	26.2	(62.7)	22.2	(44.3)
250 to 499	64	19.6	14.5	(11.2)	16.0	(11.5)
500 to 999	52	17.0	18.9	(17.6)	19.0	(16.2)
1,000 or more	60	23.2	19.3	(18.3)	19.3	(17.2)
By industry						
All manufacturing	225	48.0	20.5	(37.8)	20.0	(30.3)
Food, tobacco	20	4.8	16.6	(21.2)	12.7	(14.0)
Textile, apparel	11	2.0	26.6	(18.9)	26.2	(17.2)
Lumber, paper	26	3.0	12.7	(11.7)	15.9	(11.9)
Printing, publishing	13	1.6	17.3	(16.3)	16.7	(11.6)
Chemical, petroleum	18	3.8	22.2	(21.4)	18.2	(16.2)
Primary metals	32	1.6	15.4	(15.1)	13.4	(12.9)
Fabricated metals	21	2.4	16.6	(11.7)	16.1	(10.8)
Machinery, instruments	25	9.8	21.9	(23.4)	25.0	(29.3)
Transportation equipment	26	3.2	40.0	(100.1)	39.5	(92.4)
Miscellaneous manufacturing	33	15.4	18.6	(13.7)	17.2	(10.7)
All nonmanufacturing	114	52.0	19.9	(22.2)	18.6	(14.7)
Construction	28	8.2	20.4	(20.4)	26.1	(22.5)
Transportation services	12	3.0	16.7	(13.2)	22.6	(15.5)
Communications	4	1.2	20.6	(14.0)	27.2	(9.9)
Utilities	11	1.4	9.3	(8.4)	11.6	(10.2)
Wholesale trade	10	4.2	17.2	(14.5)	11.9	(10.8)
Retail trade	n.a.	n.a.	n.a.	n.a.	n.a.	n.a.
Finance	5	1.0	45.8	(65.3)	22.8	(6.2)
Insurance, real estate	5	1.2	23.8	(24.7)	14.0	(6.7)
Hotels	9	1.8	13.5	(10.1)	12.5	(9.3)
Business services	14	11.2	33.5	(26.2)	25.4	(10.6)
Health services	15	14.8	13.3	(11.1)	13.7	(11.5)

in that they should be measured at the beginning of the period, not the end, in order to assess their effects on subsequent job loss. These arguments suggest that the best design is to relate 1994 practices as measured by the NES to reductions in employment and downsizing from 1994 to 1997. Again, the downsizing variable is created by measuring job loss over that period and operating capacity at the beginning of the period, in 1994. For comparison purposes and robustness, I also present the results of an analysis using the 1994 independent variables to predict employment losses and downsizing from 1991 to 1994, recognizing the conceptual limitations of that design.

To summarize, I examine the factors associated with substitution within and shifts in the efficiency of production functions for job losses and for downsizing where the latter is defined as job cuts not driven by shortfalls in product demand. Because both job losses and downsizing are measured as reductions in employment, negative coefficients suggest direct relationships with the dependent variables (increased job losses and downsizing) and positive coefficients suggest inverse relationships. That is, negative coefficients imply that increases in the independent variables are associated with larger downsizing or employment losses. Relationships indicated with $\pm$ are ambiguous with respect to the predictions:

$$\begin{aligned}
\text{Job Losses and Downsizing} &= a + b_i(\text{Controls}) - b_j \\
(\text{Compensation and Occupational Shares}) &- b_1(\text{Union}) + \\
b_2(\text{Severance}) - b_3(\text{Pensions}) &+ b_4(\text{Percentage of Temporary} \\
\text{Workers}) - b_5(\text{Percentage of Part-time Workers}) \\
- b_6(\text{Management Levels Down}) &+ b_7(\text{Management Levels Up}) \\
- b_8(\text{Compete on Price}) &\pm b_9(\text{Compete on Innovation}) \\
\pm b_{10}(\text{Compete on Needs}) - b_{11}(\text{TQM}) &\pm b_{12}(\text{R\&D}) \\
- b_{13}(\text{Stock Options}) - b_{14}(\text{Profit-Sharing}) &+ e
\end{aligned}$$

There are many variables in the estimating equation because several proxy the same concept. Fourteen of the variables, for example, proxy different aspects of the same concept, the relative price of labor.

DOWNSIZING AND PERFORMANCE

These data are also ideal for examining the relationship between downsizing and establishment performance. The ability to differentiate downsizing from layoffs associated with shortfalls in demand provides the opportunity to address the selection bias issue that nags all of the prior research on downsizing. Are the firms that are laying off workers doing so because they are experiencing shortfalls in demand that would eventually lead to financial declines?

The conceptual issue behind studies of layoffs, downsizing, and performance is straightforward. First, are any reductions in associated labor costs offset by increases in other costs? Second, are any net cost reductions offset by declines in business and sales that might be caused by the cuts? If the answer to both of these questions is no, then performance improves. If both questions are answered yes, then performance declines. If the answers are mixed, then it is an empirical question. Profit data are useful for addressing this issue but are not available here because they come from establishments that are often a part of larger firms and not accountable for profit and loss themselves. Total sales per employee and labor costs per employee may offer something equivalent, especially after

Table 13.5   Employment Changes of Plants At or Above Capacity in 1994
              and 1994 to 1997

| | | | All Plants | | | |
| | | | | Mean Change in Employment | | |
	N	Share as Percentage of Worker Population	Un-weighted Mean	(Standard Deviation)	Worker-Population Weighted Mean	(Standard Deviation)
Total, at or above capacity	539	59.9 of all	5.1	(29.8)	8.6	(23.3)
By plant size						
Less than 50	59	17.9	3.9	(23.0)	5.8	(11.6)
50 to 99	76	13.2	6.2	(17.3)	11.6	(19.2)
100 to 249	100	16.2	10.6	(56.9)	11.1	(42.3)
250 to 499	99	15.4	1.6	(17.6)	5.2	(13.1)
500 to 999	80	17.2	4.8	(15.8)	8.8	(16.2)
1,000 or more	125	19.9	3.4	(19.8)	9.6	(22.4)
By industry						
All manufacturing	393	47.7	3.7	(32.4)	7.4	(29.8)
Food, tobacco	42	6.3	4.7	(20.1)	6.1	(15.3)
Textile, apparel	29	3.7	0.2	(24.5)	3.3	(21.7)
Lumber, paper	65	4.3	−1.8	(14.3)	3.0	(14.2)
Printing, publishing	32	3.0	0.3	(15.8)	−2.1	(14.1)
Chemical, petroleum	30	3.5	2.1	(15.3)	9.3	(11.8)
Primary metals	54	2.7	1.7	(17.1)	0.6	(14.6)
Fabricated metals	22	1.7	6.6	(12.0)	8.0	(11.9)
Machinery, instruments	32	10.7	7	(20.0)	8.9	(24.3)
Transportation equipment	40	3.7	18.9	(85.0)	23.5	(83.4)
Miscellaneous manufacturing	47	8.0	2.1	(23.7)	8.3	(19.0)
All nonmanufacturing	146	52.3	8.6	(20.9)	9.7	(14.9)
Construction	26	7.5	9.4	(16.3)	14.4	(20.9)
Transportation services	15	3.5	7.7	(16.0)	12.7	(18.8)
Communications	6	1.2	11	(17.4)	22.9	(15.2)
Utilities	18	1.3	1.5	(11.1)	4.6	(14.2)
Wholesale trade	15	6.0	4.5	(11.5)	4.3	(10.2)
Retail trade	7	8.7	−0.8	(6.1)	2.7	(6.7)
Finance	10	2.3	22.9	(49.8)	7.6	(11.3)
Insurance, real estate	11	2.0	2.5	(25.5)	2.1	(11.3)
Hotels	11	1.7	7.6	(9.9)	10.2	(10.1)
Business services	11	5.3	22	(29.3)	17.1	(14.0)
Health services	16	12.5	10.4	(12.9)	11.1	(13.2)

Note: Worker-population weights are calculated as sampling probability weight times 1997 employment.

controlling for industry and establishment size. Labor costs per employee provide some indication of whether labor costs are falling as a result of downsizing (controlling for other material costs), and sales per employee address the question of whether business is suffering. Job cuts when establishments are experiencing excess capacity should improve sales per employee because employers can easily cut employees—and capacity—without affecting existing sales. The relationship with downsizing—that is, when the establishment is operating at or above capacity—is less obvious because these cuts must be designed very carefully to avoid affecting production

		Plants with Decreasing Employment			
			Mean Change in Employment		
N	Share as Percentage of Worker Population	Un-weighted Mean	(Standard Deviation)	Worker-Population Weighted Mean	(Standard Deviation)
129	13.9 of at/ above capacity	− 15.8	(13.8)	− 13.9	(11.0)
13	7.2	− 18.7	(21.2)	− 16.1	(14.9)
12	14.5	− 16.2	(12.2)	− 10.8	(6.7)
21	15.7	− 16.8	(11.5)	− 14.0	(9.7)
29	15.7	− 16.8	(16.3)	− 14.5	(15.3)
17	19.3	− 13.5	(11.6)	− 13.5	(9.9)
37	28.9	− 14.3	(11.3)	− 14.6	(9.6)
110	67.5	− 16.4	(14.5)	− 15.8	(12.3)
8	6.0	− 15.8	(14.8)	− 14.9	(11.2)
11	7.2	− 21.3	(14.9)	− 20.0	(11.2)
22	7.2	− 14.9	(12.3)	− 12.0	(9.1)
12	8.4	− 12.0	(9.1)	− 14.0	(10.0)
11	3.6	− 13.3	(7.2)	− 12.8	(4.7)
13	4.8	− 16.6	(14.0)	− 14.7	(10.8)
4	1.2	− 5.6	(2.1)	− 6.3	(2.0)
6	15.7	− 17.4	(7.2)	− 17.7	(7.0)
11	6.0	− 17.0	(15.2)	− 12.7	(15.3)
12	6.0	− 24.5	(26.2)	− 21.2	(23.1)
19	32.5	− 12.3	(8.0)	− 10.0	(5.9)
n.a.	n.a.	n.a.	n.a.	n.a.	n.a.
n.a.	n.a.	n.a.	n.a.	n.a.	n.a.
n.a.	n.a.	n.a.	n.a.	n.a.	n.a.
n.a.	n.a.	n.a.	n.a.	n.a.	n.a.
n.a.	n.a.	n.a.	n.a.	n.a.	n.a.
n.a.	n.a.	n.a.	n.a.	n.a.	n.a.
0	—	—	—	—	—
4	2.4	− 17.3	11.8	− 13.1	10.9
0	—	—	—	—	—
n.a.	n.a.	n.a.	n.a.	n.a.	n.a.
n.a.	n.a.	n.a.	n.a.	n.a.	n.a.

(Table continues on p. 492.)

and sales. Labor costs per employee may fall with job losses and downsizing if more expensive labor is cut. But if less senior and less expensive labor is cut first, as in seniority-based arrangements, then labor costs per employee may rise. (If wages equal productivity, of course, then cost per unit of output does not necessarily rise even if costs per worker rise.)[6]

The relationships examined later in the chapter include job loss and downsizing from 1994 to 1997 and financial performance in 1997. For comparison purposes, job loss and downsizing are also measured from 1991 to 1994 and related to performance in 1994, with the caveat noted earlier that the downsizing measure in this period is flawed because the

Table 13.5   *Continued*

| | | | Plants with Increasing Employment | | | |
| | | | | Mean Change in Employment | | |
	N	Share as Percentage of Worker Population	Un-weighted Mean	(Standard Deviation)	Worker-Population Weighted Mean	(Standard Deviation)
Total, at or above capacity	229	56.3 of at/ above capacity	20.8	(38.4)	18.7	(25.8)
By plant size						
Less than 50	21	26.7	22.5	(23.5)	14.3	(9.5)
50 to 99	36	25.1	18.5	(15.4)	22.5	(17.6)
100 to 249	43	26.2	32.8	(81.3)	25.7	(55.4)
250 to 499	45	31.0	14.3	(11.5)	11.3	(9.4)
500 to 999	38	35.3	16.2	(13.2)	17.1	(13.2)
1,000 or more	46	35.8	20.8	(19.9)	22.2	(21.2)
By industry						
All manufacturing	153	79.1	21.4	(44.1)	20.2	(35.5)
Food, tobacco	19	12.8	17.1	(21.6)	12.8	(14.1)
Textile, apparel	9	4.3	26.6	(19.8)	24.0	(17.4)
Lumber, paper	18	4.8	11.6	(12.7)	16.2	(13.3)
Printing, publishing	8	2.1	19.2	(17.8)	15.2	(13.7)
Chemical, petroleum	12	8.0	17.4	(8.6)	14.8	(7.2)
Primary metals	21	3.2	14.7	(16.0)	12.0	(12.3)
Fabricated metals	10	2.7	16.9	(10.6)	17.7	(9.5)
Machinery, instruments	17	20.3	19.3	(18.6)	20.8	(23.9)
Transportation equipment	19	7.0	49.5	(116.3)	45.0	(102.9)
Miscellaneous manufacturing	20	13.4	19.6	(13.7)	20.4	(14.3)
All nonmanufacturing	76	101.1	19.7	(23.3)	17.5	(14.0)
Construction	16	14.4	16.9	(15.7)	24.8	(20.8)
Transportation services	8	6.4	17.5	(15.6)	23.9	(16.8)
Communications	n.a.	n.a.	n.a.	n.a.	n.a.	n.a.
Utilities	7	2.1	10.7	(10.3)	16.5	(11.5)
Wholesale trade	5	7.5	17.2	(10.9)	13.4	(10.8)
Retail trade	n.a.	n.a.	n.a.	n.a.	n.a.	n.a.
Finance	5	2.7	45.8	(65.3)	22.8	(6.2)
Insurance, real estate	n.a.	n.a.	n.a.	n.a.	n.a.	n.a.
Hotels	6	3.7	13.9	(9.6)	14.3	(9.1)
Business services	9	15.0	28.4	(28.6)	20.8	(10.9)
Health services	13	33.7	13.6	(12.0)	14.1	(12.4)

capacity measure used to define it is available only at the end of the period (1994) and not at the beginning.

RESULTS

Table 13.8 reports the results of tobit estimation techniques for explaining job loss and downsizing. It uses the log value of the dependent variables to address outliers in the values: change in employment is expressed in percentage terms (I take the log of the absolute value of the percentage change and then add the sign), and small establishments in particular sometimes have big percentage increases in jobs. The log form of the variable results in better overall fit, including larger t-statistics, although the qualitative findings are the same as those obtained from using the non-log form (results available on request). Again, because the downsizing variable is measured as a reduction in employment, negative coefficients suggest direct relationships with job loss and downsizing.

Table 13.8 begins with the panel results comparing the relationship between 1994 variables and 1994 to 1997 job losses and downsizing. The results are presented first for the variables associated with factor substitution, and then the variables associated with changes in the efficiency parameter are added. The panel data begin with a sample of nine hundred and decline sharply as establishments are deleted because information on them is missing (to keep the sample being used consistent across estimates) or because they are operating below capacity, owing to the downsizing restriction. Given that the initial survey was skewed toward manufacturing and away from nonmanufacturing, the remaining sample of nonmanufacturing establishments is too small to estimate for them separately (and for two of the compensation variables for manufacturing) the model outlined earlier. Analyses with subsets of the model indicate that the relationships are significantly different for the manufacturing and nonmanufacturing samples, making it inappropriate to pool them (see table 13.9). The results for the 1994 to 1997 panel therefore are presented only for manufacturing.

In general, the results suggest that management practices, broadly defined, do help explain job loss and downsizing, but not always in the directions anticipated. Among the factor price variables, unionization serves to increase downsizing, but severance pay seems to as well, suggesting that companies introduce severance pay in anticipation of job cuts, possibly under pressure from employees. The compensation and occupational share variables suggest no simple relationship with downsizing: establishments with higher-paid technicians and clerical employees actually downsize less than do those with lower-paid production workers. Those with a higher proportion of managers downsize more, and those with a higher proportion of production workers downsize less, consistent with the effort to move toward a "flatter" organizational structure. The compensation variables are jointly significant ($F = 2.15$ Prob $> F = .04$), as are the occupational share variables ($F = 2.75$ Prob $> F = .02$). Greater use of temporary help does seem to substitute somewhat for downsizing of permanent employees, and greater use of part-time workers has the opposite effect, as expected, because they count as part of the establishment's workforce in calculating job loss and downsizing numbers.

In terms of the variables associated with shifts in efficiency parameters, reductions in management levels are associated with increased

(Text continues on p. 495.)

Table 13.6 Variable Definitions

Variable	Year(s) Available	Definition
Operating level versus capacity		
Above capacity	1994	Dummy variable = 1 if operating above capacity in 1994; else = 0
At capacity	1994	Dummy variable = 1 if operating at or near capacity in 1994; else = 0
Below capacity	1994	Dummy variable = 1 if operating below capacity in 1994; else = 0
At + above capacity	1994	Dummy variable = 1 operating at or above capacity in 1994; else = 0
Three-year, retrospective percentage changes in employment		
Emp Chg Index 1997	1997	= −1 if "permanent employment at [the] establishment" decreased; 0 if unchanged; +1 if increased (1994 to 1997)
Emp Chg Index 1994	1994	= −1 if "employment at [the] establishment" decreased; 0 if unchanged; +1 if increased (1991 to 1994)
Emp Dn Dum (year)	1994, 1997	Dummy variable = 1 if Emp Chg Index (year) = −1; else = 0
Percent Emp Chg 1997	1997	The "percentage or amount [converted to percentage of implied total 1994 permanent employment] by which employment increased [>0], decreased [<0] over the last 3 years"; or = 0 if establishment reported employment "unchanged" (1994 to 1997)
Percent Emp Chg 1994	1994	The "percentage by which employment increased [>0], decreased [<0] over the last 3 years"; or = 0 if establishment reported employment "unchanged" (1991 to 1994)
Percent Job Loss (year)	1994, 1997	Censored percent change in employment = Emp Dn Dum (year) × percent Emp Chg (year) (note that the potential range of this variable is thus −100 to 0)
Percent Downsize (year)	1994, 1997	Downsizing (as defined here) = At + Above Capacity (1994) × percent Job Loss (year)
Establishment characteristics		
Manufact	1994, 1997	Dummy variable = 1 if primary product SIC is in manufacturing category; else = 0

Variable	Year	Description
Multi Estab	1994, 1997	Dummy variable = 1 if establishment is part of a multi-establishment firm; = 0 if single-establishment firm
Estab Age (ln)	1994	log [1995 − "Year [establishment] began operation at this location" (from 1994 survey)]
R&D_center	1994	Dummy variable = 1 if "at this or any other location in your company there is a research and development center for new products or processes in your line of business"; else = 0
R&D_priority	1994	Dummy variable = 1 if "in-house research and development" is "very important" "for your location's business"; = 0 if "somewhat important" or "not at all"
TOTEMP	1994	Maximum of (1) "total workers on [establishment's] payroll," and (2) the sum of the responses to the following three-part follow-up question: "Of those workers, how many are full-time, . . . part-time, . . . temporary or contract?"
TOTEMP	1997	Sum of reported quantities of "permanent full-time," "permanent part-time," "establishment's [own] temporary," and on-site but off-payroll "leased, temporary agency, or contract" workers
SALES	1994, 1997	Previous year's total sales or value of shipments (in thousands of dollars)
MATER	1994, 1997	"Total cost of goods and services used in the production of your [last year's] sales" (in thousands of dollars)
CAPINV	1994, 1997	Responses to question: "In [last year], how much did your establishment spend on new equipment?" (in thousands of dollars)
BKCAP	1994, 1997	Responses to question: "At the end of calendar year [last year], what was the total book value of the fixed capital stock in your establishment (for example, buildings, equipment, furniture, vehicles, etc.)?" (in thousands of dollars)
Tot Empl (ln)	1994, 1997	log [TOTEMP]
Bkcap/Wkr (ln)	1994, 1997	log [(BKCA/TOTEMP) + .1]
Mater/Wkr (ln)	1994, 1997	log [(MATER/TOTEMP) + .01]
CapInv/Wkr (ln)	1994, 1997	log [(CAPINV/TOTEMP) + .01]
ADD_VAL/WKR	1994, 1997	(SALES - MATER)/TOTEMP
AddVal/Wkr (ln)	1994, 1997	Sign(ADD_VAL/WKR) × log[abs(ADD_VAL/WKR) + 1]

(Table continues on p. 496.)

Table 13.6 *Continued*

Variable	Year(s) Available	Definition
% Capital < 1yr	1994, 1997	Percent of BKCAP less than one year old
% Capital_1–4yr	1994, 1997	Percent of BKCAP aged one to four years
% Capital_5–10yr	1994, 1997	Percent of BKCAP aged five to ten years
Establishment performance		
Sales/Wkr (ln)	1994, 1997	$\log[(\text{SALES}/\text{TOTEMP}) + .1]$
% Labor Cost	1994	Response to question: "What were your total labor costs in 1993 as a percentage of the total cost of producing your 1993 sales?" (1994 survey)
EST_LAB_COST	1994	Calculated estimate of 1993 labor costs (in thousands of dollars): $=$ (% Labor Cost/100) $\times \{(\text{MATER} + \text{CAPINV})/[1 - (\% \text{ Labor Cost}/100)]\}$
Unit Lab Cost 1994	1994	EST_LAB_COST/SALES_94
TOT_LAB_COST	1997	"Total labor cost used in the production of 1996 sales" (in thousands of dollars)
Labor Cost (ln)	1997	$\log[\text{TOT\_LAB\_COST} + .01]$
Unit Lab Cost 1997	1997	TOT_LAB_COST/SALES_97
Compensation Levels Controls[a]		
% Mgt	1994, 1997	Percentage of employees (of "permanent employees") in 1997 who are managers or professionals
% Sup	1994, 1997	As above, for supervisors
% Tech	1994, 1997	As above, for technical or technical support workers
% Ofc	1994, 1997	As above, for office, clerical, sales, or customer service workers
Comp Mgt Hi	1994	Dummy variable $= 1$ if managers' and professionals' compensation is "above average" as "compare[d] to the wages paid by other employers for similar workers"; else $= 0$
Comp Sup Hi	1994	As above, for supervisors
Comp Tec Hi	1994	As above, for technical or technical support workers
Comp Ofc Hi	1994	As above, for office, clerical, sales, or customer service workers

Comp Prd Hi	1994	As above, for production workers
Comp Mgt Lo	1994	Dummy variable = 1 if managers' and professionals' compensation is "below average" as "compare[d] to the wages paid by other employers for similar workers"; else = 0
Comp Sup Lo	1994	As above, for supervisors
Comp Tec Lo	1994	As above, for technical or technical support workers
Comp Ofc Lo	1994	As above, for office, clerical, sales, or customer service workers
Comp Prd Lo	1994	As above, for production workers
Avg Yrs Educ	1994, 1997	"Average number of years of completed schooling" of the establishment's employees ("permanent" employees in 1997) by the five occupation categories (as above), averaged across those occupations

Workforce characteristics

Union	1994, 1997	Dummy variable = 1 if "any of [establishment's] employees are represented by a union or unions"
% Part-time	1994, 1997	Number of employees at the end of the last year who were part-time ("permanent part-time" in 1997), divided by TOTEMP, times 100
% Temp_94	1994	Number of "employees on [establishment's] payroll at the end of 1993 who were . . . temporary or contract workers," divided by TOTEMP_94, times 100
% Temp_97	1997	[Number of "contract, leased, or temporary agency workers [establishment] had in 1996" plus the number of "temporary or seasonal workers on [establishment's] payroll" at the end of 1996], divided by TOTEMP_97, times 100
% Cpt Use Mgt	1994, 1997	Percentage of "managers and supervisors using computers in their jobs"
% Cpt Use Wkr	1994, 1997	Percentage of "production and nonsupervisory employees using computers in their jobs"

Work practices organization[b]

Severance	1994, 1997	Dummy variable = 1 if establishment "employees are covered by" (1994) or "contribute toward" (1997) a "severance plan"
Pension	1994, 1997	As above, for "pension plan"
Stock Options	1994, 1997	As above, for "stock options"

(Table continues on p. 498.)

Table 13.6 *Continued*

Variable	Year(s) Available	Definition
Mgt Levs Up	1994	Dummy variable = 1 if "over [1991 to 1994] the number of levels between a first-line supervisor and the top official in your establishment" has increased; else = 0
Mgt Levs Dn	1994	As above, for "decreased"
% Self Mng Teams		
Compete Innov[c]	1994	Dummy variable = 1 if, of four "factors" provided, "innovative products" is "the most important way [establishment] competes in its product market"
Compete Needs	1994	As above, for "tailoring products to specific customers' needs"
Compete Price	1994	As above, for "price"
TQM	1994	Dummy variable = 1 if establishment "has adopted a formal Total Quality Management program"; else = 0
ProfitSh Mgt	1994	Dummy variable = 1 if establishment's "company [has] a profit-sharing, bonus, or gain-sharing plan for . . . managers"
ProfitSh Sup	1994	As above, for "supervisors"
ProfitSh Tech	1994	As above, for "technicians"
ProfitSh Ofc	1994	As above, for "office/clerical/sales/customer service" workers
ProfitSh Prd	1994	As above, for "production" workers [asked of manufacturing establishments] or "sales/customer service/front-line employees" [nonmanufacturing]

[a] Percentage "production" if manufacturing establishment or "sales/customer service/front-line" employees (if nonmanufacturing) is the left-out category.

[b] The number of management levels "has stayed the same" is the left-out category.

[c] "Overall quality" as "most important" is the left-out category.

Table 13.7   Data Sources

Variables	1994 NES— Year Measured	1997 NES II— Year Measured
Job loss	1991 to 1994	1994 to 1997
Operating capacity	1994	Not available
Independent variables and performance measures	1993 to 1994	1996 to 1997

downsizing. The strategy variables are jointly significant (F = 2.25 P > F = .08), but the results are not as expected. The strongest hypothesis is that companies competing on price would have a greater incentive to cut costs than those competing on quality. The results, however, suggest a significant relationship in the opposite direction: companies competing on price actually downsize less than those competing on quality. Perhaps the former had already done their downsizing and restructuring before the period measured here; the result is otherwise a puzzle. Both TQM and the R&D variables were associated with reduced downsizing. The profit-sharing variables tend to be among the most statistically significant set of variables, although the signs on their relationships are not always consistent. Profit-sharing for managers and technicians is associated with increased downsizing, as expected, but profit-sharing for supervisors is associated with *reduced* downsizing. Firms can choose how far down the organization to extend profit-sharing arrangements, and those that extend them to various groups may have unique incentives to do so. Perhaps profit-sharing is introduced to supervisors after restructuring efforts take place. The profit-sharing and stock option variables are jointly significant (F = 2.43 Prob > F = .03).

A comparison with the set of equations examining job losses, of which downsizing is a subset, reveals some important differences. Severance has the same relationship with job losses as with increased downsizing, but many of the other variables that predict downsizing—unions, TQM, R&D—are not significant. The strategy results are also different: competing on the basis of customer needs is associated with greater downsizing than competing based on quality. Competing on price has the expected sign but is insignificant. Together, the strategy variables are jointly significant (F = 2.53 P > .06), as are the occupational employment shares (F = 2.94 P > .02). The compensation variables are not. Although it is difficult to draw conclusions from insignificant variables, one of the most surprising findings in this equation is that the two variables measuring operating capacity, included as control variables, are neither individually nor jointly significant predictors of overall job loss in the presence of the other management practice variables.[7] Excess operating capacity has been the traditional explanation for job cuts, and the fact that it adds little to our understanding of job loss in this period is interesting.

Table 13.8 Job Loss and Downsizing, 1994 to 1997 (ln) Tobit Estimation

Variable	Job Loss		Downsizing	
	Coefficient[a] T-stat	Coefficient[b] T-stat	Coefficient[c] T-stat	Coefficient[d] T-stat
Multi Estab	−.8319	−1.855	−2.174	−2.628
	1.150	2.340	2.040	2.232
AgeEstab	.0662	.2587	.4416	1.537
	.188	.730	.877	2.560
AddedValue/wk (ln)	−.0131	−.0778	−.0348	.0142
	0.195	−1.023	.398	0.168
Capital/wk (ln)	−.0915	0.1133	−.3435	−.5677
	0.504	0.593	1.090	1.813
BookCap/wk (ln)	.2316	−0.397	.2011	−.0755
	.854	0.141	.494	.187
Total Emp (ln)	−.0391	−.184	.7795	.2002
	0.138	.588	1.678	.365
%Capital <1yr	.0208	.0359	.0026	−.02730
	0.694	1.123	.070	.790
%Capital 1–4yr	.0085	.0026	.02767	.02845
	0.532	0.158	1.269	1.385
%Capital 5–10yr	.0016	.0206	−.0002	.0035
	1.10	1.349	.012	.169
Comp Mgt Hi	.1922	−.063	−.1585	−.4189
	0.229	0.074	.156	.425
Comp Sup Hi	−1.045	−1.174	−.9095	−1.552
	1.186	1.262	.849	1.505
Comp Tec Hi	1.163	2.152	1.458	3.992
	1.379	2.480	1.280	3.204
Comp Cler Hi	−.2594	−.4531	.5474	2.390
	0.341	.544	.569	1.847
Comp Prod Hi	.0434	−.1257	.4716	.6378
	.0341	0.171	.486	.632
Comp Mgt Lo	.3429	.0635	13.381	5.614
	.189	0.029	—	—
Comp Sup Lo	−1.589	−1.337	10.734	3.038
	.776	−0.561	—	—
Comp Tec Lo	.1578	.784	.3018	3.442
	.089	0.417	.107	1.303
Comp Cler Lo	.9861	1.509	−.2198	.8239
	.544	0.697	.078	.284
Comp Prod Lo	1.288	1.509	3.295	5.409
	.955	.697	1.311	1.771
% Mgt	−.0413	−.0493	−.1521	−.1715
	1.215	1.461	2.402	2.745
% Sup	.0953	.1258	.0312	.08260
	1.543	1.863	.397	1.116

% Tec	−.0533	−.0527	−.0063	.0044
	2.10	2.168	.141	.103
% Prod	−.0048	−.007	.1377	.1817
	0.159	0.211	2.282	2.438
CPU Mgt	.0231	.0333	.0181	.0247
	2.067	2.553	1.212	1.491
CPU Non-Mgt	−.0122	−.0046	−.0125	−.0176
	1.105	0.393	.814	1.081
Union	−.9844	−.8353	−.8045	−2.345
	1.472	1.116	.872	2.042
Severance	−1.334	−1.167	−1.507	−2.176
	−1.840	1.417	1.464	−1.800
Pension	−.0855	.208	−1.385	−.0673
	.095	.214	1.100	.053
% Part-time	−.0928	−.110	−.1417	−.2229
	2.182	2.471	1.814	2.779
% Temp	.026	.0158	.0864	.0640
	1.264	.776	2.342	1.697
R&D Ctr	—	1.444	—	2.235
	—	1.500	—	1.848
R&D Priority	—	.4871	—	1.926
	—	.551	—	1.711
Mgt Levs Up	—	−1.201	—	16.46
	—	.739	—	—
Mgt Levs Dn	—	−1.769	—	−2.788
	—	2.21	—	2.447
Self Mgt	—	−.0024	—	−.0163
	—	0.199	—	1.019
Compete Innov	—	−1.096	—	−1.113
	—	0.768	—	.524
Compete Needs	—	−1.687	—	−1.388
	—	2.124	—	1.371
Compete Price	—	−.0723	—	2.143
	—	.0944	—	1.849
TQM	—	.0713	—	1.541
	—	0.109	—	1.790
Stock Opt	—	−.0247	—	.7419
	—	0.036	—	.858
Profitsh Mgt	—	−1.331	—	−4.959
	—	1.201	—	2.990
Profitsh Sup	—	1.76671	—	6.013
	—	—	—	3.086
Profitsh Tec	—	−4.672	—	−5.273
	—	2.766	—	2.689

(Table continues on p. 502.)

Table 13.8   *Continued*

	Job Loss		Downsizing	
Variable	Coefficient[a] T-stat	Coefficient[b] T-stat	Coefficient[c] T-stat	Coefficient[d] T-stat
Profitsh Cir	—	2.896836	—	2.546
	—	1.998	—	1.456
Profitsh Prd	—	.5056	—	−.1436
	—	0.485	—	.108
Above Capacity	.6881	.9989	—	—
	.618	.851	—	—
Below Capacity	−.0835	−.2343	—	—
	.113	.362	—	—
Constant	.6744	2.051	−3.112	−4.357
	.301	.809	−0.933	1.329
_se	3.200	2.841	3.0327	2.244

[a] Log likelihood = 257.446; number of observations = 247; chi-squared(11) = 8.66; prob > chi-squared = 0.653; pseudo-R^2 = 0.016. Observations summary: 65 uncensored observations; 182 right-censored observations at 1_spc_e ≥ −1.00e-06.

[b] Log likelihood = 2-3.463; number of observations = 228; chi-squared(47) = 71.29; prob > chi-squared = 0.0127; pseudo-R^2 = 0.149. Observations summary: 59 uncensored observations; 169 right-censored observations at 1_spc_e ≥ −1.00e-06.

[c] Log likelihood = 147.336; number of observations = 149; chi-squared(9) = 7.15; prob > chi-squared = 0.622; pseudo-R^2 = 0.023. Observations summary: 37 uncensored observations; 112 right-censored observations at 1_spc_e ≥ −1.00e-06.

[d] Log likelihood = 100.87; number of observations = 141; chi-squared(45) = 78.60; prob > chi-squared = 0.0014; pseudo-R^2 = 0.280. Observations summary: 34 uncensored observations; 107 right-censored observations at 1_spc_e ≥ −1.00e-06.

Despite the fact that the relationships with several of the independent variables appear to be different in the job-loss and downsizing equations, the two equations overall are not significantly different.[8] The factors that explain why establishments operating at or above capacity cut jobs appear similar to those that drive establishments with excess capacity to cut jobs. It may be tempting to conclude that downsizing as defined here is in fact no different from more traditional layoffs driven by excess demand. But it is important to remember the surprising finding that excess capacity does not predict reductions in jobs in the period 1994 to 1997. Another way to think about these results, then, is to realize that, at least in this period, all job reductions are like downsizings in that they are better explained by management practices than by excess operating capacity.

The models estimating job loss are significantly different from models estimating increases in employment (F = 24.65 P > F = .0000 for the full model, and F = 25.48 P > F = .0000 for the factor price model using the manufacturing sample on 1994 to 1997 data; F = 12.33 P > F = .0000 and F = 9.8 P > F = .0000 for the full and factor price models, respectively, and the nonmanufacturing sample).[9] Job losses do seem to be explained by characteristics different from those that explain job increases, suggesting that it is appropriate to examine them separately.

A comparison of the results for downsizing from 1991 to 1994 presented in table 13.2 suggests roughly similar results to those using the 1994 to 1997 data, despite the caveats about a temporal mismatch between the independent and dependent variables. The larger sample size these data offer makes it possible to examine relationships for manufacturing and nonmanufacturing establishments separately. The data suggest that there is less downsizing in manufacturing, where supervisors are higher-paid and production workers are low-paid, and that there is more downsizing at establishments where technicians and clerical workers are higher-paid and there are proportionately more managers. The presence of unions increases downsizing, as do reductions in management levels, and the presence of an R&D operation reduces it. In this sample, the strategy variable "competing on innovation" is associated with greater downsizing than "competing on quality." The relationships in nonmanufacturing are not as strong but broadly consistent. Two that are now significant are pensions, which are associated with reduced downsizing in nonmanufacturing, and stock ownership, which is associated with increased downsizing. As with the 1994 to 1997 results, the equations estimating relationships with job losses are significantly different from those estimating relationships with increases in employment ($F = 13.03$ $P > F = .0000$ for manufacturing, and $F = 11.15$ $P > F = .0000$ for nonmanufacturing, using the full model). But again, the overall relationships between the models estimating job loss and downsizing are not significantly different.

JOB LOSSES, DOWNSIZING, AND PERFORMANCE

Equations designed to examine the effects of downsizing on firm performance should look very much like other production function equations: with controls for industry, capital structure, and the quality of labor in the establishment (education levels, average compensation, occupational mixes). The model used includes further controls: union status, computer use, the part-time and temporary help measures described earlier, and the capacity variables to control further for the initial financial condition of the establishments.

Table 13.10 summarizes the relevant results for both job loss and downsizing for 1991 to 1994 on performance in 1994 and from 1994 to 1997 and on performance in 1997. (The complete results are available on request.) The 1994 survey asked about labor costs as a percentage of total costs, which were then converted into a measure of labor costs per employee.[10] Results for 1994 are therefore presented both for labor costs

(Text continues on p. 509.)

Table 13.9 Job Loss and Downsizing in the Manufacturing and Nonmanufacturing Sectors, 1994 to 1997 (ln) Tobit Estimation

	Job Loss							
	Manufacturing				Nonmanufacturing			
Variable	Coefficient[a]	T-stat	Coefficient[b]	T-stat	Coefficient[c]	T-stat	Coefficient[d]	T-stat
Multi Estab	−0.031357	−0.089	−0.083194	−0.243	0.265269	0.563	0.662172	1.298
Age Estab	−0.247093	−1.303	−0.002520	−0.014	−0.209118	−0.847	−0.352967	−1.356
Added Value/wk (ln)	0.035576	1.389	0.015547	0.627	0.123824	3.488	0.145052	3.765
Capital/wk (ln)	0.130488	1.767	0.071282	1.005	0.261686	2.483	0.344731	3.114
BookCap/wk (ln)	−0.195279	−1.678	−0.202638	−1.775	−0.219676	−1.676	−0.157791	−1.114
Total Emp (ln)	−0.046212	−0.322	0.033547	0.231	−0.286329	−1.71	−0.010203	−0.055
%Capital<1yr	0.010155	0.623	0.023722	1.391	−0.000935	−0.051	−0.011587	−0.585
%Capital 1–4yr	0.013564	1.603	0.003804	0.455	0.007608	0.683	−0.006267	−0.536
%Capital 5–10yr	−0.001646	−0.225	0.000040	0.006	0.002766	0.243	−0.010849	−0.908
Comp Mgt Hi	0.213598	0.466	0.020185	0.047	1.15989	1.178	0.082165	0.117
Comp Sup Hi	0.196142	0.409	0.611929	1.343	−1.26355	−2.777	0.755723	1.036
Comp Tec Hi	−0.249613	−0.57	−0.295621	−0.722	0.431667	0.662	−1.273057	−1.862
Comp Cler Hi	−0.597587	−1.528	−0.538373	−1.455	0.108602	0.161	−0.341033	−0.523
Comp Prod Hi	0.145891	0.397	0.108550	0.308	−1.09574	−1.76	0.634743	1.008
Comp Mgt Lo	−0.098970	−0.135	−0.224273	−0.31	−0.712688	−1.199	1.157015	1.128
Comp Sup Lo	−0.319402	−0.373	−0.203695	−0.248	1.388096	2.314	−1.353277	−1.195
Comp Tec Lo	0.674413	0.884	1.077295	1.415	1.255798	1.263	−0.075759	−0.075
Comp Cler Lo	−1.381938	−1.976	−1.147587	−1.692	−0.964535	−0.865	0.570419	0.595
Comp Prod Lo	0.186575	0.273	0.387234	0.563	−0.239263	−0.234	0.105972	0.085
% Mgt	−0.045597	−3.066	−0.040243	−2.77	0.227494	0.254	−0.007847	−0.467
% Sup	−0.001412	−0.051	0.015962	0.602	0.792337	0.637	0.019342	0.694
% Tec	−0.036884	−2.53	−0.026083	−1.772	−0.024681	−1.776	−0.003530	−0.303
% Prod	0.006443	0.414	0.012453	0.744	0.016759	0.653	−0.017646	−1.26
CPU Mgt	−0.006523	−1.174	−0.001848	−0.341	−0.002923	−0.258	−0.005292	−0.599

CPU Non-Mgt	−0.005036	−0.896	−0.004203	−0.767	−0.008028	−0.618	0.013223	1.739
Union	−1.154543	−3.329	−1.235366	−3.558	−0.005550	−0.689	−2.243405	−3.929
Severance	−0.535257	−1.496	−0.258977	−0.721	0.003794	0.563	−1.664101	−3.061
Pension	0.342453	0.799	0.119707	0.277	−1.958168	−3.662	0.949302	1.713
% Part-time	−0.003781	−0.184	0.005380	0.265	−1.489647	−3.023	0.004858	0.374
% Temp	−0.009166	−0.421	−0.024862	−1.213	0.594360	1.165	0.021995	1.142
R&D Ctr	—	—	0.904050	2.059	0.007440	0.652	0.095644	0.127
R&D Priority	—	—	0.495240	1.245	0.019146	1.179	−0.380472	−0.415
Mgt Levs Up	—	—	0.939143	1.168	—	—	2.172907	2.017
Mgt Levs Dn	—	—	−2.372778	−6.879	—	—	−2.044151	−3.319
Self Mgt	—	—	0.000186	0.032	—	—	0.025982	2.323
Compete Innov	—	—	−1.229287	−1.974	—	—	2.263183	0.988
Compete Needs	—	—	−0.556845	−1.52	—	—	−1.424058	−2.232
Compete Price	—	—	−0.009771	−0.027	—	—	−0.532825	−0.922
TQM	—	—	−0.187693	−0.566	—	—	−0.277283	−0.519
Stock Opt	—	—	−0.222912	−0.661	—	—	−1.264616	−1.953
Profitsh Mgt	—	—	0.039827	0.082	—	—	0.406457	0.564
Profitsh Sup	—	—	1.566988	2.099	—	—	1.170573	1.175
Profitsh Tec	—	—	−1.402133	−1.787	—	—	0.113072	0.125
Profitsh Clr	—	—	0.097031	0.145	—	—	−1.294576	−1.206
Profitsh Prd	—	—	0.305896	0.649	—	—	0.279857	0.326
Constant	5.175194	4.427	3.276442	2.818	4.415104	2.587	3.595461	2.002
Standard error	3.080119	—	2.702969		3.401191	—	3.067467	—
Multi Estab	−0.522527	−0.949	−0.494172	−0.943	−0.656537	−1.002	0.303540	0.443
Age Estab	−0.664902	−2.269	−0.365706	−1.314	−0.001569	−0.005	−0.058702	−0.159
AddedValue/wk (ln)	0.056208	1.494	0.043712	1.242	0.154610	3.392	0.178355	3.663
Capital/wk (ln)	0.07551	0.607	−0.012923	−0.111	0.101994	0.705	0.269625	1.783
BookCap/wk (ln)	−0.271829	−1.545	−0.181607	−1.047	−0.242170	−1.563	−0.297187	−1.769
Total Emp (ln)	−0.234189	−1.047	−0.081240	−0.37	−0.536343	−2.368	−0.274980	−1.017
%Capital<1yr	−0.001704	−0.073	−0.006843	−0.301	0.083922	2.317	0.051300	1.388

(Table continues on p. 506.)

Table 13.9 *Continued*

| | Downsizing | | | | | | | |
| | Manufacturing | | | | Nonmanufacturing | | | |
Variable	Coefficient[e]	T-stat	Coefficient[f]	T-stat	Coefficient[g]	T-stat	Coefficient[h]	T-stat
%Capital 1–4yr	0.006198	0.48	−0.005199	−0.407	0.008196	0.55	0.005006	0.339
%Capital 5–10yr	0.008220	0.703	0.004254	0.38	0.004441	0.294	0.004228	0.269
Comp Mgt Hi	−.3667102	−0.553	−0.360935	−0.593	0.111152	0.128	−0.284614	−0.307
Comp Sup Hi	1.547134	2.076	1.917155	2.7	0.350565	0.384	1.274682	1.249
Comp Tec Hi	−1.030128	−1.622	−1.016187	−1.752	−1.103966	−1.312	−1.308968	−1.437
Comp Cler Hi	−0.900149	−1.587	−0.852282	−1.617	−0.546354	−0.672	−0.253677	−0.281
Comp Prod Hi	0.700702	1.228	0.510412	0.962	1.603819	1.935	1.288787	1.385
Comp Mgt Lo	−1.390425	−1.118	−1.65213	−1.474	−0.282686	−0.191	0.281818	0.17
Comp Sup Lo	0.131450	0.082	0.047117	0.032	1.198725	0.683	−0.307118	−0.166
Comp Tec Lo	−0.254594	−0.195	−0.144678	−0.116	−1.768842	−1.384	−1.162086	−0.89
Comp Cler Lo	−2.313438	−2.313	−2.126267	−2.208	0.314339	0.289	1.577942	1.192
Comp Prod Lo	2.646326	2.104	2.65376	2.211	1.158832	0.619	−0.009256	−0.005
% Mgt	−0.039126	−1.769	−0.037294	−1.761	−0.004176	−0.244	0.005295	0.271
% Sup	−0.017542	−0.432	0.010605	0.286	−0.007468	−0.186	−0.011643	−0.257
% Tec	−0.034633	−1.54	0.010605	−1.537	0.015863	0.982	0.016652	0.981
% Prod	0.002204	0.1	0.009689	0.375	−0.027811	−1.639	−0.041370	−2.34
CPU Mgt	−0.012728	−1.45	−0.007533	−0.891	−0.015411	−1.245	−0.008742	−0.649
CPU Non-Mgt	−0.005796	−0.716	−0.004889	−0.637	−0.000097	−0.011	0.011506	1.121
Union	−0.896381	−1.754	−1.327329	−2.625	−2.282412	−3.195	−2.635143	−3.295
Severance	−0.453833	−0.845	−0.426665	−0.82	−1.523338	−2.338	−1.807286	−2.336
Pension	−0.143700	−0.19	0.167146	0.233	1.573734	2.116	2.122314	2.623
% Part-time	−0.010952	−0.385	−0.006769	−0.25	0.005058	0.305	−0.000718	−0.039
% Temp	0.085582	1.696	0.058731	1.249	0.043632	1.341	0.039117	1.107
R&D Ctr	—	—	1.3967	2.155	—	—	−0.662710	−0.655

that are within the control of the establishment have important relationships with both job losses and downsizing. Variables associated with factor prices, such as compensation levels, unions, and severance pay, were associated with downsizing, as were other variables that proxied incentives to pursue more efficient production functions, such as business strategy and profit-sharing. Management and employment practices seem predictive of both overall job loss and downsizing. Several of the results, however, were the opposite of what was expected. One explanation is the possibility of reverse causation: firms may adjust some practices, such as severance pay, in anticipation of job cuts.

Among the most interesting observations are those that stem from the "nonresults": the factors explaining downsizing are not as a group significantly different from those that explain overall job losses, and having excess operating capacity is not related to job losses in the presence of management practice variables. At least in the mid-1990s, when these data were collected, job reduction decisions seem not to have been dominated by factors associated with shortfalls in demand. Whether this situation represents something distinct about that period—one of economic expansion when the level of excess capacity in establishments may have been too small to drive job cuts—or something more fundamental is a question for further research.

The analysis here is distinct from prior studies in its focus on establishments and particularly in its ability to distinguish establishments that were in trouble before they cut jobs. The results are broadly consistent with the commonsense view that job cuts make more sense when establishments experience excess capacity than when they do not. Even in such situations, however, the benefits of improvements in sales per employee must overcome increases in labor costs per employee. Downsizing, defined as job cuts when operating at or above capacity, appears to hurt sales per employee. In the context of this model, it is clearer why downsizing may hurt performance: it is difficult to cut jobs without damaging organizational capabilities when there is no slack to cut. In most cases, labor costs per employee work against changes in sales per employee: when job cuts make sales per employee rise, so do labor costs per employee, and when the former fall, so do the latter. This relationship may mitigate some of the gains from cutting employees, as well as the losses, and lead to an overall moderating effect on performance outcomes.

ACKNOWLEDGMENTS

Thanks to Kevin Hallock and the participants at the Russell Sage Foundation Conference on Changes in Job Security and Job Stability for helpful comments, to Bill Carter for exceptionally diligent research assistance, and to the Center for Economic Statistics at the U.S. Bureau of the Census for its continuing help with our National Employer Survey project. The research on the National Employer Survey is supported by grants from the U.S. Department of Education Office of Educational Research and Improvement to the National Center on Post-Secondary Improvement.

NOTES

1. To illustrate ways in which downsizing may be defined inconsistently, job reductions achieved through attrition may count as downsizing in one firm, while another firm may count only terminations as downsizing. Some firms may define as downsizing the elimination of jobs in order to redeploy workers in other, growing operations, while other firms may define it as reductions in total employment.

2. For example, among the best-known employer surveys, Mark Huselid's (Huselid and Becker 1996) achieved about a one-third response rate, and Paul Osterman's (1994) survey and the National Organizational Survey (Kalleberg et al. 1996) both had about 60 percent response rates.

3. One of the difficulties with this measure is that we cannot know whether employers include all contracts in this measure, especially temporary help and leased workers. The Census Bureau is undertaking separate surveys to estimate the use of such workers.

4. A related concern is whether the time period measured here is adequate to capture the true relationship with downsizing. As noted earlier, it would be ideal to know when practices were introduced and then measure the downsizing that occurred immediately afterward. For example, perhaps some of these practices led to downsizing immediately after they were introduced so that by the time the NES II survey measured job reductions, most had already occurred. Such effects would cause an underestimate of the true relationship between practices and downsizing. On the other hand, as also noted earlier, most of the practices being examined create incentives for efficiency-based job reductions that continue as long as the practices are in effect, even though diminishing returns may eventually reduce the opportunities for continuing reductions.

5. It is certainly possible that the causation with these employment practices might be reversed. For example, firms that believe that they will be laying off employees might be less inclined to introduce severance plans because such plans would end up costing them a great deal. Even in this example, however, it is the employers' anticipation of the fact that severance payments would restrict their ability to lay off employees that drives them to adjust their use of such plans.

6. I am indebted to David Neumark for suggesting the importance of the unit cost measure.

7. These capacity variables help control for the establishment's situation when the period begins (1994). They are not included as controls in the 1991 to 1994 analysis because in that context they would be representing the situation at the end of the period, after the job cuts occurred, not at the beginning.

8. The job-loss equations were fully interacted with a variable measuring whether the establishment is at or above operating capacity, and the F-tests of the resulting interaction terms were insignificant for the full model, the factor price variables alone, and alternative specifications.

9. There are several ways to test whether equations are significantly different. Here I interact the at-and-above-capacity measure with the other variables in the model and test whether that variable and its interactions are jointly significant.

10. The calculation is done by taking the percentage of labor in total operating costs, applying it to total operating costs other than labor (materials and capital investment), and then dividing by one minus the percentage of labor in total operating costs. This procedure no doubt compounds a series of measurement errors, and the resulting variable should be examined with caution.

11. The other potential relationship to examine is with changes in practices between 1994 and 1997 and downsizing between 1994 and 1997. Such an analysis offers the possibility of examining changes in practices, but it also poses considerable problems. Specifically, not all of the independent variables are available in both periods; some (such as strategy) are not easily expressed as changes; and the number of establishments in the panel that changed practices is relatively small.

REFERENCES

Abowd, John M., George T. Milkovich, and John M. Hannon. 1990. "The Effects of Human Resource Management Decisions on Shareholder Value." *Industrial and Labor Relations Review* 43: 203–36.

Allen, Stephen. 1986. "Union Work Rules and Efficiency in the Building Trades." *Journal of Labor Economics* 4: 212–42.

American Management Association. 1996. *1996 AMA Survey on Downsizing: Summary of Key Findings.* New York: American Management Association.

Baily, Martin Neil, Eric J. Bartelsman, and John Haltiwanger. 1996. "Downsizing and Productivity Growth: Myth or Reality?" *Small Business Economics* 8(4): 259–78.

Berle, Adolf A., and Gardener Means. 1932. *The Modern Corporation.* New York: Macmillan.

Blackwell, David, Wayne W. Marr, and Michael F. Spivey. 1990. "Plant Closing Decisions and the Market Value of the Firm." *Journal of Financial Economics* 26(2): 277–88.

Boisjoly, Johanne, Greg J. Duncan, and Timothy Smeeding. 1998. "The Shifting Incidence of Involuntary Job Losses from 1968 to 1992." *Industrial Relations* 37(2): 207–31.

Brockner, Joel. 1992. "Managing the Effects of Layoffs on Survivors." *California Management Review* 34: 9–28.

Cameron, Kim. 1994. "Strategies for Successful Organizational Downsizing." *Human Resource Management* 3: 189–211.

Cappelli, Peter. 1992. "Examining Managerial Displacement." *Academy of Management Journal* 35: 203–17.

Cappelli, Peter, Laurie Bassi, Harry C. Katz, David Knoke, Paul Osterman, and Michael Useem. 1997. *Change at Work*. New York: Oxford University Press.

Cascio, Wayne F. 1993. "Downsizing: What Do We Know, What Have We Learned?" *Academy of Management Executive* 7: 95–104.

Cascio, Wayne F., Clifford E. Young, and James R. Morris. 1997. "Financial Consequences of Employment-Change Decisions in Major U.S. Corporations." *Academy of Management Journal* 40: 1175–89.

Caves, Richard E., and Matthew B. Kreps. 1993. "'Fat': The Displacement of Nonproduction Workers from U.S. Manufacturing Industries." *Brookings Papers on Economic Activity: Microeconomics* 2: 227–73.

Conference Board. 1997. "HR Executive Review: Implementing the New Employment Compact." Vol. 4, no. 4.

Corporate Leadership Council. 1995. *Perfecting Labor Markets: Redefining the Social Contract at the World's High-Performance Corporations*. Washington, D.C.: Advisory Board.

Davis, Steven J., and John Haltiwanger. 1992. "Gross Job Creation, Gross Job Destruction, and Employment Reallocation." *Quarterly Journal of Economics* 107: 819–63.

Dial, Jay, and Kevin Murphy. 1995. "Incentives, Downsizing, and Value Creation at General Dynamics." *Journal of Financial Economics* 37: 261–314.

DeMeuse, Kenneth P., Paul Vanderheiden, and Thomas J. Bergmann. 1994. "Announced Layoffs: Their Effect on Corporate Financial Performance." *Human Resource Management* 33: 509–30.

Ehrbar, Al. 1993. "Price of Progress: Reengineering Gives Firms New Efficiency, Workers the Pink Slip." *Wall Street Journal*, March 16, A1.

Farber, Henry S. 1997. "The Changing Face of Job Loss in the United States, 1981–1993." *Brookings Papers on Economic Activity (Microeconomics Supplement)*: 55–142.

————. 1998. "Has the Rate of Job Loss Increased in the 1990s?" Working paper 394. Princeton, N.J.: Princeton University, Industrial Relations Section.

Gombola, Michael J., and George P. Tsetsekos. 1992. "Plant Closings for Financially Weak and Financially Strong Firms." *Quarterly Journal of Business and Economics* 31(3): 69–83.

Gorlin, Harriet. 1985. *Issues in Human Resource Management*. New York: Conference Board.

Gunderson, Morley, Anil Verma, and Savita Verma. 1997. "Impact of Layoff Announcements on the Market Value of the Firm." *Relations Industrielles/Industrial Relations* 52(2, Spring): 364–81.

Gustman, Alan, Olivia S. Mitchell, and Thomas L. Steinmeyer. 1995. "Retirement Measures in the Health and Retirement Survey." *Journal of Human Resources* 30: 557–83.

Hallock, Kevin F. 1998. "Layoffs, Top Executive Pay, and Firm Performance." *American Economic Review* 88(4, September): 711–23.

Hamermesh, Daniel S. 1993. *Labor Demand*. Princeton, N.J.: Princeton University Press.

Hammer, Michael, and James Champy. 1993. *Reengineering the Corporation*. New York: Harper Business.

Huselid, Mark A., and Brian E. Becker. 1996. "Methodological Issues in Cross-sectional and Panel Estimates of the Human Resource–Firm Performance Link." *Industrial Relations* 35: 400–22.

Iqbal, Zahid, and Shekar Shetty. 1995. "Layoffs, Stock Price, and Financial Condition of the Firm." *Journal of Applied Business Research* 11: 67–72.

Johnson, Arlene A., and Fabian Linden. 1992. *Availability of a Quality Work Force*. New York: Conference Board.

Kalleberg, Arne L., David Knoke, Peter V. Marsden, and Joe L. Spath. 1996. *Organizations in America: A Portrait of Their Structures and Human Resources Practices*. Newbury Park, Calif.: Sage.

Kalra, Rajiv, Glenn V. Henderson Jr., and Michael C. Walker. 1994. "Share Price Reaction to Plant-Closing Announcements." *Journal of Economics and Business* 46(5, December): 381–95.

Kanter, Rosabeth Moss. 1977. *Men and Women of the Corporation*. New York: Basic Books.

Kletzer, Lori. 1998. "Job Displacement: What Do We Know, What Should We Know?" *Journal of Economic Perspectives* 12(1): 115–37.

Lazear, Edward. 1990. "Job Security Provisions and Employment." *Quarterly Journal of Economics* 105: 699–726.

Levering, Robert, and Milton Moskowitz. 1993. *The One Hundred Best Companies to Work for in America*. New York: Doubleday.

Lichtenberg, Frank R., and Daniel Siegel. 1992. "Leveraged Buyouts." In *Corporate Takeovers and Productivity*, edited by Frank R. Lichtenberg. Cambridge, Mass.: MIT Press.

Lynch, Lisa, and Susan Black. 1996. "Beyond the Incidence of Training: Evidence from the National Employer Survey." Working paper. Philadelphia: University of Pennsylvania, National Center on the EQW.

Matsusaka, John G. 1993. "Target Profits and Managerial Discipline During the Conglomerate Merger Wave." *Journal of Industrial Economics* 41: 179–89.

Medoff, James. 1993. *Middle-Aged and Out of Work: Growing Unemployment Due to Job Loss Among Middle-Aged Americans*. Washington, D.C.: National Study Center.

Miles, Raymond E., and Charles C. Snow. 1978. *Organizational Strategy, Structure, and Process*. New York: McGraw-Hill.

National Center on the Educational Quality of the Workforce. 1994. *First Findings: Results of the National Employer Survey*. Philadelphia: University of Pennsylvania, National Center on the EQW.

Osterman, Paul. 1994. "How Common Is Workplace Transformation, and How Can We Explain Who Does It?" *Industrial and Labor Relations Review* 47: 173–88.

Polivka, Anne. 1998. "Changes in the Employment Relationship and Long-term Employment: Discussion." *Proceedings of the Fiftieth Annual Meeting of the IRRA* (pp. 107–9). Madison, Wisc.: Industrial Relations Research Association.

Polsky, Daniel. Forthcoming. "Changes in the Consequences of Job Separations in the United States." *Industrial and Labor Relations Review*.

Porter, Michael E. 1985. *Competitive Advantage: Creating and Sustaining Superior Performance*. New York: Free Press.

Rees, Albert. 1989. *The Economics of Trade Unions*. Chicago: University of Chicago Press.

Valletta, Robert G. 1996. "Has Job Security in the U.S. Declined?" *Federal Reserve Bank of San Francisco Weekly Letter* (96–07, February 16).

Walton, Mary. 1986. *The Deming Management Method*. New York: Perigee Books.

Worrell, Dan L., Wallace N. Davidson III, and Varinder M. Sharma. 1991. "Layoff Announcements and Stockholder Wealth." *Academy of Management Journal* 43: 662–78.

Index

Boldface numbers refer to figures and tables.